# UNHOLY TOLEDO

# UNHOLY TOLEDO

## THE TRUE STORY OF DETROIT'S PURPLE-LICAVOLI GANG AND ITS INVASION OF AN OHIO CITY

### HARRY R. ILLMAN

Commonwealth Book Company
St. Martin, Ohio

Copyright © 1985 by Harry R. Illman
Copyright © 2023 by Commonwealth Book Company, Inc.

All rights reserved. No part of this book may be reproduced in any form or by any means without the prior written consent of the publisher, excepting brief quotes used in reviews. Printed in the United States of America.

ISBN: 978-1-948986-66-3

HARRY R. ILLMAN [1918-2001] was born and raised in Toledo, Ohio. He graduated from the University of Toledo and later the Ohio State University Law School. Although a successful lawyer, his gambling troubles led to a suspension and eventually a permanent disbarment from the Ohio bar. His law career included representing Toledo gambling figures, making him uniquely qualified to author this book.

## Contents

| | |
|---|---|
| Introduction | v |
| 1. The Jewish Mafia — The Purple Gang | 1 |
| 2. The Offer That Couldn't Be Refused | 8 |
| 3. Early History | 14 |
| 4. Ohio Politics | 18 |
| 5. Early Law Enforcement | 25 |
| 6. Golden Rule Jones, An Honest Politician | 32 |
| 7. Brand Whitlock, An Honest Lawyer | 39 |
| 8. The Newspaper Game | 47 |
| 9. The Willard-Dempsey Fight | 63 |
| 10. The Million Dollar Robbery | 72 |
| 11. More Elite Lawyers and Politicians | 77 |
| 12. Vice | 89 |
| 13. Prohibition Days | 93 |
| 14. The Licavoli Takeover | 113 |
| 15. Jack Kennedy — Martyr | 121 |
| 16. The Wop English Trial | 128 |
| 17. The Auto-Lite Strike | 141 |
| 18. The Yonnie Licavoli Trial | 150 |
| 19. The Firetop Sulkin Trial and Aftermath | 162 |

20. More Reform .......................................... 170
21. Industry and Labor ................................... 178
22. A Detroit Suicide .................................... 192
23. Formation of the Syndicate........................... 198
24. The Payoffs.......................................... 210
25. A Toledo Suicide Compared........................... 232
26. The Capone Connection ............................... 244
27. The Kefauver Investigation .......................... 249
28. Denaturalization Plea Bargaining...................... 256
29. Licavoli Tribulations................................ 261
30. Gambling Characters ................................. 273
31. Some Interesting Cases .............................. 292
32. The End of Syndicated Gambling ...................... 316
33. Conclusion .......................................... 323
    Footnotes ............................................ 337

# Introduction

*by Melvin M. Belli*

Toledoans, complacent by their recent history of seeming civic quietude and rectitude, will be startled at some of the encyclopedic facts of the doings in their city by my friend Harry Illman's book.

We knew that circa the Prohibition era, Kansas City was an oasis and sanctuary for fugitives. Regardless of their record or where they were "wanted," no one would bother them. But Toledo's similar history in this regard is not as well known. It's now documented and delightfully told in this book.

I suppose only a lawyer really could do it, but it takes a gifted lawyer-historian to amass the details of a city's turbulent history, particularly the homey little details that make for such good reading.

At the top of the heap there has to be the law in any city, but it's personified for good or evil in the form of the idiosyncratic judges and lawyers who walk and stalk across the civic stage. There's a little bit of vice in every American city, but Toledo has had more than its share. Of open gambling and prostitution over the years in Toledo there was a plenty, and there seemed to be a happy medium between the kind of government (or lack of it!) the people wanted and the kind they got.

Delightful scoundrels in the trappings of criminal lawyers march across Illman's pages and more than one crooked judge apears hand-in-glove with flamboyant members of the bar. Payoffs there were legion in the police department and the whorehouses were as well-publicized in Toledo as the Opera in other cities.

Ohio, the home of Presidents, comes in for a little state history and it seems that Toledo's skullduggery didn't stop at the city limits. Whether Toledo learned from the rest of the state or the state capital learned from Toledo, is open to question.

Probably because of its geographical location on the Great Lakes and its closeness to Canada, rum-running gave a great impetus to illegal business in Toledo during Prohibition. It was a center for the rum-running trade and speakeasies and their handmaidens, the whorehouses, flourished.

The gangs came in and with them gang rule. Gang leaders became so powerful they in effect ran the city government. The history of the great Toledo newspapers, including the Toledo *Blade,* as chroniclers of the turbulent years is entwined in this story.

A narration of events without actors would be dull indeed and this book is not dull. It sparkles with the anecdotes of "honest criminal lawyers" and "honest politicians." The scoundrels were honest in their own fashion and had a code which was Toledoan to the hilt.

The Willard-Dempsey fight is delightfully told, the enterprise of the entrepreneurs. The conspiracy of weather and the fickleness of a fight crowd, the story of the actual fight iself, is history well told.

All in all, Toledo in its history was a little more of everything than most American cities. It had much more than its share of civic corruption and one wonders why Toledoans got more of the kind of government they deserved than other cities. I think the answer comes through with the description of the civic leaders the Good Lord set down in Toledo during its infamous history. One after another, lawyers, judges, politicians, businessmen, gang leaders took over. Each had his own little racket going and each contributed to the lawlessness of the city. Without these lawless, flamboyant characters holding the reins and power politics in the city, Toledo would probably have developed along the line of any other midwestern city — out of Ohio. But what makes the book so interesting is that it not only tells the history and events of Toledo, it chronicles the personalities who made the city run its course of outlawry in civic government over the years.

*— Melvin Belli*
Belli Building
722 Montgomery Street
San Francisco CA 94111

# 1 The Jewish Mafia— The Purple Gang

A new underworld personality of twentieth- century origin plagued American cities at the end of the First World War. The prejudices of previous decades were forgotten. A kind of madness followed. There was reckless abandon in the roaring years of the Charleston and jazz, of the newly rich thirsting for entertainment and amusement, of negro singers like Bessie Smith, of prohibition and a frantic, almost maniacal, interest in sports. The age of the rumble seat, plastic surgery and short hair with Marcel waves and the motion pictures had arrived.

The cobblestone streets of Detroit, Michigan, echoed with the shrill blaring of the emerging hordes of Model T Fords which, in 1914, began rolling off assembly lines at the rate of 250,000 a year. Gaslights had been replaced by electricity although a flickering few remained in the poorer sections of the city. At dusk, the nightclubs enticed the passerby with the sweet sounds of jazz.

Detroit had already developed the first haze of pollution and eventually it forced those who could afford it out to far-reaching suburbs. Another form of stench emerged at this time as they polluted, enmeshed and dominated the city for the next two decades, the Purple Gang.

Just as the word "Mafia" connoted fear, this group in Detroit created the same impression. The Purple Gang became a synonym for terrorism in bootlegging, gambling and labor rackets. The Purples acquired their colorful soubriquet in their neighborhood on Hastings Street, then the heart of the Detroit ghetto at the end of World War I. Stories on the origin of the name varied. The first story was that a Sammy Purple was the gang leader. That rumor was unfounded as the police records did not disclose any person by that name or alias. Some claimed it was for the purple of Northwestern University as a copy of the Chicago gangs model, or from their use of purple swim trunks in their summer play. Jewish shopkeepers who were looted by the gang that started as neighborhood thieves, claimed "They were a bad lot, off color, purple like the color of spoiled meat, the whole bunch." They're a purple gang and the name stuck. They might have remained petty and innocuous as thieves among their own people, or rolling drunks who came into the Jewish quarter, but for the advent of prohibition.[1]

The average age of a gang member was in the twenties with an average weight under 150 pounds. The giant gangsters of the past now were replaced by pint-sized midgets holding the new great American equalizer, an automatic or revolver.[2]

In the '20s, this all-Jewish mob — Abe Bernstein, Izzy Bernstein, Raymond Bernstein, Irving Milburg, Irwin Shapiro, Abe Miller, Joe "Honey" Miller, Abe Axler, Eddie Fletcher, Harry and Phil Keywell, and Harry, Louis and Sam Fleisher — began to specialize in bootlegging, shaking down business men and gamblers by extortion and kidnapping people in the rackets.[3] Most of the 282 unsolved kidnappings of that era in the underworld of Detroit were ascribed to the Purples. Many of these capers took place in Toledo! Kidnapping of criminals was big business. It became common in New York during prohibition, but the Purples led the country. Night club owners were snatched early in the morning and delivered safe and sound to their friends the same evening on a strictly C.O.D. basis. The growing dry cleaners businesses of Detroit were particularly vulnerable. Those who refused to pay for protection found their places of business a mass of rubble, acid was thrown into the faces of truck drivers, chemicals and stench bombs were exploded in customers' clothes. Records of the dry cleaners union mysteriously disappeared from their offices in the Detroit Temple. Records of their police encounters kept by the Detroit News were either lost or stolen.[4] In 1929 the Wayne County prosecutor had to resort to wire taps to obtain evidence that led to the conviction of two lesser members of the gang,[5] but the gangsters continued to rule the Detroit underworld.

It was the fear of this gang that prompted newspapermen Ben

Aronoff and Ben Harris to start their later numbers and handbook business in Toledo, regarded as a suburb of the Motor City at the time.[6]

In the spring of 1926, the control of the Purple underworld was challenged by an invading St. Louis gang who tried to take over by preying on downtown gambling houses that were Purple customers in that they were paid regularly to prevent such incidents. Paying customers complained that their protection was a flop. The competition between gangs was costly. The Purples received heated complaints; gamblers balked at paying both gangs.

Such competition had to be eliminated. Twelve gunmen were imported form New York, including a couple of nice Jewish boys named Abe Axler, alias Abe Gold, alias Harry Levine, fresh out of his second trip to Sing Sing, and Eddie Fletcher. These two Purples lived at the Milaflores Apartments. One day in March 1926, they invited three of the St. Louis gang, Rube Cohen, Joe Bloom and Frank Wright, to discuss some business deals. For the first time in Detroit history, machine guns were used in gang warfare as other Purples broke into the parlor and rubbed the competitors out in what the papers called the "Milaflores Massacre." Thereafter, Purple domination was unchallenged.[7]

The crimes of extortion of business people, kidnapping or gangland warfare were beyond police protection. While vice or prostitution could be watched and controlled, the acts of the Purples in these other areas created consternation and hate. This big-time criminal action had originated in Chicago and was being copied in Detroit. The gangs fighting for control were ruthless and uncompromising. Neither politicians nor police could intervene successfully. The Purples' methods, brutality and continued immunity from the law brought fear to the public, police and their political affiliations. Rumors spread that when Al Capone was in Florida on February 14, 1929 he asked the Purple gang to do a job for him on St. Valentine's Day. The modus operandi — brains, daring and mass murder — was typically Purple.

None of the Purples was ever convicted of the gruesome or maniacal murders of their rivals nor of the numerous killings involved in the labor rackets. Their new tactics and wanton cruelty created anxiety and tension in the underworld and police department.

The police were losing control. The Purples had escaped justice too long. Ironically, two of the gang, Philip Keywell and Morris Raider, were apprehended and sentenced to life imprisonment for the senseless murder of a 14-year-old negro boy whose childish curiosity in

*UNHOLY TOLEDO*

sticking his head under the door of a Purple brewery resulted in his untimely death.

In the afternoon of September 16, 1931, an incident occurred that James E. McCarthy, Chief of Detectives, described as the greatest accomplishment of the local police in years in gathering evidence that helped temporarily break the gang and close their reign of terror in the city.[8]

Newspapers called it the "Collingwood Avenue Massacre." Three leaders of the Jewish "Little Navy" gang were found shot to death in an apartment rented a few days before on Collingwood Avenue in Detroit. They were originally called the Third Avenue Navy, getting their name from their place of action as they used the Third Avenue Pier in Detroit for delivery of illicit liquor. Hymie Paul had eight bullets in his back and head. In the living room "Nigger Joe" Lebowitz was lying face down near a bedroom doorway where Joe "Izzy" Sutker had fled in an attempt to escape the bullets of the three Purple assassins.

The police were aroused. The modus operandi of the killings smacked of Purple techniques and the biggest shakedown of the underworld since the former "Milaflores massacre" was under way.

It was well known that the Little Navy had been out of line by peddling booze throughout the city without respect for areas controlled by other gang factions. They had approached the Purples to become distributors for them and meetings were arranged to conclude the details.

Joe Sutker's 18-year-old girl friend stated that she had dinner with him the night before and he had been in good spirits, unaware of any danger. Because the three were found unarmed, her statement indicated that they expected little trouble. Besides, one of their partners, Solly Levine, was a school chum of Ray Bernstein, the Purple Chief. Scores of gangsters were rounded up for questioning. Writs of habeas corpus accompanied each arrest, so most were quickly discharged.

Solly Levine was picked up within an hour and a half of the discovery of the murders at the Little Navy handbook. He told the prosecutor he didn't know who did the killings, or why, and gave several different versions of the shooting. There was an intuitive feeling he was being evasive and it was felt that Solly's testimony could be obtained. Prosecutor Harry Toy kept him in a cell while the investigation continued.

Police found no sign of occupancy in the massacre apartment, no furniture, clothes or personal property. There was an open bucket of green paint in the kitchen where police found three revolvers, spent cartridges and serial numbers mutilated. Ballistics showed another gun was involved. This missing gun was why Solly Levine decided to talk.

He was there all right — so were Irving Milberg, Harry Kaywell, Ray Bernstein and Harry Fleisher, Purples deluxe. After the shootings, they ran to a car Bernstein had ready, then after driving around for a while, dropped Solly off at his handbook. As the car stopped, a gun fell to the floor, it was the missing murder weapon. Solly was told to pick it up and when he touched the gun, he realized his own death warrant was signed; he would be found dead with the murder gun on him. Solly decided to live, even if it meant a life of oblivion and seclusion.

At one o'clock Saturday morning following the massacre, Norton Custer, court reporter and attorney, finished taking the notes on the confession statement of Solly Levine. He was visibly shaken, appalled by the horrendous tale just related to him. Under police guard, he was hustled out of the police station to his office in the Majestic Building where he typed the notes for signature. The police grabbed the notebook, carbon papers and all papers and rushed back to get the signature of Solly Levine so that arrest warrants, already being prepared, could be executed.

The court reporter called a friend, Irving Meiland, asking to spend the weekend with him; he was too frightened to stay alone.[9] Within an hour police arrested Irving Milberg, his suitcase packed and ready in his car. Another police detail surrounded a house occupied by Ray Bernstein and Harry Keywell. They had over $9,000 on them at the time of arrest but their departure had been delayed while they entertained a 26-year-old vaudeville dancer from Newark.

The fourth killer, Harry Fleisher, had disappeared. He was still on the lam a year later when the Lindbergh baby was kidnapped. Nationwide bulletins were broadcast because of his notoriety, propounded by the fact that he may have been in need of funds.

The toughest job for the police was to protect Solly Levine until he could testify. Twelve handpicked officers were assigned as personal bodyguards.

A reporter, Ralph Nelson, described the trial that started in late October, 1931, before Judge Donald Van Zile.[10]

"When the trial began, only 250 spectators were allowed each day. There were rumors that mobsters would storm the court room to take their gang chiefs.

"Every male spectator was searched for guns by police at the door of the court room. Every woman's handbag was opened and inspected. A heavy sprinkling of plainclothes officers mingled with the spectators.

"On November 3, Solly Levine took the stand. Pale, and obviously frightened, he slumped in the witness chair, flanked by eight of his twelve-man guard. He steadfastly refused to look at the three Purples, whose murderous eyes never left Levine's face.

"Levine told the court that he had been in partnership with the three slain men. They had been negotiating with the Purple Gang to take over the distribution of fake liquor labels, wine bricks and wholesale alky for them.

" 'I saw Bernstein two days before the killing,' Levine said.

" 'I'll give you a call in a couple of days.'

" 'Then Bernstein called the handbook on September 16, and told me to bring the boys and come to the apartment on Collingwood. We didn't expect trouble. We were supposed to become distributors for the Purples . . . . We figured this was it.'

" 'Bernstein met us at the door. We shook hands all around and went into the apartment. Irving Milberg was there, and Harry Keywell. So was Harry Fleisher. We were surprised to see him because he was on the lam from the Feds and hadn't been around.'

" 'We talked for a while; mostly we kidded Fleisher for having the Feds on his tail. Then Fleisher said, "where's the guy with the books for our deal?" '

" 'Bernstein said he would go down into the lobby and call him. He went out, and pretty soon we heard a car backfiring in the alley.'

" 'That was the signal. The noise was to drown out the sounds of the shooting and to heat up the car for a quick get-away. Fleisher jerked out a gun and shot Lebowitz. Milberg and Keywell started firing at Sutker and Paul.'

" 'Fleisher ran over to me and said, "Are you hit, kid?" He seemed worried about it. I told him I didn't think so. He said, "Come on, then," and he dragged me out of the apartment. We all ran downstairs and into the alley where Bernstein had the car ready.'

"The three Purples were convicted and sentenced to life in Marquette prison. And the day the trial ended, Levine's sentence became effective. But instead of prison, he was condemned to a life of flight. His conviction was based on the statute of gang law that prescribed flight or death for the squealer.

"Eight months after the trial, Harry Fleisher surrendered. But after weeks of court room bickering, Prosecutor Toy decided he could not prosecute Fleisher without the testimony of Solly Levine, and Levine could not be found. So the charge against Fleisher was dismissed and he was turned over to the Federal authorities. He was sentenced to Alcatraz Prison on a liquor-conspiracy charge."

With the power of the Purples eroded, they merged with the Italian gangs. Control of Detroit went to its major competitors, the Unione Sicilians, headed by Sam Canta La Notte.[11] He was commonly called Sam-sings-in-the-night or Sam-Singing-in-the-night-time, owning the most mellifluous nomenclature ever encountered in such nefarious business. Sam had been the ruler of his empire until his death at the time of the Purple demise. When he died, airplanes were hired to circle the cemetery, dropping garlands and petals of flowers as a last farewell to a fallen monarch. Even in death, Sam violated the laws on littering.

Meanwhile, another young Italian gang, members of the Licavoli family, began making waves in the Detroit circles of power. Sam's death left the throne of gangdom open. Big Chester LaMare, the apparent successor, was killed in his home while another ambitious pretender, Black Leo Cellura, had to take it on the lam shortly thereafter. The Licavoli Gang had started like the Purples and were indoctrinated into the ruthless tactics used by their peers.

A few years earlier, 1927, in the Detroit Fort Shelby Hotel, Thomas (Yonnie) Licavoli had already met with Al Capone. "Stay the hell out of Detroit," the six-foot, 210-pound Yonnie warned the shorter, squat Capone. "It's my territory."[12] He made his order stick and the underworld remembered and the word on Yonnie's prowess spread.

Even in this famed outburst, people said Yonnie never talked above a whisper. His tone was soft, menacing and convincing. When Yonnie Licavoli talked, people listened.

Yonnie planned to go far.

# 2 The Offer That Couldn't Be Refused

The name Licavoli became synonymous in the public mind with the Purple Gang of Detroit. Fear was their stock in trade. Most newspapers claimed that the Licavolis were associated with the Purples and vice versa. In a business based on intimidation, such comment was a compliment. This connection was never denied, but never confirmed either. If the people thought they were Purples, it didn't hurt. As far as the victims were concerned, threats from either spelled death or fear of death.

Three Licavoli brothers, Pete, Thomas (Yonnie) and James, were born in St. Louis. Yonnie was first arrested in St. Louis in 1915 at the age of 12. The Juvenile Court of that city later described him as "incorrigible." Yonnie had to flee St. Louis to avoid prosecution on a concealed weapons charge. He joined the Navy and promptly deserted. As a tribute to his good political connections and leadership abilities, he was granted amnesty by President Harding. In 1924 he began a whiskey running operation in Detroit. Here, with his two brothers, his life in crime began.[1] A Pete (Horseface) Licavoli of Detroit was a cousin of the St. Louis family. The Detroit Pete had been convicted of the murder of Harry Tupency, a petty competitor, and died in the Marquette Branch Prison in 1951 after serving 21 years of a life sentence. Shortly after arriving in Detroit, St. Louis

Pete, as gang leader and elder brother, formed an association known as The Down River Gang. Their income came from bootlegging, extortion, protection of gambling for a cut of the action and other related racket activity.[2] The Licavolis became a faction in The Unione Sicilione, an ethnic organization, led by powerful gangland leaders such as Joe Massie and the Bommorito family, among others.

In 1930, an ambitious Yonnie married Zena Moceri. Her father was a member of the Detroit family. In a lavish wedding at the Tuller Hotel during the Great Depression, Yonnie received $20,000 in cash and a $16,000 limousine as wedding gifts.

The gang had connections extending into Ohio. When Frank Commorata of their mob received a 15-to-30 year sentence for a Detroit bank robbery, the sentence was commuted so that he could be deported. He was smuggled back into the United States via Canada and hid in Ohio. He went to the Cleveland and Youngstown area where Alfred (Big Al) Polizzi, head of the Unione Sicilione, protected him. Pete Licavoli had been best man at Big Al's wedding.

In 1930, after 22 murders in one month, Detroit was screaming for reform to clean up the crime cesspools and recall mayor Charles E. Bowles for permitting the corruption.

A crusading radio announcer and reporter, Gerald E. (Jerry) Buckley, was a prime force in the recall movement. The underworld acted to protect its connections. On July 23, 1930, at 1:40a.m., while he was seated in the lobby of the old LaSalle Hotel, Jerry Buckley was shot to death. Three gunmen entered. One stood in the lobby doorway. The other two walked within two feet of the unsuspecting victim and emptied their revolvers into his reclining body. Eleven bullets were taken from the victim. This crime galvanized the city into action.[3] The mayor was immediately recalled. Gunmen, frightened by the city's wrath, fled from the general clean-up following the recall. The heat was on the Licavolis for alleged complicity in the Buckley murder.

Within days, Prosecutor Harry Toy arrested three Licavoli gangsters, Ted Pizzano, Joe Bommorito and Angelo Livechi, for the Buckley slaying. Warrants were also issued for Pete Licavoli, Frank Commorata and Joe Massie.

On October 6, 1931, Pete was brought from Toledo by a carload of detectives. He waived extradition as his Toledo lawyer, Harry G. Levy, said he had an alibi. Police claimed Pete's girl friend allegedly lured Buckley to the hotel on the telephone promise of a story.[4]

Pete Licavoli and Joe Massie were also later accused in the 1932 death of Milford Jones, a St. Louis gangster well known in Toledo gambling circles, who was shot to death at the Stork Club in Detroit.[5] In addition to the accusations of murder, several members of the gang were sought for kidnapping wealthy people, but most witnesses in such cases refused to testify before juries or at trials.[6]

The Buckley murder made conditions too hot for the gang to continue operations in Detroit. No convictions were obtained in the Buckley murder case. Pizzano and Livechi were later convicted of slaying two Chicago racketeers who were mowed down in a parked car. Charges against Pete were dismissed for insufficient evidence. In the Milford Jones murder, witnesses fled to Canada and charges against Pete and Massie were also dropped. Yonnie and Jimmie moved south to Monroe, Michigan, where they maintained a successful bootlegging operation in the area between Toledo and Detroit.

Yonnie, the underworld claimed, was a genius at organizing criminal action. News of such talent reached the ears of Jacob (Firetop) Sulkin in Toledo.[7]

Firetop's nickname was obviously derived from the color of his hair. He grew up on the streets of Toledo as a typical hustler. He was streetwise, flip, arrogant, ruthless and greedy. He was small, wiry, but quicker with his fists than with his brains, they used to say.

Firetop was born in 1890. He was a newsboy during the mayoralties of Golden Rule Jones and Brand Whitlock, when Toledo had little or no social morality. It was known then as a city where "everything went." Firetop was regarded as a leader. The founder of the Newsboys Association, John E. Gunckel, liked the brash, outgoing, tough little Firetop. At age 12 he was made drum major of the Newsboys Marching Band. Very little music was played as the group paraded through the streets carrying signs and making noise to attract attention to their cause. The whole city grew to know Firetop as the leader of the band. Firetop dominated those about him. He became a bully. He refused to accept "No" for an answer. It became a style of his life. He always wanted to be on the winning side or have an edge in his favor.

At an early age, he was exposed to vice, gambling and prostitution. He learned a great deal of money could be made through politics. He became intrigued with politicians and politics, first as a ward leader, vote getter and "fixer." His original mentor was Sam Cohn, a venerable Jew transplanted from Louisiana. Walter F. Brown ran the party from behind the scenes, but Sam Cohn was the nominal head of local Republican activities for twenty-five years. Sam led his lawyer son, Aaron Cohn, to a later Municipal Court judgeship.

Cohn never maintained an office. He would sit on a box at the

Court House or in the lobby at city hall, dispensing patronage, advice and counsel to those who sought such favor. In that era, it was financially fruitful for those who could deliver favors from judges or police.

Firetop, with only a grade school education, was ambitious, unscrupulous and capable of learning the ropes of politics as it related to vice for that was his forte. I lived across the street from Firetop and his family. I saw him regularly in and about the city for years. I talked to him regularly.

Firetop had employment in the street sales department of the *News Bee,* then the leading newspaper of the city. With such exposure on the streets, he continued to achieve recognition by the police and public. On election days he delivered the ward vote for his party candidate. On the counting of ballots on election nights, some claimed Firetop destroyed as many opposition ballots as he counted. When Cohn died in 1915, Firetop was 25 years old and rising. He established a reputation as the best "fixer" in town. With the entry of the United States into World War I, he volunteered for service with his friend, Harry G. Levy, who later became an attorney for the Licavolis and a well-known politician.

After World War I, Firetop became very close to Walter F. Brown, head of the local Republican Party, who later would become Postmaster General under Herbert Hoover, nominally a position for the head of the national Party. Evenings, Firetop could always be found in Bowles, a downtown all-night restaurant, kibitzing with important people and politicians. People liked him. Politicians regarded him as a civic leader. They thought he had a following as a vote-getter and could be used. They encouraged him to be active as a ward leader, raising money for candidates and controlling ward votes. With such encouragement, Firetop became a "jail house lawyer" and fixer. He could get better results in certain criminal cases than most lawyers. So he charged accordingly. He followed the credo of his mentors, "a politician never does a favor for anybody for nothing."

When Firetop, or "Jake" as he was often called, was called upon to fix a case, he would take the Judge handling the matter to lunch or dinner and arrange a result. Most Republican judges were obligated to him for votes and contributions. Eventually Firetop could walk right into the mayor's office or judge's chambers unannounced as he felt he belonged.

Firetop developed an avid interest in criminal matters. He bought and read every newspaper article, crime book or story printed. He studied gambling, vice, prostitution, systems of police payoffs, handling of politicians and the like. He knew at that time that a triumvirate of politicians, police and criminals had developed to operate in every major city of the country.[8] He knew each part of the triangle depended upon the others for success. Firetop knew Capone had most of the police, city fathers and the courts under his thumb. To be honest was to be a fool in an imperfect world.[9] Firetop also knew police took payoffs, city bosses split their loot with the political powers. Crime could only exist because it paid off.[10]

Firetop owed a gambling joint of his own known as The Villa. He had first-hand experience and information of what was required to function outside the law.

Firetop had become unhappy with his lot. He had dreams and aspirations for greater success. With the advent of prohibition, he read about the empire Johnny Torrio had built in Chicago by the use of a ruthless henchman known as Al Capone. He was envious. Firetop felt he had all the right political connections. The police were in his vest pocket. He needed a gang with guts and guns to intimidate rival gamblers and bootleggers. Licavoli would be an ideal leader, he thought.

When Pete Licavoli hid out in Toledo after the Buckley murder, Firetop sought him out and talked to him. He introduced Pete to his boyhood friend, Harry G. Levy, whom Pete retained as his lawyer in the case.

Firetop was impressed by the glowing praise of Yonnie Licavoli's genius for organization. Detroit was sizzling after Buckley's death. The Licavoli gangsters were on the lam. Firetop figured the Licavolis, like the Purples, could take over certain operations he could finger. With that type of gang, he could make it big. He became enthralled with his ideas.

Firetop did not consult the politicians or police on this new venture. He knew they would not like it. He felt his popularity, personality and weight would overcome any adverse criticism of his negotiations with Licavoli. He was so determined that advice against his overtures would probably have been ignored. So Firetop acted on his own in his deal with Licavoli. He went to Detroit for a conference!

"I want you to come to Toledo," Firetop began. "I'll protect you."

"I'm doing OK where I am," Yonnie answered.

"No you're not, you have competition. There are no rival gangs in Toledo." Yonnie became intense. "Trust me, Yonnie," Firetop continued. "Look, I read every book on the subject. I know everything that's going on. Toledo is a perfect set-up waiting just for you."

Yonnie began to like the idea but remained silent as the pitch continued.

"Do you know Walter F. Brown?" Firetop asked.

"No, who's he?"

"He's Postmaster General of the United States, that's who! That's the job given to the top man in the party — and I'm his right-hand man," Firetop bragged.

"What has he got to do with me?"

"He loves money — a lawyer and politician who loves money can be moved. He and I can fix anything. I got the judges and cops in line. I get tipped off before anything ever happens."

Firetop knew Walter F. Brown was spending most of his time in Washington and could not be approached but he also knew Yonnie didn't know that.

"Look Yonnie, you scared off Al Capone, didn't you?"

Yonnie brightened. "Yeah."

"Well just the mention of your name will scare the shit out of people in Toledo — you got the reputation!"

"OK. I'll line up some of my men," Yonnie replied, encouragingly.

The former newsboy-drum major had formed a new band. With his brother on the lam and three other members of his gang under various murder indictments, the beleagured Yonnie now had an offer that could not be refused. He decided to accept Firetop's proposition and move on in Toledo.

This new band would soon be traveling South. Their instruments were pistols, revolvers, sawed-off shotguns, machine guns, bombs and dynamite. They would play a tune Toledo never heard before or since.

# 3 Early History

The gore and bloodshed the Purples and Licavolis wrought in Detroit and, later, Toledo, may have been foreordained. The area had a history of violence, as it was wrested from the Indians successively by the French, British and Americans.

Sixty miles south of Detroit at latitude 41-40 North, the Maumee River flows in a general southwesterly direction from Lake Erie. After the French founded Montreal in 1640, they extended their trading and exploration southward into what is now Michigan and Ohio. A tribe known as the Miamis greeted the early French traders. All the tribesmen were called "mon ami" by the French, but the Indians and later the British, could not nasalize French words and so called the river Maumee. When in 1863 the French settled Detroit (De 'Twa), meaning the straits, the name was not nasalized and pronounced Detroit by the British. Many other French names were prominent in the early development. Bon Eau, meaning "good water," became Bono. Frenchtown was a part of the city of Monroe. Michigan, however, was a name derived from two Indian words meaning "Great Lake," and Ohio was an Iroquoian word meaning "Great River."

At the end of the Revolutionary War, the treaty of 1783 with the British ceded this territory to the United States. But the British refused to honor the treaty. Then, President George Washington sent General "Mad Anthony" Wayne, commander of the Legion of the United States, to suppress the British and their Indian allies. In the famous battle of Fallen Timbers of 1794, Wayne crushed the Indian forces and humiliated the British.[1] At the time, it was felt that Wayne's victory brought peace to the area. But that impression was short-lived.

Despite a treaty with Wayne, the Indians joined the British and renewed hostilities against the United States in the War of 1812. Once again the area was involved in bloody battles. After early setbacks at Detroit — where American General Hull surrendered without "a gun being fired in defense" — and a "massacre of 700 Americans at River Raisin" in Monroe, the new nation's forces turned the tide. In September 1813, Commander Oliver Hazard Perry defeated the British fleet in the Battle of Lake Erie, capturing the brig *Adams* surrendered by Hull at Detroit, and cleared the English ships out of the Great Lakes. At Fort Meigs, the present site of Toledo, the American General William Henry Harrison defeated the British in two engagements. Following their retreat to Detroit, Harrison chased the fleeing Indians and English into Canada. Then in October 1813 at the historic battle of the Thames, 60 miles east of Detroit, wars in the Northwest Territory ended British occupancy and rule in the area.[2] Thereafter, the international boundaries were established.

When the Indian hostilities subsided, the westward migration of pioneers continued. By 1803 Ohio had 60,000 residents and thought it had become the 17th state when its legislature met in Chillicothe on March 1, 1803. One hundred fifty years later, when Ohio was about to celebrate its 150th birthday, it was discovered that Congress had ignored Ohio's resolution for admission so that it was never legally admitted to the Union.[3] Politicians had a field day for jokes when they learned Ohio's formal application for statehood had never been accepted by Congress. "If the mother is illegitimate," they asked each other, "what, if anything, do we say of her progeny?" The innocuous faux pas was corrected by a resolution passed by Congress in 1953 to admit Ohio retroactively.[4]

The significance of treatment of error by Congress was shown in the aftermath of the famous Ohio-Michigan Boundary War. Toledo was originally in Michigan and the northern peninsula of Michigan was part of Wisconsin, but the Ohio-Michigan War changed all that. The bellicose, contentious nature of the area's inhabitants was clearly manifested in the most ludicrous entanglement ever recorded between the states.[5]

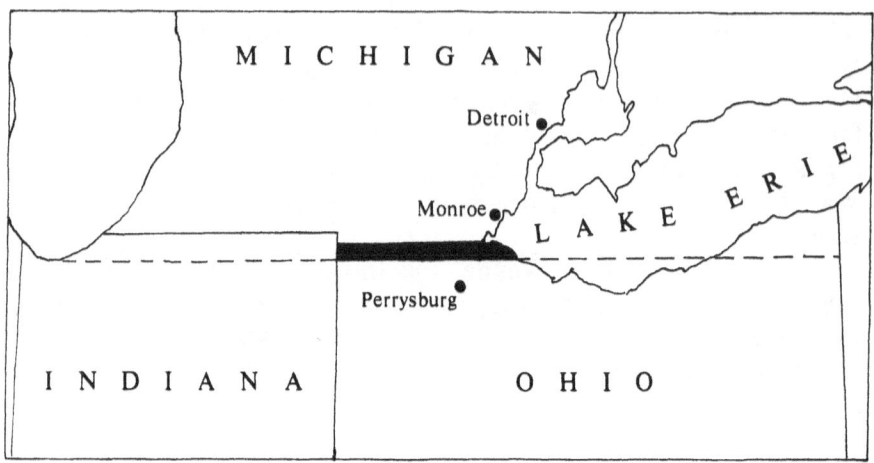

Map showing part of the area surrendered in the Ohio-Michigan War. Courtesy *Escanaba Daily Press*.

The ordinance of 1787, which created the Northwest Territory, provided in part that the lands north of the Ohio River have defined boundaries. The boundary line between Ohio and Michigan was not to intersect Lake Erie. The early French traders showed Lake Michigan smaller than it really was and the line drawn from its southern tip eastward did indeed intersect Lake Erie, placing Toledo north of the disputed area lines. The people of Michigan and Ohio knew that the pioneer railroad of the West, Erie and Kalamazoo Line, with Toledo as a terminal, was nearing completion. (The first locomotive ran in June 1837). The Erie Canal was in progress. (Officially, it was started in 1837. Completed in 1843, it was called the Miami Erie Canal.) Since 1818, steamboats had been appearing on the Great Lakes. The original Erie Canal through New York connected the Hudson River with Lake Erie. River and lake commerce was twice as large as foreign trade. Grains, meat, lumber and furs from the west flowed along the Great Lakes through this canal to New York City. Manufactured goods from the east went westward along the same route. Each state built its own canals and the Ohio venture was such an extension. The canal terminus at the mouth of the Maumee River would be a valuable governmental and trade area. Both states wanted Toledo within their jurisdictions.[6]

In 1835, the Ohio-Michigan boundary war broke out. Armed bands of men wandered about the border, and it looked like blood would be spilled. Surveyors from Ohio who were attempting to re-mark the state line were fired upon by Michiganders and had to abandon their work. The situation looked more grave when Michigan called out a militia of 1,000 men while Governor Lucas of Ohio recruited 600 volunteers. The Niles, Ohio, *Register* of May 2, 1935, copied an article from a Michigan paper published near the seat of war: "We are sorry to be compelled to state that since individuals in the disputed ground have been base enough to erect, in the village of Toledo, a flag on which was ostentatiously displayed the name of Ohio, some patriotic citizens of Michigan, indignant at the disgusting exhibition, tore the disgraceful badge of freedom from its perch, dragged it through the streets over which it had waved, and after arriving with it at Monroe, finally burned it with suitable demonstrations of contempt."

When Judge David Higgins rendered a preliminary decision in favor of Ohioans, a rebellion started. A James Wood of Monroe, Michigan, tried to arrest Two Stickney of Toledo. (Major Benjamin Franklin Stickney was one of the founding fathers of the city not yet named Toledo. He named his sons One and Two in numerical order and wanted to name his daughters after the various states. His wife remonstrated as to the first two daughters but he succeeded in naming his third girl Indiana). Two Stickney stabbed his assailant to escape arrest and was compelled to flee. This was the only blood shed in this comic opera war that has raged periodically since that date.

At that early date, political corruption came upon the scene. Ohio was a state, Michigan was not. The electoral vote of Ohio meant more to President Andrew Jackson than the embarrassment of Michigan.[7] It was not expedient to admit Michigan to the Union while the boundary dispute raged. Congress had jurisdiction because Michigan was still a territory. The area in question was awarded to Ohio with compensation of northern territory to the loser. A petition by Michigan for statehood in 1835 reopened the boundary question but was rejected by Congress — a stinging humiliation. Because the erroneous boundary lines awarded six more miles of territory to each of them, Indiana and Illinois blocked further moves by Michigan to reopen the debate on boundaries. Two years later, in 1837, Michigan reapplied, recognizing the new boundary lines demanded by Ohio. Their admission was then granted.[8]

Toledo, Ohio, was politically tainted from its very beginning.

## 4 Ohio Politics

After the settlement of the Ohio boundary in 1837, the two villages nearest Lake Erie on the right bank of the Maumee River, Port Lawrence and Vistula, were incorporated into the municipality of Toledo, Ohio. The popular Washington Irving was writing his *Alhambra* sketchbook series, which included "Rip Van Winkle" and "The Legend of Sleepy Hollow", in Toledo, Spain. (Irving, a newspaperman with the New York *Morning Chronicle,* served in the American legation in Spain in 1832.) He suggested the city's name to his brother for use as there was no other American city by that name at the time. Today there is a Toledo in Massachusetts and another in Iowa, but the Ohio city became the biggest and most notorious of the three.

The growth of the city and county was steadily upward from the date of its organization. In 1840, the first United States census year, the population of the county was 9,382. Fifty years later, in 1890, it was 102,296; and by 1900, 153,559. In 1840 there were 79 counties in Ohio; 65 were reportedly larger than Lucas County. And by 1900, Lucas County occupied fourth place, being exceeded in population only by Cuyahoga (Cleveland), Hamilton (Cincinnati) and Franklin (Columbus), in the order named.[1]

In the 1800s, city life attracted more and more people. Many Toledo residents were transplanted citizens who arrived to work on the commerce generated by the location of railroads and the advantages of the harbor and shipping facilities of the river and Great Lakes. Its first mayor was John Berdan, originally from New York.

The West was growing lustily. Indiana, Illinois, Iowa, Kansas and Nebraska, and the forest lands of Michigan, Wisconsin and Minnesota were producing vast surpluses of corn, wheat and pork. Iron ore factories of Michigan and Minnesota needed the soft coal of Pennsylvania, Ohio and West Virginia. California and Colorado mined gold; Nevada, silver. All required large-scale marketing and distribution in manufacture and sale. In the prosperity that followed the Civil War, Ohio became the crossroads of the nation. The canals carried the East's shipping across the Great Lakes. The Ohio River connected Pittsburgh and the East to St. Louis and New Orleans, while railroad centers grew in Cleveland and Toledo. It was held by many that Toledo would be the Chicago of the Midwest as Ohio grew to become one of the largest states in the Union.

The Civil War was the first conflict in which railroads played a major role. It was claimed then that the railroads became of age. The Civil War burdens on railroads were relieved when steel was introduced in the post-war period to replace the worn-out rails. Mark Twain labeled the period after the Civil War up to the end of the century "The Gilded Age" because of the ostentatious wealth acquired by the nouveau riche in this monumental expansion.[2] The initiators became known as "Robber Barons" because of their large financial coups in railroads, mining, gold and franchises. The emergence of industry in the northern states, the taming of the West and change in the rise of a new South gave the new nation a vitality that attracted immigrants from all nations. By 1900 the national population stood at 75 million. The United States became the great supplier of goods to the world.

As the railroads began to criss-cross the country in all directions, Toledo developed as one of its largest railroad centers. It became the largest soft coal loading port in the world. Cheap natural gas in northwestern Ohio later led to its further distinction as the Glass Center of the world. Industrial development in the 20th century brought the automotive industry, weight scales and auto accessories to increase its importance as a lake port and great industrial metropolitan community.

The political situation in Toledo was typical of all newly-formed cities.

In 1831, Alexis de Tocqueville, a young French magistrate and lawyer, came to America to study our prison system. After submitting his report (a major source of French prison reform), he wrote an analysis of democracy as a working principle of society and government. De Tocqueville came to America to study the actual functioning of democracy in action in a country that had never known aristocracy. His book *Democracy in America* was described as the greatest work ever written about one country by a citizen of another.

De Tocqueville wrote:

> The government of democracy is favorable to the political power of lawyers; for when the wealthy, the noble, and the prince are excluded from the government, the lawyers take possession of it, in their own right, as it were, since they are the only men of information and sagacity, beyond the sphere of the people, who can be the object of the popular choice.[3]
>
> In America there are no nobles or literary men, and the people are apt to mistrust the wealthy; lawyers consequently form the highest political class and the most cultivated portion of society. If I were asked where I place the American aristocracy, I should reply without hesitation that it occupies the judicial bench and the bar.[4]
>
> The more we reflect upon all that occurs in the United States, the more we shall be persuaded that the lawyers, as a body, form the most powerful, if not the only, counterpoise to the democratic element.[5]

In the hierarchy of social rank, a lawyer as a squire, called esquire, was one rank above a gentleman. In becoming the aristocrats of American society, many lawyers became snobbish and arrogant, with supercilious airs for all except their peers.

History proved de Tocqueville's analysis of a legally-dominated government to be correct. From inception, colonial governments, city or state, needed laws. Lawyers were essential to the democracy from origin. Thirty-three of the first 56 signers of the Declaration of Independence were lawyers. Twelve of the first 16 Presidents were lawyers.[6] Thomas Jefferson, James Monroe, John Q. Adams, Andrew Jackson, Martin Van Buren, John Tyler, James A. Polk, Millard Fillmore, Franklin Pierce, James Buchanan, Abraham Lincoln and Rutherford B. Hayes were all of the legal aristocracy which emerged to dominate the three branches of government in the growing democracy. The United States became known as "a nation of lawyers."

They numerically abounded in the legislative and executive branches. The judicial branch was exclusively theirs. Lawyers drafted, debated, revised, enacted, proclaimed, decreed, defined, construed, interpreted, declared, upheld, enforced, defended, abrogated, repealed, nullified, amended, struck down, attacked or averted law upon laws needed as the growing country expanded in population, size and commerce.

When others sought to encroach upon this province, lawyers organized to monopolize. The first bar association, the Association of the Bar of the City of New York, was founded in 1870; eight years later, the American Bar Association was organized.

The original bar associations were formed partly in response to rising competition by laymen. "Competition from outside the profession began to figure as a material element in the economic situation of the bar."[7]

As the practice of law grew to serve national or interstate business, organizations such as title companies, collection agencies, trust companies, banks and accountants became intimately engaged in business traditionally performed by lawyers. The bar responded to this competition with a doctrine called "unauthorized practice of law," which has been used to justify use of legal sanctions against others to maintain inviolate the territory of lawyers.[8]

Harry M. Daugherty, attorney to the later Ohio gang, wrote, "Law and politics go hand in hand." Many lawyers, seeking their fortunes, turned to politics as a business in which huge returns could be realized. It was inevitable that those seeking political favor, franchise or privilege would have to turn to lawyers for advice or grant. Lawyers, by the nature of their profession, were the first to learn of the areas of crime or corruption. Those seeking to escape sought advice, those caught in the violations of law exposed their mode of operation and the nature and extent of wealth involved.

Lawyers became the first peddlers of influence and favor in exchange for fees. When asked, "How do I know you can produce?", lawyers went to strongboxes with secret lists of men they controlled in the legislatures. It was common knowledge up to Teddy Roosevelt's administration that a Southern Congressman's vote could be had for as little as ten dollars. Lawyers could advise on what the state of the law was or how it could be circumvented. Theirs was an enviable position of being on the inside or both sides in a system of democratic government that supported free election to all city, state and federal offices.

Just as the nation flexed its industrial muscle and might, Ohio politicians exerted political machinations of intrigue that dominated the country for half a century after the Civil War. Ohio was known as the "Mother of presidents." Beginning with the election of Ulysses Simpson Grant in 1868 to the Warren G. Harding election of 1920, seven native-born sons, all Republicans, entered the White House during these 52 years to epitomize the fact that Ohio was indeed the hotbed of national political activity and intrigue. The city bosses, county bosses and state bosses nationwide exchanged ideas on political manipulation. As long as they held the power to nominate, they could control.

General Ulysses S. Grant began the parade of Ohio presidents to the White House in 1868. Rutherford B. Hayes in 1876 and James A. Garfield in 1880 made it three in a row. Running for Governor of Ohio was equated to running for President of the United States. After election of Benjamin Harrison as 23rd President, the "Ohio Gang" came into power. This was a newspaper term applied to the group of shrewd politicians who were years ahead of the rest of the country in political machinations. Graft was prevalent in each administration as it knew no party or politics. Bribery and corruption were not accidental and occasional, but general and deliberate. For every bribe given, there was also a taker. Machine politicians, as organized by party, believed the end-all of the game was to win power and spoils. They accepted corruption and graft as a necessary part of politics.

Marcus Alonzo Hanna of Cleveland became the first prominent "business man in politics." He learned that granting of favor and franchises to political friends was lucrative business. It was a form of public privilege that he wanted. His companies and colleagues in gas and street railway corporations had to appeal to city governments for fees, rates and use of public streets and facilities. They needed to make peace with the parties in power.[9]

Like the businessman in politics, there also developed the elite lawyer, a man who stood at the top of his profession and had political power as well. It was these men who took control and supervision of candidates for office, supporting those who were tractable and thereby taking over cities, states and finally the government nationally.

Walter F. Brown became one of the most famous names in Toledo politics. Born in Massillon, Ohio, in 1869, he moved to Toledo where his father was a member of the bar and local postmaster. Brown started his career as a newspaperman. Later, he despised newspapermen, claiming "there's not one I trust," as he avoided publicity of any kind. All his activities were kept in a low profile. Upon graduation from Harvard in 1892, he turned to law and politics. Brown was brilliant; he had psychological insight into group behavior. He made a dignified, conservative appearance, was soft-spoken yet a persuasive talker. His word was always good. Once his promise was given, it was kept. Brown learned that politics was a form of business. A lawyer having political leverage (commonly called clout) with judges and government officials would make a formidable opponent. Few, if any, could stand up against such a lawyer. Just as Hanna became the businessman in politics, Brown became a lawyer in politics. Local newspapers claimed Brown turned to politics to make money.[10] If love of money was the root of all evil, the early lawyer-politicians had enormous greed and cupidity. History would prove their sense of integrity and honor was lost in the lust for power and money. Emerson wrote, "The word 'honor' in the mouth of Daniel Webster was like the word 'love' in the mouth of a whore." Walter Brown was of this ilk. He was penurious from the start in politics. Stories about his tightfistedness were legion.

Brown, the lawyer in politics, dominated Toledo Republican politics for half a century. He encouraged Firetop to join his ranks. Firetop learned from him that the political segment of the triangle of corruption of police, politicians and underworld was the strongest. No enterprise of police and criminals alone could operate without a prosecutor, sheriff or mayor, who appointed a chief, being privy to the action. Even a strong newspaper could ruin an enterprise if the elective officials or the politicians behind the scenes were remiss in their duty.

Before the 1890s, William McKinley, as Governor of Ohio, had incurred huge personal debts. He was considering a return to his private law practice to pay his creditors. Mark Hanna, later labled "Kingmaker," as national political leader and head of Ohio Republicans, bailed him out. Hanna called up a group of wealthy men including Andrew Carnegie, Henry Frick, Charles Taft and John Hay to raise a fund of $130,000 to pay McKinley's creditors. With his career restored, he won election as the 25th President in 1896. He repaid the Ohio Gang in favors and privilege. McKinley was reelected to a second term in the election of November 1900. His term was aborted as he became the third martyred President. He was shot on November 6, 1901, at the Pan-American Exhibition in Buffalo, New York. Teddy Roosevelt succeeded McKinley for the balance of his second term and was reelected in 1904. The Golden Age of the Republican Party lasted from just after the Civil War until the death of the national Boss Mark Hanna in 1904.

The Ohio Gang succeeded in electing still another lawyer, William Howard Taft, as the sixth Ohio Republican President. Taft was defeated for reelection by Thomas Woodrow Wilson, an attorney who turned to academia in 1912.

After an eight-year absence from national power during Wilson's terms, the Ohio Gang again went to work. With another elite lawyer, Harry M. Daugherty, campaign manager, Walter F. Brown predicted that their candidate, Warren G. Harding, would be nominated and elected by 15 men in a "smoke-filled room." When Harding asked his campaign manager, "Am I a big enough man for the race?" Daugherty told a friend, "The day of greatness in the presidential chair is over. . . . Greatness in the presidential chair is largely an illusion."[11]

Politicians of that era knew they could put any person on the ballot. Then by the ballyhoo of promotion and publicity, get such candidate elected. History will credit the Ohio Gang for starting the chain of mediocrity of men in public office that continues to the present time

Examination of all the administrations from Grant to Harding indicated in each shocking and scandalous graft.[12]

Republicans alone were not to blame. In New York, William Marcy (Boss) Tweed and his cohorts at Tammany Hall in 1869-1871 were swindling the city and state of millions.

In 1871, Thomas Nast created his best cartoon of Tweed showing the Tammany Tiger gouging on a prostrate human in a Roman carnival-like arena. The New York *Times* called it the most impressive political picture ever written.

"Stop them damn pictures," Boss Tweed said. "I don't care what the papers write about me. My constituents can't read. But damn it, they can see pictures."

Tweed's philosophy was, "Take all you can get — and spread it around as much as possible." He felt the more people involved in his manipulations, the safer the practice. In protecting themselves and each other, such protection, Tweed contended, would also extend to him.

During that same post-war period, Mark Twain, as a Washington reporter, wrote: "America has one habitual criminal class, the . . . Congress of the United States."[13]

Politicians as a group recognized their superior position and took best advantage of it. As part of the group, Ohio politicians took graft as part of the established system. The political thought at the time was that an election by the public was a mandate from the people to "get even" for the cost of election. The ripping-off of the public and lying were accepted ways of American political life.[14]

"Graft" is the general term given to any political activity that involves unjust enrichment in exchange for privilege or favor. It came with the election and the territory. For Toledoans in politics, this acceptance of graft would continue to be an accepted way of life.

# 5 Early Law Enforcement

Westward expansion of the Untied States was lead by hardy, rugged men seeking fortunes in gold, silver, farming, mining and land. They were a sturdy lot loving drink, gambling and women. Most modern western movies correctly depicted life of a frontier city. At the first crossroad of any new town, the first structure was a saloon. Loose men and loose dollars lured loose women. The flourishing of prostitution in modern Las Vegas and Atlantic City was preordained. Gambling, prostitution and social drinking were established early as American ways of life. As the cities were established, churches, law and order came. When the authorities wanted to stop the unlawful activity, the "Underworld," as the newspapers named them, turned to the police for protection. The early police were simply too stupid to know what to do. The chief usually went to the mayor who had appointed him, and together they plotted with the Underworld. As long as payments were made, operation was permitted. In every city of any size, Toledo included, a triumvirate was established where, in the beginning, the Underworld worked for the police and politicians.

This background information in the development of police protection is essential to understand the ultimate triumvirate. The police were the weakest segment of the structure, for they served at the sufferance of the politicians. Police chiefs were not elected, only appointed. Frontier citizens were permitted to carry guns to protect their families and property against the Indians and roving gangs. As townships and cities grew, government law enforcement agencies and personnel relieved the townspeople of the burden of protection. Early history was correctly depicted in the movie versions where justice was often meted out by a sheriff who told the criminal offender, "If you are not out of town by sundown, I'll shoot you on sight."[1]

The first law enforcement officer in Lucas County was the sheriff. The position was first created by appointment and later changed to an elective office. Historically, some claim the name was derived from the Arab word "Sharif" (nobleman). Some historians claim America was named for the Sheriff of Bristol, Richard Amerycke, who helped John Cabot's New World explorations.[2]

An early sheriff in America was John Nixon of Philadelphia, who gave the first public reading of the Declaration of Independence. George Washington's father, Augustine, served as an early sheriff of Westmoreland County, Virginia.[3]

In 1838 the first jail was accepted and $25 was appropriated by Lucas County for bedding and furnishings.[4] The sheriff, like most American officials, had county-wide authority in criminal matters, but his prime responsibility was outside the city limits.[5] Later, when police departments were organized, the police handled crime in the city while the sheriff took care of the rest of the county. This anomalous situation was used to advantage by politicians when city reformers chased the gamblers out of the city into the county. There, immune from police harassment, the gamblers needed only the sheriff's patronage to continue their operations.

In the city, the police or marshalls had jurisdiction. The first law enforcement officers of the City of Toledo were city marshals.[6] The origin of marshal is from the old High German words "marah", meaning horse, and "scalc", a servant, hence "marahscalc", a farrier or groom. In England the marshal had the duty of escorting (and later summoning) persons before the King.[7] The duty of the marshal in Federal Courts is a similar one to bring parties properly before the court in their proper districts. Sheriffs in the early years performed both duties.

The original authority of the sheriff as an officer of the court was in service of civil process, holding county prisoners, return and service of indictments and posting of court notices. In New York today, the function of the sheriff is strictly civil, in service of court process and subpoenas. There, a virtual bloodbath occurs every three years to obtain the Democratic nominations in each of the five boroughs. The office pay is $25,000 but the costs of services and subpoenas, taxed as court costs, bring in an additional $150,000 annually so that a sheriff of any New York borough could retire at the end of one term.

As Lucas County grew, the sheriff became more important politically. Staffs of 40 to 50 people were required at the turn of the century. Since the office was elective, an incoming sheriff would sweep out the entire staff of deputies of the defeated incumbent to satisfy his campaign obligations. The early elected sheriffs were usually police officers whom politicians urged to run. Since the politicians controlled the office, they fought change because the office was rich in patronage. Because they had no civil service protection until after 1954, police officers could be fired at any time.

In 1867, the office of elected city marshals was abolished by an act of the state legislature which created a paid police force for the City of Toledo.[8] Four men, one from each ward of the city, were made police commissioners by appointment of the Governor. They in turn appointed the police department. The mayor had no power to change these appointments — hence the police were controlled by the politicians.

The first superintendent, Henry Breed, received an annual salary of $1,500. The salary of Captain Michael C. O'Conner was $900, Sergeant William P. Scott $800 and 14 patrolmen received $720, or $15 per week. The state act provided for an additional policeman for each 1,500 increase in city population.[9]

The unattractive wages made it difficult to find educated or competent men of good moral character.[10] To encourage building of a workable force, the superintendent or chief, as he was later called, was given great latitude in running his department. In later years, he was answerable only to the mayor, an elected official. Generally, any male applying would be accepted provided he did not have any serious criminal record. Old-timers describing the early police said, "There was no degree of respectability attached to the job — which few wanted. There were no tests, no scholastic requirements, no screening, no compulsory target practice on the job. The physical requirements were minimal and if passed, an applicant was usually hired."

The classic tale of the early Toledo rookies was about one apprehending a criminal on Tecumseh Street. The story was the cop couldn't spell "Tecumseh", so he dragged the culprit over to Dorr Street to complete his report. Another classic tale was that of a rookie who apprehended two men in the crime of sodomy. Being unable to pronounce, spell or report "sodomy", he dismissed the pair with the admonition, "Don't let me catch you two doing what you were doing again." Another anecdote: a man bent on suicide dove into the river. A policeman nearby ran over, pulled out his gun and shouted, "Come on out or I'll shoot." The would-be suicide, thus thwarted, climbed out and prolonged his own life.

The budget for public safety may have been deliberately kept at a minimum by politicians so that they could control the police.

Police salaries remained less than $1,500 a year for 50 years. Salaries were raised to $150 a month in the middle 1920s and to a minimum of $175 after one year's tenure. Thereafter, staffing of the police department, promotions and placement of men was left entirely to the chief. When applicants were hired, they were given a club, a gun, a badge and uniform, and an assignment sheet outlining their general duties. The state law provided that a book of rules be read by the captain to the men each week. Usually a rookie worked with a veteran for a month and then was on his own. When an arrest was made, the criminal had to be led from the place of arrest to the police headquarters. There were no precincts. The first police station was built in 1873 when the city's population was 47,000.[11]

"Poverty corrupts and abject poverty corrupts absolutely", is the maxim to describe early abuses. The low pay made all policemen vulnerable and always on the take. Derelicts and drinking men were prevalent. A few drinks or a few dollars could bribe most of them. The men were not above temptation, asking or taking anything of value, for they felt as a group that society, by reason of the wage scale, owed them something — a handout of an apple from a stand, a drink in the back room of a saloon, a few cigars. None were above sticking their collective hands out at Christmas to the business people in their precincts. "Police began to justify their own conscience for the taking of a bribe where the lawful punishment was out of proportion to the offense committed. The bribe operated as a small fine, he decided, and that is all the offender deserves to pay."[12] Just as graft was later accepted by politicians as a way of life, bribery of police and corruption appeared early in the local history of such departments all over the country.[13]

All police transactions were subject to financial appraisal. There was a systematic and pervasive impact of bribery. In addition to bribes from the public, promotions could be purchased from a scale of $100 for a patrolman's advance to $1,500 for a captaincy.[14]

Prostitution and gambling were commonplace in the early community growth. The American lust to work was matched by the lust to gamble. The need for protection from harassment or arrest was realized by the underworld elements. When an individual policeman was approached with offers of bribes, he would often confer with his chief or with legal advisors in the law department charged with enforcement. The law departments of the city and county became the hubs in the wheels that turned the favors and privileges. All political leaders kept colleagues in these offices to be advised of any problems so that the machinery of "fixers" could go into action. Operators knew that without protection from prosecution, their rackets or illicit activities could never continue operations.

Partnerships between politicians, police and criminals in all types of business, legal and illegal, became commonplace. The political fixer Firetop knew all the ropes. His function was to control judges and other public officers to see that they did not perform their legal duties and to see that protection for the whole scheme worked. [15]

"It was the money that gave these people power."

"He who has money and friends can sneer at the law."

Endemic of all cities, police bribery was condoned and nobody seemed to care.

A good relationship with the chief and a chance for placement on the vice squad was the goal of each man in the department. The city hierarchy of rank and organization placed a service director over the police and fire departments, answerable to the mayor. This relationship never seemed to have much effect for the vice squad personnel could take even when a service director did not.

As the city grew, precincts and substations were established. Call boxes were installed to facilitate delivery of criminals by wagon and later by motor vehicle to the city jail. Later, when fully mechanized, command officers were assigned chauffeurs. Field promotions from the chief were common — he could and did appoint as he desired — particularly on acts of bravery or where great publicity or credit was given to an officer.

With the growth of the city and county, more courts were established.

Justice of the Peace courts, as elective offices in the townships, were created for handling minor traffic violations, minor breaches of the peace and small civil cases. Municipal courts were established to handle traffic violations and crimes involving penalties of less than one year in jail. These crimes were called misdemeanors. Crimes involving penalties in excess of one year in jail were felonies. These distinctions were prior to the adoption of the new Criminal Code and Revisions in Ohio.[15] The Common Pleas Courts of each county disposed of all felony cases. As arrests occurred more frequently, police would make the reports and then detectives would take over investigation to develop the necessary facts and evidence for prosecution or court work. The police department of the city prepared misdemeanor court cases. In the handling of misdemeanor cases, a law department appointed by the mayor was the legal advisor for the police. The city (municipal) courts could and did hear all criminal cases. Those in which the courts found probable cause of the commission of a felony would be bound over to the Common Pleas Court of Lucas County. If an indictment was returned, the matter would then be tried in that court.

The prosecuting attorney, an elective office, was the legal advisor for all county officials. His staff included attorneys of various specialties who would prepare the cases for court action or trial by jury. On conviction of a misdemeanor, city prisoners went to the city workhouse established in Whitehouse, Ohio. In felony convictions the criminals were usually sent to state reformatories or penitentiaries but were housed in the Lucas County Jail until conviction.

The use of police to detect crime and prepare court cases, both city and county, had adverse ramifications.

Some officers, envious of the income of vice and morals squad personnel, were easily corrupted or bribed to secretly report evidence received to criminal elements or their counsel paying for the same or to bondsmen or court clerical personnel to determine risks on bonds or to "fix" or lessen offenses charged.

It was easier for an accused to obtain probation on a misdemeanor than a felony. The police, however lacking in intelligence, were quick to learn these ropes!

In the later Licavoli murder trials, it was claimed that "There were more leaks in the Toledo Police Department than in the men's room of Grand Central Station."

Such was the accepted state of affairs in the first 70 years of law enforcement in Toledo. The Toledo triumvirate was able to share in the epidemic of corruption that followed from the end of the Civil War to 1900. The vast reaches of a magnificent continent were looted on a scale unrivaled in the history of human greed."[17] The time was ripe for exposé. A furious President Theodore Roosevelt deplored the massive injustices and corruption and that "an American society, in its greed, had cast overboard all concept of honor and most of the principles of true democratic government."[18] TR coined the phrase "muckraker" for those who collected filth, from Bunyan's *Pilgrim's Progress*. He attacked the journalists who had aroused the American people over the wrongdoings that prevailed. McClure Magazine became the vehicle of such writers. The magazine proposed to write a series of articles about the Underworld to tell it the way it was. Such series began in 1900 under the title "True Stories from the Underworld." The articles were later collected into a book, *The Powers that Prey,* followed by *Notes of an Itinerant Policeman.* The purpose of disclosure was in the hope of reform.[20] McClure wanted articles on every city in which corruption was rampant. In 1901, Lincoln Steffens joined McClure. Steffens had risen to the top of his profession with his writings of police corruption in New York, told through the reformer, Dr. Charles H. Parkhurst. The famous Lexow investigation of 1893 followed these sensational exposures. Steffens became America's premier muckraker. The search for muck caused Steffens to travel to Ohio.

# 6 Golden Rule Jones, An Honest Politician

"There are things going on in your police department that you and the Chief ought to know about," Lincoln Steffens wrote to Sam (Golden Rule) Jones, the best-loved mayor of Toledo.[1]

There is no record of any response to this letter.

When Steffens originally set out from New York to write his muckraking stories of the corrupt cities at the turn of the century, he mentioned that he intended to write about Toledo, for the infamy of the city was well known. Toledo, Spain was one of the earliest centers of Christian culture. That place originally was the source of the enduring exclamation "Holy Toledo." The Ohio city could never earned such acclaim.

Steffens had written "Tweed days in St. Louis,"[2] and of corruption in Minneapolis,[3] Chicago[4] and New York.[5] He described Pittsburgh as "Hell with the lid off,"[6] and Philadelphia as the "City of Brotherly Loot."[7] The prominence and respectability of the lawyers and politicians who interceded for crooks aroused the American conscience.

Steffens learned more about cities than he ever wrote, much that he could never write. Every major city was suspect.

In his tours of the country, Steffens looked for good men who had the caliber of leadership. In Ohio, he found such men: Tom Johnson of Cleveland, Samuel Milton Jones and Brand Whitlock, mayors of

Toledo. All were pioneers in the Reform movement sweeping the country at the turn of the century.

Steffens' stories clearly demonstrated that criminals, police and politicians had formed a working triumvirate, each dependent upon the other.[8] Steffens found Jones and Whitlock basically honest and not in privy with wrongdoers. Neither shared in any political spoils. Consequently, out of friendship, Steffens did not muckrake Toledo,[9] although there was ample evidence of its corruption.

As the country's third-largest railroad center, Toledo serviced more than 30 different railroad lines.

Toledo was less than a day from New York City, six hours from Pittsburgh, four hours from Cleveland, two from Detroit and six from Chicago. Crooks could, and did, hop out of the city, commit a robbery or burglary and return to the city within hours.

Many crooks lived in Toledo and were protected as long as they behaved. They would not be picked up or harassed for minimal provocation. This was the policy of "Silver Jack" Carewe, Chief of Detectives, and Mayor Jones agreed.[10]

A man was not arrested in Toledo for mere suspicion or because he was known to have a past record. Many criminals on the lam sought the sanctuary of Toledo police or the sheriff. For a stipulated fee, fliers from other police departments were either ignored or received a response of "not known, or not found." Sometimes the police would take an inquiry to the local underworld, apprehend the wanted criminal, and "arrange" for his protection in the city.

Del Kaufman, known as the Delmonico Kid, an internationally known confidence man, was a frequent visitor to the Toledo streets and hangouts. In his youth, the Kid was reportedly shot in the leg by a disgruntled victim and amputation of a leg below the knee was required. An artificial limb gave Kaufman reason to sport a diamond studded gold handled cane, which he displayed ostentatiously. A suite at the Waldorf Hotel, then a fashionable downtown residence, was always reserved for his use when in the city. Friends claimed the Kid had over 150 different suits and he would change clothes three times a day.[11]

Sam Hessler, an unscrupulous riverboat gambler, was also a frequent visitor. As a professional card shark and con man, he was permitted to hide out as long as he cut the police in on a share of his winnings. Sam dressed like a country banker or preacher. He appeared as the essence of integrity, with his low, soft voice, smiling face and clean-cut features. He wore high, stiff collars and had his dark hair parted in the center of his head. He would venture daily down to the railroad station to "size up" likely prospects or have hired stooges make inquiries about newcomers to the city. He would invariably learn where such guests stayed, engage them in some conversation and eventually inveigle them into some games of chance where such victims never had a prayer. If they complained to police about their losses, they were threatened with arrest themselves for participating in games of chance.[12]

Even the ladies were welcome. The incredible Chessie Chadwick, alias Betsy (Elizabeth) Bigley, also known as Madam Lydia DeVere, clairvoyant, also known as Mrs. Wallace Springsteen and Mrs. John R. Scott, plied her trade and charms at Clayton and Broadway Streets in Toledo.[13] Many bankers, whom she ruined, claimed her to be the most incredible forger and swindler ever encountered. After conviction and a term in jail, President McKinley pardoned her in 1896. Chessie then moved to Cleveland. There she made claims of being the love child of Andrew Carnegie. Using fake documents, she duped various bankers into loaning her huge sums secured by her alleged potential inheritance. Such escapades led to reconfinement in the Ohio pen. There she paid for a gravestone to be erected before her death and, incredibly, prepared her own obituary which was eventually read at her funeral.

Lefty Louie (Rosenberg), one of the gunmen involved in the 1912 murder of Herman Rosenthal, the cop-baiting New York gambler, was reported to have hidden out in Toledo for months while New York police and Burns detectives searched in Denver, Boston, Tallahassee and Fargo, North Dakota.

An accomplice in the same murder gang, allegedly implicated by Police Lieutenant Charles Becker, was Harry Horowitz (alias Gyp The Blood). In her book "Against the Evidence," Andy Logan, wrote "Gyp The Blood was the favorite of the feature writers. He had been a bouncer in Bowery dance halls and liked to boast that he could break a man's spine with his two hands. It was even said that he kept in practice by demonstrating his prowess from time to time on some harmless bystander. He had once explained that his favorite assignment was throwing bombs because "I likes to hear da noise."[14]

Ironically, Rosenthal was gunned down because he had written letters to New York newspapers implicating police officers as grafters who were preying on the city's gamblers. Small wonder Toledo quartered Rosenberg!

In downtown Toledo, Dominy's Bar had its entire cellar dug out and redesigned as a long term hide-out for the most wanted. Criminals could eat, sleep, drink and gamble for months without fear of being apprehended. Joe Muzzio, alias Cowboy Bill, a notorious gunman, spoiled his stay in Toledo by a shoot-out with local police in the Jewish neighborhood on a Yom Kippur Day in 1920.[15]

Later Jack (Legs) Diamond, Bennie Singer, John Dillinger, Pretty Boy Floyd and the Purvis gang used Toledo and the islands of Lake Erie as hide-outs or escape routes. Alvin Karpis claimed Toledo was his refuge. He had contacts here. He and Harry Campbell shacked up at Edith Barry's whorehouse.[16]

Toledo was wide open with an enormous welcome mat.

Mayor Jones was tolerant of gambling. He regarded it as a social habit. He felt police action was aimed at the "little fellow" who was easy to get. Saloons didn't close on time. Jones called saloons "the poor man's playground," and he said if private clubs could open for the rich on Sundays, then saloons could serve the poor workingman. A segregated vice district with widespread prostitution flourished. In Toledo, it was called The Line. Some cities called such areas the Tenderloin as the area from which police took graft in order to eat Tenderloin steak. Jones took clubs away from police to avoid brutality.[17]

Steffens was obviously deterred from writing about Toledo because of his friendship with Brand Whitlock, a fellow novelist and journalist, and one of Steffens' disciples in the old guard of muckraking and reform.

It was Brand Whitlock who wrote, "The great problem is to make the government of a city 'human'."[18]

Whitlock took Steffens to meet Samuel Milton Jones. Steffens was favorably impressed by this big, strong, intense man. His black and gray hair, flashing eyes and large mustache gave Jones a dignified appearance. Jones had to go to work at an early age. He had become a day laborer in the Pennsylvania oil fields. His formal education was meager.

He moved to Lima, Ohio, in 1876 where he became interested in leasing oil lands and drilling wells during the famous Ohio-Indiana oil boom. Jones applied his inventive mind to producing better petroleum appliances and invented a tool known as the Acme suckerrod. He formed the Acme Sucker Rod Company to manufacture the appliance, later changing the name to the S. M. Jones Company.[19]

After his first meeting with Jones, Steffens wrote, "Jones, for all his money, remained as work-toughened as those of his employees. He also retained a bardic, visionary quality which came from his reading of Walt Whitman but which people were apt to trace back to his Welsh origins. He ran his factory by the Golden Rule which was painted on a large sign nailed to the wall; it was the only regulation he posted, and it replaced warnings, supervisors, time clocks, and even Golden Rule Jones' first name. During the depression of the nineties, Jones paid a living wage instead of the going wage, and he introduced an eight-hour work day, hot lunches at cost, vacations with pay, profit-sharing, sickness and disability insurance. On Sundays, in the factory's Golden Rule Hall or under the willow trees in the park and playground, there were concerts and addresses by outside speakers on themes of brotherhood, equality and the social gospel."[20]

Jones talked less about politics and administration than about poets and prophets — "He was practicing what they preached," Steffens was to say — and he read aloud passages from *Leaves of Grass* and the *New Testament*.

"I do not believe that we are to get very much relief from the evils that distress us by legislation," Jones said. In time, according to his scheme of things, society would regenerate itself and become a true commonwealth.

Later, as he walked along to the railroad station with Whitlock, Steffens mused aloud, "Why, that man's program will take a thousand years."[21]

Still, the first steps, at least, were visible in Toledo, even though the city's businessmen had opposed Jones and called him utopian, socialist and traitor to his class when he fought for home rule and municipal ownership, expanded recreational facilities, lower transit fares and a city administration free of party politics.

According to the clergy, he was the tool of the liquor interests because on Sundays he disregarded the ordinances and permitted the saloons to stay open, arguing that the people had earned their pleasures. He fought "police-court justice" as it was dealt out to gamblers, prostitutes and petty thieves. When he sat as magistrate, he sometimes let them off. "What was the point of punishing the victims of a system?" he asked. He was often to be found visiting the workhouse and the prison. Vagrants came to his office for help.[22]

In politics, Jones was primarily responsible for the so-called independent movement — an office free from party control.

In 1897 Jones was elected mayor after being nominated by the Walter F. Brown-led Republicans. His conduct during his first term in office lost him the support of such party leaders who were determined to prevent his renomination. Where the politicians couldn't control the mayor, their ability to obtain the plunder of victory was lost or impaired.

Jones was determined to get a second nomination in 1899. He had no intention of withdrawing from the race. After losing the Republican nomination in May of that year by a very close vote, he announced himself as an independent candidate. On election day he received twice as many votes as the Republican and Democratic candidates combined and carried every precinct in the city but one. "Nobody loves me but the people," he said.

He tried to govern the city by the rule he used in running his factory, "And as ye would that man should do to you, do ye also unto him." Unfortunately, Jones did not understand the basic nature of democratic government. He interpreted non-partisan to mean anti-party, and much of his political energy was used in an unremitting war upon both political parties. He refused to permit his followers to organize as a formal political unit. When they did so, they were without his support to organize or control the city council. It could be equated to a Presidency with an opposition party-controlled Congress. Consequently, his accomplishments in his eight years of office were meager.

His first plank in his platform of municipal reform was public ownership of public utilities.[23] Jones felt patronage, franchise and favor to private owners was a form of graft and corruption. Jones could not see or understand "profit" from politics. He believed good government meant honest government as he practiced it.

During his fourth term, Jones vetoed a council bill for a proposed street railway franchise. A political storm erupted. City council was preparing to override his veto when a vast, protesting crowd stormed into City Hall. This incident, entitled "Petition in Boots," prolonged Jones' fight against private ownership of utilities.

The attorney for the street railway company asked Jones, "I suppose this is an example of government under the Golden Rule?" "No," Jones replied, "it is an example of government under the rule of gold."[24] Jones may have been referring to Tweed days in St. Louis of 1902 where wholesale bribery of the entire legislature led to granting of the franchise. Such privilege as in utilities were monopolitic in character — without competition — in the allotted geographical area.

One of Jones' earliest reforms had been the lowering of transit rates. There was a poignant tribute to Jones' memory in the mere fact that the day after his death, stocks in the Toledo Street Railway Company ran a twenty-four point gain.[25]

As to the other vices, Jones was opposed to public gambling — touts and capers. His intimates explained, "but he could not see a system where the police raided some small place in which half a dozen men were gambling for a few pennies while men gambling for much more in hotels or clubs went unmolested. That, he would point out, was not suppressing gambling but merely persecuting those who were easy to get, who didn't have the means to make them difficult for the police to reach. He also would point out that gambling on the stock markets was permitted and that a church might conduct a lottery or drawing."[26]

Whitlock relates in his autobiography how a committee of men and women once called upon Mayor Jones with a demand that he obliterate prostitution, "offhand and instantly."

"But what am I to do?" Mayor Jones asked. "These women are here."

"Have the police drive them out of town and close up all their houses," they replied.

"But where will I have the police drive them?" Whitlock quotes Jones as replying. "Over to Detroit or Cleveland, or merely out to the country? They have to go somewhere, you know. I'll make you a proposition," the mayor continued. "You go and select two of the worst women you can find and I'll agree to take them into my home and provide for them until they can find some other home and some other way of making a living. And then you, each of you, take one girl into your home under the same conditions, and together we'll try to find homes for the rest."

The members of the committee looked at him, then at each other, Whitlock relates, then, seeing how utterly hopeless this strange man was, went away.[27]

The years 1902 to 1912 were the banner years of reform.[28]

Jones, in his unique fashion, became a Reform leader. Inept by reason of his inability to understand politics, and frustrated over the lack of progress toward Reform, the "humanizing" mayor died suddenly at age 58 during his fourth term in office. His last hope was that Brand Whitlock or others would pursue the ideals he fostered.

# 7 Brand Whitlock, An Honest Lawyer

Toledo's most famous mayor, Brand Whitlock, won international recognition for his courageous role in Belgian Relief during and after World War I.[1] He had been appointed minister by President Woodrow Wilson in 1913 and was elevated to ambassador after the end of hostilities.[2]

Born in 1869, the son of a Methodist minister, young Brand was brought to Toledo as one of the cities served in his father's circuit. In high school, dominant Walter F. Brown lured him into his first campaign by successful management of the election of senior class president. The two were close friends until Whitlock became a protege of Golden Rule Jones.[3] Thereafter he and Brown remained life-long enemies. Whitlock learned of Brown's political clout and machinations and would not be privy to it. The two were diametrically opposed. At 18, Whitlock was a reporter for the Toledo *Blade*. Later, Congressman Frank C. Hurd befriended the young journalist by helping him join the staff of the Chicago *Herald* in 1891. There he became part of the Whitechapel Club, which included some of the finest political satirists and writers in the nation. Finley Peter Dunn, author of the Mr. Dooley series, humorist George Ade, Charles Seymour, Alfred Henry Lewis and muckraker Lincoln Steffens were leaders of this elite group. Whitlock joined as its musical and piano playing member.[4]

After a year of intensive reporting, Whitlock was asked to write speeches for Illinois Governor John Peter Altgeld who became famous for his pardoning of the "alleged anarchists" convicted in the Chicago Haymarket Riot of 1886. The pardon doomed Altgeld's advance in politics.

From his experiences, exposure and writings as a young man, the impressionable Whitlock became disenchanted with his Democratic Party. He wrote, "He had turned to the Democratic Party and trusted it to redeem its promise to reform . . . evil . . . only to have leaders in the Senate betray such trust . . ."[5] He despaired of his chosen party and of the party system as it developed in America.[6] His steadfast later reluctance to run politically can be traced to his early experience and repulsion by its corruption.

Whitlock turned to the study of law. He hoped to use it as a tool of reform. In 1894 he gained admission to the Illinois Bar. Three years later he returned to Toledo to begin a practice with "sincere concern for the common man and all his problems." He started with a developed wit, poise and charm that opened the doors of the elite everywhere. Continuing his literary career in his leisure moments, he wrote a series of articles, short stories and a money-making novel on politics, "The Thirteenth District." He was tall, slender, of scholarly appearance. He wore Norfolk jackets and elegant clothes. He talked at the level of the common man with humor and charisma. Golden Rule Jones visited him when he learned of his work on the cases of the poor. The two joined forces in the Reform movement. Whitlock became Jones' chief counsel in 1902.[7]

In a murder case where Whitlock won an acquittal for his client, the Toledo *Bee* said: "He made one of the best arguments ever heard in Toledo. It was characterized by clear, incisive English, careful and logical arrangement of facts, penetrating analysis and keen sarcasm."[8]

One of his noble characteristics was his command of himself. Never did he lose his temper or utter anything derogatory to even the most unworthy of his opponents. His ambition was to teach men by example that political campaign could be conducted without abuse or hatred.[9] Whitlock's idealism led to other ends. Neither political party "blew the whistle" on corruption of the other. Both declared, "We don't campaign that way in Toledo," thus perpetuating abuses rather than ending them through exposure. Whitlock refused to degrade lawyers or politics by public comments. He fictionalized them in his writings, hoping for change.

As a Progressive, Whitlock advocated equality for women who had heretofore been "just sort of cleaning up after the men."[10]

Whitlock became a frequent Sunday speaker at Golden Rule's park. When Jones died, Whitlock delivered a moving eulogy at the funeral. A municipal holiday was declared. 55,000 people from all walks of life paid their last respects; many wept, openly and unashamed.

Following the death of Golden Rule Jones, Lincoln Steffens urged Brand Whitlock to run for mayor, calling him "the most advanced leader in America politics today." Steffens himself had become a national reform hero after his magazine publication on the "Shame of Minneapolis: The Rescue and Redemption of a City That Was Sold Out." His articles described the intricate workings of a system of corruption that "for deliberateness, invention, and avarice has never been equalled." The Minnesota bosses had franchised blackmail, theft, confidence games, crooked gambling and prostitution; they had invited known criminals to come in and rob the people. No one would call Steffens "liar" or cry "libel" as he had facts, names, dates, figures and documents to satisfy the editor and publisher of McClure's magazine completely.[11]

The Oscar Wilde case in England a few years before had taught a bitter lesson to those who sued for damages in libel. Wilde had lied to his lawyer when he filed civil charges against the Marquis of Queensbury for his allegation that Oscar had "posed as a sodomite."[12] Wilde lost the suit, had to pay costs and fees. Moreover, the evidence adduced at the original trial was the predicate for his later criminal conviction on morals charges ending in imprisonment and eventual exile.

Steffens' writings and ever increasing investigation of cities revealed municipal governments could not reclaim integrity during their years of rapid change. Whitlock himself concurred in writing: "Government of cities was a conspicuous failure in the United States."[13]

Steffens, Whitlock and colleague Frederick C. Howe agreed the "city was the hope of democracy."[14] "One city was all cities" and their hopes were to create national concern for the success of democracy in Toledo.[15] They naively assumed that the problem of one city literally applied to another.[16]

Whitlock visited Steffens at the McClure magazine offices. They were both coming heroes of the progressive era. Whitlock had combined his literature with politics and law. Steffens boasted, "Whitlock has seen everything and he can tell it."

The articles by Steffens had turned the tide of public opinion in favor of reform. "Reform costs nothing so everybody asks for it, provided the costs remain the same."

Whitlock wrote, "as long as his (Steffens) writings exposed only the low and vulgar politicians, ward heelers and bosses, and the like, he was quite popular; ... even asked to deliver addresses ... but when he went more deeply, when he exposed the respectable connections of the machine politicians, some of his admirers fell away . . ."[17]

In a short story entitled, "Fowler Brunton, Attorney at Law," written in 1907, Whitlock deplored the conduct of his fellow lawyers. "Lawyers were only liked by businessmen to advise them how, and with skill, cunning and address, they could commit crimes without violating the law."[18] Whitlock hoped his public admonitions would have a therapeutic effect towards reform.

He wrote, "People were delighted when some other city other than their own was under scrutiny, but there was an uplifting of hands in pious horror when a local study came. Reform is popular so long as someone else is to be reformed."[19]

Reform means end of graft with wise consideration of good government. How could one write "literature" about business and politics, the controlling institutions from which American intellectuals were alienated and excluded? The Steffens group saw the answer in a concept of truth-telling. The new reform non-partisan movement was to be the vehicle of change. As the new champion of the non-partisan movement, a reluctant Brand Whitlock was induced to succeed Golden Rule Jones as mayor. He was by inclination a Democrat, but he found the role of Independent much to his liking.

To free himself from the power and discipline of the Republican and Democratic parties of the period, he organized an Independent Party. A constitution was drafted to insure maximum participation of the people and to prevent the rise of a strong mayor. Privilege, cloaked in the form of partyism, was the great fear of Whitlock and his contemporaries.[20]

"Privilege" was a source of evil.[21]

In his campaign, Whitlock urged voters to elect Independent Party candidates, stating: "The most important thing in this campaign is to elect men who can be trusted." This was the truth-telling that won most Reform campaigns.

The city responded as Independent candidates and Whitlock were swept into office.

With Whitlock at their head, they took and held control of city council. However, the Independents were uniformly beaten when they attempted to extend their influence in elections for county and state offices, for here the Republicans remained strong.[22] The Republican party under Walter F. Brown, his nemesis, provided the principal opposition for the Independents. During the Whitlock era, Democratic strength dwindled almost to the vanishing point. In 1911, for instance, at the time of his last re-election for a fourth term, the Democratic candidate for mayor ran fourth, behind the Independent, the Republican and the Socialist. The Democrats elected only one candidate to the 18-man city council.

It was evident later that the non-partisan enthusiasts had ignored a number of important factors in their analysis of municipal governments.

The Independent non-partisan movement in Toledo, for all the theoretical soundness of its position, was in reality based upon the outstanding personalities of Jones and Whitlock. Men of this caliber could not be counted upon to appear with sufficient frequency to insure continued success.[23] For another thing, it was plain that city governments did not function in a vacuum. A man who was an efficient and able non-partisan mayor would also be a man ambitious for higher posts, and these could not be had without party affiliation.[24] It was apparently impossible to completely disengage the politics of the city from the politics of the state and nation.[25] In retrospect, the reformers failed to reform, for their actions were limited to the geographical areas in which reformers were elected.

Reform had to be first statewide and then nationwide for complete effectiveness. Tom Johnson, the great Cleveland Reform Mayor, proved the point.

Johnson was a teacher and a preacher. His power as a public educator was so great that everybody in Cleveland at the time could talk intelligently about franchises, property rights and taxation. He was not aware that a revolution in texts on teaching politics was needed.

"When the history of America is written, if ever it is properly written," Brand Whitlock was to tell Steffens, "Tom Johnson will tower high above all the other personalities it has flung up into the skyline. I should really be afraid to say just how great I think he is." Johnson's old enemy Hanna called him a "socialist-anarchist-nihilist." Roosevelt called him a "ruffian," an extremely undesirable person "from the moral standpoint." Steffens too, when he first came to Cleveland in the spring of 1902, had been prepared to dismiss Johnson as "a dangerous theorist with a dangerous ambition" — at worst, a demagogue, possibly an eccentric; at best, just another businessman playing at reform. "My ambition," Johnson told him then, savoring the reporter's disbelief, "is to make Cleveland the first American city to get good government." Everybody had heard that one before.[26]

"No man can finish a municipal reform job without going to the state," he told Steffens. When Steffens saw him in 1903, Johnson was running for governor.[27]

Ironically, Whitlock shared Jones' view on crime and criminals. When petitioned to clean up the city, he replied with a long discourse that is something of a classic. "It is a waste of time," he argued, "to attack crime by arresting criminals." The source must be attacked, and the source was poverty which, in turn, was the result of privilege and monopoly. Furthermore, it would be unpopular to enforce the law; had not he and Jones been regularly re-elected despite their failure to do so? He cited Havelock Ellis and other authorities to prove that moral crusades against prostitutes were futile.

Whitlock had little use for those people who self-righteously damned the poor prostitute. In a short story, "The Girl That's Down," he wrote: "There were lawyers who sold their brains for prices far higher than these girls who sold their souls."[28]

"Puritanical laws, the hounding of the police, and all that sort of thing have never lessened prostitution in the world, but to the contrary have increased it."[29]

Unlike Jones, Whitlock ordered professional gambling stopped,[30] but the police were remiss in enforcing his orders. "Working men never gambled," he said, and drew a parallel between stockbrokers and the gamblers. "You can not make people good by law," Whitlock declared, and concluded with the Jonesian sentiment that "Inequality and the denial of brotherhood were at the root of the problem." To critics who complained the city was wide open, Whitlock said, "A city is just as good as the people in it."

Jones and Whitlock were never privy to graft or corruption. Their injudicious political naivete on such was inconsequential — compared to the ruthless conduct of other mayors scorned in Steffens' epic work on political wrong-doing. Their inability to control the vice continuously rampant through the city during their terms in office created a reputation for the city equal to the most heinous Steffens described. Jones and Whitlock proved that honest but inept politicians could in some ways be more harmful than the corrupt, and often more undesirable. History records a preference for scoundrels over fools or sinners over saints.

How do you define corruption in politics? A need for special privileges! Corruption is neither of men nor of politicians. It is a system where those who seek privileges corrupt; those who possess privileges defend corrupt politics. It is these privileges that cause evil, not wickedness.

Big business monopolies in street car franchises, television and radio stations, utilities, trusts, railroads, banks — those with percentages in their favor or guaranteed profits, having the best of it — these are the privileged characters, corporate or personal. It is the struggle of the haves over the have nots; the resultant conflict that inevitably follows and demonstrates inherent problems.

To understand vice, prostitution or gambling, one must first understand that it is a form of business. Politics is a business; politicians are businessmen with a specialty.[31] The operators seek political corruption to obtain the privilege of breaking the law. These small businesses pay or share the profits as bribes for leniency or protection in the enforcement of laws, calling for "pulls" with judges, prosecutors and police, all controlled by political bosses.

It is obvious that continuous harassment by police would ruin any such business by driving away customers, increase costs or arrest, bond, attorney fees, court costs and so forth.

Once privilege is acquired, the corruption grows with time. Politics then represents the greatest power — the power to create, grant, alter, extend, renew, revoke, amend, enlarge, detract, suspend or increase the privilege — this is what it's all about.

In an article on city government, Whitlock argued: "The trail of graft leads always to privilege. The only way to eliminate graft is to eliminate the father of graft, which is privilege."[32]

As Lincoln Steffens observed a few years later, "Business and politics must be one — it was natural, inevitable and, possibly, right that business should — by bribery, corruption, or — somehow get and be the government."[33]

Upon lack of recognition in the state or nation, Whitlock again became disenchanted. This time it was public apathy to the Reform movement.[34] The American voter repeatedly returned to the two-party system. In Cleveland, after eight years of leading the best-governed city in America, Mayor Tom Johnson was defeated.[35] Broken in health and fortune, he returned to private life, doubting whether he had accomplished anything of value.[36] At the same time, Reform Independents were being beaten in San Francisco, Jersey City and Philadelphia.[37]

Despairing over the death of the Reform movement, Whitlock refused to run after his fourth term expired. Instead he accepted President Wilson's appointment to war torn Europe. His food program was universally acclaimed. Most Belgian cities named streets in his honor.

Whitlock was angered when stories circulated that Georges Clemenceau, the Tiger of France, spat on Wilson for his idealism during the peace treaty talks. He saw the President's vision of a League of Nations rejected by an ill-advised United States Senate which would reverse itself after a second holocaust. He despaired over the Republican "smoke filled room" selection of Harding, the scandals and the ascension of Walter F. Brown to the position of Postmaster General under Herbert Hoover. He knew such appointment was to repay those who financed the campaign.

Whitlock remained in Europe after the war. His literary output consisted of 18 books, numerous articles and short stories. His work continued to reflect his disenchantment with his fellow lawyers and American politics.[38] The New Deal under F.D.R. gave a hint of greater good for a greater number but Whitlock died before it could be evaluated. Following surgery at Cannes, France, he expired and was buried there on May 24, 1934. No heirs survived this disillusioned giant of the Reform era.

# 8 The Newspaper Game

Perusal of a newspaper has long been an American pastime. Most families held it was a pleasure to leisurely read the daily news in the era before radio or television. The job of delivery and supply to the public was left to newspaper circulation departments. Thousands of dollars were spent to keep customers satisfied, for it meant retaining circulation and continuing advertising revenues. Newspaper wars raged in every major city at the turn of the century.[1] The most violent was in Chicago in 1910 between the *Tribune* and *Examiner*. From these wars, the personnel for future gangs and liaisons were assembled.[2] The circulation battles offered a training ground for the system of gang warfare and racketeering that emerged in major cities in the 1920s and 30s. Newspaper wars formed only one source of personnel and techniques. From these exposures, many newsmen entered into gambling rackets and prostitution, with gangsters as partners and allies.[3]

Both sides in newspaper wars made use of underworld toughs, muscle and cash, encouraging their help to use intimidation, bribery, violence or trickery to prevent the rise or success of effective competition.

A city became a circulation battlefield. Newspapers had always gone to great lengths to establish critical newsstand locations; now they had

*UNHOLY TOLEDO*

to fight to keep them. The circulation business was traditionally tough; circulation men became their publishers' shock troops. The papers maintained crews of men who acted as field generals to control their newsboys with military authority as they dominated desirable corners. They were the muscle, or used muscle men or professional criminals. They depended on muscle and intimidation.[4]

An example of the rise of underworld elements to neutralize business opposition was described to a Senate committee in 1951 by Arthur B. (Mickey) McBride. At 24, McBride was a veteran of the Chicago newspaper battles. In 1913, the Cleveland *News* and *Leader,* both owned by the Hanna family, were engaged in a fierce circulation war with the city's two other newspapers, *The Plain Dealer* and *The Press.* McBride was hired as street sales manager to head the *News* forces. He explained, "The trouble was because they were chasing our boys off the streets, not permitting them to sell papers in Cleveland." Beating up on opposition or causing papers to disappear were common forms of action. Circulation managers earned reputations for ruthlessness. These tactics had to succeed because publishers would not stand for failure.

The method McBride employed to deal with the problem was the hiring of young toughs to push the sales of the *News* and *Leader* and make the work of the competition more difficult.[5]

Among those used by the Hanna papers were several future syndicate leaders including Alfred (Big Al) Polizzi, and Morris "Mushy" Waxler. Working opposite McBride in Chicago was James M. Ragan. When Moses Annenberg left his job as circulation manager of the Chicago *Tribune,* he took Ragan with him. In the '30s, they ran a highly successful wire service of horse race information to gamblers. They also published *The American Racing Record* which later became *The Daily Racing Form.* When Annenberg went to prison, Ragan took over, until his bitter battles with the Capone gang.[6]

In Toledo, two daily newspapers, as watchdogs of the public and critics of politics, were in competition at the turn of the century. The city needed a good press as its image was notoriously bad. The Toledo *Blade* was the Republican organ, the *News Bee,* the Democratic vehicle; both were afternoon editions. The Toledo *Times* was the only morning and Sunday paper.

The Toledo *Bee* and Toledo *News* combined on June 8, 1903, to form the Toledo *News Bee,* selling for one cent a copy until July 1, 1918. It had a circulation at the time of merger of 44,000, much larger than its rival, the Republican-oriented Toledo *Blade.*[7]

Cornelia Otis Skinner in her book "Life with Lindsay and Crouse" vividly described Crouse's father's life as editor of the *News Bee*.

> Hiram Powers Crouse had run his paper with unflagging public spirit. His editorials were perceptive and fearless, and through them he brought about a number of civic reforms which for long had been glaringly needed. He had the courage to realize that Toledo needed a complete political clean-up, one that should totally break with the professional politicians. As a consequence of his campaign efforts, the city elected its first non-political mayor in the person of Brand Whitlock. Hiram Crouse was by now one of Toledo's most respected citizens and, being an amiable man with a warm smile, he had a host of friends. Under his excellent guidance the *News-Bee* was running successfully — so successfully that the Scripps-McRae newspaper syndicate bought up a half-interest. It also bided its time until Crouse went on a trip to Europe. During his absence the syndicate, through some clever finagling, bought enough further stock to put it in the powerful position of being able to dictate the *News-Bee's* policies. These policies were at complete variance with those of its high-principled editor who, in disillusionment and disgust, sold off his own remaining shares and resigned.
> His many friends, plus a number of civic-minded citizens, distressed at the prospect of the city losing an editor of such integrity, banded together, raised enough funds to buy the Toledo *Press* and placed Hiram Crouse's name at the top of the masthead. The Scripps-McRae syndicate, regarding this paper as an upstart challenge, launched an overwhelming assault on the Toledo *Press* which, helpless against such competition, simply expired. Its unhappy editor-publisher all but expired with it. He had lost one quarter of a million dollars of his own money and owed a similar amount. Hopelessly bankrupt, he was forced to sell his house and possessions, including every book in his beloved library. His health gave way and he had a complete physical and emotional breakdown.
> This Toledo fiasco was the first of a series of financial disasters which, throughout his professional life, plagued this kindly, brilliant but improvident man. He was eventually to die owing thousands."[8]

In 1918 the *News Bee*, with Negley (Neg) Cochran as editor, sold for a penny and had a daily circulation of 86,000. The *Blade* sold for two cents and had 40,000 while the Toledo *Times*, later taken over by the *Blade*, had a circulation of 15,000.

On November 7, 1918, the *News Bee* ran a false story of the World War I Armistice. The erroneous calling of an end to hostilities was based on a report received from the United Press. The *Blade*, which used Associated Press releases, neither printed the story nor resorted to boasting when the true Armistice was signed four days later. The *Blade* in bold print typed "The *Blade* is the only afternoon paper carrying dispatches of the Associated Press."[9] The *News Bee* circulation further declined after another false extra on the Dempsey-Willard fight less than a year later.

The *Blade* was founded in 1835, originally as a weekly newspaper; later it was tri-weekly. Washington Irving previously suggested Toledo as the name for the American city. Toledo, Spain was famous for its weapons of beauty and quality. The Toledo *Blade* was named in reciprocal honor of that city. One of its original owners was Jessup W. Scott, businessman, builder and capitalist whose philanthropy made possible the founding of the University of Toledo. In 1865 David R. Locke, writing under the pen name of Petroleum V. Nasby, gave the *Blade* nationwide status by his brilliant and witty commentaries on American and world affairs. The humor of his speeches and writings was in great demand at the White House. Lincoln claimed the *Blade* articles made a war-weary President laugh.[10]

In his lifetime, publisher Paul Block, Sr. owned many newspapers — the New York *Evening Mail,* Newark *Star Eagle,* Brooklyn *Standard Union,* Los Angeles *Express,* Duluth (Minnesota) *Herald,* Memphis (Tennessee) *News Scimitar,* Lancaster Pennsylvania *New Era* and the Milwaukee *Sentinel.* He was also an owner of the Newark Bears of the International League, a triple A minor league baseball team one step below major league status.

In 1916 Paul Block, Sr. bought the Detroit *Journal.* He admired the journalistic abilities displayed in Toledo at the time by Grove Patterson, managing editor of the *Blade* and *Times.* Patterson, born in Rochester, Minnesota, in 1881, came from the position of night city editor of the Cleveland *Plain Dealer.*[11]

Short and stocky with a square jaw, Patterson looked and acted the part of an editor. He was young, smart and fiercely competitive. He knew how to run a paper although circulation and delivery had to be someone else's problem. Grove Patterson was named traveling editor of the Detroit *Journal.* The *News* was their primary competition.

At that time, the *Blade* had in Abe Joffa one of the toughest circulation managers in the country. Joffa stood 6'3", weighed more than 230 pounds, was powerfully strong and athletic with hands like bushel baskets. He was a punishing street fighter. He had a hard, long, lean face with deep-set eyes, and barked when he spoke. Everything he said was an order. Everybody feared him. When he needed help, Abe would call on his muscular brother Jules for assistance. The pair were the roughest scrappers in the city. Jules eventually was sent to the Ohio penitentiary for killing a man by running a knife up his rear and twisting it until he bled to death. Jules Joffa and Firetop's brother, Charlie Shulkey, were reported to have been instigators in the 1930 Easter Sunday fire at the Ohio Pen where 322 prisoners died.

Abe kept two other assistants, Raphael Kest and Joe (Yussel) Friedman in street sales. The *News Bee* circulation men were Glenn Morris, Benny Hoffman and Jew Kelly. The latter died in action during World War I. (Mickey) Rubin succeeded him, taking on Firetop as one of his street sales managers.

Block sent Joffa to Detroit on a part-time basis to circulate his *Journal.* Sales were needed to entice advertisers. The struggle for national advertising was always a challenge to all newspapers in competition. While in Detroit, Joffa met the four Aronoff brothers - - Ben, Joe, Walter and George of that city. Walter was circulation manager of the Detroit *Times,* a Hearst newspaper, which later was purchased by the Detroit *News* in 1960. Ben Aronoff and his first partner in Toledo rackets, Ben Harris, were with the Detroit *Herald* and later with various scandal sheets that thrived on yellow and sensational journalism.

Abe Joffa kept abreast of circulation manager roles by word of mouth from other cities. Like Ragan in Chicago and McBride in Cleveland, he had contact with the underground. When his boyhood friend, Tony Paul, alias Neufio Scott, wanted the Union Station as his corner for sale of newspapers as it was a lucrative spot, Joffa beat up two tough Walton brothers, chased them off the corner and gave it to Tony. When Tony later became a strong man and leader in the Syndicate, Abe Joffa was repaid.[12]

With his own political connections and police friends, Abe Joffa owned a horsebook at the Meyerhof Cafe. When the scandal sheets and the five star final papers of Detroit folded, Ben Aronoff and Harris were looking for employment. The Purple gang encroachment on gamblers in Detroit did not appeal to them. Abe Joffa recommended that they move to Toledo. In the late '20s Joffa sold them his horse book and introduced them to his local connections. The two Detroiters liked the deal from the start. Harris had a calculating mind for figures. Aronoff was a front man, a fixer and negotiator. He knew how to handle police. It was claimed that when Aronoff had a fix, there were no arrests or raids. A few over-zealous cops later tried to use the publicity of a raid as a springboard to the vice squad. Aronoff crushed them permanently. When mobsters and gunmen tried to muscle in as partners or demand a part of the action, Aronoff claimed the police already were partners and would not care to be consulted. He countered, "The police will kill you if you interfere."

In the '20s Joffa sent his assistant, Raphael Kest, to Detroit to help *Journal* circulation. Originally a native of Riga, Latvia, Raphael came to Toledo as an infant. He was stockily built, heavy above the waist in chest, arms and shoulders. Like his mentor, he talked in an imperative tone — short sentences ordering things to be done. Ray was dark with black hair, bushy eyebrows and round facial features. He was tough and consequently feared. In his early years, he ran a crap game among the young men who played at Macomber playground on Sundays. Ray was big, abrasive, but tough enough to intimidate the players to either play in his game with his dice or there wouldn't be any game at all. He loved craps and loved to rake part of the action. When force was required, Ray often recruited Mendel Kozman as his aide. "Loudmouth", or Crazy Mendel, as he was called, was invariably in trouble with the police. After numerous encounters, one judge gave Mendel a suspended sentence on condition he stayed away from the downtown area. Sometimes Ray and Mendel would start crap games at Scott High School during the lunch periods. The school then had children of the finest families in the city. Ray always brought in crooked dice. The story was often told of one time getting caught. He was getting his brains beat out by a youngster his size. Ray kept screaming in Yiddish for Mendel or somebody to help but it was one-on-one and everybody was rooting for the "goy." They said Mendel was crazy but he was not crazy enough to interfere that day with a big crowd around.

The street-wise Raphael did a good job in Detroit. He became friendly with the Aronoffs in the circulation field. Grove Patterson and Paul Block, Sr. grew to like the aggressive and hustling Ray Kest.

The Detroit venture was successful. In 1922 the *News* bought out the name and good will of the *Journal,* without the physical equipment, for a substantial price. Grove Patterson was rewarded with a $35,000 bonus which was promptly lost in the stock market.[13]

In 1925 Paul Block, Sr. purchased the *Blade.* He called Grove Patterson to his "Friendship House" in White Plains, New York. There, 45 minutes from Broadway, he had 186 acres, partly wooded and partly under cultivation, with miles of bridle paths, a private golf course, tennis courts, swimming pool and conservatories. The brick mansion house stood on a knoll. After that first conference, Grove Patterson emerged as editor-in-chief of the *Blade.*[14]

Ray Kest also began to rise in the world. After the sale of his Meyerhof Cafe to Aronoff and Harris, Abe Joffa became Toledo sales manager for several out-of-town papers including the Chicago *Tribune*. With his connections to the former circulation managers, Ragan and Annenberg, Joffa took on the additional duties of collecting for the wire services rendered to the horse books on their behalf. Frank Newell then succeeded Joffa as circulation manager. He made Ray Kest street sales manager. In gratitude, Ray named his son Newell. Ray loved his new job. At every opportunity he tried to ingratiate himself with the owner and his superior in every manner. Paul Block, Sr. Usually traveled by private railroad car.[15] When he came from the east, Kest would board the train at Pittsburgh and tell PB, as he was then called, his circulation successes. When the train came from the west, Ray would join it at South Bend to again ingratiate himself with his employer. When a strike was threatened at the offices of the Pittsburgh *Morning Post-Gazette* (another Block paper), Raphael took a group from an ever increasing assortment of friends in labor, Mafia and numbers to Pittsburgh on an errand for the Blocks. Through his intervention and influence of his friends, Raphael was able to avert the Pittsburgh strike.[16] The deal was settled when the managing editor, among other things, was permitted to throw a rock out of his office window into an alley adjoining the building. To the rock was tied the numbers of the day from the three houses, race, stock and bond, for use by the large contingent of Pittsburgh operators to prevent their being "past posted" by bets after the numbers came out. The arrival of the numbers of the day hastened the service of daily play. For an accurate throw, the mob paid the editor $50 a day. The Block family was deeply indebted and grateful to Raphael. When Frank Newell resigned as circulation manager in 1944, Raphael Kest was appointed by Paul Block, Jr. to succeed him, bypassing some who felt more entitled by reason of seniority. Raphael had found ways for the Block family to dearly pay for past favors.

Grove Patterson had a free rein and fared very well. He loved the sound of his voice and his name in print. As a Republican in political thought, Patterson claimed Walter Folger Brown of Toledo and Ed Schorr, Ohio State Republican Chairman, as old and good friends.[17] Maurice Allen, an attorney who joined a predominantly Republican law firm, was appointed secretary of the *Blade* in 1923. Thereafter, the *Blade* endorsed every national Republican candidate until Patterson's death on August 7, 1956. Patterson made the nominating speech for Robert Taft of Ohio for president at the 1940 Philadalphia convention. When Paul Block, Sr. died in June 1941, he helped "conduct services at Temple Emanuel."[18]

The ownership of the *Blade* and other publications passed by will to his two sons, Paul, Jr. and William Karl Block. They did not change policy. Patterson became one of the founders of the American Society of Newspaper Editors and was twice its president. His editing and syndicated column, "The Way of the World," led the Hearst syndicate to offer him 10 times the salary earned at the *Blade,* but he refused. His national writing, speeches and appearances gave him the title "Mr. Toledo," which nomenclature has never since been repeated.

Big business, industry, bankers and the Republicans looked with favor on the Toledo *Blade* after Patterson's takeover. The advertising they purchased far outweighed that given to its rival. In turn, a good press relationship existed. Unlike its rival, the *Blade* never became a crusader or reformer, for it was not profitable or business-wise for them to do so.

A word should be inserted about the real battlers of the circulation wars, the newsboys. Both newspapers were hungry for circulation in the early years. The front line for the battle was on the streets where newsboys were paid a dollar a week to "buck" each other by selling against each other on every available corner or place where the public could be reached. Contests, with prizes, for increased sales or subscription, were always in vogue. Sales managers were continuously on the streets prodding newsboys to "get up and hustle" or admonish them when resting with traditional cliches like "The building won't fall down if you quit leaning against it."

Behind the editorial offices were the press rooms. The press area usually consisted of a drab, unpainted, large, high-ceiling room with newspapers of former days pasted on the walls yelling headlines of famous stories of the past. Wire cages formed lines for the day's hustlers to line up to receive their sheets on credit.

The press men or mailers could be easily detected by the square-shaped hats they wore with a tiny apron like those of a crap dealer to keep the news print off their clothes. Before the street sales, an earlier edition had been stamped and mailed to rural subscribers. It was late editions, sports, race and market results as sheets that required hustle. Invariably, before the presses started to roll, crap games would be held on the cement floor of the room. Mailers, pressman, street sales staff and outsiders indulged in play while kids, like me, watched in silence. When the roar of the presses was heard to start, they sounded

"They're off" and all bets were cancelled as everybody scrambled to their jobs.

The press men or mailers, as they were called, took the papers in packets of 50 each hot off the presses and sent them by dumb waiter to the mailing rooms for distribution. The linotype inventions of 1885 permitted high-speed printing, folding and handling of newspapers at the rate of 16,000 per hour. Later changes permitted twice that number for a 64-page edition.

With the yell "They're off," fleets of panel type trucks, open-ended, equipped with hand rails and steps on the open rear warmed their engines to push the latest news to the substations in the city. With a fresh load, the street sales people drove the trucks like wild men in the race to get an edge on the opposition. A policeman, operating traffic by semaphore signal, would have the signal device knocked over if he failed to turn it in time to yield traffic to an oncoming newspaper truck.

I think I became a compulsive gambler when I started to work on the streets as a newsboy. I was fascinated by the entire rigmarole of craps by daily exposure. The milieu, trappings and action were always there. I never learned the value of a dollar or of anything tangible. I became a rank sucker earning money only to have the means to gamble. Maybe in fact I came by it naturally; my father was an inveterate gambler. He abandoned a wife and seven kids to carry on that pursuit. We were a working family. My mother would shuffle us off to school then go to work in a laundry. After classes we all went to various jobs except my kid sister, Gitty, who would sit on the stoop after school until someone came home to let her in. There was no family life; everybody came in at different hours for meals. My mother often complained, "This isn't a house, it's a restaurant."

As a newsboy on the streets, I felt I knew almost everybody in town. I knew all the ethnic groups — Poles, Hunkies, Syrians — from membership in the Newsboys Association. I attended three different grade schools, Warren, La Grange and Sherman, and Scott High School, all of which were on the fringe of the downtown area and I knew many of the families and students. The Toledo Barber College gave out movie passes to the Hart Theatre to customers who allowed students to practice shaving heads. For two summers I was bald. In seeing the shows, I would sit in the open space between the front row and the stage, looking up at the screen. I ruined my eyes and had to go to sight-saving classes at La Grange School.

For years I had a corner where I was paid a dollar a week to "buck" an adult, Split-lip John, who sold the *Blade*. He spent his life on the streets, living in a flop house and existing on five-cent breakfasts and 10-cent dinners. He had the habit of hailing all prospective customers by name, calling out "Paper, Mr. Brown?" etc. After a few years, I learned from him the who's who of the city.

One incident I recall illustrates the hardness of circulation personnel. Once John gave me his sheets while he went to answer a call of nature. It was a courtesy we exchanged. Ray Kest came by. I had the *News-Bee* on the outside, the *Blade* on the inside and I continued to yell the *News-Bee* headline. Ray didn't like it. He scowled at me, "Put the Blade on the outside," he ordered as he raised his foot as if to kick me. I quickly put John's papers under a rock on the walk and explained, "I sell the *News Bee!*" My loyalty and defiance impressed him for he never troubled me after that.

Each paper sold for two cents. When a customer paid a nickel, we tossed for the extra cent. When things were slow, there was often penny pitching as part of the constant exposure.

Joe "Bugs" Weisberg, a life-long family friend, would often let me sell on one side of the Interurban Station. I would go through all the phone booths to check for the five-cent coin return and all slot machines for forgotten coins. Sometimes I got lucky. When I sold papers on a bus, heaven help the customer who wanted change. I always had to leave for change. The bus would be in Sandusky by the time of my return. It was hard to be honest in a dishonest world.

I learned about the birds and the bees on the streets of the city. Drunks and prostitutes were good tippers but they could not be approached in the brothels or speakeasies. "People don't come in here to read," I was told. "This is not a library. Scram."

At age 11, I sold copies of the murder confession of Dr. Snook. As a professor in the College of Veterinary Medicine at Ohio State, he was injecting drugs into his abdomen and groin to delay ejaculation while feeding his student, Theodora Hix, Spanish fly. She was in such a frenzy of sexual arousal, he had to beat her to death to stop her advances. The confessed lurid details of the sex crime of the decade sold for a quarter.

Some older newsboys selling the *Blade* would shove a paper near the boobs and face of a sweet young thing and ask, "Be laid today, lady? Wanna B-lade?" They did it for the amusement of the younger kids like me and I enjoyed the scene.

The two-cent receipts were divided between the newsboy and the paper. At six o'clock we were to settle up for the day's action. Street sales people would take returns and handle payments. The check-out room could be a chamber of horrors, particularly if a kid came up short. The street sales staff, as a deterrent to others, would put the offender on a box, place a rope around his neck and threaten to hang him even if seven cents short. A few sadistic street sales people beat kids that came in with too many returns. Slaps and kicks were common because that was what kids understood. Some were never hit twice for parents and brothers came in to intercede. Fist fights were common. Fortunately for me I was a good hustler and was never reprimanded.

In the same area the mailers and press men held their crap games, similar games were initiated by the newsboys, including me. Small games of black jack, rummy at a penny a deal or poker would be played on the mailer's benches. The *News-Bee* never permitted anybody to "rake" or "cut" any games, knowing the kids always gambled. The *Blade* had a mustachioed "Bruce" who thrived on the games for years. In such games the participants would lose a day's earnings while the raker made a living from his Fagin activities.

There were times when we held crap games under street lights or in lighted alleys after the offices closed. Often during such games, Allie Brown, one of the most brutal cops in the city, would suddenly appear. He was built like a gorilla and seemed as ferocious. He yelled at all the kids, scattering them in all directions while he pocketed the loosely lying, hard earned pennies and nickels of the players.

There were days when I lost everything and didn't have a nickel to take home. I would take an armful of papers and bootjack. Since everybody had checked in, I could cover the whole downtown area without molestation because there were no protected corners. I entered every restaurant, poolroom, bowling alley, store, card room or business in hope of selling papers. The hours were long. Maybe it was the way a compulsive person punishes himself. I didn't know. Sometimes I didn't reach my quota of a quarter until midnight. The downtown was the center of the city night life and social life. Saturday nights when we sold the Sunday *Times,* we were where the action was. I saw the who's who of the night life then.

In every place that a penny could be earned, I could be found. I hustled on Wednesday nights at the Armory wrestling matches. The next day I thought I was sent to school to entertain the class. I got up and recited the name of every wrestling champ at every weight. I also sold programs at the Mud Hen games. "How much?" they asked. "Fime", I stammered, "Fime." It meant a nickel or a dime in an instructed prepared answer. It was hard to be honest when one had financial advisors.

I sold the weekly copy of the *Sporting News* that Hy Blitz regularly gave me for helping him at half price. On Sunday nights during the winter I worked the Redman Tobacco pro basketball games, staying after the games passing out ads for indoor miniature golf or going through all Coca Cola caps for prizes. On the Fourth of July, it was work at Walbridge Park and peanuts - but the money to me was only a vehicle to gamble, typical of the compulsive.

As long as I can remember, everybody close to me called me Rebbi. That's my nickname. In Hebrew it means "learned one," "master" or "teacher." I started Hebrew school at age nine to prepare and study for the usual Bar Mitzvah at 13. The teachers used to have weekly and monthly contests. I won all kinds of prizes in contests on reading or scholarship. We held our own Sabbath services below the main synagogue. I was appointed shammes in our children's shule. It was an honorary position. In the Old Country, a shammes was the janitor, while a Gobi was an elder or advisor. In this country, most shammes were custodians and members of the "minyun," The requisite 10 men required for full services. On High holidays, the shammes could be seen with his arm about the biggest tippers helping them in stentorian tones to recite the traditional Kaddish for the repose of the soul of the departed parent or taking gratuities to recite the memorial prayers for men who could not attend.

As Gobi I kept records in my head of all who had donated, recording them the next day as no writing was allowed on the Sabbath. As shammes, I always picked out the strongest to take the Torah out and carry it around the sanctuary. The teacher had warned that if the Torah was dropped, we all would be compelled to fast for 30 days to atone for this sin.

I chose those who would go up to the alter, often taking the Levy aliyah going up myself. Aliyah means "going up."

My mother was so proud that she would give me a nickel to schnudder (donate) rather than let me go sell papers on Saturday. As in grade school, I acted up in Hebrew school too. One day, while shooting marbles outside at the window of the classroom, Mr. Micklin, the teacher, yelled at me to come into class. "I don't have a yamulke," I replied, "I can't." Mr. Rosen, the head of the congregation, overheard the colloquy and the very next day gave me a beautiful skull cap so that I never could use that excuse again. Another time I had Manny Hurley, a goy, sit next to me one Sunday morning. This was a no-no. The teacher was furious after evicting him. I was blamed. So I got kicked out of cheder classes with regularity too. A year before, I was dismissed from the Boy Scouts for "cutting up" and refusing to buy Scout wear because I had dissipated the money in gambling. Maybe rejection was a way of life.

In Hebrew School I was a charity case, a non-paying student — too poor for that too. Besides getting expelled there were also regular beatings. One of the slats from a chair was used as a ruler to beat me across the hands and shoulders. All of the old-time teachers beat the students — it was traditional. Mothers always upheld the teacher. "You are wrong and he is right."

Sometimes he kept me after class. I sat in studies with the advanced students. Most were from better families, snobbish and unfriendly. They called me "Little America," referring to the fact that I was the wild one at the time and would often laugh at my predicament at having to remain and sit silently in the back row as the teacher went over more complex Biblical teachings as Rashi and Gomorrah for these older students who had already been Bar Mitzvah.

During the many times that I had to stay over, hungry and without supper, I dreamt of greatness among my people. The Jews always held there would be 36 wise men among them chosen to rule their world. Those selected were secret. Those 36 were called Lammed Vuv, while the word "Nistorem" meant hidden or secret. In Hebrew my name was Herschel ben Moishe Mordecai, Harry the Son of Max. Unknown to my tormentors during those hourly periods, I adopted an additional name of Hanina ben Dosa, a renowned scholar of the first century, who was also very poor. I became Rebbi Hanina ben Dosa ben Moishe Mordecai esch mi Lammed Vuv Nistorem, one of the Secret 36. The others were never to learn that I was destined to become the greatest among them — nor could I tell the snobs of my fore ordained place in the world despite adversity. The last laugh, I surmised, would inevitably be mine.

On a Passover Sabbath about 10 weeks before my 13th birthday, I was still holding both offices. The congregation brought in coconut cookies and candy as Passover goodies to be passed out after services. This was also one of my duties. Naturally, with all the friends I had, there was nothing left of these sweets. When the teacher discovered everything gone, he became incensed. I was berated, scolded, excoriated, expelled from school and fired from both positions. The words he used did not descend with Moses from Mount Sinai. My buddy, Mal Straus, tried to defend me and called him an S.O.B. and Mel, too, was expelled. Mal was soon to be Bar Mitzvah but his father was very learned in Hebrew and would teach him Moftir, which was the sermon of prayers of the event. I did not have any other person I could turn to, nor could we afford one. My mother begged the teacher for another chance and again, for what was the last time, I was permitted to return to classes. Another student, Hilary Sax, had the same Moftir as his Bar Mitzvah date was the same as mine so there were no extra lessons involved.

Now I had a very poor voice because of my daily selling of papers, and I lacked musical training. Mr. Micklin thereafter began to find more and more fault with me. He again decided that I should be expelled from the Hebrew school within three weeks of my scheduled Bar Mitzvah. I can't describe the despair that the news of my being evicted from the Hebrew school brought to my mother. Maybe she felt it was because of our financial condition and our inability to contribute a gift to the Rabbi or to the teacher, or to the hall for the celebrants. My mother came over from her job in the laundry with the wetness and dampness from the hot June sun and the wetness of the laundry still upon her, humbly pleading in front of our afternoon class, shaming and embarrassing herself and me in her humiliating request that this particular teacher show some mercy toward me and continue teaching me the Moftir that was being prepared. I was bitter, but I could not bring myself to cry. The teacher was adamant in his position and refused to yield to my mother's poignant pleas. There was no one else she could turn to as the Rabbi could not interfere with the teacher-student relationship.

Of all the many sad days of my life that I have encountered before and since, I think that the saddest was that particular day when I watched my little mother pitifully ask for the merciful teaching of Bar Mitzvah lessons for her youngest son, and being ignominiously denied before a classroom of fellow students.

I had broken my poor mother's heart. I wanted to punish myself. I had all kinds of feelings of guilt. I didn't know it then, but a compulsive gambler is like a naughty child who expects to be punished for performing a forbidden act.

Psychiatrists write: "He revels in the suffering and misery of his plight and feels self-pity and righteous indignation."

How much this rejection contributed to the ultimate result, only psychiatrists could tell.

No chapter on newspapers could be complete without mention of the Newsboys Association founded by John E. Gunckel in 1892. His book featured pictures of Firetop and told stories of the fun furnished to the newsboys by him and his fellow philanthropists.[19] J.D. Robinson, an eastern transplant active in the Libbey Glass Company (later

Libby-Owens-Ford), carried on the work of Gunckel and instilled the same charitable spirit into his two sons, Joseph Warren Robinson and Jefferson Davis Robinson.

The Newsboys was like a second home to me. I learned to swim there, receiving a ribbon for swimming the 40-foot pool underwater. I took lessons in typing and journalism. I regularly got a new suit from John Moffitt at Christmas and a dinner at a downtown hotel, after which our entire gang would go to Ad Thatcher's party for candy, ice cream and toys.

On Saturday nights there were movies that we always attended before going out to sell Sunday papers. Whenever there was a change of reels, the words of the Notre Dame fight song were flashed on the screen. We sang that song six or seven times those nights and everywhere we went. I became so enamored with Notre Dame that a Niagara of tears flowed down my cheeks as I cried the headlines of Knute Rockne's death in a 1931 plane crash. The tips I received were truly earned, for the tears were genuine.

The director of the Newsboys, Earl G. (Chief) Cook, had a stiff middle finger of his right hand. At all meetings, including the movies, he would raise his hand and wave. The stiff finger to the newsboys became the forerunner of what the raised middle finger is today. Newsboys used that expression for years. Chief, as he wanted to be called, was eventually replaced by one of the finest men the city had ever known, Homer Hanham, my lifelong friend.

Later the Newsboy name was changed to Boys Club, joining the national association of Boys Clubs of America.

In 1939, an Old Newsboys Goodfellow Association was formed. The Old Newsboys took over distribution of clothes and food to the city's needy families at Christmas through proceeds raised in an annual newspaper sale. The *Blade,* as part of its public relations, published such charity editions. Raphael Kest, with his extensive knowledge of circulation and mass placement, became an integral part of the group.[20]

He later was a link to the Mob who ran the city. Since Raphael provided them with good press, the Mob in turn, wanted to make him look good in public. They instructed all tradesmen dealing with them to buy Charity editions from Ray. He had a ready made list of contributors each Christmas that enabled him to bring in top dollar without too much effort.[21]

As time passed, local advertisers favored the local *Blade* rather than the nationally syndicated *News Bee* of the Scripps-Howard chain. Both

*UNHOLY TOLEDO*

Toledo dailies depended on politics as an important source of revenue. Local politicians and business people predominantly patronized the *Blade*.

*Blade* advertising executives started a trend of slanting ads toward the housewives who searched for money-saving bargains. The housewife was the first comparative shopper. The *Blade* prospered while increased production costs and decreased circulation and advertising revenues caused the *News Bee* to fold. On August 7, 1938, the city was left with only one daily newspaper. The *Blade* owned the *Times* and controlled its policy. This later proved to be a deplorable situation in a city of such size.

In repayment of its obligations of prior years to Raphael Kest and others, the *Blade* left a blot on its journalistic record that would be difficult to explain or defend.[21]

# 9 The Willard-Dempsey Fight

The most publicized event in Toledo's history was the World Heavyweight Championship fight between Jess Willard and Jack Dempsey held on July 4, 1919. International coverage of the event had the sportswriting world in attendance. Ring Lardner, Rube Goldberg, Bob Edgren, Grantland Rice, Frank G. Menke, Damon Runyon, "Bat" Masterson and others came to report the fight news.[1] James L. Corbett, one-time heavyweight champion, Al Wolgast, a lightweight titleholder, Battling Nelson, Jack Dillon and other boxing greats were present in the fighters' camps, working out with contestants or giving opinions to the writers.

The champ, Jess Willard, was one of the first giants of boxing. He stood 6'7" and weighed 250 pounds. He became a Pro at twenty-eight when a boxing man, Tom Jones, saw him handle a 500-pound bale of cotton by himself and suggested he become a boxer.[2] He had the true size of a champion but lacked love of combat or a killer instinct. His long left could hold off an opponent, and his right hand punches, a straight right and an uppercut, could finish the job. His record of 23 wins included 20 by knockouts. He became the Great White Hope and answered such challenge by beating Black Jack Johnson for the heavyweight title on April 5, 1915, in Havana, Cuba.[3] There were claims made that Johnson took a dive and newspapers rapped boxing thereafter. Willard's response to these reports was: "If he did take a dive, why did he wait until the 26th round to do it?" Because he came from Potawatomie, Kansas, he was called the Potawatomie Hercules by the press and public. It was this same original tribe of Potawotamis who ceded their territories in Ohio after the War of 1812 in exchange for researvations in Kansas and the West. None of the writers at the time exploited this story of the return of an old warrior to his former stamping grounds.

After winning the title, Willard did everything but fight to cash in on it. He made public appearances and boxing exhibitions, but it wasn't until Tex Rickard, fight promoter, offered him $100,000 for a title bout that he agreed to fight again. After binding the champion, Rickard looked for a suitable challenger for the 36-year-old champ. Jack Kearns, manager of Jack Dempsey, suggested his man. Dempsey, age 23, stood six feet tall and weighed only 180 pounds and looked even lighter because of his excellent condition.

Rickard didn't want to match Dempsey with Willard because of the size difference. It would look like an overmatch. To make matters worse, Willard had killed a boxer, Bull Young, in the ring some years before, and had such great fear of killing another with his tremendous right that he might balk at fighting a little guy.[4] It was later reported Willard asked for legal immunity in the event he killed Dempsey or anyone else.[5]

Whenever Rickard went looking for an opponent, it turned out that Dempsey had been there first. Kearns had used sports page pressure, money, ridicule, trickery and every other known device to trap the big man in the ring with his Jack.

Jack kayoed Gunboat Smith in two, Carl Morris in one, Battling Levinsky in three, Bill Brennan in six and Fred Fulton in one. There was really no one else.[6]

The challenger was to get $19,000. Other reports were Dempsey signed for $25,000 plus $2,500 training expenses. Kearns was to get half. The title fight match was announced.

Rickard, promoter and master of publicity and ballyhoo, had a rough time finding a site for the match. Paris, France, recuperating from World War I, didn't want it. Most newspapers and churches were against boxing. In many states, fights were illegal. Cumberland, Maryland, and a number of small towns rebuffed his overtures.

Word of this difficulty reached Addison Q. Thatcher, owner of a diving and salvaging firm and of a gym called the Toledo Athletic Club, and part-time fight promoter. Thatcher, who was later to become Toledo's 37th mayor, went to New York to induce Rickard to bring the fight to Toledo. As he told *Blade* reporter George De Gregorio in 1960, "I showed him the map and explained Toledo's fine location." At the time, Toledo was the second largest railway center in the country. "What do you want out of it?" Rickard asked. "Seven per cent of every dollar for the Mayor's charity fund."

"How many politicians do I have to take care of?" the experienced Rickard asked skeptically. "Not one," Thatcher assured him.[7]

Ohio had no boxing regulations or laws but it did have strong reform and church movement. Governor Cox would not interfere in Toledo, as no other governor had not for decades before. As Rickard continued to encounter heavy anti-boxing sentiment in other states, he finally agreed to come to Toledo.[8]

Bay View Park, a municipally-owned plot of ground consisting of sixty acres, was turned over to the promoters for the fight. Located four miles from the heart of the city, the site was bounded by Bay on the north and the Maumee river on the east. It was flat and treeless, making the job of construction of an arena easier.

Construction of a huge bowl-shaped arena costing $150,000 and capable of seating 50,000 people was started on May 17, six weeks before the fight. Add Thacher advanced $46,000 for the costs of lumber. Rickard engaged James McLaughlin, an industrial engineer of San Francisco, as builder. When the Jeffries-Johnson fight was switched to Reno, Nevada, McLaughlin built an arena with a seating capacity of 20,000 in seven days.[9] The new arena was to be four times as large. Seats were scaled from $10 to $60. Boxes at ringside went for $60. Seats a few rows back sold for $50, then a circle of seats back of the first two went for $30 to $40. Halfway up the wooden embankment, seats were $15, while the upper edges of the arena, not more than 270 feet from the ring, were scaled at $10. Gate receipts were expected to reach over one million dollars.[10]

The advance sale was so good Rickard decided to build 100,000 seats instead of the 50,000 originally planned.[11]

Several hundred discharged soldiers, all having seen service in France, were engaged as ushers and guards at the arena. Armed guards were to be used to protect the bank clerks hired for handling of ticket sales at the arena. Precautions against rushing the gate were taken by construction of a barbed wire fence eight feet high and a half mile long to keep crowds away from the entrances.

On Memorial Day, with the fight a month away, the ballyhoo of publicity began. Referee was to be Toledoan Ollie Pecord, an old-time ball player and boxer, veteran of 400 bouts. Two judges were to be seated at ringside, A. J. Drexel Biddle and the imperturbable Tex

Rickard. The timekeeper chosen was a former amateur heavyweight champion, Warren Barbour of New York. Alternate referee was Jack Skelley, old-time New York fighter. For the first time in the history of the ring in a title match, the bout would be limited to twelve rounds.

Although a champion is usually regarded as a favorite to win in any title bout, the betting quoted by the local bookmakers was even money.[12] Other sources showed Willard a 10 to 8 or 5 to 4 favorite.[13] The short twelve-round aspect held betting back. The two judge system aroused controversy. If both men were on their feet at the end, the judges would decide. If they differed, the referee Pecord would have the deciding vote. Opinions by veterans failed to change the odds. Veteran Tommy Ryan said Dempsey had no defense. Jack Dillon, the 158-pounder who earned the name,"Jack, the Giant Killer" by beating a lot of big men and winning the light heavyweight championship, worked out with Willard and announced he was too slow for Dempsey.[14] Grantland Rice reported three out of four sportswriters favored Dempsey.[15] Jack Kearns asked his fighter if he thought he could knock Willard out in the first round. "I don't know. Why do you ask a question like that," Dempsey replied. "Because," Kearns said, "I got a chance to get 10 to 1 if you win in the first." So Kearns wagered $10,000 of his share of the purse with John (Get Rich Quick) Ryan that Dempsey would win by a first round knockout.[16]

In preparation for handling of the traffic, the city announced that the Summit Street thoroughfare leading to Bay View Park would be one-way going to the arena before the fight and one-way toward downtown afterwards. Several command officers and two hundred police were assigned to the fight arena. Detectives from other cities were invited to help the local force seek out pickpockets. In addition, Safety Director Chris Wall had sworn in 300 civilian police to patrol the city at night on the lookout for auto thieves and holdup men.[17]

Local newspapers announced fight extras would come out immediately after the fight.

The Boody House and Secor, downtown hotels, anticipating thousands of fight fans, announced minimum rates of $5.00 to $10.00 a night for rooms that ordinarily cost $1.50 to $2.50. Other hotels bought or leased beds and cots and placed them in the corridors. Add Thacher and Ed McDaniels leased an empty warehouse and equipped it with 1,500 beds. Smaller entrepreneurs set up 150 cots in the Schackne Dancing Academy, another 50 cots in a large room nearby.[18]

While everyone was making plans, few gave little thought to the weather. Ralph E. Phelps, a *Blade* staff writer in a story entitled "Toledo's Most Exciting Day," on March 31, 1957, wrote: "Toledo was hit with a terrific heat wave July 1. It was above 92 on Wednesday, July 2. The mercury soared to 95 the next day and on the day before the fight.

Although Rickard announced on July 3 that 200,000 were expected for the fight, as a matter of fact he was worried. The heat was playing havoc with the sale of seats. Early Friday, rumors were heard that 28,000 seats remained unsold, that the arena was not the sellout expected.

Scalpers became frightened and began unloading their tickets. But the public was too hot to buy. Some panicky scalpers even began offering $60 tickets for $50 — and finding few takers.

July 4th — the day of the big fight — dawned and almost before the sun had peeked over the horizon, the city was sizzling. Hour after hour the mercury soared upward. By noon it was 95; by fight time the mercury had passed the 100 degree mark in the shade.

Summit Street, which was to have been a milling mob of spectators, seemed almost deserted.[19]

Back at the arena the sun was getting in its work. It was so hot there that the resin began to ooze from the ring platform. A single tarpaulin had been used for the preliminary fights. A second one was draped over the ring for the main event. It fell across the fight bell which promptly became useless.

As good as the story of the fight is the story of the concessions.[20]

Two characters, Thomas V. Bodkin and Billy Carney, somehow or other managed to obtain concession rights for everything except the programs. These included rights to sell near-beer, cushions, lemonade, ice cream, opera glasses, cigarettes, sandwiches, and practically everything else offered in the stadium.

Both of the men had many other duties including the handling of press relations for Kearns, so they immediately opened a campaign to sell off the concessions to locals. This was wise. They advertised the concessions for sale in the paper and had no trouble getting rid of them.

The one concession which had a chance of making good, the lemonade concession, was sold to a Chicago handicapper for $1,000. Unfortunately the story, true or not, got around that Battling Nelson who never could see lemonade as a drink, decided to take a bath in the stuff the night before the fight. There were a number of tubs of lemonade on the grounds but no one was certain in which tub the old Battler had bathed so the stuff just didn't sell.

Some of the youngsters found that they could get water from a firehose on the premises and that they could get ice from their cronies in the idle lemonade concession. They did a big business of peddling ice water for whatever the traffic would bear, although even this trade was deflated somewhat by the fact that all customers had to drink from the same glass.

Bodkin and Carney were particularly glad to get rid of the cigarette concession. Having been around this sort of installation before, they were confident that the fire marshals would allow no smoking in the stands on the day of the fight — and they were right.

The heat virtually destroyed the cheese on hand for sandwiches, and the ham didn't go so well inasmuch as this battle was taking place on a Friday.

Selling the pillow concession was a masterpiece in salesmanship. Bodkin and Carney invited a man of wealth into the stadium and asked him to be seated. The newly nailed lumber, still oozing sap, made a hard, sticky, and uncomfortable seat. How would he like to buy the pillow concession, along with thousands of Japanese-made pillows that he could sell easily for 50 cents each? The man leaped at the opportunity but sold few pillows inasmuch as they were on sale at stands outside the grounds for only 10 cents.

The day of the fight, less than 20,000 attended. The enterprising people who put up cots reported few takers. Both promoters blamed low attendance on newspaper stories of the expected crush of humanity on the city's limited hotel facilities. Had 100,000 or more arrived, there would have been no way to handle them.

The champ kept the challenger waiting. The fight was delayed for two hours, until four o'clock. The timekeeper had to use a whistle to start the battle because the bell was unusable.

Seymour Rothman, *Blade* staff writer, described the fight: "It started slowly with Willard pawing at Dempsey with his left. Suddenly Dempsey found an opening and hooked Willard right over the heart with a right hand. Willard threw a right in hopes of evening up matters but did no damage with it. Dempsey countered with a right to Willard's stomach and a looping left to Willard's eye. Willard was stunned but didn't go down. Now Dempsey went after Willard with both hands. Finally, he crashed a right to the chin and Willard went down."

Ollie Pecord, the Toledo referee who always credited that looping left hook with winning the fight, recalled that Willard went down for a count of 6, then for a count of 5, then for 4, then for 5, and then he lost track. At one point, he recalled that Willard indicated that he wanted him to count louder although Pecord already was shouting. He was quoted before his death in 1941:

"I was counting 7 when I made out the shout that the round was over. (It was Willard's seventh trip to the mat.) No one had heard Barbour's whistle. I waved Dempsey to his corner and called for someone to help Willard. I saw the crowd rushing toward the ring. They all thought the fight was over. Dempsey's seconds thought the same thing. Dempsey was hurried from the ring. I had trouble getting them back together... It was the tightest corner I ever was in during my ring experience."[21]

The story is that Kearns knew very well that the round was over and was trying to win his bet. While it is hardly likely that Kearns would make such a bet without heavy odds, it also is hardly likely that he would hustle the winner and new champion out of the ring without his hand being raised unless he had some ulterior motive.

Many reporters wired the fight was over. The *News Bee* released an extra "Dempsey Wins in First" and the papers arrived as the fight ended two rounds later.[22] Kearns called frantically to his man to get back into the ring or he would forfeit the bout.

Rothman continued his anniversary story:

"Early in the second round, Willard caught Dempsey with one of his famed uppercuts, and all ideas of this being something just for movies disappeared. Dempsey went at Willard again. Both men now were concentrating on the chin, looking for the big knock out punch. Willard took an awful beating but remained on his feet.

Late in the third round, just before the bell sounded, Willard slumped to the floor under a rain of blows. His seconds helped him to his corner. The seconds worked on him. "Can you stand to go to center again?" one asked. Jess shook his head negatively. A bloody towel floated to the center of the ring." The fight was truly ended.[23]

Kearns made good his gambling losses out of the $19,000 guarantee. Training expenses and extras ate up almost all the rest, but Jack was Champion and could write his own ticket. Thereafter Doc Kearns fought bitterly with the champion. He continuously showered abuse upon him. The two split and never really made up. The last piece of nastiness that Kearns used came virtually from the grave.

"Shortly before Kearns died in 1963, he had completed the manuscript for his autobiography. In talking about the Willard fight, Kearns described how he had started worrying about the $10,000 he had bet on a first-round victory, and how he had decided to help the results along. Unknown to his fighter, he asserted, he had sprinkled the wrappings that go under a boxer's gloves with plaster of Paris, and had then doused them with water before lacing on Jack's gloves.

The first that Dempsey knew about this was in January, 1964, when *Sports Illustrated* published Doc's account with the headline "DEMPSEY'S GLOVES WERE LOADED." Dempsey promptly sued for libel. Dempsey had evidence to support his case. One man turned out to have the actual bandages which he had picked up off the floor of Dempsey's dressing room and kept for a souvenir. Another fan, an ex-fighter, had kept the gloves Dempsey wore in the fight. Manufacturers of plaster of Paris wrote to say that it would take about five layers of their product to create a rock-hard wrapping, and that anyway there had not been time for it to set. Various doctors and experts assured Dempsey that had Kearns' charge been true, he would have broken all the bones in his hands, let alone every bone in Willard's face. In short, the story seemed preposterous. The case was settled out of court.[24] Three years later, when Kearns' book was published, the charge had been deleted. "From wherever he was," Dempsey said, "Jack Kearns had managed to give me one more good swift kick in the butt. The man was not to be believed!"[25]

Years later, Sam S. McConoughey of the Toledo-Lucas County Public Library staff wrote to Willard's wife, asking her to contribute or display any documents on the fiftieth anniversary of the event. Mrs. Willard sent back an article that appeared in the Sydney, Australia, *Daily Mirror* on August 1, 1966.[26] Movie film taken at the time of the fight 48 years before disclosed an object lying near the fallen Willard which many people claimed was an iron bolt. It was about five inches long and dark in color. The object was seen at Willard's feet as he was dragged to his corner at the end of the first round and then disappeared. There is no evidence that Dempsey ever used the object or that it fell from his gloves. Such an object could have got into the ring in a hundred different ways. At the time he saw the 48-year-old pictures at age 84, the gentle Willard seemed to gesture bitterly as if to say "It's too late now."

The fight was a financial success as everybody made money. Official attendance was 19,650 persons with receipts of $452,224, a record up to that time, and still a record for boxing in Ohio.[27]

The city received $28,751.25 although Rickard had turned over a check for $30,000. The two promoters wound up with $85,732 profit. The effect of the fight enhanced the reputation of the city as a sport town. The success enabled Rickard to get financial backing to build Madison Square Garden in New York and to restore respectability to boxing as a spectator sport.[28]

The big fight marked the beginning of the golden age of sports as part of the Roaring '20s. Spectators and readers alike showed renewed interest in display of masculine virility and power. This type of reaction develops after any holocaust such as World War I.

Professional football soon after started in Ohio at Canton, where the present Hall of Fame is located. Toledo's entry in the league was the colorful Maroons. Massillon, Ohio, also competed. In scholastic football Toledo Waite in 1919, with gifted Louis Ray Scheets, later Police Lieutenant Scheets, as quarterback, won a national title. Toledo Scott, with an equally great quarterback in Eddie Evans, dominated national scholastic football with a championship team a few years later.

In basketball, Toledo had high quality teams in high schools and colleges. The old New York Celtics, later the Cleveland Rosenblooms, came to Toledo as the Red Man Tobaccos in a professional league that preceded the formation of the NBA players. Joe Lapchick, Dutch Dehnert (originator of the pivot play), Davey Banks, Lou Spindell, and Cookie Cunningham were part of that quintet.

In baseball, the city always was in the American Association, a triple A league one step removed from major league caliber. Toledo won its only pennant in 1927 under the managerial aegis of the colorful Casey Stengel.

In boxing and wrestling, the Shea brothers, Steve and Jimmy, promoted club fights where spectators could drink or gamble. Add Thacher's gym was always filled with boxers and wrestlers in daily workouts. Professional wrestling matches were held weekly at the Armory under the promotion of a former wrestling champion, Johnny Hurley. The Dempsey fight and its aftermath proved that a "sporting town" could also be a good sports town.

# 10 The Million Dollar Robbery

With all the crooks hanging around the city, it was only a matter of time until something big was bound to happen.

Toledo again hit national headlines on February 17, 1921 when its main post office was robbed of eleven mail sacks containing $880,000 in Liberty Bonds, $37,000 in new currency from the Cleveland Reserve Bank and a quantity of expensive jewelry. Labeled by newsmen as the "million dollar robbery," it was the biggest in the history of the city and ranked among the top two up to that time in the United States. Only the Leonard Street mail robbery in the same year in New York outranked it in scope.[1]

Gerald Chapman and "Dutch" Anderson, principals in the famous New York mail event, had frequently used Toledo as a hideout in previous years. It was claimed Chapman was also planning to rob the local post office but the locals beat them by a few days.

In the underworld of the city, Joe Urbaytis was considered one tough Polack. His buddy, Charles (Split-lip) Schultz, was not a slouch either, according to the records of the local police. Seated with the two at a downtown tavern some time before the heist were Eddie O'Brien, a friend of Joe, George Rogers, an escaped lifer from San Francisco, and Jimmy Colson, a Chicago hoodlum, all of whom were in Toledo for "health" reasons, meaning if they were caught elsewhere, they would be jailed. A news story of that day reported a mail sack had been stolen from a Mt. Vernon, Illinois, railroad station and that employees handling the mail were not armed. They knew substantial cash and valuables were sent through the mail.[2] The idea for a holdup was born. Joe appointed himself to mastermind the job.

Urbaytis and Schultz agreed to check out the mail train schedules. For days they checked the time of arrival of trains, loading, and the time it took mail trucks to drive from the Union Station to the downtown main post office. Jimmy Sansone, a Detroit felon, was added to the gang. As a hideout, the group selected a garage off an alley in back of the home of Jimmy Feese, a smalltime Toledo hoodlum, which was located less than eight city blocks from the post office.

On the day of the robbery, Urbaytis brought out a large touring car that had been stolen four days before. They drove to the Union Station. There Joe went inside to ask if the mail train from Kansas City was on time. Two postal employees were also waiting for the same train which they reported was on time. Mail sacks containing cash, bonds and jewelry were tossed into a Postal truck and the two employees, W. H. Milroy and Paul Weinrich, departed for the main office. They were unaware of a large, curtained touring car that followed. On arrival downtown the truck was backed into a loading dock at the post office. Milroy unfastened the wire gate on the back of the vehicle as Weinrich went for a hand truck. Inside, less than fifty feet away, in a large room, twenty-five postal clerks were busy sorting mail. One had just finished and went out the back to drive his car home. At the same time, across the street where the Toledo Club was located, a state senator was emerging, but in the snowy weather he did not notice any handkerchiefs over the faces of any of the men. Suddenly the three outside postal employees were facing guns of four of the gang. With one holding the victims at bay, the mail sacks were quickly loaded into the car which was parked adjacent to the truck, motor running. The event took seconds. Not a shot was fired. No one was injured. As the car sped away, the three ran inside to sound an alarm.

Within minutes thereafter, the sacks were thrown into the garage of Jimmy Feese. All but the driver went into his apartment in front. The car was driven to a remote section of the county and abandoned.[3]

The next day the gang, including Feese, had a rendezvous in an apartment where the cash and jewelry were divided. A wrist watch was given to Feese and later some other jewelry to a taxi cab driver who took them to the apartment.

Feese was ordered by Urbaytis to destroy the mail sacks. He obtained the services of Harry Thrush, a smalltime bootlegger, who burned the sacks and tossed the ashes and metal into the Maumee River.

A taxicab driver gave the police their first clues. When he learned that nearly $1,000,000 was involved in the loot, he was scared. He had been given a watch. He dumped it in a sewer. Then he read about the heavy rewards being offered for apprehension of the robbers. He tipped a rookie policeman who, in turn, told Detective Captain Ralph Murphy that a watch had been given to him by Feese. Feese was arrested.

Because the mail sacks were U. S. Government property, the crime was a Federal one under jurisdiction of the Secret Service although the Toledo Police Department did intervene. Since the government needed Feese's testimony, he was given immunity.

Newspaper stories during the investigation resulting from "leaks" in the use of Toledo police, resulted in the Federal government calling in a Columbus lawyer, Stuart Bolin, to be special prosecutor with secret service men doing the investigative work.[4]

On evidence supplied by Feese, several participants were arrested.

A short time later there came another break, this time from Chicago. Postal agents revealed they had arrested a priest, the Rev. Anthony Gorek, of New Chicago, Indiana, and two of his parishioners, Albert Murzyn and Stanley Bartnikowski, for having sold some of the Liberty Bonds stolen in the Toledo robbery.

Father Gorek told the agents that while he was at the Englewood station of the New York Central, he met Wanda Urbaytis, sister of Joe Urbaytis, who gave him a package and asked him to keep it for her. He said that when he read of the robbery, he became curious and examined the package. Inside he found $80,000 in bonds. Because of the 1921 depression and the economic plight of his parish, he asked the two men to dispose of three bonds so he could use the money for charity. They were arrested when they did so, and implicated him.

Father Gorek revealed he once had been an assistant priest at St. Hedwig's Church in Toledo and thus had met the Urbaytis family.

The three, together with two other Chicago men, John J. Epps and John Paulek, were brought to Toledo.

The Grand Jury indicted 18 people on charges of conspiracy and charged six with robbery. The principals in the robbery, according to the indictment, were Urbaytis, Sansone, Rogers, O'Brien, Schultz and Colson.[5]

On June 6, 1921, in a heavily guarded courtroom, the group went on trial before Federal Judge John M. Killits. Armed guards patrolled the corridors and more than a score were scattered in the courtroom.

The principals were found guilty and lodged in the Lucas County jail awaiting sentence by the Court.[6] As there was no jail for Federal prisoners, the Court contracted with the county for holding and keeping of Federal prisoners.

On Labor Day 1921 Urbaytis, Rogers and Schultz staged a sensational escape.[7] There were claims that it was politically arranged in exchange for some of the cash taken in the robbery because few people were downtown and many deputies and police were handling huge crowds at the grand circuit races at Fort Miami Fairgrounds that day.

Sheriff John Taylor said, "The escape is the result of momentary negligence on the part of my deputies." (It was known before the escape that Rogers had escaped two years before from the fifth floor of a jail in San Francisco where he was held after his conviction on a murder charge.)

The three escapees were placed in the same cell block. Urbaytis' mother had brought him some lunch in a pail. When Deputy Andrew Szemtko opened the cell door to remove the pail, the trio jumped on him and beat him. The cries of Szemtko attracted the attention of Deputy Sammy Zimmerman and Dr. William Shapiro, jail physician who was visiting that day. Deputy Zimmerman rushed up the stairs where he encountered the fleeing criminals. With cries of "Kill him, hit him," they attacked Zimmerman as he threw his keys to Dr. Shapiro who ran into one of the cells, slamming the door behind him, thinking the escape could be thwarted as they had no keys. But the trio had grabbed Szemtko's keys; they dragged Zimmerman to the first floor, opened the door of the office and went to the front desk drawers where they took four revolvers. They knocked another visitor, J. C. Alfred of Dayton, to the floor with a blow from a pair of icetongs; then they ran through a barred door between the office and corridor which had been inadvertently left open, into the yard to a picket fence at the rear. Schultz and Urbaytis scaled a fence while Rogers went down another street in another direction.[8]

W. J. Burns, Chief of the U. S. Secret Service and America's foremost criminal hunter, was called in to investigate the escape and take charge of hunting down the fleeing robbers. Post Office inspectors intimated a $5,000 reward would be offered for apprehension of the fugitives. The Lucas County Commissioners refused to back the sheriff's request for a $500 reward.

The Secret Service and Federal Judge Killits were furious over the escape. Deputies Zimmerman and Szemtko were indicted and convicted for negligence in allowing Federal prisoners to escape.[9] Both were sentenced to the Federal penitentiary in Atlanta, Georgia, for twenty-one months.[10] While out on bond pending their appeal, the convictions were reversed as there was no showing of criminal intent or culpability.[11] Stephen Fazekas, defense counsel for Szemtko, said, "I know there was no payoff. It was just poor judgment. My client didn't get any money. I defended him without a fee."[12]

Two days after his escape, Schultz was captured in a farm house near Crissey, Ohio. He was sentenced to 50 years imprisonment. Sansone got 40 years. Wanda Urbaytis got seven years, Harry Thrush 6-1/2 years. Because they had testified for the government, Father Gorek and Feese were sentenced to one hour each in custody of the U. S. Marshal. Albert Murzyn and Stanley Bartnikowski got 30 days each.

Rogers was recaptured in Palos Park, Illinois, two years later. He received a 67-year sentence with a provision that upon completion he be turned over to California authorities to finish his life term.

Undetected for two years, Colson and Eddie O'Brien were subsequently found and brought to trial by jury. Both were found guilty and given 50 years each.

Only the leader, Joe Urbaytis, remained free. On May 5, 1924, in Columbus, Ohio, 39 months after the robbery, Joe's freedom ended. Two detectives raided a home to arrest Frank Urbaytis and two women. As they were about to leave, Joe appeared. A gun battle ensued in which Joe was shot and captured. After several weeks in a hospital, he was brought to Toledo and sentenced to 50 years imprisonment.

Appeals by the principals were successful in getting sentences reduced without new trials. Each of the principals had his sentence reduced to 25 years, making them eligible for parole after 18 years.

After his release in the '40s, tough Joe Urbaytis became involved in new legal entanglements that led to his later being shot to death, allegedly by a gun stolen from Toledo Police Detective Captain George Timiney. The latter was a name to remember: Timiney played important roles in city and county police action thereafter.[13]

# 11 More Elite Lawyers and Politicians

Firetop reentered politics after his war service under the tutelage of one of the shrewdest politicians in the country, Walter F. Brown. Weaned on Ohio philosophy of "To the victor belongs the spoils," by his father, S. M. Brown, a prominent Republican leader, the younger Brown was later acknowledged to be national leader of his party by his being appointed Postmaster General of the United States by President Herbert Hoover in 1928.

Political writers could claim Brown was capable of getting a Ku Klux Klan candidate elected in the Harlem district of New York.

Brown never sought public office but preferred to direct campaigns and candidates from behind the scenes. All of his actions were in a low profile, advising followers "never to attract attention" so that impropriety could never become an issue of any kind. Brown named candidates he expected to control. Where resistance occurred, as under Golden Rule Jones, Brown opposed reelection.

From 1906 to 1912 Brown was chairman of the Ohio Republican State Central Committee. An example of his organizational ability occurred in the presidential campaign of 1912. The Taft candidates in the Toledo district were John North Willys and Edward Drummond Libbey, two of the city's most famous and leading industrialists. Willys was head of the Willys-Overland, leading car producing company, while Libbey, with Mike Owens of the Owens Bottle Machine Company and Edward Ford of the glass family and owners of the Pittsburgh Plate Glass Company, consolidated to make Toledo the glass center of the world.

Libbey was also the city's most renowned philanthropist. In 1909 he founded the Toledo Museum of Art, one of the finest in the world. In his will, executed in 1909, he arranged to dispose of an estate in excess of nine million dollars. When he died 16 years later, without changing such will, his estate then exceeded 21 million dollars. Legatees argued that their specific shares should be increased proportionately. In the protracted litigation that ensued, the Museum of Art as residuary legatee fortunately prevailed.

Under Brown's machinations in the campaign of 1912, two lesser-known candidates sponsored by him easily won over Willys and Libbey.[1] Brown's authority became so well established that on any major political issue, "Ask Walter" became a byword.[2]

With George P. Hahn and Sigmond Sanger, he founded the law firm of Brown, Hahn and Sanger in 1908. President Harding and the Ohio gang offered him positions in Washington, but he preferred to remain in Toledo to guide local affairs. Will H. Hays, an Indiana lawyer and congressman, became Postmaster General. This office was used to pay off political favors. Later, Hays became counsel for the new motion picture industry to protect from federal regulation or censor.[2]

In 1928 when Federal Judge John M. Killits resigned, Brown was responsible for his associate, George P. Hahn, being appointed to succeed him. Killits had authored a three-volume history of Northwestern Ohio consisting of compilations of personal data on all the prominent persons in the area. It consisted primarily of short articles which read like an obituary, listing birthplace, schooling, politics and profession of the area people. It was interesting to those enjoying obituary columns.[3] When told that a set of books cost $17, Brown refused to subscribe. As a consequence, this most prominent character was not mentioned in the Killits' historical collection.

Another example of Brown manipulation occurred in the election for mayor in 1922. After defeats by another Independent, Cornell Schreiber, later Licavoli lawyer. In 1918 and 1920, Brown induced Judge Bernard Brough, age 51 and a bachelor, to run as Republican candidate for mayor. The *News-Bee* wrote "Political machines utilize a respected citizen to carry the banner ... to cloak city government with respectability. It is an old trick. The Republicans tried it ... to get men of high reputation to stand as figurehead — to be the goat. Some refused. Judge Brough gave in."[4]

The *News-Bee* argued, "a mayor must be considered tractable by a machine headed by Walter Brown, for Brown was a man whose business is to make money out of politics."[5] Despite these articles, Brough was elected and reelected by the greatest majority ever given a mayoralty candidate.[6]

Firetop listened and watched Brown's office control election of new judges, city and county officials. Patronage and favor were asked and received. Informants claimed that Brown used an obscure, unknown black, Clarence Venia, among others, as a bag man. He was a person nobody would suspect. Every Thursday during Brough's two terms, Venia would carry a large satchel type case known to be filled with cash to the Civic Center parking garage and place it in Brown's car. Brown would come within minutes, enter the car as Venia watched, and take off. Firetop often was perplexed about the lectures on low profile when he heard about this well-known payoff.

Brown would breakfast regularly at Mike Evedemon's Manhattan Lunch. He invariably sat at the counter so that he would not have to tip. They featured a 29-cent and 39-cent meal. He always ordered the cheaper meal, stating, "I have to watch my pennies."

Most of the newsboys knew him. If one ever tried to sell him a paper that was torn, wet, faded by the sun or otherwise soiled, he would repeatedly demand a perfect copy. He never was known to have given a penny tip, even at Christmas.

When Brown's wife died, she left an estate of 2.4 million dollars. He died a year afterward and left three million dollars in trust funds not subject to probate and an additional $177,000 that could be part of his estate. No appraisal was mentioned of properties in other states. Sig Sanger, his law partner, left a more modest estate of $443,903 at his death.

During Brown's absence from the city from 1928 to 1932 as Postmaster General, Firetop acted without Brown's advice or counsel. He was on his own in acquiring a gambling joint known as the Villa where he operated a crooked roulette wheel. His manager was Hank (Manure) Blumberg, who acquired such unusual nickname because everybody continuously told him he was full of it.

If he had known in time, Brown would surely have vetoed Firetop's contacts with Licavoli. By then, Firetop was consumed with envy, greed and ambition. He looked upon the Independents as stupid, for they were untouchable. The Democrats had proved pathetic opposition for the preceding 30 years. While Independents like Jones and Whitlock dominated for a period of 15 years, the Democrats hung gloomily on.

John Augustus O'Dwyer, called the Napoleon of Democratic politics, led the opposition party during this era. In 1904 he was a member of the Lucas County Board of Elections and served as president. He served as secretary and chairman of the Democratic executive and controlling committee, heading his party for a period of 21 years thereafter until his death in 1925.

Before the turn of the century, his father, Edward O'Dwyer, entered the police force to rise from a rookie cop to captain. In those days, captain was the ranking officer. While captain, the A.P.A. movement, an anti-catholic hysteria, was sweeping the country. The "Apes," as they were called, elected a completely new county and city ticket, including a police board which controlled the police department. Captain O'Dwyer was stripped of his command and reduced to the rank of lieutenant. Only the intervention of Mayor Guy Major saved his job on the force. The proud Irish blood of his family was aroused by this insult. Since the Apes held control in the Republican party, the O'Dwyer clan turned Democrat to use that party as an instrument of revenge. The Apes were turned out in 1904. On St. Patrick's Day, the new police force board met to vote on dismissal of 23 members of the department. All 23 dismissed were A.P.A. members. Thereafter, O'Dwyer ruled with an iron hand.[7]

O'Dwyer's philosophy created disfavor. His "Never forget an insult" or "Never forgive or forget an enemy" have been supplemented by modern-day thoughts of "Don't get mad, get even." His tactic of sticking strictly to party lines in all matters of patronage and favor became a salient part of Democratic policy during his terms and endures today.

Unrefined and unpolished as the Republican leaders, O'Dwyer operated in the manner of the formula used by Boss Tweed. He dealt in city and county businesses with percentages for the political bosses. This was the accepted graft of politics where the people could expect such activity to occur. O'Dwyer headed the board of elections and was paid a salary. He formed an insurance agency, Goldberg and O'Dwyer, which insured most of the county buildings. When word was sent to county commissioners to renew insurance through his offices on all county buildings, two of the three balked. O'Dwyer refused to recommend the recalcitrants for renomination and they were not renominated. Instead, John Mathias, a workman for a construction firm owned by Mike Hannin, a close friend of O'Dwyer, was nominated and elected to the office of county commissioner. When the commissioners awarded contracts for repair, maintenance and construction of all county streets and roads, O'Dwyer saw that friend Hannin got most of the work. Republican opponents charged that O'Dwyer took fees for bookkeeping for saloon keepers. He was accused of sending examining physicians directly to saloons to examine applicants for insurance at work, of applying funds raised politically from saloonkeepers and others to his bills for "services" and of paying like fees to his brothers and relatives. Republicans claimed several O'Dwyer relatives held sinecure positions at the court house, drawing $300 per month as salaries, which were the same as those paid to elected officials.

Upon his death in July 1925, some members of the executive committee of the Democratic party wanted the position of chairman to go to John O'Dwyer's widow for his unexpired term. His brother, Kevin, favored Peter Ragan with an understanding Ragan would retire at the end of the term so that Kevin could take over.

In a vote of the committee, Ragan won by 10 votes. Later, every member of the committee who voted for the widow was removed from the committee and excommunicated from the party. Thereafter, for a period of seven years under such demonstrated leadership of Kevin O'Dwyer, the Democrats failed to elect one person to public office. Kevin, like Walter F. Brown, never made speeches and never issued public statements. Eventually a New Deal split in the Democratic party under Franklin Delano Roosevelt and his national Democratic landslide of 1932 created political changes that ended the local reign of the O'Dwyers.

Steffens wrote: "Politicians are the enemies of the people." In Toledo, with such leaders, it could be true!

If there was one man in the city who could genuinely dispute the Republican party leadership of Walter Brown, Edwin J. Marshall was such a person, probably as powerful and as influential as Brown in local and national affairs. He was one of the elite.

"E.J.," as he was popularly called, was a big man in size, stature and mentality, an outstanding lawyer with a keen legal mind, particularly in the field of corporation law. He started a lucrative partnership with Harold M. Frazier, one of the leading trial lawyers in the city. Like Brown, E.J. loved money and power and the prestige that money brought.

Informants reported that both Frazier and Marshall were vain; each had enormous egotism.[8] It was inevitable that a split occur. Marshall's greed and love of money manifested itself when Frazier obtained a verdict of over $100,000 against one of the railroads. Their client was a famous circus performer.

When Frazier refused to pay E.J. his share of the fees, Marshall literally tore into his associate, throwing him out of the office. Later he told clients that he had never regarded Frazier highly, saying, "I can hire a trial lawyer when needed any time."[8]

Marshall's anger and the rift were precipitated by Frazier's brazen and abrasive conduct in court. In a case where Brown's office was on the other side, with Sig Sanger as counsel, Frazier commented to the jury in response to Sanger's final argument, "What does that Jew know about anything?" E.J. apparently valued Brown's association more than that of such a partner.[9]

Thereafter, E.J. organized and headed a larger firm known as Marshall, Melhorn, Marlar and Martin.

As a young lawyer in the new office, Edward Lamb later wrote of his recollections of Marshall. "E.J. was a towering, slovenly 250-pounder who roamed the offices in his stocking feet. He had 25 of us writing briefs, typing up cases, drafting wills, planning memoranda, and figuring out ways of cutting down somebody's taxes. He was cold and calculating, and his fees were enormous. 'Let's soak this client,' he said. 'He's a rich son of a bitch, so let's distribute his wealth.' The distribution always ended up in E.J.'s pocket."[10]

Marshall's greatest influence came through the banks and controlling them in their relations to corporate clients.

E.J. was a paradoxical character. He wore two hats in a dual capacity as counsel for corporations, business and industry, while retaining behind the scenes connections with the gambling characters.

Many claimed his gambling connections, where no tax problems existed in deposits and savings, with a large cash flow, aided E.J. in obtaining such prominent retainers. He was a great personal friend of Henry Lawrence Thompson, president of Bostwick and Braun, international wholesale and jobbing distributor of hardware equipment, chairman of the board of Willys-Overland, and also chairman of the board of The Toledo Trust Co., the city's largest bank.

His office also represented A.E. Reuben, millionaire realtor and owner of Hasty Farm Stables of outstanding stake race horses.

With E.J.'s guidance, Reuben controlled the sale of large tracts of industrial and commercial properties. Both acquired and held onto valuable tracts of land, awaiting huge increases in price before sales.

When the banks crashed in the 1930s, Marshall's inside information on banks helped many clients escape without financial losses.

As legal advisor to many newly formed corporations, bankers referred new businessmen to him.

Like Brown, Marshall never held public office but dealt from behind the scenes in election campaigns, locally and nationally, for years. The newspapers claimed, "When E.J. roared, city hall shook and judges trembled as he could make or break anyone down there." Both papers referred to Marshall as the man who called the shots on most local issues. He used political clout wherever required. Operating through emissaries and third parties, he continuously manipulated Republican strategy.

When E.J. died on January 15, 1946, he left an estate estimated "in the millions."[11] His first partner, Harold Frazier, left a far less modest estate.

A third politico-lawyer, also an elite like Brown or Marshall, was John B. McMahon. Born in Ellicottville, New York, in 1888, his family moved to Toledo in 1902 where his father became general manager of Northwestern Ohio Natural Gas Company.[12] A Harvard graduate, he entered the practice of politics and law in 1912 in Toledo. His father put him in the law firm of Cohn, Northrup and Morgan.

The Gas Company needed to use city streets. Political alliances were helpful.

Sam Cohn had practiced since 1880 and was a wealthy owner of real estate. Charles Northrup was an excellent lawyer with influence politically. Northrup was also a close friend of Neg Cochran, editor of the *News-Bee,* and of John O'Dwyer, dominant head of the local Democratic party. McMahon's acceptance into the firm drove Northrup and Morgan away.

In addition to the Gas Company retainer, McMahon represented most of the gambling crowd. Jimmy Hayes, owner of the biggest crap game in the city, Ben Aronoff and Bennie Harris, owners of a horse book then, called for his services whenever needed.

Marshall, McMahon and Brown remained good friends and confidants throughout their political and legal careers.

McMahon was the most gregarious of the trio. Standing 5'11" with brown-grey hair, stockily built with handsome facial features, the Irishman was a pleasantly good speaker and a better listener. He could have captured public office but, like his friends, never tried.

With fellow lawyer Oscar Smith, McMahon engaged in a number of civic ventures. They bought the Toledo Mud Hens of the American Association, a baseball team slightly below major league caliber. Despite becoming a pennant winner under manager Casey Stengel in

1927, the franchise lost heavily and had to be sold. Both invested in the Steamer Greyhound, which operated boat rides on the Maumee River and Lake Erie. When the boat was destroyed by fire, it was grossly underinsured.

The same McMahon and Smith introduced the first talking pictures in the city at the Temple Theatre. Lacking foresight into the future value of movies, McMahon sold out early, but Smith retained his RKO stock and recouped his losses, plus much more.

McMahon later brought Joel Rhinefort and Thomas J. Mattimoe into his law offices. Both were later prominent in the entanglements of the gambling fraternity and Licavoli connections.[13]

The advent of the Depression of 1929 brought on a change of the nation's gambling habits. In Toledo, nickel, dime and some quarter slot machines were installed for use by those who formerly bet with currency. Slot machines were regarded as sources of legitimate income. Hundreds of units were on locations throughout the city and county.

Virgil Gladieux, head of Ogden Foods with restaurants on the Ohio, New York and Pennsylvania turnpikes, was one among many who derived financial benefits from slots.

Numbers on policy betting became in vogue. The city had five prominent establishments with the most income going to the Buckeye Club owned by Aronoff and Harris. Numbers became big business. It was known in gambling circles as lockup action, meaning there were few payouts or great returns. Five dollars or 500 to one was paid on every penny bet. The public loved the action even though they knew the odds should be 1,000 to one as the policy numbers were bet on three figures in Race, Stock and Bond series. The middle three figures in sales reported in the market closings determined the winning combination. The major number houses would buy 600 to 800 copies from each newspaper and distribute them free to patrons in their various places of business, delivering many to outlying districts to be used particularly by the blacks. Aronoff had a policy of excluding negroes from his house at that time. Blacks were permitted to bet on horses but they would receive a slip in the front of the house in the restaurant. Payment would be in the same place and manner on winning. Newspaper results stimulated further betting and saved the operators from being deluged by phone calls asking for the day's number in all three plays.

Every day, either Aronoff or Harris would call Ray Kest to verify such numberes to avoid being "past posted" or having bets placed after the winners were determined. Ray got paid for such services.

The Depression brought the city finances to new lows. Rather than send out police to make arrests on numbers runners, operators or slot owners, arrangements were made to have arrests and court appearances set by phone. Operators would be called on a regular basis by police. "We need ten for arrest tomorrow," operators would be told. "Bring three in the next day," others were ordered. City revenues were enhanced by court fines and costs. The fine was pre-arranged, $10 per man and $3 costs. Sometimes when a large group appeared, only one would be charged court costs.

Appearances were by appointment. The numbers people were summoned early so that they could make their rounds of collections.

Detective Art Ness, a police desk sergeant during the period, never made a physical arrest in his entire career, yet his record showed he was credited with more arrests than any other member of the force for he was credited with all those pre-arranged numbers cases on the docket. Many records disclosed individual runners with 500 to 2,000 separate convictions or violations.

The gambling fraternity wanted representation and protection in court. Attorney fees were usually $10.00 per man so the income could be sustantiated. The gamblers went to McMahon; he in turn consulted his friend, E.J.

Neither Marshall nor McMahon desired to be in the middle to represent or appear in front of such activity. It would impair relations with other more important clients.

McMahon and Marshall arranged to have a disbarred attorney, Dan McCullough, reinstated into the practice of law within a year after the Toledo Bar Association had obtained a court order of permanent disbarment against him based on eight charges involving moral turpitude.[14] Both wanted to use him as their courtroom emissary. Neither cared to be directly involved, so they selected a tainted lawyer they could trust who would be indebted to them to do their dirty work in representing the gamblers, yet give them a share of the loot.

Abraham Lincoln once said, "A disbarred lawyer becomes a lonely man." Dan H. McCullough was saved from social oblivion by the action of McMahon and Marshall, two highly-respected leaders of the local bar. Since the large law firms controlled Bar actions and elections, few, if any, would object. Just as leaders in the bar could act in reinstatement, another occasional adverse action also could be instigated to strike down and destroy a fellow lawyer.[15]

Dan McCullough was grateful to his benefactors but forever bore a grudge against many others in the bar. He never became active or held office in the local association. Later he manifested his resentment by comments referring to those in charge as "sanctimonious sons of bitches."

While everybody called him Dan, for some unexplained reason his mother always called him Harold.[16] Born in 1898 on the east side of the city, he was the son of a railroader father. Though a poor Catholic as far as church attendance was concerned, Dan attended St. John's High School, College and Law School. He interrupted his education to serve with an army cavalry unit overseas in World War I.[17]

Tall, lean with a prominent proboscis and deep-set eyes, he emerged from law school in 1922 with the idea that fighting cops meant physical as well as legal battles. He was of a belligerent nature, aggressive, with a quick temper and a powerful physique. When frustrated in the courtroom, he would seek satisfaction in the hallways or nearby bars or speakeasies. He drank, he fought, he caroused.[18] He used his fists once too often on his wife, Virginia Williams. She consulted E.J.'s partner, Harold Frazier, and obtained a divorce and custody of Dan, Jr. She claimed Dan was a loner and a difficult man to live with. Virginia became the wife of Jack O'Connell, theatrical entrepreneur, and Dan Jr. used his stepfather's name in school for years as a de facto adoption.

One of the best known stories on Dan's pugnacious conduct occurred when he tried a case in Findlay, Ohio. After an outburst in the courtroom, the judge asked his bailiff to conduct McCullough to the railroad station and stay with him until the train departed. As he boarded the train which was about to depart, Dan spoke to his escort. "You have a beautiful set of teeth. There's about four of them you won't use," he said, swinging a haymaker to the bailiff's mouth. When the Findlay police sent a flier requesting an arrest, the Toledo police accommodated Dan with the same courtesy shown others on the lam. "Not known or not found" was the reply.

Another fracas involving Dan occurred when he acted in defense of bonus marchers on Washington, D.C. in 1932, to the dismay of Republican members of that organization. Dan was in line for the presidency of that group, but others decided that because of his bar problems it was not to be. When an opponent took the platform and tried to take over a meeting by parliamentary procedure, Dan tossed him out bodily, shouting, "You use Roberts Rules of Order, I use the Marquis of Queensberry Rules."[19]

This and other nefarious conduct created a poor image in the bar. Dan was disbarred. E.J.'s and McMahon's efforts were first unrequited. Dan was again in trouble with one of the local judges for contempt of court. McMahon, a fellow Catholic, marched Dan into E.J.'s office. There, after promising to apologize to the judge, Dan emerged the local emissary of the powers behind gambling in the city.[20]

When asked about his disbarment proceeding, Dan often commented, "You'll never find any trace of it." The papers on disbarment cases were kept in a secret vault in the office of the clerk of courts. The documents in Dan's proceedings had disappeared. The clerk was required by law to send a copy of the original court order to the Supreme Court for permanent filing, so the loss of documents did not destroy the record.[21]

With McMahon's support, Dan was soon handling all of their criminal cases. He was not an elite lawyer and never became one although under the protection of elitism. He was not an outstanding trial lawyer. His high, shrill voice and aggressive courtroom tactics frequently offended jurors. Most of his early cases were "fixed" or settled; many of those tried were often lost. Under his two sponsors, he soon enjoyed a good press. They called him "Dapper Dan" as his newly-found wealth allowed him to become a clothes horse. If a man was in custody with money, the police called Dan.

He retained his cavalry experience and love of horses, becoming a noted rider and polo player. Society ladies, particularly the matrons, accepted him as he joined the leading clubs of the period. While handling the gambling cases, he earned the nickname "Silver Dollar Dan." When the police raided Benny Aronoff's Buckeye Club, Dan ran over to help. He saw three bags of silver dollars which the police, in the unannounced raid, had placed on a table. Dan picked up the bags and walked out.

Some say that Dan took the money to a popular restaurant and passsed out dollars as souvenirs. Others claimed he took the evidence up to McMahon's office a half block away. In either case, no charges were ever filed. The evidence was never reclaimed. The newspapers loved him for such defiance.[22]

In time, Dan became cocky, bolder and oozed with confidence. He joined the local Y to keep in shape. There he regaled the regulars with stories about law and sex.

Dan developed a peculiar and warped sense of humor. He would send out dunning letters to prominent people under another lawyer's name. Often phony invitations were sent to unwanted guests. One time he sent a letter to Judge McCabe complaining that his bailiff, Eddie Newmark, was campaigning for the opposition. Newmark intercepted the letter before it cost him his job. An alarmed Dan confessed to the prank before the judge could act.[23]

Dan was the acknowledged gamblers' mouthpiece. Now he could

truly plan revenge. His social contacts were many and varied. For those in the bar who had sought to destroy him professionally, he planned to make each a cuckold. It was stated that Dan kept a diary or portfolio of his successes with the ladies and wanted to publish it. No newspaper friend would touch it. While the prominent ignored and rejected him, Dan found that their wives did not. Dan revelled in the thoughts of being able to get rich and also get even with the social snobs whose ostracism hurt him so deeply.

# 12 *Vice*

Vice is defined as "indulgence in degrading pleasures or practices."[1] In early America, gambling was closely associated with crime. In the rugged tradition of the frontier as well as on the more sophisticated eastern seaboard, local gambling flourished unchecked.[2] The modern phenomenon of organized crime in gambling was a product of the Prohibition era. Illegal gambling did not produce the gangster, but it proved an activity suited for him to take over and develop.[3]

Just as Toledo had a segregated district of bordellos long before the end of the 19th century, there were also numerous organized gambling houses, all protected by police. The word tenderloin was given by newspapers to those areas of a city from which police obtained graft enabling them to buy tenderloin steaks.

The Parkhurst investigation in New York of 1894,[4] and the Steffens stories eight years later revealed similar corrupt states of affairs rampant in most major cities.

Crap games and blackjack were and still are the most lucrative games. In the 1920s, Jimmy Hayes' 631 or Jovial Club made him the King-pin of Toledo. He brought St. Louis friends, Pat and Joe Morrissey with Ed Warnke to assist him. The only other major crap game was at the Dugout, under the auspices of prominent Tom Worland.

Smaller houses using the names of owners as Dugans, Worlings or Sailors were also allowed to run.

Hayes would never brook further competition. When Ben Aronoff and other newcomers to the city wanted to open with craps and blackjack, Jim was adamant in blocking them. "I paid too much protection ... I did too many favors." Police used Hayes too much to deny him. Hayes was backed up in his actions by his attorney, John McMahon. It was not until after his brutal murder in 1934 that his luck in craps changed.[5]

Slot machine franchises were by competitive bidding.[6] Joe Fretti[6] bid annually and paid $25,000 a year to the mayor's office for the annual right to operate 2,500 nickel, dime and quarter machines in the city. They were located everywhere change was given. Because the mayor controlled appointment of the police chief, there was no interference. A later attempt to cut off revenue from slots resulted in one of the most famous leaks in the city police department.

In the county, several operators, including the enterprising Tom Worland, paid similar rights of protection.

Booking off-track horse bets was lucrative. Ben Aronoff and Harris took over a large book. When the Depression increased the play and volume of business in policy or numbers, a downtown numbers house known as the Buckeye Social Club was opened. Six other houses with runners all over city factories, stores, business offices and homes brought in daily clandestine collections. For the five days of the week that the stock market was open, business in small change — and there was plenty of it — boomed.

Smaller cigar stores and pool rooms throughout the city had "stusch" (a form of Faro), poker, pinochle, bridge and rummy. A few downtown bars had several card tables for rummy at a quarter a deal with a five cent rake from the winner of each game. A few also maintained Western Union tickers for sports results.

Wherever a loose dollar is found, looser women will abound. The two social evils coexist and have always done so in the 200 years of this country.

Gambling breeds prostitution.[7] "Where there's gambling, there's easy money, where there's easy money, there's whores."[8]

The number of bordellos in the city could cover a page of listings of a phone book. From the fringes of the downtown area, a string of over a hundred residences, known as "the line," extended for several blocks throughout the city.

The most notorious establishments were Jean Ford's, Mother H,

Three Aces (which featured black and white), Chicken Charley, Palm Gardens, Gypsy Joe's and Pappy's.

The best-known girls were Silver Tongue Elsie, Blonde Dottie, Gracie, Gypsy and Little Egypt. Sadie Sherman, Stella Hoffman, Tilly Diamond and Jean Ford were the most notorious madams. During Prohibition, some places serving booze and broads acquired a newspaper named *Blind Pig*.

Pearl Barber, a black pimp, was used by the police chief as bagman for collections in the vice circles. Jimmy (Highpockets) Carr reputedly had the best-looking girls working at the Boody House Hotel in the center of the city.

The Freudian obsession with sex brought consternation into every American home after World War I.[9] A new code of ethics and morality came in with Prohibition. Having gained the right to vote earlier, the women now exhibited new independence. Skirts were lifted far beyond any modest limitation.[10] Hems were nine inches above the ground.[11] Short hair styles were in vogue. Girls wearing provocatively thin dresses and low-cut gowns were regarded as flappers. Use of rouge, the abandonment of corsets, smoking and drinking oneself into a stupor were part of the "in" scene.

The new code of ethics brought an inevitable change in morals.[12] Boys and girls were becoming sophisticated about sex at an early age. The state of morality was "a single standard, and that a low one."[13] Movies with heavy kissing and love-making brought on petting parties and promiscuity. The automobile was called "a brothel on wheels." Concerned parents were unable to stem the tide of new sexual freedoms.[14] As hems went up, pants came down.

It was claimed so many were "giving it away" freely, brothels suffered financially. But after the Depression of 1929, when the poor working girl could not find employment, many turned to the oldest profession as a means of livelihood. At a dollar per trip or trick, brothels became places of social rendezvous among the working classes and college students.

Dating was expensive then. Saturday nights would find the single stud out on the town. After trying to make out at one of the dancing emporiums such as Tabernilla, Recreation, Coliseum, Chateau La France or Madison Square Gardens (later Trianon), the frustrated youths would gather to watch the girls in diaphanous gowns display their charms in hope of a score.

During the weekdays whole fraternities and youth clubs would frequent the larger houses. With the economy being as it was, students took turns lending each other a dime or two until a dollar was acquired. At least five or six out of a group of 20 could thereby obtain some biological relief. One father, on hearing of his son frequenting a bordello, exclaimed, "I'm increasing his allowance to $5 a week. He needs it."

Gambling and prostitution were policed by the vice squads. Newcomers and neophytes to sporting houses often reported seeing members of such groups regularly. Stories told by first-time visitors were often of shock and laughter. While seated in the living room, they were often surprised by the appearance of a young policeman in uniform entering through the front door, strolling directly through the living room into the kitchen. "It's a pinch. He's barring the exits," excited youngsters would cry out.

Fears or alarm about arrest were quickly allayed by the girls or madam present. "There's nothing wrong. It's lunchtime." A short time later, the youthful officer would reappear, munching a sandwich or drinking a beer which he usually finished before going out on the street. It was common practice for rookies to take free meals or drinks on their beats in such manner.

Raids by vice squads were always pre-arranged to make the police look good in the public eye. Advance notice was always given to the gambling joints. When police and newsmen would arrive thereafter, no action of any kind could be seen. All tables and paraphernalia were covered or hidden. Slot machines were contraband — that is, they could be seized or confiscated on sight wherever found — but the police always insisted that actual "play" be taking place before an arrest would be made.

In the bordellos the scene was the same. Vice squad cops would order "a raid" at an early morning hour when no girls were working and no customers were present. Newspaper photographers were tipped to cover the story of the raid. Pictures of police chopping the door to the House into splinters would make the daily pages. Milkmen, making daily deliveries, often reported the "ax act" as a common occurrence. The pimps, on seeing the reluctant milkman, would yell out of an upstairs window over the noise of the hacking, "It's OK. Three quarts of milk and a pint of cream. Put 'em in the refrigerator. Pay you tomorrow." The next day the milkman reported a new door had been installed and "it was business as usual."[15]

Morality in the police ranks was low because of the great advantages given to vice — the chief's pets, as they were called.

In exchange for the privileges of conducting gambling and prostitution, the operators kept the city free from crime. It was part of their bargain. This was one factor that Firetop unfortunately overlooked.

# 13 Prohibition Days

Prohibition gave greater impetus to the growth of crime, graft and corruption than any other law ever enacted. Will Rogers often quipped, "When Congress makes a joke, it becomes law, when they make a law, it becomes a joke." Prohibition proved his point.

The Volstead Act, more commonly known as the Eighteenth Amendment, also proved that it was foolish, if not impossible, to try to regulate public morality on liquor or drinking. Two-thirds of the states ratified the Eighteenth Amendment (prohibiting the sale and use of intoxicating beverages) after its first proposal on December 18, 1917. The ban was to become effective nationally on January 17, 1920. Ohio jumped the gun by setting Monday, May 26, 1919, at midnight for the official death of liquor business in Ohio. The events of the final day in Toledo were repeated in the same manner in other cities and states the following January 16, 1920. The *Blade* described the last day:[1]

> As dawn came, hundreds of Toledo saloons unlocked their doors for the last time to admit the thousands already clamoring for their last morning drinks.
> Early interurbans brought hundreds of roisterers to the city; Michigan sent delegates by the thousands. Many carried jugs and other receptacles in which wine and whisky might be carried home.

*UNHOLY TOLEDO*

> Women, in many instances, walked boldly into saloons and ordered their wet goods over the bar — some stood there and brazenly indulged while the shouts of male approval sent the flush of excitement into their cheeks.
> "Yo, ho, ho, and a bottle of rum" was the theme song of the weekend revelers in the 163 Toledo bars still selling their wares. Monday, the last legal "wet" day, was a day of liquor auctions and sales as saloons and warehouses sought to clear their shelves.
> Between Saturday afternoon and Monday morning there were 150 arrests on drunk and disorderly charges. The Central Police Station was so crowded that prisoners had to sleep on the floor, benches and chairs.[2]

On Thursday preceding the last weekend, the *Blade* reported that "prominent Toledo citizens, particularly county officials," were receiving invitations something like this: "Last rites of our Old Friend and Companion, John Barleycorn. On Saturday evening, the twenty-fourth of May, one thousand nine hundred and nineteen, at nine o'clock, at the Boody House. Flowers accepted. Make reservations now. Pallbearers — Prominent and Influential Toledoans."[3]

On the day the bars closed there was panic in the land, the records show. Many citizens had been buying and storing liquid refreshments in warehouses and vaults, intending to withdraw them as needed for thirst-quenching and party-throwing.

But a Federal District Court case on January 15 spoiled the plans. The decision upheld a U.S. Prohibition Bureau ruling that such stored liquor would be subject to seizure as soon as the Eighteenth Amendment and Volstead Act went into effect at 12:01a.m. on January 17, 1920.[4]

Hip flasks were forbidden and Prohibition authorities proclaimed that pants in which a flask was carried would be classed as a vehicle and could be confiscated.

That started the frantic last-minute movement in the big cities on the 16th to rescue all stored liquor and move it safely. Moving vans, children's wagons and baby carriages were pressed into service to haul away the liquor. Children on roller skates helped their families.

One little Chicago girl, it was reported, made 50 trips to a warehouse and carried home 50 bottles of whisky without breaking one. Her father gave her a bottle of ginger ale and a pair of new skates as a reward.

A Massachusetts brewing corporation, which had bought liquor on speculation, distributed the stored booze pro rata among its stockholders.

As the wets hoarded liquor and had their last public flings, the drys celebrated the coming of Prohibition. There were thanksgiving and watch night services in every town with a WCTU chapter., There were parades and mass meetings to hail the victory of the Prohibition forces of the land.

In Norfolk, Virginia, evangelist Billy Sunday preached a "funeral" for John Barleycorn before more than 10,000 people. Old John's "body" in a 20-foot casket arrived on a special train from Milwaukee, the nation's beer capital. Twenty pallbearers escorted the coffin to Billy's tabernacle. A man dressed as Satan, moaning in grief, followed. Satan and a score of his ragged followers occupied the mourners' bench. And the evangelist preached.

"The reign of tears is over," he orated. "The slums will soon be only a memory. We will turn our prisons into factories and our jails into storehouses and corn cribs. Men will walk upright now, women will smile, and the children will laugh. Hell will be forever for rent."[5]

There were other "funerals" too, such as the one in Toledo in the old Boody House the previous May, where bartenders wept, liquor was served in black glasses, napkins were black, walls and tables were covered with black cloth. Orchestras played the Funeral March and "Goodbye Forever."[6]

Thus one era ended and another began. There were no more golden fizzes, sloe gin rickeys and whisky sours served legally and properly from bars. Gone were the days of "rushing the growler" to saloon doors to get brimming pails of draft beer to carry home at supper time.

Evasion of the law began immediately.[7] Drinking became the thing to do,[8] and grew in popularity. The use of the hip flask, the cocktail party, and general transformation of drinking from a masculine prerogative to one shared by both sexes together were a further aftermath of the public revolt.[9] Under the new regime, not only were the drinks mixed, but the company as well.[10]

Prohibition was not prohibiting.

The new social order saw the birth of speakeasies and the rise of organized gangs in the larger cities, controlling the highly profitable bootlegging business.

On Harding's election in 1920, the Ohio gang had their fingers in the affairs of attorney George Remus, known as the gentle grafter. Remus, a multi-millionaire, became known nationally as "King of the Bootleggers" by reason of his Cincinnati operations. Remus organized drug companies and obtained medical permits for liquor which he resold. It was claimed that his bribes totaled twenty million dollars as his sales were nationwide of legitimate distilled whisky. The whisky permit enabled him to withdraw liquor from bonded warehouses. The medical formula was copied where resale was profitable, otherwise bootleggers made and sold their own. Ohio also boasted the largest distillery during and after Prohibition at Zanesville, Ohio, where over 36,000 gallons of mash were produced every day.

Toledo followed the national trend. Prominent speakeasies replaced former bars. The Villa, Tabernella, Chateau LaFrance and Casino, operated by Heini Billiter, brother of Johnny Billiter, world light-weight wrestling champion were among the leading hangouts. Chicken Charlie's in the red light district was unique, for patrons could obtain both booze and broads.

Enforcement of the new law was difficult if not ludicrous. Yet one of the first persons arrested while using Toledo as headquarters, was Sherman Billingsley, then labeled in an era of kingmakers as "King of Whisky Runners." He was apprehended by Michigan authorities while escorting a party of five automobiles carrying 1,500 gallons of whisky from Toledo to Detroit. Authorities said that within a month Billingsley and his associates had smuggled from Toledo 46,000 bottles of whisky worth $168,192, costing him $3.00 a quart and selling for $8.00.

It was said that Billingsley and his three brothers, Fred, Logan and Orrie, operated exclusively in dry states from the Pacific Coast through the Southwest; reportedly they were headed for a clean-up when New York was declared dry. At the time of Sherman's arrest, Fred and Logan were "doing time" for their activities while Orrie, also wanted, was at large.[11] Sherman later became famous as an outstanding night club host at the Stork Club in New York City.

Monroe, Michigan, was ideally situated for bootlegging activity. Located between Toledo and Detroit, its harbor could accommodate speedboats bringing in Canadian brands past border patrols that concentrated on Detroit and Toledo. Papa Joe Bedelementi, Rough Manuel Bedelementi, John Costello and the Gallino brothers handled 90% of the incoming liquor for reshipment to Detroit and Toledo.

The nation learned of the gangland's interests through news reports on the Capone activities. Chicago set the formula which was repeated in other cities until the Twenty-first Amendment repealed the ill-advised Eighteenth Amendment on December 5, 1933.

It was in the Prohibition era under Licavoli that Toledo acquired its reputation as "Chicago on Lake Erie."

Legitimate people feared moving to Toledo. Local officials claimed "it was no worse than others." In a way they were right. Before Licavoli there were no organized gangs taking over distribution with hijackings or forced sales. Gangland killings or murders were virtually unknown. Local crime was under control.[12]

Yet the city was like the others nationwide. Every bathtub became a potential still. Those who were unable to produce sometimes stole from others. Since the goods so stolen were contraband, theft would not be investigated or reported. Gangs of kids were paid 50 cents each to peek into basements, garages or sheds to detect and report a potential still or cache of goods that could be heisted.

The Cleveland *Plain Dealer* wrote a front-page story proclaiming the success of a raid by federal agents under the direction of U.S. Marshal Charles W. Lepp of Cleveland in which 1090 arrests were made and more than 80 resorts closed.[13] The article stated, "When the Volstead Act went into effect, Toledo quite naturally became a bootlegging headquarters. Its infamous resorts, low grade hotels, gambling joints, pool rooms and bawdy houses afforded sanctuary for the operators, while crooked taxicab drivers aided in the illicit business of liquor running.

"Certain lawyers, some of whom boasted of official pull in many cities and who were known to almost every crook in the country, had headquarters in Toledo and were recognized as 'legal advisers to the fraternity.' They had their agents or representatives in other citys.[14]

"Official laxity is not wholly to blame for Toledo's reputation or its record of crime and vice. Its location made it an ideal center and it possessed unusual facilities for crooks seeking speedy hiding places or quick getaways."[15]

The Cleveland publicity and investigation resulted in the ousting of safety director Chris Wall. In the hierarchy of city government, the safety director superseded the chief of police and fire chief, but his removal made little difference.

In addition to vice and gambling, bootlegging brought a new dimension to police graft. There was a great need for police protection or privilege in operation of a location, in production of stills and in protection of finished products from thieves and hijackers. Drinkers far outnumbered all other illegal enterprises. Prohibition easily brought more illegal revenue and graft to police than any other source.

Harry Jennings, chief of police during the early '20s, used only two officers, Whitey Winkleman and Paul Howser, on his vice squad. Their jobs involved, among other duties, collections for the chief and politicians. Police scrambled for a chance to join the vice squad. Officers associated with that division could earn an estimated $30,000 a year in addition to their $2,100 yearly salary. The secretary to Jennings, Roy Scofield, was responsible to political bosses for their share. All graft was carefully collected. Immunization by indirect acquisition was the key. Obscure, unknown, low-key personnel were used to perform in these perfunctory tasks for high pay. Graft in bootlegging was also accepted as a way of life in Toledo.

"Give the people safe streets, orderly nights and security in their homes. They will overlook graft," politicians advised.

"American people don't mind graft but they hate scandal, so operate in a low key and don't get caught," police were told.

While Prohibition violations became federal offenses, the city and state were quick to enact their own laws. Seventy five hundred arrests for violations occurred the first year. The Federal prosecutors did not have sufficient personnel to handle their volume. Federal prisons would have been filled with liquor violators but the courts were lenient to first and second offenders by suspending sentences and imposing fines. Federal agent L.F. Hansbrough, stationed in Toledo, deplored the fact that his force was insufficient for the requirements of the city. He claimed the main defect in the Crabbe Act was that it had no provisions for reaching violators who escape jail penalty for a third offense by naming a dummy operator after two prior convictions by the offender. "As long as liquor dealers can sell and be let off with fines, they have no fear of the law," he declared.

The increased traffic in liquor and the enactment of state and city laws required increases in vice squads. Jimmy Ford, Earl McBride, Harvey Kleiber, Allie Brown, John Michalek, George Timiney and Ralph Murphy also became big-shots on the early squads.

Patrons of the Casino grew accustomed to seeing the entire vice squad meet there regularly, as did patrons of Mother H's quarters. They had to make arrests for the sake of appearances and such visits were to show the public they were doing their jobs.

Police themselves sometimes criticized the chief or entire department for putting young policemen in positions on the vice squad where they could be corrupted with bribes, broads and booze. It was argued that when police were corrupted, the thieves, pimps and underworld refused to trust contaminated police for fear that confiding in them would result in further extortion. Many police on the vice squad subsequently became drinkers, gamblers and whoremongers. Ralph Murphy, who later became head of homicide and an excellent detective and witness for the prosecution or defense, became addicted to gambling to such an extent that reports circulated around City Hall that he was betting heavily on the horses and bet $500 or more on one race.

As a consequence of favoritism, morale on the police force was low. Envy, jealousy, petty bickering and conniving prevailed. Don Cockran, a newspaper reporter turned policeman, in 1926-27 inveigled himself onto the vice squad, walking right in because he knew the ropes and where to look if he needed a story to tell. He never wore a uniform and his sudden emergence added to the already growing dissention.

With the volume of arrests, proceedings in the police court (criminal branch of the municipal court) were equally hectic. The minimum liquor case sentence in federal court was 10 to 90 days in jail and big fines. If prosecuted by one jurisdiction, the city, an offender could claim double jeopardy in federal court so police and their cohorts worked fast to get the bootlegging cases heard or disposed of before federal charges were filed. Police prosecutors from the city law department were paid $100 a week, but were often offered bribes of four times that amount on an annual basis if favors could be granted.

Judge Aaron Cohn, a Republican whose father was prominent in politics at the turn of the century, was reputed to be a harsh judge. Defendants and their lawyers would try to avoid his discipline and ruling by frequent continuances, delays and dilatory tactics to maneuver cases to more favorable judges like Ira Cole or Homer Ramey, who were inclined to do favors for their friends and fellow lawyers. Although basically honest and popular, it can not be said that either judge received anything beyond funds for re-electon. Judge Ramey, however, loved the girls and stories of his nightly escapades in their emporiums were legion.

Homer was a stout, short, heavy-set man with heavy jowls and a jaw to match. He loved food, booze and broads. He could eat nine or 10 chicken halves at one sitting and wash them down with a gallon of beer. He would take his father, a country farmer, with him on rounds in the vice district. There, singing, boozing and carousing until the wee hours of the morning, Homer would tell his friends, "I fixed Dad up for another year."

Some lawyers handled Homer easily. They could get him to reduce a fine or bond although he had sworn he would not do so. Such attorneys would follow him into his office after court sessions and plead. When he fled, they followed him home, usually arriving ahead of him in time to explain their problems to his wife, Ruby. Before he could say a word, Ruby would blurt out on Homer's arrival, "Now, Homer, you take care of this case so this nice man can be on his way."

Homer was a devout student of the Bible. If a criminal defendant gave an intellingent response to something from the Bible, Homer would dismiss his case on payment of cash. Homer enjoyed preaching. He was popular as a speaker and humorist, frequently called upon to deliver speeches at funerals, parties and Bar functions.

Judge Ramey told his wife everything about his court cases, word for word, as he possessed a remarkable memory. Whenever court was not in session, phone conversations ensued. The classic story is told that one day Homer was out on the town and came home loaded with vomit all over the front of his pendulous abdominal girth. He recovered in time to tell Ruby, "Now, honey, you know how popular I am. Well, I was at a Republican Party meeting and some drunk did this to me. But don't worry, they arrested him and I'll get him good in court in the morning." With that explanation, he went to bed. The next day, as he waited for court to convene, the phone rang a few minutes before nine. "Homer, dear," Ruby began, "remember that man who vomited on you last night?" "Oh, yes," Homer interruted, "he's coming up this morning and I'm really going to give him hell." "Yes, Homer, do that. Give him double hell because there's shit in your pants, too."

During this era, Firetop frequently acted as front man for offenders in criminal cases as he became acutely aware of the enormous amounts of money to be made.

As for "fixes," local bondsman Louie Wittenberg seemed able to get better results than anybody else in town, including lawyers. Newspapers hailed Wittenberg as "King of Canton Avenue." Born in Poland, he came to Toledo from Port Chester, New York, and opened a saloon in 1889 on Canton Avenue, then the Jewish sector of the city. People then knew each other and their affairs; they helped neighbors in all kinds of trouble, legal or financial. So many people involved in infractions of the law appealed to the kindly Wittenberg for help, that he started a professional bonding business. For a premium of 10% of the bond set by the court, which he retained as a fee, he put up the rest of the security for bail set by the court. Louie's closest friend became the "Golden Rule Judge," police court judge James Austin, Jr. For most of the 50 years he spent on the local bench, Austin had a strong, perverted sense of sympathy for the underdog. He gave most of those coming before him a second chance. Judge Austin once gave a banquet in honor of men with criminal records trying to go straight. The judge claimed the men had reformed but he didn't like to use that word himself. He invited Louie Wittenberg as a guest together with other friends and newspapermen. After a banquet and a few short speeches, the diners went home. Then the judge discovered his newly-purchased hat had been stolen.

The *Blade* commented "A picturesque feature of his [Austin's] career has been his personal friendship for Louie Wittenberg." Austin once appointed his friend Louie to the position of probation officer of his court, which brought on great public criticism. For years, Wittenberg was friendly with other police court judges such as Ira Cole, Len Donovan and Homer Ramey. Moses McClosky, a Jewish captain of detectives, was also a great pal. Consequently, over the years, the bondsman could get results in police court cases. Incredible "fixes" were performed. One judge would forfeit a bond; another would vacate the order and save the bondsman's money. An irate Judge Cohn warned one city prosecutor, "Stay away from the bondsman; he can get you in trouble."

The bondsmen were reported to have the vice squad in their pockets. They could ask for and set any bond and the police would not object. A bondsman could go into the clerk's office and remove any file to take to a favorable judge. It was claimed that while Lou Wittenberg was charitable, he was a bad loser. When he lost heavily in craps, he would ask the vice squad to stage an unannounced raid so that he could recoup his losses in bond fees, and they did his bidding. Where one judge would order a $500 fine, another would reduce it after it was paid, and then the bondsman or clerk would pocket the money as records were sparsely kept. The number of cases in which judges were asked "to go easy" were astronomical. Usually the police had no objections to any court findings. Weak cases were dropped, strong ones fixed, maneuvered or reduced.

Many police themselves became unknown or known accessories when they raided a still and confiscated the liquor; sometimes it would be stored in places other than the police property room, then used or sold. Police were silent partners with dealers as with the numbers game.

Sometimes police "framed" evidence to enforce tribute. In some reported cases, the vice squad placed bottles of whisky on victims' premises. They would then make an arrest for possession. When the defendants protested innocence, police prosecutors pressed their investigations to discover that the police had connived to compel payoffs.

The stage was set in the previous panoramic history of the Toledo scene.

Firetop felt he could handle all the politicians, police, bondsmen

## UNHOLY TOLEDO

and protection devices. All he wanted was a little muscle to organize and take over the illicit operations of the city.

Firetop knew this city. Toledoans had always taken kindly to visitors from other places. He said, "They bend over backwards to make strangers welcome. They would do more for a complete unknown than for a neighbor in order to make a good impression." It appeared to the disgruntled Firetop that Toledoans habitually pushed newcomers to the top. "Anybody who ever amounted to anything in this town seemed to have come from some place else," he said. It was time for a hometown boy to make good.

He felt the city would accommodate the now-arriving Licavoli friends from Detroit. In his zeal, Firetop failed to take cognizance of the fact that Licavoli and associates were not the type of people that would endear any place, any time, anywhere! He would learn what it was all about very soon.

*Firetop Sulkin hears the court pronounce his death sentence. Courtesy Toledo-Lucas County Public Library.*

*Purple Gangsters Keywell, Milberg and Bernstein on trial, with lawyers Kennedy and Baxter. Courtesy Detroit News.*

*Joseph W. Robinson presenting gold medal for journalism to author Harry R. Illman. Courtesy Toledo-Lucas Public Library.*

Brand Whitlock, Toledo's greatest mayor. Courtesy Toledo-Lucas County Public Library.

Sam (Golden Rule) Jones, the "Honest Mayor" of Toledo. Courtesy Toledo-Lucas County Public Library.

*Walter F. Brown (center) at 1936 Republican National Convention. Courtesy Toledo-Lucas County Public Library.*

*Jackie Kennedy: at 24, a martyr. Courtesy Toledo-Lucas County Public Library.*

*Sister Jean, beauty queen: depression settlement, $1500 for loss of eye and facial disfigurement.*

*Scab in the famous Auto-Lite strike, stripped by the angry mob. Picture courtesy of the late Brandon Schnorf, Sr.*

"Mr. Toledo", Grove Patterson, editor of the Toledo Blade, who felt syndicated gambling did not hurt the city's image. Picture courtesy Toledo-Lucas County public library.

*Gang leader Thomas (Yonnie) Licavoli (left) on trial for murder. Shown with attorney Cornell Schreiber. Picture courtesy Toledo-Lucas County Public Library.*

# 14 The Licavoli Takeover

A happy, peacock-proud Firetop strutted among his associates and friends as the Licavoli gang moved to Toledo in the Spring of 1931. He became the cock of the walk. Arrogant, snotty, he was called "Flip" by many who knew him. Firetop realized he was to play an important role in the gang action and he wanted the town to know it.

Crime in most big cities was acknowledged as a way of life. It could only exist because it paid off.

In the 1930s and the years that followed, organized crime linked with corruption in government. Society was at the mercy of organized crime.[1]

Toledo police had never previously experienced encounters with an organized gang of armed killers. Thus they were unprepared for what was to follow. The city had tolerated vice, prostitution and bootlegging on the promise of the operators that the streets would be safe for the public, with crime and criminals controlled. But the Licavolis changed that concept as Yonnie transported his brother Jimmy, alias Blackjack, his brother-in-law, Leo Moceri, along with John Mirabella, Ralph Carsello, Russell Syracuse, Ernest LaSalle and John Rai as the nucleus of his gang. With Firetop acting as his fingerman, he added four local hoods, all known to the Toledo police, to help in his takeover. Joining were (Chalky Red) Yaranowsky, alias Harry Leonard,

*UNHOLY TOLEDO*

Sebastian (Buster) Lupica, Anthony (Whitey) Basase and Joe (Wop) English alias Serifina Sinatra.

Of the four, Chalky Red became the most notorious. Like Firetop, his nickname came from the color of his hair. Born to a poor but honest fish peddler and his wife, Jacob and Sarah Nemerowsky, the newspapers constantly referred to Chalky Red as Yaranowsky.[2] Some sources stated the error developed and was never corrected after Red gave a false name at his first juvenile arrest to avoid embarrassment to his family. As a big muscular kid with sandy red hair and pasty white skin, he began his life of crime as a kid. One can't fool kids: those who knew him instinctively disliked him. When he sold newspapers, he held the corner where the Ann Arbor Railroad passenger trains brought commuters to the city. He was known then as Ann Arbor Red, nervously yelling all the time, even when talking. Red had a lucrative spot and he would never tolerate competition. In the days when the news boys bought the papers in advance to resell at two cents apiece, they had to sell or "eat" them — no returns were taken. The story is told that one stormy, winter day, my oldest brother Ben came past Red's corner enroute home after a day on the downtown streets. Red approached him, "I don't think I'll wait for the next train. If you want, Bennie, I'll sell you these twelve sheets for a dime, double your money, what do you say, buddy?" There was no reason to mistrust him. The two poor families knew each other intimately, Red's older sister was Ben's and my older sister's best friend, so the deal was made. Two hours later, Bennie was still waiting out in the cold and snow for the late train. The bad weather had caused a cancellation. Red knew it all the time. It was too cold to go back downtown to hustle. "That's what happened to today's money," Ben told our understanding mother. "Don't do no more business with Red," she admonished. "He's no good." Indeed, Red was destined to be one of the Jewish members of the Licavoli mob, growing richer, bolder and colder, ruthless, brutal and more powerful as he aged.

(Rough Manuel) Badalamenti ran a grocery store in Monroe, Michigan. When prohibition came, he went into bootlegging and rum running. He asked Chalky to be his partner, promoting him from the numbers rackets. Red became a rum runner of whiskey from Canada to Monroe and Toledo. He soon developed a love for boating, flashing his new prosperity with sports cars, speedboats, and hustling broads. When the vice squad ordered Rough Manuel out of town, his long-time friend, Firetop, asked Red to join the new Licavoli team and bring his customers with him.

Former taxi-driver Firetop took the gang on a cook's tour of the city, pointing out favorable locations for his friends' various activities. In the after-hours life of the city, in downtown restaurants where many congregated nightly to kibitz over depression "panic steaks" of toast and coffee, the newcomers got a "feel" for the city. Finally the gang set up temporary headquarters in the Cleo Apartments located on the fringe of the downtown area and at the Argonne Hotel three blocks away from the County Court House.

At daily meetings, Yonnie, using an alias of Lasser, presided; but Firetop did most of the early talking. "First," he advised, "let's take on the bootleggers. That's where the big money is." "Right," Yonnie echoed. "Because I'm not yet well known here, just tell them we're the Purple Gang from Detroit." Yonnie knew from his past as a member of the Purple Gang that the very mention of Purple to Toledo victims meant instant diarrhea. "Tell them they'll be smart to make us 50-50 partners." Thus Yonnie instructed his henchmen in the new city.

Al Capone had calling cards which he ordered henchmen to hand out on a take-over. Lacking such credentials, the gang came down hard on most approaches. "We're 50-50 partners or else." Few, if any, resisted such well-known pressure. One of the first to renege was Jimmy Leahy, a long-time Toledo bootlegger. On May 5, 1931, Leahy was out driving with his friend, Aaron Harris, when a deluge of bullets flew at them. Leahy escaped injury but Harris, an innocent victim, was killed immediately.[3] Leahy attempted to retaliate by hijacking a Licavoli truck, but ten months later, on March 16, 1932, his lead-loaded body was found along a ditch on Stearns Road, outside of Monroe, Michigan. "No outsiders get into Toledo" Yonnie told the underworld. This was all the warning he felt was needed.

When Cleveland competition tried to sell in the Toledo area, Licavoli's men knocked off Harry Gertzlin and Al Joffe of that city on July 17, 1931.[4] Licavoli then took over their out-of-town customers. Martin Schweitzer, a Canton, Ohio bootlegger, was one among many who paid $100 a month protection on an "or else" threat.

Licavoli learned that Ray Swayne of Mansfield, Ohio had one of the finest stills in the area. "I'll give you 40% commission on all stock sold," Yonnie promised Swayne, a part time automobile dealer and full time bootlegger. After taking two vehicles, without payment, and being advised of the location of his still, the Licavolis dismantled it and relocated it in Toledo without paying Swayne one cent in return. With proper equipment, Licavoli needed other ingredients for massive production.

Sugar was essential to production of whiskey. Licavoli ordered Russell Syracuse "Take over the General Importing Co. owned by George Petcoff." Thousands of dollars' worth of sugar were taken without payment. When legitimate people demanded pay for their goods, Licavoli instructed his men "Just pull out your guns and ask them — are we even — or else?"

In a short time, Licavoli had a still within three blocks of the downtown police station capable of turning out a thousand gallons a day. A second location installed in the area of a furniture store held a complete aging plant capable of hiding 10,000 gallons valued at $100,000.

With money coming in, the gang opened their own night club, the Golden Rose, taking its name from the new manager, John Rose, a former police court bondsman.

Local businessmen, gamblers and bootleggers put pressure on the local police to get rid of Licavoli. Led by Captain George Timiney, nightly raids, sometimes as many as four a night, were conducted in harassment. Customers of illicit businesses did not like the idea of constant surveillance by police. They stayed away and the Golden Rose was deflowered as a business venture. Undaunted, Licavoli tried for another tavern in the downtown area. He selected The Show Boat, owned by Chet Marks and Lou Greiner, as a site for their action. The owners resisted gang pressure for a piece of the Club (without pay). On July 17, 1931, Chet Marks was found shot to death in the rear of his home. Three weeks later Licavoli was running The Show Boat. Captain Timiney again appeared driving the widow's car to tell Yonnie he did not intend to tolerate his gang in the city.

Timiney's threats were ignored. Firetop had told Mrs. Edith Marks, "If you're smart, you'll keep quiet" and she did not press the matter.[5]

Among others, Ken Willard, owner of Danceland, complained to police that he was told by Chalky Red and other Licavoli gangsters that his place would be blown up if he did not put in their slot machines, whiskey and beer.

Bootlegger Charles Merea had to split his money 50-50 with the gang and a Licavoli man was installed in his business place to see that there were no hold-outs.

An incident later occurred at the Show Boat that may have led to the murder of two more Toledoans. Abe (The Punk) Lubitsky, was originally associated with Ben Harris in his numbers operation. Lubitsky had received friendly treatment from Federal Judge Killits. Firetop, then twice the age of The Punk, accused Lubitsky of squealing to the Feds and police about their operations. The Punk resented the accusation. A bitter argument followed and the near combatants parted bitter enemies. Two weeks later on October 6, 1931, Lubitsky left Bowles downtown restaurant to drive to his house. Seated in the middle of the front seat was Norman (Big Agate) Blatt and on the right side of him was Hyman (Nig) Abrams. The Punk stopped for a traffic light behind a car being driven by Attorney Morris Lubitsky, an older brother. As Morris pulled ahead, another car, with three male occupants, pulled alongside the Punk and showered him and his vehicle with bullets.[6] Morris ran back to find his brother and Agate in a pool of blood, mortally wounded. The Punk's last words were, "Morris, it was the Dagos."[7] Abrams had rolled out the right side of the car and recovered from his wounds. While in the hospital, Abrams claimed he could not identify any of the killers. It was rumored he had been advised that if he made any incriminating statements, he would not live to testify.

Firetop did not allow friendship, faith or allegiance to deter his ambitions with the gang. He grew haughtier as the revenues swelled. He adopted a dapper dress. Everyday nattily attired, he showed up at Licavoli's home to confer on new plans and meetings.

Fellow Jew Sam Schuster owned a deli and take-out store in Canton Avenue adjoining that of the deceased Punk. Everybody on the Avenue had been approached for a $50 monthly protection fee. "Protection from what?" Schuster asked. "I'm a World War vet, I don't need protection!" "If you want to operate you do." A few days later, Schuster was visited by three Licavoli men. They beat him unmercifully, throwing him through a window cutting his head open necessitating hospital treatment. Later, when Schuster came into the cigar store next to his place, he was confronted by Firetop. "Why didn't you pay off? You got what you deserved, you stupid bum." "My friends downtown will answer for me," Schuster replied as he left. When Licavoli learned that he had assaulted a man with political connections, he personally appeared to settle matters with the victim. "He wore a silk shirt — monogrammed — beautiful cuff links, a watch chain with diamonds in each link. He talked in a soft voice actually apologizing. He gave me $250 cash ... a lot of money in those days so I told the police to drop the charges against Wop English, one of the guys I identified."[8]

Another Avenue merchant also complained. Harry "Butch" Petler owned a gas station where the gang used to fill up without paying. He was ordered to pay $50 a month. One winter day, two of the gang came in to collect. "I don't have it," Butch told them. "I only have $43 and I need it for gas." "Open that furnace door," one hood said to the other. "Let's see if his head will go in the fire." Then he pulled a gun and demanded the money Butch held. Indignant over this incident, Butch raced downtown to the police station, where Captain Emmett Cairl listened to his complaint. Immediately upon his return from headquarters, Firetop confronted him with "Why did you complain to Cairl about us?" The police captain placed two men in the gas station to get the alleged extortionists if they would appear again, but with the leaks in the department, the arrangement was ludicrous.

Yonnie took on the biggest slot machine operators in the city at that time, Joe and Ben Fretti. Despite all their police connections, the Fretti brothers were deathly afraid of Liciavoli and backed off on his orders. Licavoli was able to take a big percentage of this gambling action. William Poulos had choice locations in which he placed 115 slot machines worth thousands of dollars. He had been splitting his take with Joe Fretti because Fretti had the political connections. Later he was told to split with Licavoli. Paulos was told to bring all the money out to Licavoli's new luxurious home. Once in a while Yonnie, who always claimed he was short, gave him $10. After a few months Paulos was told "You're out completely. Don't come back, that route is no longer yours, it's mine, 100%."

When the gang tried to muscle in on Aronoff and Harris in numbers, they were told "The police are our partners, ask them!" Jimmy Hayes would never brook any cut on his action. Yet Licavoli prospered. He purchased a plush home on a double lot in the Ottawa Hills secluded residential section of the city. A gardner and bodyguard were kept constantly in attendance. Yonnie was a good family man for his father-in-law would have disapproved misconduct. With wife Zena, he raised a family. Some claimed he wanted to set an example for the gang. He held frequent parties. Many civic leaders attended. Municipal Court Judge Ira Cole was a frequent overnight guest.

The gang also took over the Tabernilla Club in east Toledo as the closest point to Lake Erie shipping and made it a second rendezvous and warehouse.[9]

The Tabernilla Inn was built in 1917 by Fred Wescott, an engineer who worked on the Panama Canal. The local inn was a replica of the one in Central America. After Licavoli took it over, he had the bay dredged so boats could land the smuggled whiskey from Canada, Detroit and Monroe. The gang members became more prominent in the city. They developed new hangouts such as the Hill Avenue Gardens, Bancroft Grill and the home of Ralph Carsello. They frequently attended sports events and went to University of Michigan football games. There they laughed at the antics of Firetop's lifetime friend, Hank (Manure) Blumberg, who always seemed able to get in on a Press Pass. Hank would parade up and down both sides of the playing field taking pictures of players and coaches with a box camera that never contained film. Often the camera would be pointed at the gang in jest as they knew the film would never be printed.

When the authorities tried to cut off gambling income, extortion became part of the Licavoli program. At a meeting of dry cleaners of the city in the fall of 1932, Licavoli and two of his henchmen suddenly interrupted their meeting in a downtown building. Christopher Engel, one of the proprietors, demanded to know who they were. The Licavoli name had grown so that use of Purple would have been superfluous.

"My name is Tom Licavoli. Me and my friends here are dry cleaners from downstate and I think your business in this city needs protection under a director." Those present knew what he meant — that he wanted monthly tribute or take over. Engel refused to be cowed and announced his intention not to accede to the demands. Three days later on October 24, 1932 his plant was bombed.[10] The shock was heard for miles. Although guarded at night, a heavy fog allowed the perpetrators to get away. L. W. Schmitz, a downtown dry cleaner, had two front store windows broken and 25 suits slashed by the racketeers. Two more bombings in dry cleaning plants occurred the next month thirteen days apart. Cleaners were wary of accepting any new business. Clothes were being brought in with solvents sewn in the armpits or hems to avoid detection. When mixed with the chemicals and solvents in the cleaning vats, small explosions occurred. The number of cleaners paying for protection at 25 cents per garment was not capable of determination.

Clifford Roach, owner of the Pearl Barber Shop, was muscled out of gambling after his room was bombed twice. He claimed Louie The Lug, a Detroit Licavoli associate, took over his operation.

At this time, Jimmy Licavoli was being sought for a train killing in broad daylight in Detroit. Seven witnesses had identified him as the killer from police mug shots. Jimmy sought Toledo sanctuary but the policemen, Louis Ray Scheets and Chris Brennen, who had never been on the vice or racket squads, apprehended him for Detroit authorities. They reported Yonnie offered them $20,000 each to turn Jimmy loose but they refused to do so. Jimmy fought extradition as he needed time to get to the witnesses. Governor White of Ohio sent his secretary to Toledo. The hearing officer decided there was an improper arrest, ordered Jimmy released and the extradition warrant returned — denied. Yonnie later told Scheets and Brennen it had cost him over $40,000 to straighten the matter out. "You could have taken it and saved me a lot of problems."

Toledo police Captain George Timiney, infuriated by the legal entanglement, took Jimmy to the state line where Michigan authorities were waiting to grab him. Jimmy was arrested and detained in a Detroit jail; but by the time of his trial, witnesses had fled.[11] His absence during this period saved him from a life sentence in later murder trials.

Other small names in the rackets, Augie Armerino, Clayton Knor and Rolland Lampert were found shot to death on nearby county roads. Ike Bracker, a big-time Jewish bootlegger, serviced many prominent Toledoans with the best Canadian brands. He also refused to divulge his customers, sources or cut the Licavolis in. His name was added to the list of unsolved murders when he was found shot to death near the garage of his home.

Newspapers claimed at least fifteen other unsolved murders were attributed to the gang during their short reign of terror.[12] No detailed investigations, arrests or criminal proceedings started until the entire city became aroused by the brutal murder of youthful Jack Kennedy, the only man who actually fought back and attacked Licavoli's gang.[13]

# 15 Jack Kennedy— Martyr

Toledo's Jack Kennedy was as handsome as the later martyred President of the same name. This earlier version could have been a movie star. He stood an inch under six feet in height. There was not an ounce of fat on his 185-pound muscular frame. With wavy brown hair and brown eyes to match, his sensuous dimpled smile made him attractive to most women.

Jack's grandfather was born in Ireland. He came to America at an early age and settled in St. Louis. While working for the railroad, he lost a leg. He used the money from settlement to bring Jack's father and six brothers to Toledo from St. Louis as part of the "mule skinners" of that city. Joe and Pat Morrissey of the same group were then associated with Jimmy Hayes Jovial Club. With police connections, all the Kennedy clan branched out to various bars, taverns or gambling rackets.

Jack was born in 1909, an only child. He was described as a real hellion. He became the toughest kid in every school he attended and the toughest guy in any neighborhood in which he lived. Friends said, "If Jack didn't like you, look out." His school recess and lunch periods were often spent in fighting. He was a natural athlete. Friends claimed he could have been an outstanding football star as he was very fast, shifty, coordinated and loved bodily contact, to hit or be hit. But he dropped out of high school rather than be disciplined by training or coaching. Jack never backed away from any scrape. He loved danger. As he grew older, he continuously looked for thrills. On winter days, he would speed his car down an icy street, suddenly brake and count the number of turns the car would make on the ice. He packed mud on his license plates to aggravate the police, then defy arrest.

When prohibition came, his family went into speakeasies and operated a Soldiers and Sailors Club in the downtown area. Young Jack thrilled to the action. He wanted to be a dealer. Sometimes he would hide the crap game paraphernalia. His uncles had to come to the Catholic High School to call him out of class to start their games. Jack would refuse to reveal or produce the hidden equipment unless he was permitted to deal. His youth was spent around the joints. Often when he saw a shooter he didn't like, he would get down on the floor, place a metal paper clip in a rubber band and shoot his victim in the legs. If there was an outcry, Jack would admit the offense and challenge the complainant. "What are you going to do about it? Want a piece of me?"

Fortunately for his father and uncles, Jack found love at age nineteen, married and had a son, whom he named Jack, Jr. It was time for him to provide a living for his family and he turned to what he had seen and learned — bootlegging.

Jack Kennedy, youthful, athletic, muscular, handsome man-about-town, known as an extravagant spender, good mixer, with daring, guts and charisma galore then became the city's most popular operator.

Jack was good to the Church, helpful to the poor in the depression times. He never refused to give a handout, a drink or meal to anyone who asked. He gave "walk-around money" to anyone down on his luck. Any police officer could talk to him on a financial problem, whereas an approach to Licavoli was impossible.

With encouragement from his friends and police, Kennedy became the most defiant competitor of the Licavoli gang. He challenged them whenever possible. With many personal friends in the police department, like Captain George Timiney, the Licavoli gang never dared to approach Jack with their "50-50 take it or else" propositions. They were forewarned what would happen if they tried as Jack loved any kind of fight. When Licavoli started selling beer for a quarter, Jack reduced his price to fifteen cents. Their rivalry developed early.[1]

Charles Merea, one of the bootleggers taken over by Licavoli, complained to Jack. Licavoli was told, "Merea is now my partner, leave him alone."

Roy Swayne sought him out for help after Licavoli had dismantled and hijacked his still from Mansfield and moved it to Toledo. With the aid of three men using high-powered binoculars, they located the still in a rural area. Jack and Swayne rushed the operators, herded them into a shack in the nearby woods, and bound them securely. Then they quickly dismantled the still, loaded it on a Swayne truck and took it back to its former location.

Swayne also complained that he had not been paid for vehicles the gang purchased from his car agency. Kennedy grabbed John Mirabella in broad daylight, forced him to surrender the keys to the car he was driving, then turned it over to one of Swayne's men.[2]

The gang's hatred of Kennedy was further intensified by the constant raids on the Golden Rose and Show Boat conducted by Captain Timiney. Licavoli complained, "Kennedy is behind these raids. You don't raid his businesses."

Two stills controlled by Licavoli were raided and destroyed, the one within three blocks of the Court House and the aging plant worth one hundred thousand dollars. The income of the gang was seriously impaired by these seizures for which Licavoli also blamed Kennedy. The unfavorable police discrimination in favor of Kennedy inflamed Licavoli and his allies.

One night, two of Yonnie's henchmen tried to barge into one of Kennedy's downtown clubs known as the Black Hawk. Jack was warned by buzzer as they entered and started to climb the stairs to his office. Jack stood at the top of the stairs. In true movie fashion, he grabbed a large beer barrel bound by metal hoops and hurled it at the two, causing both gangsters and full barrel to hit the bottom together. The noise attracted an immediate audience. The gangsters, fearful of recognition, fled into a closed car, as Jack laughed derisively behind them.[3]

A story is told by the Kennedy family that when Jack heard the Licavoli gang had rumored threats against his life, he decided to determine the truth of such stories. One night Yonnie and three of the gang were reported to be in a Crescent Club fixing it up for future use. Kennedy and an armed accomplice climbed an iron stairway at the back of the Club, opened a window and stealthily crept into the room in which Licavoli was working. "Jack," it was reported, "had the drop on them and had Yonnie where he wanted him with his pants down." His associate kept saying, "Let's give it to 'em. Let's let 'em have it." Jack hesitated, they said. Yonnie, sensing his life in danger, made his greatest pitch. "Look Jack," he joked in an easy manner, "what will my friends say when they see me like this — in my work clothes. They'll laugh at me, know what I mean?" Tough as he was, Jack could not kill in cold blood. Jack was a fighter, not a killer. Jack laughed lightly. "Yeah, I know. What's this bullshit that I'm responsible for all your troubles? I don't run the police." Licavoli, sensing a reprieve, interrupted, "Jack, nobody accused you. Honest."

"And what about stories that you're gonna knock me off?"

"Jack, my word of honor, it didn't come from me. Did it boys?"

Thus assured, Jack let Yonnie go. He would never get another opportunity. Licavoli was livid with rage. "He's crazy enough to try again. Kennedy is responsible for all these losses. Now I know. He's got to go." — and the word was out to get Kennedy at the earliest opportunity.

Jack's mother was still disturbed over the rumors of death for her son emanating from Licavoli sources. To allay her fears, Jack muscled Joe (Wop) English into his mother's home. Forced to his knees before his mother, Wop said, "I've known and liked Jack all his life. I promise I'll never harm a hair on his head, so help me God." Later Jack's mother swore she didn't believe him. Wop, she thought, was humiliated by Jack's action.[4]

When his wife also intervened to quarrel about his nocturnal affairs and the safety of their child, Jack could not take the continuous bickering. He consented to a divorce, making ample provisions for alimony and child support. Soon Jack was seen squiring many beautiful women in the night spots of the city.

On November 30, 1932, Jack and his date, Louise Bell, drove to a theatre. From there he planned to drive to his Black Hawk Club. The downtown streets were crowded with people, as the social life of the city and the center of night life was in the downtown area; two or three all-night restaurants were always crowded with customers and kibitzers. As Jack drove by a cigar store, Firetop, standing on the sidewalk, waved and yelled, "Hiya, Jack." Some claim he was fingering Kennedy by the salutation. Jack stopped for a traffic light. As he did so, a car swept alongside, bullets hailed into Kennedy's car; he instinctively leaned forward or ducked to escape injury, but Miss Bell was shot several times and died two hours later.[5] Jack vowed revenge. He said he knew the killer and would testify if he was ever apprehended. Jack paid all the funeral expenses of his sweetheart and promised to drape her grave with the body of her killer. Jack acquired citywide sympathy. His actions were acclaimed as heroism. Storms of protest to rid the city of Licavoli arose. "If there is anybody who can get rid of those hoods, Jack can," the city said. Yet the police were fearful for him. They urged his restraint.

The Bell murder stirred authorities into action. Federal authorities took the first steps by arrest and indictment on December 8, 1932 of Licavoli and some of his henchmen, for violation of prohibition laws. On March 10, 1933, he was found guilty, fined $5,000 and sentenced to two years. While the case was being appealed, prohibition, the experiment that failed, was repealed at the end of the year and charges were dismissed.

Prosecuting attorney Franzier Reams then ordered all slot machines out of the city, hoping to cut the Licavoli revenue and drive them elsewhere. Some claimed this action forced Licavoli to find other income so that extortion tactics against dry cleaners followed thereafter.

Because of the failure to procure arrests or convictions in the Bell murder, Chief of Police Louis L. Hass was reduced in rank to Captain of Detectives and replaced by Chief Daniel T. Wolfe on January 2, 1936.[6]

Aware that he was in danger, Jack imported bodyguards from St. Louis, members of the Egans Rats of that city. His chief bodyguard was William Seath Browning, frequently described as "the man with the smoked glasses." Browning wanted to wade right in and shoot it out with the Licavoli mob but was advised by local associates to avoid open gang war. "The public and police are appalled at what is happening on the city streets. Another outburst could ruin us all."

Jack practiced regularly with a machine gun at a local range. He frequently drove around town with a shot gun or machine gun in his lap. He carried dead rabbits on the floor. If stopped by the authorities, he could claim he had been hunting. His actions received wide notoriety as he was regarded as a local hero.

Realizing fervor created in public sentiment after the Bell murder and the Federal conviction thereafter, Licavoli did not press a Kennedy confrontation. He was advised prohibition was in the process of repeal and new enterprises would be needed for income. Kennedy would no longer be a competitor in such event. The Licavoli change of attitude was not known outside the gang. Two hoodlums, Frank Vacchiano of Dayton and Albert Bruno of Pittsburgh, wanted to be accepted into the Licavoli gang. They thought if they killed Kennedy for Licavoli, they would surely be accepted. On March 29, 1933 the two men, armed with revolvers, staked out a table in Kennedy's Studio Club waiting for him to enter. Their plan was to start shooting on sight, then escape to Licavoli protection. Forewarned by employees about armed men in the Club, Jack failed to show up that night. Frustrated in their failure to get Jack, the two gunmen proceded to get drunk. They went to the Park Lane Hotel, a fashionable residential property near the Toledo Art Museum. Vacchiano had been there before and had been evicted when he tried to register. An argument ensued with night clerk John L. McLaughlin. The bullets originally intended for Kennedy went instead into Mr. McLaughlin in a wanton, senseless murder. Both men fled to Richmond, Indiana where they were apprehended with the weapons still in their possession. Ballistics tests proved they were the murder weapons. Vacchiano tried to escape trial in Toledo by pleading guilty to second degree murder in the death of Sam (Gyp) Valentine in a Dayton barber shop.

The legal tactics of the pair were aided by Tony Paul, alias Neufio Scott, then an accomplice to the Fretti brothers. Vacchiano, age 24, was going out with Tony's sister, Ann Scott. Both men were represented by Dan McCullough, tried separately for the Toledo murder, and convicted.[7]

In the psychiatric query on the sanity of Vacchiano, it was reported the psychiatrist asked him, "Is it true you have killed seven men?" "No," he replied, "it was only five!" One of his victims was his own father. Vacchiano died in the electric chair on December 29, 1933 and Bruno followed on February 6, 1934.[8] The convictions and death penalty sentences were sought as warnings and deterrents to the Licavolis; at least the authorities hoped so.

On March 25, 1933 Kennedy's bodyguard, Browning, was shot and killed in a shoot-out with police in Marion, Indiana. He was replaced by Kenneth (Punkin) Francis, whom the family claimed was primarily a babysitter for Jack's son, now four.

The tempers that had cooled between the parties were reheated in an incident that occurred on June 10, 1933.[9] Jack, his bodyguard and a black employee were driving downtown in his expensive roadster. As he passed the Acme Sales Co. offices of Joe Fretti, he was given a Bronx cheer by some Licavoli gangsters standing on the walk. As he drove back to the same area a short time later, the razzing increased. The challenge lit Jack's short fuse. He stopped his car in front of the store and quickly ran toward the jesters. John Mirabella rushed to intercept him. Jack's first punch broke John's jaw and several teeth. As Mirabella reeled in pain, he was pummelled with more blows about the head and body, sustaining a severe beating. Ralph Carsello and Johnny Rai were present but did not interfere in the fight, which ended in seconds. Jack ran back to the car and sped off. Several shots were fired into his car. Absent this incident, many claim, the feud would have ended at repeal of prohibition within six months. The police were afraid for Jack. "Protect yourself at all times until prohibition is over," they advised. Jack gave the Licavolis wide berth.

Morale in the Licavoli group was low. There was resentment against those who had refused to join in the fight. Nobody had ever previously openly attacked a member of the gang and survived. Jack was hailed as a hero while the public called the gang "bums." Word leaked out that revenge was being planned. Friends from all over the city warned Jack, "Please be careful." Every night Jack took a different route to his home. Sometimes he drove in one car with his bodyguard. Sometimes he and Punkin would take two cars and alternately drive in front or behind each other. His family begged him to leave town. "I can't," Jack said, "I never ran from anybody before and I am not running now. I can take care of myself."

A small cottage in Point Place, then a sparsely settled, secluded area, was rented for the summer. Jack hid out there. The Licavoli henchmen staked out an around-the-clock vigil.[10] When Yonnie's father-in-law died on July 5 in Detroit, Jack learned Yonnie left the city. Jack felt safe. On Friday, July 7, 1933 he took Audrey Rawls, a beauty contest winner, to his cottage. Leaving his bodyguard and son at home, unarmed and unguarded for the first time since the fight, Jack left his house after 9 o'clock to take a leisurely stroll along the beach. The young lovers walked hand-in-hand softly singing among the darkened shadows of the trees. Suddenly, without warning, rough hands shoved Miss Rawls aside. Two men rapidly emptied their guns into the defenseless Kennedy.[11] As he fell mortally wounded, the assassins continued firing so close to his head that his right ear was powder burned.[12] Attracted by the noise, a crowd gathered. Many thought the shots were belated Fourth of July fireworks. Immediate witnesses said Jack's muscular body convulsed, twitching and twisting like a newly-butchered chicken.

The police were late in arrival. Some claimed it was because they were afraid of encountering the Licavolis on return, as Summit Street to the scene was two-lane traffic. Word spread rapidly. The public was now actively aroused. At 24, a hero was dead. Huge crowds gathered the next day outside the funeral parlor and later at Calvary Cemetery.

Two carloads of heavily-armed Egans Rats gunmen came from St. Louis. They cruised the downtown streets searching for the now departed killers.

The course of the future was clear. Public authorities could not deny the wrath of the city. Prosecuting attorney Frazier Reams angrily declared, "Yonnie and his gang will be stopped!"

# 16 The Wop English Trial

Kennedy's death was the talk of the town. Hundreds of curious spectators were attracted to his funeral. Licavoli and company temporarily fled the city. Sheriff David Kreiger, not knowing what to do, did little or nothing.

By law, the sheriff was the chief investigative officer for crimes in the county. While the new prosecutor, Frazier Reams, anxiously waited for arrests or statements of witnesses, none were forthcoming. When questioned by the sheriff the day following Kennedy's death, witnesses allegedly told the sheriff they could not identify any of the killers. Kreiger leaked this valuable information to the gang and within a few days they were able to return to the city.

Under orders of Reams, Audrey Rawls, the 20-year-old beauty queen with Kennedy at the time of murder, was held in the county jail, without bond for her own protection. She claimed that at the time of the shooting she turned away, covered her eyes and could not make any positive identification. Her attorney, Dan McCollough, threatened to get her out on habeas corpus unless charges were filed.

A few days later, the sheriff said he received a tip called in by Licavoli. To make him look good, Kreiger was able to apprehend Joe (Wop) English, Ralph Carsello and John Mirabella at Licavoli's home. They were playing croquet at the time of arrest. When booked,

English, age 34, said he was a salesman; Carsello, age 29, a barber, and Mirabella, age 28, a fruit merchant. Each had an alibi of being elsewhere on the day of the shooting. Later that same day, Yonnie again called Sheriff Kreiger to pick him up. He said he had been in Detroit since July 4th, attending the wake and funeral of his father-in-law. On questioning by he sheriff, Yonnie said, "I met Kennedy only once. I couldn't recognize him if I saw him again. I know nothing of the murder. Somebody took advantage of my absence to kill Kennedy knowing I would be blamed." The four were held without bond. Harry G. Levy appeared as attorney for the group.

After service in World War I, with Firetop, Levy entered politics as a Republican protege of Walter F. Brown. He was appointed to the office of U.S. attorney in the Toledo district by the Republican administration in 1926. He had been a boyhood friend of Firetop and cast his lot with the underworld characters he grew up with as Firetop, Chalky Red, Louis (Paddock) Walker and others. Levy never married; he became a loner socially except for the drinking parties and sex orgies provided by the Licavolis during their better years. He had previously appeared as counsel for Carsello and Mirabella in federal court on liquor violations. After the arrested men were locked up four days, Levy appeared at the office of Prosecutor Reams to inquire how long the men were going to be held on suspicion. When the prosecutor asked him bluntly if he represented them, Levy replied, "I am interested in their welfare only as a public spirited citizen."[1] This type of low-key approach characterized Levy's later handling of problems involving his underworld friends and clients. He would attempt to cover up association with them, insulate himself from inquiry and direct the action from behind the scenes through intermediaries. In later events, comments were frequently made that the "heavy hand of Harry Levy was on the case."

In the interim, Sheriff Kreiger talked to 14 witnesses. Three indicated they had information about Kennedy's murder. Robert Schwaite, the witness closest to the scene, was not interrogated. Yet after 11 days in jail, through error, Licavoli and his men were released without bond. They were driven out to the Licavoli house. The prosecutor ordered them to be picked up immediately but police leaks beat the sheriff out to the house. Although lights were found on during a search of the premises, Kreiger did not locate the missing men, so he left.[2] Later searches revealed a secret, specially built, inaccessible, air-conditioned compartment located off the basement wall in the Licavoli home. It was well stocked with food, water and facilities to keep a gang secreted for months, if required.[3]

The gang then fled from the city. Prosecutor Reams was furious. He had campaigned for the office in November 1932, as (Democrat) independent, without being bound to political bosses, "to rid the city of crime."[4] Born and raised in Franklin, Tennessee, he graduated from Vanderbilt University College of Law. In 1921, he came to Toledo to visit a brother who was in residency as an intern at a local hospital. He liked the city and returned a year later to start the practice of law. Tall, thin, erect, with a shock of prematurely white hair, he made a fatherly, benevolent appearance. His slower pace and southern drawl was a welcome change in contrast to the sharp staccato voices of many Toledo lawyers. Society opened doors for him. He won election in his first race in the 1932 Democratic national landslide headed by F.D.R.

True to their custom of advancing newcomers over locals, Reams was first elected president of his Toledo American Legion post. Veterans campaigned vigorously for him. The job paid $400 per month, a substantial wage in Depression times. After election, legionnaires served notice on the criminals that if Frazier or any member of his family was injured, Licavoli and Company would be exterminated without due process of law.[5]

The young and ambitious Reams knew conviction in these murder cases could further his political career. He was determined to go all out to keep his campaign promise and eventually earn the appellation of "The man who saved Toledo."[6]

Lack of cooperation from the sheriff stirred Reams into action.

He asked Detective George Timiney of the Toledo police to be assigned to the case. Timiney had a vendetta against the Licavolis. He constantly harassed them. He went to their home, many times before, checked license plates of cars of visitors and entered the home to peruse their affairs. One time, he was called by police radio and told to call a certain telephone number. A prominent political figure identified himself and told Timiney, "We don't persecute people like that in Toledo." Although his job was on the line, Timiney loved Jack Kennedy and he persevered in harassment of Licavoli. Timiney was one cop Reams trusted, but he did not trust many others. Reams then called Prosecutor Harry Toy of Detroit, who had successfully broken up the Purple Gang, for help. Toy sent two of his biggest and best detectives, Leonard Smith and John McDonald, to aid Timiney. Local newspapers kept the identity of the Detroiters secret, calling them "the Clarke brothers."

Slowly, leads on the Kennedy murder developed. Two young boys found a .38 caliber revolver along the Ottawa River, a half mile away from the scene of the crime. The gun had been pawned in a downtown pawnshop. A .38 caliber bullet had been taken from Kennedy's body. Two .45 caliber bullets were also removed from his body, which had been perforated with 11 holes. A day later, a .45 caliber gun and bullet with copper jacket was found 200 feet from where Kennedy was shot. The bullet had passed through his body. Another bullet tore the watch off the victim's wrist, then ricocheted a half block away. The bullet fit the hole in the watch as confirmed by Detroit ballistic experts. These two guns were the death weapons. Four men and two women answered an appeal for eye witnesses. They were promised protection by Timiney, who recruited two other Irish officers, Chris Brennan and John McCarthy, to aid in obtaining evidence. Witnesses brought in newspaper pictures of four gangsters. They identified Joe (Wop) English and John Mirabella as two of the killers at the Kennedy scene. Other witnesses claimed they saw a man with bandages on his head leave the death car. Mirabella had worn bandages since the Kennedy beating a month before.

Sam Stein, a former clerk at the pawnshop where the .38 was pledged, was picked up. He first stated he had stolen the gun from his employer and was fired. Then he later said he sold it to some bootlegger whom he didn't know. Stein was booked as an accessory to murder and turned over to the Clarke brothers for grilling. They worked him over for hours. Finally, on August 1, 1933 Stein said "Firetop borrowed the gun and loaned me $5.00." Later, Stein told the Clarke brothers, "I sold the .38 to Firetop for $17.50." Charges against Stein were dropped as murder charges against Firetop were filed. Immediately after such confession, a tip went out from inside sources that Stein implicated Sulkin. He left town. His attorney, Harry G. Levy, also took a week's vacation at the same time at Atlantic City. Sources said they needed time to prepare defenses. Firetop could deny the Stein accusations. The witness had told three different stories. This evidence, they knew, was obtained under duress. Stein could recant and word was sent out for him to do so! The source of the mysterious sender in and out of the county jail baffled the authorities. A note was found indicating that "a fix" with that fellow (meaning Stein) and Firetop could be arranged. The party carrying this note which was found in torn parts in a waste basket in the sheriff's office was the same person who had tipped off Firetop to take it on the lam. In an effort to strangle the Licavoli gang into submission, on August 3, 1933 Reams ordered all slot machines in the county confiscated. Joe Fretti had paid politicians $25,000 for a year's privilege to operate slots. Licavoli had become his partner. A leak received the night before again beat the police. Of the 3,200 to 3,500 slots in the city and county, the sheriff found four, two of them of the penny variety, while the police only located three others. Infuriated by leaks, Reams ordered all gambling joints closed because they "helped finance the Licavoli mob." The sheriff and chief of police indicated they would cooperate but in a few days it was business as usual for the regulars at these haunts. A week after the Stein confession, Harry C. Levy brought Firetop in to surrender.[7] A few days later he pled him not guilty to Kennedy murder charges.[8]

Firetop was then escorted by Kreiger to the court house from the county jail to be questioned by the Clarke brothers, because they claimed Firetop knew "everybody and everything."

Unknown to the gang or their lawyers, Reams had used wiretaps on Firetop's phone for months.[9] Within minutes in the room with the Clarkes, Firetop yelled out to his friend the sheriff, "Dave, help!" A swift shoe to his groin almost ruined his sex life. Sheriff Kreiger opened the door, looked at his stricken crony, but said nothing. The interrogation continued as the Clarkes refrained from violence while the sheriff lingered by. Firetop then openly bragged of his political connections in the city — that he delivered the votes of the seventh ward — he knew everybody, sheriff and prosecutor, intimately. Even Walter F. Brown, his mentor, would bail him out. The first session was unfruitful. Two more sessions were held, one from 7:45 p.m. to 2:00 a.m. the next day, in which, attorney Levy contended in later habeas corpus proceedings, "Firetop received the worst treatment in the history of the Courthouse." His client complained that his right ribs were bruised yet showed no marks although he labored on every breath. His groin ached and he expressed difficulty in walking.

Prosecutor Reams refused to let up on Firetop. He took a new tack seldom used at that time in a murder case. He arranged to take Stein's deposition in the Sulkin case. This is a procedure where the witness (Stein) is sworn by a notary or court reporter to testify under oath. His testimony, taken in question and answer form as in trial, is filed with the court to be used as evidence at trial in event the witness can not attend. Levy objected, but appeared at the deposition with the defendant. This new dilemma placed Firetop in jeopardy. If Stein was killed or disappeared, his testimony might be used at trial. It would be better for Stein to appear in person, for the egotistical Firetop felt he could crack or discredit Stein's different stories. A big nose and shifty eyes made the youthful Stein appear less believeable. Firetop further felt that in a confrontation of the two before a jury, his testimony would be more acceptable — particularly after Stein admitted that the

Clarke brothers brutally beat him into giving incriminating statements. In his deposition under oath, Stein said the Clarke brothers beat him from 6:00 p.m. one day to 4:00 a.m. the next. They forced him to admit he sold the gun to Firetop. He claimed Firetop was his life-long friend. In truth, "I really sold the gun to a Morris Asher," (then deceased). Stein had further confided he would change his testimony at trial to protect Firetop because "he was popular with the tough guys," an innuendo leaving what he meant to conjecture.

As the Clarke brothers persevered, they found four eyewitnesses to tell a grand jury ordered by Frazier Reams that English and Mirabella were the gunmen killing Kennedy. Russell Syracuse was named as the driver of the death car, while evidence came in of a second car at the scene. All three were promptly indicted. To prevent leaks, identities of all witnesses were kept secret as they went before the grand jury at different times, while a large group of witnesses for other criminal cases were present in the same offices. Proof was given that the car used by Syracuse and Ernest LaSalle to escape to Akron was the murder car, provided by Sebastian (Buster) Lupica on the day of the killing. Chalky Red also had lent a similar car to the gang, which may have been the second car. More warrants were issued. Harry G. Levy also represented Chalky Red. Since he was not at the scene, he asked for a bond, promising to produce Chalky Red for trial, if released. The trial court agreed and released Red on $5,000 bond! Similar bonds were approved for the rest of the Toledo contingent, Besase and Lupica.

Reams demanded that Yonnie's wife be brought in. He knew a wife could not be compelled to testify on matters involving her husband, but he wanted to pressure the gang or flush them out, if possible. Zena appeared before Reams with Harry Levy at her side. She remained silent. Reams warned, "Warrants are out. We'll find them and put them away."

On August 29, 1933 police found Wop English hiding under the bed of a woman companion in Akron, Ohio. Two guns were found in his clothes. At arraignment in Toledo, a trial date was set. Mirabella disappeared after the indictment and was never brought to court. He was reported to have died in a Youngstown hospital on April 5, 1935 under the name of Magnine. Russell Syracuse also escaped. Reports indicated he was still alive and living somewhere in the United States.

On September 14, 1933 Yonnie Licavoli also was arrested in Akron with a .32 revolver on each hip. A week before, his gang with Leo Moceri, English, Ralph Carsello and Mirabella had been running a local walkathon. They had muscled in on a similar show at the Coliseum in Toledo a year before. An invalid bailiff of the Akron Municipal Court tried to attach the proceeds of a day's receipts to satisfy a judgment against one of the gang when they beat him up and fled. When questioned by Reams, Licavoli had Harry Levy by his side. He told the prosecutor that the imprisoned "Firetop was only a messenger boy. He took my money to pay bills."

New federal charges were also placed against the gang. Attorney Levy arranged $27,000 in bond security and obtained Yonnie's release on such charges. In Akron, a municipal court judge fined Yonnie $100 on the charge of possession of firearms. The prosecution there charged "every racketeer in town tried to intervene in his behalf. It was a disgrace."

Johnny Rai was found and jailed. On November 6, 1933, Ralph Carsello tried to break into a house where a former girl friend lived. An Akron pilot, Glenn Clark, politely told him she didn't live there anymore. Carsello insisted on coming in to look around. A fight ensued. Carsello was subdued and when the Akron police checked his fingerprints, he was also brought to Toledo to face murder charges. Moceri remained at large.

Reams had to get a conviction! His strategy was to try the strongest case first. Since there were eye witnesses to Wop English being one of the Kennedy killers. He scheduled an early trial date for English on November 8, 1933.[10]

U.S. Supreme Court Justice Holmes wrote, "The life of the law is not logic, but experience." Reams was not an experienced trial lawyer. He called in his two chief assistants, Joel Rhinefort and Arnold Bunge, to prepare the prosecution case against English. Bunge was the most able, intelligent and best trial lawyer of the trio. He was assigned to plan the strategy of trial and order of witnesses. Rhinefort had come to Toledo in 1922 from a position of prosecuting attorney in Lawton, Oklahoma. He was tough, seasoned and ruthless. Rhinefort was accused of misconduct in more trials by lawyers in Lucas County than any other prosecutor before or since. Misconduct of counsel covers a wide range of action, speech or conduct during trial. It may be prejudicial to such an extent that a claim could be made that one party was deprived of his constitutional right to a fair trial. Injection of inflammatory, prejudicial or inadmissible statements or evidence into a record may constitute misconduct of counsel. Rhinefort had a habit during trials of repeating damaging statements made by witnesses from the stand. The effect of repetition constituted argument before the allotted time as repetition of certain statements could make a greater impression on juries.[11] Inflammatory remarks or inadmissible statements likewise could turn a jury even though the judge might tell the jurors to ignore such evidence — the impression had registered. Students in law schools were usually taught "that the mind is not a black-board from which an idea or impression can be erased." The Ohio law held that a continuous asking of improper questions or attempting to introduce inadmissible evidence constituted misconduct which was none the less reprehensible and inexcusable because it was spoken by counsel of standing and ability.[12] The courts also held that misconduct was waived if no objection was made. This meant the defense had to object to every tactic, remark or statement that they felt was inadmissible or prejudicial from counsel or witnesses, if they hoped to use such error of misconduct on appeal. Defense attorneys for English were A.J. Bianchi and DeWitt Fisher of Akron, Ohio. They soon learned that the local prosecutors would stop at nothing. On voir dire questioning of the jury, the defense brought out that the defendant acquired his nickname "Wop" through his boxing career. Bunge interjected that the name was acquired through his criminal career. The effect of the prosecutor's remark was to let the jury know English had a felony record. This was before he or any other witnesses took the stand. An objection was made by the defense together with a request to dismiss the entire panel. The judge told the jury to disregard the remarks of counsel relating to acquiring nicknames and overruled the motion to dismiss the panel.

    The defendant in a criminal case alone opens up the issues of character. If he was going to testify, his lawyer could tell the jury on opening statement that English had a record, to take the sting out of cross-examination later. The opening of the use of the name "Wop" by his own counsel made the court ruling proper. English had a record of 33 arrests, which was inadmissible because only his three convictions could be mentioned on cross examination, if any, in trial. He served a term in the Ohio pen for robbery, again in the Atlanta federal pen for liquor violations and a term in Pennsylvania for receiving stolen property. The court record was replete with objections made into the record as a predicate for appeal. Rhinefort later admitted, "We had to use some tactics that we can't use in the ordinary case."

    The witnesses for the State paraded to the stand. The coroner established the bullet wounds as the cause of Kennedy's death. The two boys who found the guns along the Ottawa River testified as to where the guns were found. Ballistic experts identified these two weapons as those firing the bullets taken from the victim's body.

Vern Taylor, a Monroe County deputy sheriff who was visiting in Point Place at the time of the murder, gave the police the license number of the getaway car. A Ford V-8 bearing Ohio license U 9299 belonged to fellow gang member Sebastian Lupica. Principal witnesses Robert Schwaite, age 19 and Harry Craig, age 25 both testified they were seated on the running board of a car at the murder scene conversing. They saw a car stop, two men emerged and the men and car followed Jack Kennedy and Miss Rawls. The youths followed at a discreet distance. A hat of one of the two men fell off. A bald head was exposed. Both witnesses identified English as the bald man wearing such hat. They pointed him out in court. Schwaite told his mother the same story that night. Craig said, "Kennedy and his date were singing 'Love in the Moonlight,' a popular song at the time. English pushed Miss Rawls aside, then with one man on each side of Kennedy, they emptied their guns. The get-away car backed up to turn around. The two killers jumped in and sped away. Both witnesses said Mirabella was the second killer. The driver was Russell Syracuse. A similar-looking car loaned to the gang by Chalky Red was at the scene, purportedly to abet the crime or getaway. Leo Moceri was identified as the driver of the second car. Moceri had rented a cottage within a mile of the Kennedy cottage several days before the killing and moved out the day of the event.

While the trial was pending, the prosecutor was aghast at another leak to newsmen from his office — this time that two brothers of Mayor Thatcher were secretly indicted.

Craig admitted on cross-examination that he was taken by the sheriff to a line-up with English in it a few days later but refused to identify him "for fear of being involved." He did identify such defendant for the Clarke brothers. Sheriff Kreiger later appeared as a defense witness to testify that Craig failed to identify English at the line-up four days after the shooting. "The explanation went to credibility of the witness and was an issue for the jury," the court said. Both Craig and Schwaite admitted they were convinced it was their duty to testify by Captain Timiney and the Clarke brothers. Both were guarded in rooms at the Argonne Hotel by policemen Chris Brennan and John McCarthy during the days preceding trial.

The defense claimed English had an alibi in that he was in the slot machine warehouse of Morris (Mose) and Arthur (Huntz) Shapiro. When the defense revealed the names of six alibi witnesses, the sheriff was ordered to arrest all six named and the prosecutor's staff cross-examined them before they took the stand, Morris Shapiro said he was in jail 14 days and was threatened by the Clarke brothers.

When I questioned Mose, whom I knew as a newsboy, Morris Shapiro said, "My memory is bad. I can't really think. I get terrible headaches. I am sorry but I can't help you." The other alibi witnesses' testimony placed English away from the scene of the murder at the time of commission. Kenneth (Punkin) Francis, Kennedy's bodyguard, was taken to the County Jail as a material witness and held for 33 days until the trial ended. He was later awarded $35 in witness fees by the court on release although never called to testify.

Wop English took the stand to swear to his innocence and alibi. It was brought out on his cross-examination that he was in the city on the night of the murder. He admitted going up to Detroit about 2 a.m. the following morning and telling Yonnie Licavoli of Kennedy's death. He admitted that other gang members were also present in Detroit and that they also discussed the killing. The jury apparently refused to believe him or his witnesses. Five days after the trial began, the jury returned to a packed but silent courtroom. The bailiff intoned their verdict of guilty of murder in the first degree without recommendation of mercy.[13] This meant the death penalty. English had faced many opponents in the ring and in gun battles. He had knocked out his opponent in a preliminary bout at the Willard-Dempsey fight 14 years before in 72 seconds of the first round. Yet when he heard the verdict, English fainted at counsel's table. He was carried into the judge's chambers by court attendants. On reviving, he said, "The Prosecution would set me free in five minutes, but I don't dare tell. I don't. They would rip out my guts and feed it to the dogs." English was cautioned to await his counsel at the County Jail. Later his only comment was, "I didn't do it but I know who did."[14]

Joseph (Wop) English was sentenced to die in the electric chair on April 20, 1934 by Presiding Judge Roy A. Stuart. On the day of the sentence of English, Firetop Sulkin was released on bail of $10,000 in a first-degree murder case! He had been in jail since August 8, 1933. His petition for a writ of habeas corpus was heard by the Supreme Court of Ohio.[15] In an opinion written by Justice Howard L. Bevis, a legal precedent was adopted 30 years before it became popularly accepted, holding that "the trial court had jurisdiction to hear applications for admission to bail in first-degree murder cases before trial . . . except when proof of guilt is evident or presumption great." Apparently the English conviction took some heat off the court.

Within three days of the death verdict, defense counsel filed various motions to forestall the penalty or obtain a new trial. Their briefs complained of repeated acts of misconduct of counsel for the State. It was claimed the State was allowed to reproduce the fight of

June 1933 where English was absent, yet the prosecutor promised to connect him to such fight but never did. The defense contended, among other things, that evidence that English had guns in his room when arrested in Akron was inadmissible; that Timiney was erroneously permitted to testify as to the places he went to try to find the defendant yet didn't find him; that the State charged the defendant was a member of a gang, yet there was no evidence of gang association brought out; that the arguments "strike down the gangs that makes witnesses afraid to testify" was prejudicial. It was also claimed that the State withheld exculpatory evidence in English's favor from defense counsel and the jury, particularly regarding a variance in the testimony of Craig and Schwaite. The prosecution countered this by an affidavit from Ben Mendoza, a reporter for the Toledo *News Bee*. Immediately on hearing the news on radio, Mendoza went to the scene by cab. He interviewed both witnesses and stated the testimony given at trial was substantially the same as given to him by the witnesses on the night of July 7, 1933.

The defense then produced a letter from Punkin sent to Wop English while both were in jail telling him the names of witnesses in the area who could aid his defense.[16] After release, Punkin denied such letter existed.[17]

In the interim while the motions for a new trial were pending before the court, five pounds of notes and papers from the prosecutor's locked files on the case were mailed to defense attorney Bianchi in Akron! Reams was aghast. Prosecutor Bunge claimed he knew later of the source of the leak that caused 35 pages of witness statements to be stolen from his locked files and mailed to defense counsel. In a newspaper article, Bunge indicatated "he would give this information to Frazier Reams" who was in Columbus at the time.[18]

They never uncovered the leak or sender, frustrating the prosecutor's office. Bianchi claimed the leaked information clearly showed that the prosecution did not deliver documents that would help English. They claimed United States Supreme Court decisions held that "suppression of evidence helpful to a defendant in a criminal case constituted denial of a fair trial and was a denial of due process." The trial court disagreed, upheld the conviction, and overruled all defense motions.

To cut off leaks and further revenue, Reams indicted 16 slot operators in the county including Licavoli and his two partners in gaming, Ben and Joe Fretti.[19] Bonds of $500 were posted as these were misdemeanor charges.

Reams hoped English might weaken to testify or release evidence on other murders. He received numerous stays of execution on his penalty. While on death row, English occupied a cell next to Albert Bruno, who was scheduled to die on February 7, 1934. Frank Vacchiano, his accomplice in the Park Lane murder, was previously executed on December 29, 1933. Both had planned to kill Kennedy to get Licavoli's approval. Vacchiano marched by the pictures of other killers pasted on the walls of death row and the electric chair without comment. His attorney, Dan McCollough, said, "He was the gamest guy I ever defended." Vacchiano died a bitter enemy of Bruno because he thought Bruno had squealed on him. At the trial he knew differently, but the reports persisted. Police officers Owen Green and Ray Scheets had tried to prevail on Bruno to testify against Vacchiano to save his own life. Bruno, in his last hours, called the two officers his best friends. All the way to the chair he denounced Dan McCollough who had defended both in separate trials. He damned McCollough for an inadequate defense, for refusal to allow him to testify to save his life.

The stories of the electric chair march of Bruno had some influence on Dan McCollough's estranged son, Dan Jr. For years he maintained a replica of an electric chair with a 10-volt charge in the basement of his fashionable River Road home.[20]

Vacchiano had murdered a number of people. Bruno claimed he was merely a pimp who never committed any crimes of violence. Vacchiano got him drunk after the scheme to kill Jack Kennedy failed. "Shooting a gun while drunk," he said, was his only crime. He cried out in agony while being led to the chair, "Me, a murderer? Why I wouldn't kill a chicken." The story of his execution was poignantly told on the front pages in both Toledo papers the next day.[21] As the condemned man entered the death chamber filled with 35 witnesses he said, "I'm sorry about going out this way. I'm sorry for my mother." He was seated by the guards into the chair. He glanced about the room. "Wait a minute," he yelled, "can't I have a drink of water?" The prison chaplain extended a tin cup. He tried to reach for it but was pinned down. A guard held the cup to his lips. He sipped twice and licked his lips. His eyes darted about the room. He took a deep breath, wet his lips and said bitterly and slowly, "This is a miserable way to die ... that's all."

The guards closed in quickly, placed the electrodes, made a cursory examination of the connections then stepped back. A mask was slipped over his head. A priest patted Bruno's tightly-clenched left hand and stepped aside. There was an appalling silence as the spectators stared. A dull metallic crunch was heard, then came a whine of high voltage with a high-pitched "wee" sound, Bruno's body stiffened and strained against the straps. The whining stopped and started twice, making cracking noises. A thread of smoke curled up from Bruno's bare right leg. The sounds stopped. The prison doctor made a quick examination. The windows were quicly opened for air to aid witness William Harding, a Toledo jeweler and expert marksman, who fainted at the scene. The doctor announced "Albert Bruno is dead. That's all, gentlemen." A guard stated, "step lively, please."

Wop English remained silent when asked to comment on the executions. The prosecution hoped he would break. Yet while Wop remained in death row, on September 12, 1934 two Dillinger gangsters, Charles Mackey and Harry Pierpont, made a break for freedom. They unlocked the cells of the other eight men under death sentences. English was the only convict who refused to leave. He knew he would get further commutations and would never sit in the chair, if he kept his mouth shut! His gang political connections told him so!

# 17 The Auto-Lite Strike

In the spring of 1934, the eyes of the industrial world were on Toledo. A monumental milestone decision in the field of unionism was to ensue.

President Franklin Delano Roosevelt desired to be a champion of the masses. In 1933, his New Deal legislation was pushed through Congress to give bargaining power to labor. Section 7a of the National Recovery Act (NRA) contained provisions which permitted organization of factory production lines, without interference from owners or management. A brilliant young Toledo lawyer, Brandon Schnorf, studied the new law. He left a large firm to represent a local union.[1]

The Automotive Worker's Union, with Thomas Ramsey, business agent, selected as their target the Toledo Electric Auto-Lite Co. This company produced starting motors, generators and related electrical lighting equipment for passenger car manufacturers. Organized in 1911, the company manufactured 12,000 different parts in complete lighting and ignition systems. It sold 90% of such parts to major auto factories. On January 1, 1934 a 27-million dollar deal was announced when Auto-Lite merged with Moto-Meter. Seven months earlier, on May 6, 1933, the company announced a profit of $1,364,000 for the past year making it one of the most successful auto concerns in the country at the time. It was also one of the city's largest employers.[2] More than 50 other companies would be directly affected by a strike. The target choice was an ideal one for the workers. This began as the first strike in the United States involving the right to organize production lines or factory workers under the provisions of NRA. The seeds sown in his notorious affray would have national ramifications.

The eventual strike surged up from a long series of abuses against the workers in this open-shop town. The Great Depression started on Black Tuesday, October 29, 1929. It was called the worst and longest in the nation's history. Twenty-three hundred banks collapsed in 1931. Manufacturers were overstocked and cut employment. Thousands were laid off each week. Those with jobs had wages cut. In the year before the strike, unemployment reached 16% and was going up. The mayor of the city in 1929 was William T. Jackson, a maverick Republican who won the election over the party candidate with a campaign slogan "Down with Brown." His victory demonstrated the continued affinity of the city's voters for maverick politicians. He was defeated two years later by another maverick Republican, Addison Q. Thacher. At this time the city suffered from heavy debts, virtual bankruptcy and other acute Depression-related problems. One hundred and fifty policemen were laid off. Others had salaries reduced to $100 per month. An investigation into the city relief rolls which were at their peak, revealed may irregularities. Although a grand jury inquiry failed to produce indictments, there was an aura of corruption. In the 1933 election a Socialist candidate, Solon T. Klotz, received the unofficial endorsement of the Republican Party as a rebuke to Mayor Thacher, who had challenged Walter F. Brown's leadership. Klotz received 38% of the vote and defeated Thacher by 2,619 votes. The city was defaulting on its bonds, paying salaries in script, and began to hear bellows from R.J. Marshall's office voicing authority for bond deals and financial changes.[3]

My sister Jean was a high school beauty. While enroute home from night classes at the University of Toledo, her car struck a hole in the street. There were no guardrails or lights. There was a state ordinance that required "the cities to keep the streets open, in repair and free from nuisance." This was a case of clear liability. My oldest sister, Sadye, recommended Harry Levison because he did her legal work without charge in exchange for dry-cleaning services. Levison was not a personal injury lawyer. He obtained a $1,500 settlement from the debt-ridden city for the loss of an eye and permanent facial disfigurement. He took a fee of 50% of the gross recovery. Jean had to pay her own medical expenses. Levison did not know that as long as a city had the power to tax, recovery could always be made later. This was strike one in his three times at bat for our family.

Laborers were at the mercy of employers. They took whatever pay they could without complaint. From low-paid workers, C.O. Miniger, executive head of the Auto-Lite, made huge profits.[4] He became a banker, associated with the Ohio Bank and the Security Bank, both of which were involved in banking scandals and litigation at the time. A grand jury was questioning loans to insiders, withdrawals before failures by bankers, industrialists, lawyers and others with inside information. Miniger had paid his double indemnity as a stockholder but his holding companies had withdrawn money under highly questionable circumstances. Thousands of thrifty Toledoans had suffered financial hardships in the bank failures.[5] The mood in the city was an ugly one. During the strike, the *Blade* carried a front-page story, "Vice Rampant."[6]

With 50% of the men unemployed, many poor unemployed girls turned to prostitution. No arrests had been made by police in vice for two months. In the same news article, payoffs were openly admitted. The underworld complained, "We take in nickels and dimes while "the fixers" (unnamed) still want $100 bills." The paper stated that the underworld complained because members were compelled to pay more for protection than their profits warranted. This was the most apparent rift in the graft arrangements ever recorded. It was an ideal time for ties to be broken, but they were not. The grand jury inquiry of the Thacher brothers during the Licavoli trials was the first and last into political corruption. Only one elected official, city or county, police officer or politician ever faced criminal charges involving graft or corruption in office during the years of this history!

Bishop Karl Alter printed a full-page editorial plea, placing blame on major industry for the 50% payrolls of the city. The Central Labor Union of the A. F. of L. claimed low wages, bad working conditions and a conspiracy by factory owners to destroy local unions by creating a cheap labor market were the basis for concerted action in the Auto-Lite strike.

As a background to this alleged "civil-war" strike, on February 1, 1934, Auto-Lite workers walked out. Simultaneously, two affiliated plants, Logan Gear and Bingham Stamping, also struck.[8] With the fervor of new unionists, the pickets showed great militancy. Picket lines were maintained day and night. Tents were pitched at strikers relief stations. In March, the companies capitulated. The agreement was a compromise.[9] The 10% increase in wages was cut to 5%. Shop committees were recognized. The issue of "Union" was deferred to

April 1, Auto-Lite stating that on that date, it would negotiate further on the union contract. When the date arrived, the companies reneged.[10] They refused point-blank to discuss unionism. The management ordered the business agent, Thomas Ramsey, out of the company offices. Eleven days later the three plants struck again with mass picketing. The strikers appealed to the Lucas County Unemployed League for aid. The Unemployed League movement, fostered by the American Worker's Party, pledged to aid union actively in strikes by preventing the jobless from strike-breaking.[11]

In a famous 1919 strike at the Willys-Overland, an injunction against mass picketing was issued by Federal Judge Killits. It was called the most vicious in American labor history, breaking the strike by limiting pickets.[12] Labor learned lessons of mass picketing in the next 15 years. One of the purposes of mass picketing was to stop, hinder or delay entry or exit by scabs, strike-breakers, factory personnel or trucking to the struck plant. This, in turn, would impede production.

The companies fought back, obtaining an injunction signed by Judge Roy R. Stuart against the unions and the Unemployed League. The order limited 25 pickets at each gate.[13] At first, the strikers decided to observe the injunction but oppose it in court. Mass picketing ceased. The strike ebbed lower and lower. With the unemployment situation as it was, hundreds of strike-breakes, willing to work, broke through the small, inadequate picket lines.[14] For a while it appeared that the srike could be broken.

Two of the leaders in the strike were Ted Selander and Sam Pollock. Both had leftist learnings. With Edward T. Cheyfitz, I often saw them on the grounds of Cherry Park spreading the Communist gospel. Nightly singing of their songs attracted large crowds. The newsboy gang sang the following words:

> Beans, bacon and gravy,
> They almost drive me crazy.
> When I wake up in the morning
> And another day is dawning
> I know I'll have another cup of beans.

Eddie Cheyfitz eventually married Director Sam Pollock's sister Julia. He became a giant in local and national labor affairs, as related in later chapters. Cheyfitz visited Russia to see, hear and adopt Lincoln Steffens' proclamation on their revolution: "I have seen the future and it works." Eddie, as a non-religious Jew, remained a Communist for years until the Hitler-Stalin pact of 1939, when he renounced membership. The Communists saw an opportunity to advance the cause of the working man, the proletariat. They infiltrated the local unions, supplied stimulating slogans or incentives and adopted positions of leadership and responsibility in furtherance of the strike.

Upon suggestion of Cheyfitz, they talked to Louis Budenz, a Communist lawyer who had smashed many injunctions in his career as a labor organizer. Selander and Pollock took the initiative to beat the limiting injunction. On May 5, 1934 the Lucas County Unemployed League sent a letter to Judge Stuart saying, "the union, in protest against the injunction issued by your court, will deliberately and specifically violate the injunction enjoining us from sympathetically picketing peacefully in support of the striking auto workers' federal union." They described the injunction as "an abrogation of our democratic rights" which contravenes "the spirit and letter of Section 7a of the NRA."

On the morning indicated, the "mass" picketing was carried on by Selander, Pollock and two other members of the union. The four were arrested, charged with contempt of court and held for 24 hours. Released on bail, they promptly returned to the picket line and were joined by others. A few days later 46 men were arrested, including the irrepressible Selander and Pollock. When their trial for contempt came up, an attempt was made to isolate these two leaders and three active union members, sentence them, and let the rest go. The other 41 insisted that they were "guilty of the same offense" and that it must be "46 or none."[16] They were backed in their demand by hundreds of union members and sympathizers who took possession of the courthouse, cheering and singing while Selander expounded the principles of militant labor from the witness stand.[17] After this amazing scene, the court recessed for lunch. The court enjoyed a long lunch hour and later in the afternoon, after two hours of confusion, mumbled what was supposedly a decision, but which no one to this day has been able to explain. Those who had been cited for contempt walked blithely out of the court and back to the picket lines!

Selander, Cheyfitz and Pollock retained Edward (Ted) Lamb, its local party lawyer, to represent them on their contempt charges. Like Schnorf, Lamb was also a scrapper. Only a few months before he had been bodily ejected from the offices of City Law Director Irv O'Conner, after an exchange of challenges in city council chambers earlier that day. Lamb said "union workers asked me to represent them." He wanted to take over hearings on injunctions and the numerous contempt citations. Brandon Schnorf, attorney for the striking unions, did not relish being associated with or tainted by an alleged Red label. Schnorf allowed Lamb to represent individual members while he stayed on to represent the union interests only.[18] There was bitterness between counsel. When he wrote of the strike in his book, Lamb never mentioned Schnorf.[19]

The assets of the local unions were depleted. The national could not help until the strike was settled or an organization occurred. "We have to accept help from any source," Fred Schwalke, the union treasurer, said. The leftist, Ted Lamb, sent for Louis F. Budenz, lawyer and executive secretary of the American Worker's Party together with Arthur Garfield Hays of New York, counsel for the American Civil Liberties Union, to insure representation of the workers. Both had considerable experience in trial of radicals and in breaking injunctions in contempt cases. Hays was to represent the right to strike, Budenz the strikers.

In his book, *This Is My Story*, Budenz wrote, "In labor history the name 'Toledo' signifies the beginning of successful permanent union organization in the automobile industry. The right of association was there made a living thing."[20]

The strike took on new dimension as both sides remained intransigent. Skirmishes between strikers and scabs were daily occurrences. Bricks were catapulted out of stretched rubber tires through plant windows, breaking 90 of them.[21] The factory was one city block in length, half a block wide, and four stories high. Most of the exterior had glass panelled windows. Thousands of them were knocked out or shattered. The strikers explained, "They wanted an open shop, now they got it."[22] The notorious Floyd Dillinger was then at large. Pickets carried signs reading, "You can have Dillinger. We got Miniger."[23] Communists came from all over the country to participate, agitate and stir up the strikers. Since the city had a Socialist as mayor, the Reds felt they were not too far behind. This could be a springboard to national prominence. They used the strike as a vehicle to propagandize their movement, "to proclaim the justice of their cause under the guise of aid to the working classes." They told the crowds, "The Communist Party is the party of the proletariat. Wasn't force used to overthrow the Czarist rulers?" Fires were set. Personal property outside the factory was destroyed. Syndicated columnists like Heywood Broun came to cover the event.

On Monday noon, May 21, attorney Louis Budenz of the American Worker's party spoke at the plant gates, stating that he would defy the injunction. Behind a large banner, he called for "peaceful mass picketing," on one side while on the other, "1776, 1865, 1934" blared out. Budenz headed the picket lines. At the conclusion of the picketing that day, the numbers present had risen to 2,000, whom Budenz addressed again. Tuesday he spoke and again led the line, 4,000 supporters were before the plant. On Wednesday, he addressed 6,000.[24]

Sheriff Kreiger refused to deputize union workers as guards around the plant, as suggested by the Central Labor Union. Instead he appointed company choices, paid by the company and not by the county, for this task. As the Wednesday picket line began, these deputies had placed tear gas receptacles on the roof of the plant. Shortly thereafter, the strike breakers began throwing long iron bolts from the plant windows. One of these struck a girl picket behind the ear and she was hurried to the hospital. The leaders of the line urged, "Don't be provoked. Continue the peaceful mass picketing, no matter what the scabs may do."[25] The crowd observing had risen to 10,000.

Suddenly Sheriff Kreiger ordered the arrest of Budenz and four other pickets carrying banners. Police took them to the city jail, then to the county jail, where they were kept until noon of the next day.[26] The five arrested were cited for contempt.

While he was in jail, Budenz' wife had a baby girl and gave her the middle name "Toledo."[27] At court, Sheriff Kreiger stated on the witness stand that he would have charged Budenz with "inciting to riot" if he had not been "too busy" that day. Immediately after the Budenz arrest, a deputy sheriff arrested an old man in the middle of the street, in full view of 20,000 eyes, and hit him unmercifully. The crowd could stand the terrorism no longer. They surged around deputies and police. Clouds of tear gas rolled from the roof of the plant, felling many men and women. Scores lay in the streets.[28]

The crowd quickly reacted. Hurling bricks and stones into the plant, they cut off the light supply, rammed the doors of the plant with great timbers, and continued a battle with police and deputies all through the night. Strike breakers meanwhile were imprisoned in the plant.[29] The officials of the company had called for the National Guard on Tuesday, without apparent reason. On Wednesday, observers from that body were present. Jointly with the sheriff, they called for the militia. Sheriff Kreiger testified in court that he had decided to "take the offensive on Wednesday," lending color to the strikers' charge that the attacks from within the plant were "a frame-up" to get the aid of the troops.

At 5:30 a.m. the next day, Ohio National Guardsmen came into the city in a heavy rain, which had fallen all night. They attempted to disperse the thousands gathered before the plant. Skirmishes between guardsmen and workers began immediately.[30]

Later that first day, militia, with fixed bayonets, fired a volley into the crowd, killing two and wounding scores of others. I was there that day. My friend Danny DeWood was stabbed in the thigh. I ran so fast I was two blocks away before he said, "Ouch!"

A protest meeting was organized at which Budenz and Heywood Broun spoke. Charles P. Taft, President Roosevelt's personal mediator, came to Toledo. He declared, "The strike should never have been called. Outside agitators were responsible for the trouble."[31] The Toledo *News Bee* agreed in a series of editorials. The Communist Party of Toledo took out a full-page ad calling for a meeting to explain its position.[32] Both sides still refused to budge. Previously a strikebreaker was pulled out of a car, stripped naked and marched from the Auto-Lite plant to the Inter-urban Station downtown, a distance of 12 city blocks.[33] Two hundred and sixty angry sympathizers intended to throw the scab into the river, but a kindly policeman talked them out of it.[34]

The violence subsided on May 31, 1934. One-third of the National Guard left town. The rest were removed from the strike zone and quartered in the local armory in reserve for any emergency.

Finally, mediator Taft brought both sides to the bargaining table. The Auto-Lite now brought in its top people. The antagonists glared at each other, defiance and hatred oozed from both sides. The vitriol dripped. Chances of agreement were nil, but they were there to supposedly try.

Royce Martin of the Moto-Meter Department of the Auto-Lite took out his false teeth and placed them in the center of the large oval table. "For years," he said, "I've had trouble with my teeth. Finally, I got a pair of dentures that cost me thousands of dollars. I am so happy with them, I wanted you all to see them." That broke the tension in the room.[35] They were able to negotiate in earnest. Martin had been an advisor to Pancho Villa during the revolution in Mexico. With such experience, he became suitably equipped to deal in settlement of rebel causes. With men like Martin and Schnorf at their best, terms were agreed upon, collective bargaining and rights to unionize factories and production lines were recognized. A truly monumental precedent had been made. The date was June 5, 1934.

The company was smarting under its defeat by the union. At the last minute, one detail had been overlooked, the date of return to work. The company wanted to save face and call back the scabs first and let the strikers wait. "Out we go again," Schnorf declared. Taft came to him in an appealing tone. "You can't do this to me. I have worked too hard. Please." "You're right, I can't," Schnorf replied. Taft promised to hasten the strikers' return, which he did as it worked out.[36]

Both union and industry developed a new respect for each other thereafter. The strike was costly for both, as well as to the State of Ohio. There were no funds in the local union treasury for payment of attorney fees; nor could the International help, for the strikers had depleted its kitty. A picnic was planned to raise money to pay Brandon Schnorf $1,000 for his splendid legal services. Not knowing that the picnic proceeds were to benefit him, this exemplary attorney bought tickets to the picnic. Schnorf deserved accolades of praise for the magnificent result.[37]

Thus ended one more chapter in the city's already violent history. These foundations in labor and the lessons learned gave impetus to new vistas for the Underworld.

# 18 The Yonnie Licavoli Trial

Forty years before Watergate, Democrats in Toledo wiretapped the phones of Republican sources.

"Wiretapping is dirty business," U.S. Supreme Court Justice Oliver Wendell Holmes wrote in a dissenting opinion in 1928.[1] This 5-4 decision was overruled almost forty years later.[2]

Harry Friberg, on the prosecuting attorney's staff since 1933, concurred in 1955, telling the Toledo *Blade* that "wiretapping was a sneaky way of obtaining evidence."[3]

Ohio had a wiretapping statute as early as 1892 that made it a felony to intercept calls. Then penalty was a fine of $200 - $1,000 and one to three years in prison.[4]

Regardless of the law, Reams began using taps for 15 months beginning in January, 1933. Police vice squad members Merle Uncle and James H. Ford placed taps on phones at the homes of Ernest LaSalle and Firetop. The authorities felt Firetop would be a prime source of information. The recorded revelations were embarrassing to the Republican Party, particularly to a few incumbent judges, but the true nature and extent of the political intrigue was never publicized nor were criminal charges of any kind filed except as related to the murder cases.

Most of the police hated Firetop. They resented his conduct of bringing Licavoli to Toledo. They had been paid to protect local interests. Through him, their customers were lost or forced to share. This ruined their end of the take as well.

Listening to calls, the police knew Firetop had become more arrogant, uncontrollable, belligerent. They heard Firetop pontificate rather than advise on petty fixes to his cohorts: "Always take care of yourself first; never do a favor or fix for anybody for nothing, find out how we get paid and get the cash up front."

The wire tap evidence showed conspiracy of the group. In a conspiracy, the crime of one can be charged to all. The whole gang could go! But learned lawyers claimed the Ohio law at that time did not permit a charge of conspiracy in murder cases. All crimes in Ohio were statutory. If there was not a specific law prohibiting the conduct or acts in the Criminal Code, there could never be any prosecution for something that was not a crime.

Frazier Reams consulted an outstanding criminal law authority, J.B. Waite at the University of Michigan.[5] Through his advice, Reams felt a common law conspiracy would hold up in court. On March 8, 1934 Yonnie Licavoli, Firetop and 12 others including Anthony (Whitey) Besase, Ralph Carsello, Leo Moceri, James Licavoli, Ernest LaSalle, Russell Syracuse, John Mirabella, Joe (Wop) English, John Rai, Sebastian (Buster) Lupica and Harry (Chalky Red) Yaranowski were indicted and charged with four murders of Jack Kennedy, Louise Bell, Abe (Punk) Lubitsky and Norman (Big Agate) Blatt.[6]

A charge of first degree murder and conspiracy would allow the state, as prosecutor, to bring in a varied amount of circumstantial evidence that would ordinarily not be allowed in a single murder trial.

Firetop and Yonnie as principals were both picked up at home. Yonnie said he was surprised. There was evidence of another leak as he was caught hastily packing to travel when apprehended. John Rai was already in custody; Ralph Costello had a detention holder sent to the Federal Pen at Milan, Michigan, to turn him over to Toledo authorities on termination of his sentence. Wop was in death row, Moceri was at large while all the Toledo contingent were out on prior bonds.

After being placed in separate cells in the Lucas County jail, Harry Levy first appeared as attorney for both principals, Firetop and Licavoli. Preliminary motions ordered separate trials to be scheduled. Levy was not an outstanding trial lawyer. He retained Cornell Schreiber, a former Toledo Independent Party Mayor, and Elmer G. McClelland of Cleveland for the defense. Both were excellent trial lawyers.

## UNHOLY TOLEDO

A trial date in October, 1934 was scheduled for Yonnie Licavoli. As he languished in jail, with his gang in hiding, Licavoli was hard-pressed for income. His threats to muscle in were now being ignored for there was no strength behind him to fear. For years, Gerald James (Jimmy) Hayes, the king pin of Toledo gamblers, with his associates Ed Warnke, Joe and Pat Morrisey steadfastly refused to give a piece of their action to the Licavoli gang. With police and political connections of long standing, Hayes simply defied all overtures of any kind. Jimmy Hayes had become extremely wealthy over the years. He had a fashionable home in the best residential area, owned downtown properties, many residences and had valuable properties in Petrosky, Michigan, and other states. He also became a little careless. The Licavoli family was originally from St. Louis. Hayes did not fear them for he had connections there and in Detroit. His muscle in gambling circles had protected him for many years. In October, 1934 he drove up to Detroit to see a World Series game between the Detroit Tigers and the St. Louis Cardinals. As a former St. Louis "Muleskinner" he had a large bet on his home town team. It was the year of the "Me and Paul" Dean brothers, Jerome (Dizzy) and Paul, each winning two games for the Cards. Fans will recall the final seventh game, won by Dizzy 9-0, where Joe "Ducky" Medwick was pelted with debris by disgruntled Detroit bleacher fans.

On October 4, 1934 at about 7:00 the bloody, battered body of Jimmy Hayes was found in a Detroit alley.[7] Examination revealed it had been there for hours, jammed up against the door of a garage and partly hidden by a fence. There were several bullet wounds from a sawed-off shotgun in his head and heart.

The condition of his dirty, ruffled clothing indicated the body had been thrown from an automobile. A large amount of money found in his pockets indicated that the motive for the death was not robbery. Hayes had been badly beaten before he was shot, indicating that he was killed by someone who had a personal interest in his death. It was surmised that the killers either wanted to see him suffer before the shooting or that they may have sought to extort trade secrets or political information from him by torture.

Newspapers claimed Hayes was the 15th Toledoan murdered by gang warfare in the past five years. Some claimed the murder was a dying gesture of the Licavoli gang to obtain revenge because Hayes frustrated their attempts to levy tribute. Another theory advanced was that Hayes had to be silenced as a warning to other witnesses in the forthcoming murder trial of Yonnie as Hayes had been scheduled to appear as a witness for the State.

Ben Aronoff, Joe Fretti and Bennie Harris had been subpoenaed in the Yonnie murder trial for the State, but they were never called. It was believed that their testimony would have concerned the extent of extortion or threats made by Licavoli or his gang on them.

Pressure was on the Detroit police to solve the Hayes murder. The Unione Sicilione of that city was suspect. Joe Massie, Charles Bracco and Joe Bommorito were called in by the investigators. These three were wanted because Hayes was seen in their company at the Club Maxine about five hours before his body was found. The fact that all three were connected to the Licavoli gangs in Toledo and Detroit strengthened the police theory that it was a Licavoli murder.

Massie and Pete Licavoli had been suspected in the murder of Milford Jones, a St. Louis gangster friend of Hayes, who had been put on the spot at another Detroit night club years before. Bommorito was a body guard of Pete Licavoli. Brocco was a partner of Ted Pizzino, one of the Licavoli men accused in the murder of Gerald Buckley two years before. Witnesses told police Joe Massie left early in a car driven by his wife and Hayes was not with them. Others reported Hayes was seen with the three at the Roosevelt Democratic Club about 6:00 a.m. or 70 minutes before his body was found. They claimed Hayes had been drinking and started an argument over the death of Milford Jones. Some asserted his death resulted from this argument. Brocco alone was taken into custody as Massie and Bommorito went on the lam. Charges were filed but no conviction was obtained. The Hayes murder, like the Buckley case, remains unsolved to this date.[8]

Even after Hayes' death, Joe and Pat Morrisey with Ed Warnke refused to cut Licavoli in. John McMahon's office represented Hayes and his estate. It took him three full years, to complete probate.[9]

With the death of Hayes, Benny Aronoff and Joe Fretti began putting pressure on McMahon to allow them to open up with craps. "If we can't join 'em, let us go on our own," they cried. McMahon used Fretti's J and B Realty Co. to handle Hayes' real estate. Joe Fretti was a trusted name in gambling circles. The police and politicians always liked him. The word was finally given for Aronoff, with Ben and Joe Fretti, that it was OK to open up with craps and blackjack. The second floor of Aronoff's Buckeye numbers house on Superior Street was remodeled to accommodate the action. Tony Paul, alias Neufio Scott, had been a Fretti strongman. He joined the group as one of the bosses. Since Yonnie had previously been a partner with Fretti, it was easy for the new venture to siphon off income for the Licavoli trial and living thereafter. The Hayes death became a financial windfall to

Yonnie and Firetop as they knew they would be relieved of money worries as their hours of true jeopardy approached. It was the custom of the underworld to take care of the interests of members of the gang even those serving life!

The most sensational trial in Lucas County history, *State of Ohio vs Thomas (Yonnie) Licavoli,* and others began before Judge John M. McCabe on October 8, 1934.[10] Many claimed that the notoriety of the case was to distract public attention from the bank scandals of preferred withdrawals and shady ventures that had caused great financial losses the year before. Reams was up for re-election, a month away.

Anti-Licavoli feelings ran high in the City. Both newspapers and the radios carried daily front page stories on the progress of the trial. The reports were that the State would produce the same witnesses that resulted in English being given the chair, plus new evidence that the gang was in a conspiracy to run roughshod over business and rackets in the city.

From the Licavoli camp the word was that he had an alibi. He planned to use as character witnesses numerous prominent citizens who had enjoyed the enjoyed the hospitality of his elegant Old Orchard home. His booze flowed like a Niagara, freely given to every Bar Association function during his short tenure in the city. There were no security guards for most prosecution witnesses as in the Detroit Purple Trial. Word was out from Reams that he would not tolerate tampering or assaults on witnesses. A warning was issued that "if one witness got hurt, every member of the gang would die in the chair." The inference was that once principals like Licavoli and Firetop were convicted, deals on the others might be made. Sam Stein went unprotected during and after the trial of both Licavoli and Firetop.

"Licavoli and his kind have to go. They are not wanted here," the prosecution team stressed.

The State had the burden of proof to show beyond reasonable doubt that the defendant, Licavoli, with others, conspired to kill Kennedy and the others. Reams, with Bunge and Rhinefort, knew that they would have to present all the evidence in a jigsaw manner but that they could fit it all together if the conspiracy was established and accepted by the jurors. The prosecution would prove that the gang was organized to take over bootlegging, gambling and extortion in the city. After the jury was empanelled, they were taken out to the Licavoli home to view the premises.[11] "The defense objected that this was improper for it would create an impression of acquisition of wealth by the defendant, prejudicial during such Depression years. When overruled, the jurors toured Licavoli's home, also seeing his newly-born daughter, Concetta, in her baby carriage on the front porch while his two-year-old Gracie peacefully played with a doll almost as big as herself. [12]

Testimony that the defendants-conspirators were known to each other and frequented business places together covered over 100 pages of the voluminous record.[13] Bernard Hastings told the jurors he went with Jack Kennedy to meetings on bootlegging business. Chalky Red, Rough Manuel from Monroe, Corrado from Detroit, Wop English and Licavoli were there for the gang. At other meetings of bootleggers, Chalky Red and Pete Corrado usually attended. Police officers Brenner, McBride, Green, Scheets, McCarthy and others identified the various members of the gang as having been in various places in the city in company of each other. Clara Osborne testified she lived in the lower half of a duplex rented to a Ralph Cross identified as Carsello. He frequently entertained Firetop, Syracuse, LaSalle, Chalky Red, Besase and the others. She claimed the group was gone all night and came home on the day of the Kennedy murder, she was told that they were all going to a funeral in Detroit. At about 10:00 p.m., she saw her neighbor Carsello drive by but fail to get out of his car. LaSalle came over shortly thereafter and she heard Mrs. Carsello say, "You were told to stay away from here tonight."

The two police wiretap witnesses were allowed to testify that Syracuse called a number of times looking for Licavoli, who was on the lam. Syracuse and Ed Beck promised to get money to Firetop. Licavoli's wife Zena called asking for money. Firetop, in turn, arranged meetings with Joe Fretti. When Joe asked if Firetop had seen "that party," his answer was "that party is on the duck." Other conversations described involved Ben Fretti, Mose Shapiro, several "fixes" where money was to be left at the downtown R & K (Romanoff and Kaplan) Smoke Shop frequented by Firetop and the others. Chalky Red and Rough Manuel also called regularly.

Myrtle Dunn, a maid at the Argonne Hotel, together with the manager and a bellhop, identified Yonnie as the man to whom 10 or more of the others would come to see. Yonnie, they said, did most of the talking, usually in Italian. They heard him give orders, saying, "You are paid to do this." She said Firetop once told her "Licavoli was boss." Police Captain George Timiney related the many encounters he had with the defendant. He said Yonnie told him "The others are merely messenger boys for me." After establishing the existence of a gang, the prosecutor brought in proof of extortion.[13]

Chris Engle testified about English and Licavoli attending the dry cleaners meeting. English had followed Engle out of the room and warned, "If you know what's good for you, you better sit down."[14]

Edith Marks testified her husband was killed and shortly thereafter Licavoli took over operation of his Show Boat Niteclub. When she complained, Firetop told her, "If you're smart, you'll keep still." She never received a dime for her husband's interests.[15]

An owner of a barbershop which also had gambling on the premises, said he was muscled out after his room was bombed twice. His business was taken over by a Louie The Lug from Detroit.

Harry "Butch" Petler had resisted the protection of $50 per month. He repeated the story previously told.

One winter day he was tending a fire in the furnace of his station. Licavoli men came in and demanded payment.

"I told them I didn't have it. I only had $43 and had to buy gasoline. By that time the fire was going pretty good and one of the men said if I didn't pay they'd have to stick my head in the furnace. Then one of them stuck a gun in my ribs and took the $43."

Petler said he immediately went down to police headquarters and complained to Detective Inspector Emmett Cairl.

Twenty minutes later on his return to the station, Firetop drove up and scolded, "What the hell business you got going to Cairl and telling him a story about us?"[16]

Petler further complained Licavoli men drove in for gas but never paid. He said Chalky Red checked receipts from his filling station and made regular accountings to Licavoli on collections.

A beauty shop operator paid Wop and Mirabella to stay open.

Ray Swayne told the jury he had met with Licavoli, Mirabella, Rai and Firetop. He said the gang kidnapped him and stole his still. He was held in a flat overnight when he finally escaped.

George Petcoff of General Importing Co. told how Syracuse took thousands of dollars worth of sugar without pay and later took over his business.[17]

Jack Kennedy's mother, Sadie Gromintz, was permitted to testify Wop English came over to her house and swore he would not harm her son. She testified she didn't believe English and told him so. She also was allowed to say, over objection, that her son had characterized the Licavolis as a bad bunch of people who were not good for Toledo.[18]

After proof of gang action, conspiracy and extortion, the Prosecution proved the gang was responsible in the four murders. A cab driver, Clarence F. Ash, came forward to testify Leo Moceri was the driver of the car from which bullets were rained on Louise Bell. John Rai and Ralph Carsello were the gunmen in that car.[19]

Ernest LaSalle was named as the driver of the car which left a restaurant near the scene of the Lubitsky-Blatt murders at a high rate of speed. This was after LaSalle received a phone call about the time Lubitsky left the downtown Bowles restaurant. Pete Corrado and Rough Manuel were reported to have left with LaSalle and returned within minutes after the shooting.[20]

Morris Lubitsky was allowed to tell the jury he heard his brother's dying declaration "Morris, it was the Dagos." Ordinarily such a dying declaration is only admissible in evidence against the person named. Here a group, instead of an individual, was involved. Since the test of admissibility was that a dying declarant would not want to go to Heaven with a lie upon his lips, the Court had no trouble in permitting the jury to have that statement.[21]

John Henry Brown, Licavoli's gardener, testified that he saw members of the gang disguising license plates of a car on the day of the Kennedy slaying. He had fled from the city when he learned from leaks of a subpoena for him. He was taken to Akron where he worked as a gardener for A.J. Bianchi, one of the defense attorneys for English. Later Brown was transferred to Monroe, Michigan, then to Port Clinton, Ohio, where he was finally apprehended. After first testifying for the State in the Licavoli trial, he was arrested for perjury. Recalled to the stand, he was asked if he had told the truth before. He answered: "I was protecting myself ... word was sent to me what to say on the stand. A man was standing in the court room and I was afraid of him."[22]

Brown recanted and identified Moceri, Carsello and LaSalle as the men changing plates that day. All carried guns. A month before, Moceri, using the name Leonard Caresi, rented a cottage near Kennedy in Point Place. He gave as a reference the name of Henry Freshman. Firetop had contacted Freshman and told him to say "Caresi was OK" in event inquiry was made. Moceri moved out the day of Kennedy's death. All the plate changers, together with English and Mirabella, were placed at the scene of the Kennedy murder by the youthful Craig and Schwaite. Their testimony was bolstered by Thelma Boost, Ernest Reid and Helen Buder, who identified both vehicles and occupants at the Kennedy shooting.

Sam Stein's three different versions of his sale of the gun used to kill Kennedy went to the jury. The Court held the discrepancies brought out on cross-examination didn't affect the right to use such evidence but was a question on credibility of the witness for the jury. Chalky Red and Whitey Besese's cars were mentioned as being involved on the dates of the slayings. In all, 75 witnesses testified for the State.

Defense counsel had preserved all the conceivable errors in the record for purposes of appeal. Defense motions for dismissal of alleged conspiracy as a crime were overruled. Licavoli could not take the stand for he would be forced on cross-examination to incriminate the others or himself. Yonnie had a criminal record consisting of a felony and sentence in Canada. This could be brought out on cross-examination, among other things, for it was said if cross was needed, the prosecution was loaded.

If he took the Fifth Amendment while on the stand, the jury would resent it and penalize him for it. It was too risky. The defense wisely kept Licavoli from testifying.

The defense tried to make the best of what they had. Two witnesses testified that Harry Craig, who identified Ralph Carsello as one of the killers, had once mistaken Abe Kipperman, an attorney in Cornell Schreiber's office, as Carsello. The witnesses admitted Craig was frightened at the time and had to be accompanied home.

The highlight of the trial occurred when the defense called Sheriff David Kreiger as their witness.[23] The inference was previously made that the sheriff informed Licavoli in a telephone call that he had examined alleged witnesses to the Kennedy murder, none of whom named the gang, so it was safe for them to come back to Toledo. Kreiger was not running for November reelection. His conduct in the Auto-Lite strike coupled with the Licavoli escapes ruined all chance of voter approval. The sheriff is represented by the prosecuting attorney of the county. Here, a disgruntled sheriff was taking the stand against his own counsel. Tempers were short. A life was at stake. Rhinefort's acerbic tongue touched off a three-minute fist fight, a courtroom one-rounder, between the bigger Democrat Rhinefort and the smaller Republican sheriff.

The colloquy between the two participants was:

Rhinefort: "Dave, you're in big business now."

Sheriff: "You're a liar when you say those things about what happened at the jail."

Rhinefort: "Why you," then he slapped the Sheriff across the face. Kreiger grabbed the larger man.

Sheriff: "I'll bust you — you big sap. (He smacked the prosecutor twice.) "Take off those glasses." (Before they could be removed, the sheriff knocked them off.) A cut appeared on the right side of

Rhinefort's face. Then the fighters were parted by the attorneys and Deputy Sheriff William Jacobs. Blows were exchanged as the participants were separated. Deputy Jacobs told Reams, "He's my boss and I'll take care of him. Why should you get mad when he stands on his own feet?"

Reams: "Shut up."

Jacobs: "You shut up. Who are you?"

Counsel Elmer McCelland told them all to shut up. The judge called the combatants into his chambers and chided both for their disorderly conduct.

The purpose of the sheriff's testimony was to impeach the testimony of Harry Craig for Craig had told him at the original lineup that he knew nothing about the case. On cross-examination, the prosecutor asked: "You drink liquor?"

A. No.

Q. Weren't you at a party at your jail where liquor was served?

A. That's a lie.

Q. Did you give Licavoli freedom of the jail?

A. No, I defy you to prove that! I never played cards with him either.

Q. Didn't you get a phone call from Licavoli that Carsello, Mirabella and English were coming in from Detroit and you could arrest them at Licavoli's house?

A. I went out there with two carloads and arrested them.

Q. And your son as a deputy went along.

A. Yes.

Q. And the arrests were made before most of the deputies arrived?

A. Yes.

The Sheriff admitted he had known Firetop for 20 years. It was brought out that Wop English had a mysterious key to the handcuffs he was shackled in during the police lineup. The key fell out of his pant cuffs and was an exhibit in the trial. A mysterious "fix" note was found torn to pieces in the grand jury room. The note was to Firetop and read, "Phoned Fire said making a fix tonight with that fellow." The sheriff admitted attending police lineups but did not know how Wop got the key.

The sheriff shouted during one part of the cross-examination: "I didn't come here to get insulted by you, Mr. Rhinefort." The retort was "No, you came here to help the defendant."

Q. You were in the grand jury room on July 7 [shortly after the Kennedy murder]?

A. No.

Q. You brought prisoners over?
A. One, I believe.
Q. (Handing him the torn fix note) Have you ever seen this before?
A. No.
Q. Didn't you say you tore the note up in the grand jury room?
A. No, I don't remember. I may have torn it up.
Q. You tore the note up and put it in the basket in the grand jury room, didn't you?
A. I may have. I wouldn't say I did.[23]

Licavoli had an alibi. He was not in the city on the date of the Kennedy or other murders. The State did not prove he was present. They went on the leadership evidence. These facts must have bothered the jurors.

The jury thinking may have been influenced in consideration of the harshness of the penalty. The final arguments from both sides were anti-climactic. The Prosecution hammered on the campaign of terror created by Licavoli to resistors of his demands. Such tactics were incongruous to the traditional underworld that had lived in Toledo for years.

Defense lawyers sometimes use tactics, muddying up the waters, by shifting responsibility from the defendant. Since many police officers testified, the principal police witness, Detective George Timiney, was accused by defense counsel in closing argument.

They said "When Prohibition was enacted some law enforcement officers seized the opportunity to participate in the liquor industry and those who did not see fit to share profits were blacklisted."[24]

When the Golden Rose opened under Licavoli, Timiney raided sometimes four times a night and told Licavoli "It looks like you won't be running the place."

The defense argued strongly on the points of partiality of the police officers who arrested Licavoli time after time, yet did not arrest Jack Kennedy or Charley Merea. Merea was arrested twice by Federal Officers but never by the city or state.

"What was the relationship between Timiney and the widow Mrs. Marks that permitted him to use and continuously drive her new car?" The defense put the police on trial![24]

The unfairness of the police and their bias had an impact on the jurors. Licavoli was found guilty of complicity and conspiracy in the four murders with a recommendation of mercy making a life sentence mandatory unless commuted or reduced to second degree murder, a lesser offense.

When the verdict was read to a packed courtroom, Yonnie's wife Zena, cried openly. His mother, Grace, became hysterical and collapsed crying, "Tommy, Tommy, my son, my son!" She was aroused by attendants after her fainting. She resumed screaming for her son. She was forcibly led from the Courtroom and taken to the home of a relative living in the city.

There is a doctrine in the law known as prosecutional discrimination. For the same charge, English got the chair, Yonnie got life. If Yonnie appealed and won a reversal at best, there was a risk at that time another jury, if any, might not recommend mercy. His life had been saved. There were other factors to consider.

On the basis of difference in penalty the Governor could commute the death sentence of English and others that could follow. With political connections, there were always possibilities of release or reduction of sentence. Lawyers advised Yonnie not to appeal at the time Consequently he did not appeal the verdict within the time prescribed by law! He was to later claim in habeas corpus proceedings, "There was so much publicity going on at the time, not only about me but others in the country, I felt my life would be in jeopardy if I went any further with appeals."[25]

After the conviction, Court officials became fearful of gangland reprisals or attempts to free Licavoli in a massive jail break. Newspapers depicted deputy Bill Jacobs seated in the jail hallway with a machine gun in his lap. Special arrangements were deemed advisable to transport the prisoner to the Ohio State Penitentiary. Judge McCabe ordered county funds allocated to pay twelve guards to escort Licavoli on a special Community Traction bus to Columbus. Once confined, the State waited for the statutory period of appeal to expire. Then Reams turned to try the third culprit, Firetop, whom the Prosecutors regarded as the alleged brains and fix for the gang — the fingerman who pointed out their unfortunate victims.

# 19  *The Firetop Sulkin Trial and Aftermath*

Jacob (Firetop) Sulkin described by the *News Bee* as "a political ward healer for the Republican Party for twenty years"[1] went on trial for his life on February 26, 1935.[2] Because Firetop was Jewish, Reams named his assistant, Harry Friberg, a fellow Jew, to the Prosecutor's team. Cornell Schreiber and Paul Regan were retained as defense counsel.

The issues were the same as the Licavoli case. Much of the former testimony would be repeated. Only some new witnesses gave the case a fresh flavor. Martin Schweitzer, a Canton, Ohio, bootlegger, told of being forced to pay Firetop and Yonnie $100 a month for protection. He said he paid Chalky Red three times and Firetop thereafter.

Ken Willard, owner of a dance emporium called Danceland, said Chalky Red and others told him his place would be blown up if he did not convert it into "a boot joint." He said they would put in slots, whiskey and beer. He was told to look up Firetop at the R & K Cigar Store. There Firetop warned he could get protection to stay in business for $100 a month.

Bootlegger Charles Merea split 50/50 with Licavoli after threats to him. Yonnie, he said, sent over one of his men to check on receipts to see that there were no hold-outs. After six months he went to Kennedy for protection. He also told of an argument another bootlegger,

Arnetto, had with LaSalle and Syracuse when he refused to deal 50/50. Later Arnetto was found shot to death.

Witness Irving Knab rented a home to Mirabella. The gangster tenant used all his plumbing fixtures to make a still. When the lease expired, he sued Mirabella for property damages and signed a warrant for malicious destruction of property. Every time he went to Court, Firetop, acting as Mirabella's lawyer, was present talking to Judge Ira Cole. The case was dismissed. The Bar Association questioned Cole's qualification, but nothing developed because of his political friends.[3] The gang said Knab was lucky for had he pursued his claim to judgment and collection, he could have been killed.

William Poulos owned a slot machine route. The Licavoli gang hijacked a number of his machines worth $8,000. He saw Firetop, Buster Lupica, Chalky Red and Whitey Besase constantly with Licavoli. For two years he had 115 machines on locations throughout the city. His deal was to split 50/50 with Joe Fretti. In 1933, he was told he had to split with Licavoli as Fretti made him a partner. Poulos brought his collections to Yonnie's home. Once in a while he got $10 with the explanation Yonnie was short. Finally he was told he was out completely.

City merchants testified Firetop bought all the equipment for the Golden Rose operation. Ray Swaney said he dealt with Firetop who introduced Licavoli to him as an attorney. He told the story of recovery of his still through Jack Kennedy.

A cook at the Bancroft Grill, located near the scene of the Lubitsky-Blatt murders, identified Firetop and Chalky Red as customers frequenting his place and getting phone calls. All 13 indicted attended various meetings there.

So it went as in Yonnie's trial, the conspiracy, the participation by Firetop, the murders and his involvement. Sam Stein's testimony provided the most dramatic incident before the crowded and hushed courtroom. He was unprotected. His deposition, if required, would have been used and was probably more damaging than personal appearance.[4] "Yes, I sold gun number 541282 — sold it to Firetop — sometime before the Kennedy slaying." He held an index card aloft taken from the pawn shop where he was formerly employed upon which was written the serial number 541282. The number had been obscured partially from the frame of the gun by someone after Stein sold it. The manufacturer of the gun had placed an identical serial number underneath the blue steel plate between the grip and cartridge chamber. A ballistic expert took the gun apart and found the second secret number. That piece upon which the number was stamped was shown to the jury. On expert cross-examination, Cornell Schreiber brought out that Stein had also been charged with the Kennedy murder and spent 61 days in jail on that charge. Three different stories regarding the sale of the gun had been told. When taken by Reams to see one of the Clarke brothers[5] where "he beat me ... struck me ... kicked me ... asked me questions until my head whirled ... twisted my arm ... hit me in the face ... in the ribs ... stepped on my back."

Question: "And while he was doing this he was crying Firetop, Firetop, Firetop, wasn't he?" Answer: "Firetop's name was mentioned several times during the night." On rebuttal Rhinefort asked, "But you will say that you are now telling the whole truth?" Stein relied: "I am."

The first witness for the defense was Raphael Kest, street sales manager of the *Blade*.[6] He served as a character witness for his pal, Firetop, stating he never saw Chalky Red and Firetop together. Members of the circulation departments of both newspapers had friends in the rackets and responded to calls when one of their people was in trouble.

Unfortunately, Firetop took the stand in his own defense. He was his usual nattily-dressed, cocky, defiant, arrogant self. Being on trial for murder did not cause him to become humble or a supplicant. He admitted he visited in the Cleveland home of William Harper, a United States Secret Service agent, after Stein squealed. He boasted that the Probate Judge, former Mayor. Ad Thatcher and others came to him for help. He admitted entering the gambling business to make a better living and that his relationship with Licavoli was prosperous.

He spoke voluminously, frequently overstating answers to questions from his own counsel. He was glib, but shifty. He denied purchase of the gun from Stein.

Assistant Prosecutor Harry Friberg delivered the final argument that all Toledo wanted to confirm. Friberg argued "Licavoli's gang could not have operated without his assistance. He betrayed his fellow citizens and neighbors by leading the gang into new feeding grounds in Toledo. The guiding hand of Firetop Sulkin was in the thick of every move of the gang. He was as much responsible for instilling terror in the victimized as any of the others. . . ." The state proved beyond reasonable doubt, Firetop was responsible for Licavoli coming to Toledo. The jury hated Sulkin for that. When Jimmy Hines was convicted in 1938 the highest New York Court defined the role of a fixer as one which made the operation of illicit activity possible.[7]

After two and a half hours of deliberation, the jury returned a verdict of guilty of murder in the first degree. There was no recommendation of mercy, making the death penalty obligatory. As he was led from the court room, Firetop was still defiant yelling to friends in true gangland fashion. "It's a bum rap. It's not true. I'll beat it. Don't worry."

When the jury of eight men and four women were questioned by reporters later, those interviewed unanimously agreed Firetop's attitude and defiance on the stand convicted him. They felt he would have done better if he had never testified. The jurors believed Stein sold him the gun. The first ballot was unanimous for guilt, only two held out for a short time for a recommendation of mercy.

Licavoli told the *Blade* on the date of conviction "It's a shame. He's a nice boy and as far as I know never did anything wrong."

A few days later, when called upon by Judge McCabe, Firetop had nothing to say why sentence should not be pronounced upon him. The Judge set the execution date of July 8, 1935 and ordered "a current of electricity to be passed through his body until he was dead."

Firetop stood up, his face pale, fists clenched, but void of other emotion.

Rhinefort announced he had a strong case against the entire gang. The day after Firetop was sentenced, Anthony (Whitey) Besase was captured by Toledo police while driving a car with stolen license plates. He had tinted his hair an auburn color to escape detection. Buster Lupica also surrendered and was released with Whitey on $5,000 bond. Chalky Red had been represented by Attorney Harry Levy at an earlier hearing. He had promised the court he could produce his client. Now the absence was embarrassing as it reflected on his attorney's word to the court. Release in a murder case on minimal $5,000 bond made it obvious that the prosecution and court wanted to give some break to the Toledo contingent of the Licavoli gang. Chalky Red had to be returned for a deal on the remaining Toledo members.

The adverse publicity from the trials was disturbing. Even in hiding Red didn't like the bad things people were saying about him. Previous to the trials, police took his revolver in a raid on his Black and Tan Cafe on Canton Avenue. There were four notches in the handle of his gun but he refused to explain what that meant. He admitted being a frequent visitor to the Carsello apartment. He lent his black coupe to friends the day of the Kennedy murder but claimed it was black, not maroon, as was the Ford V-8 used by the killers. He was twice arrested, once for interfering with an officer but was released; a second arrest as a suspicious person violating prohibition was dropped. He had no criminal record. When he joined Licavoli, he had used the name Harry Berson when a still belonging to a person of that name was knocked off. To gain a new image, Red changed his name to Leonard, Harry Leonard; two first names were always good. The gang didn't like that. There were already too many Harry's around. His pasty-white complexion was perfect for naming him Chalky Red. That name caught on and stuck with him the rest of his days.

Harry Levy went to two mutual friends, Izzy Schall, Republican protege of Ad Thatcher and Louis (Paddock) Walker. He told them to arrange to see attorney Samuel Z. (Zeke) Kaplan and retain him at a fee of $3,000 to represent Red. Kaplan a respectable lawyer, a former Prosecutor, said that office owed him a favor. They would deal with him.

Levy's modus operandi was to lurk in the background, directing the action. The intermediaries would report to him and he would advise of the action to be taken. A retainer was paid. Then Izzy Schall, Paddock and attorney Kaplan drove to the Akron - Youngstown area where they located Red in hiding under a new alias of Anthony Mangino. Induced to return to Toledo by the trio, he plead not guilty and was also released on $5,000 bond.

The disposition of the cases of the three Toledoans invites considerable comment or controversy. Within two weeks of the date scheduled for Firetop's execution, they were permitted to come into court, waive reading of the indictment and enter pleas of not guilty and be released on bonds of $5,000 each! There was ample evidence to connect each of them as active members of Licavoli gang.

The Court of Appeals of Lucas County, in passing on the appeal of Firetop, unanimously stated, "The proof, as shown by the record, fully established this unlawful and criminal purpose. Any person who takes part in a conspiracy, whether as a party to the agreement or by willfully doing an act in furtherance of a common design, is liable as a conspirator.

"The general rule is well settled that, where several parties conspire or combine together to commit any unlawful act, each is criminally responsible for the acts of his associates or confederates committed in furtherance of any prosecution of the common design for which they combine. In contemplation of law, the act of one is the act of all. The law considers that wherever they act, they renew, or, perhaps, to speak more properly, they continue their agreement, and that this agreement is renewed or continued as to all whenever any one of them does an act in furtherance of their common design. It is immaterial, as affecting the question of co-equal responsibility, that one or more were not actually present at the consummation of the preconcerted design, or that the conspirator who committed the act cannot be identified, or that the act charged may not have been arranged for. Each is responsible for everything done by his confederates, which follows incidentally in the execution of the common design as one of the probable and natural consequences, even though it was not intended as a part of the original design or common plan." [8]

In September 1935 the docket sheet of the court record in the case indicates the three Toledo members of the gang were permitted to enter pleas of guilty to the crime of extortion and were given five year sentences for such crime.[9] There was no record made of the plea to the court. Learned attorneys asked, "Why extortion?" The charge was murder — four lives had been taken — others unaccounted for. There are lesser included crimes in the crime of murder — second degree, manslaughter, all the way down to assault and battery. Extortion was not an included offense.

Nothing can be done about it now. All three have since died. Yet "When talk is of all the fixes that went on in the Toledo Courts this was a situation to remember." The claim was "all three got away with murder." Friends countered they were under duress to join Licavoli, but such claims were never proven.

Murder indictments against Red and others were nolled with consent of the prosecutor. Red was sentenced to Mansfield Reformatory on October 24, 1935 as an extortionist for a term of five years. Red thought he was entitled to probation after a year. When his petition for parole was rejected,[10] he refused to pay Kaplan the balance of his attorney fees. With time off for good behavior, he was released on June 14, 1940, in time to become a prominent leader of the local syndicate.[11]

As for the other members of the gang, the joint trial of John Rai and Ralph Costello was scheduled with the same court and counsel on January 28, 1936. Both defendants claimed alibis. A torrent of abuse from Rhinefort rained down on defense attorney Schreiber when the defendants were allowed to introduce alibi testimony even though the law required the defense to give notice of an alibi three days in advance of trial. Because of a stipulation during trial, notice was deemed waived by the Court. The alibi witnesses, a dentist from Buffalo, New York had records of treating Rai in his office on the dates of the murders. Relatives testified he was in their homes on other nights.

Costello was at the wake with Licavoli on the night Kennedy was killed. Neither defendant took the stand. On February 22, 1936 the jury returned verdicts against Costello on four counts and against Rai on Two. Mercy, probably because of the mitigating circumstances of alibi, was recommended for both, meaning life sentences. This reflected on the death penalties of English and Firetop.

Firetop and English remained on death row in jeopardy of electrocution. Within weeks of his scheduled death set November 13, 1935, newspaper friends of Firetop came to his aid. Newsboys and business people circulated petitions on the downtown streets to "Save Firetop." 25,000 names were sent to the Governor imploring a stay of execution. Before leaving office in January 1936, Governor Dewey commuted the sentences of English and Firetop to life. Of the five under life sentences, only Yonnie and Firetop were to become "privileged prison characters."[12]

Ernest LaSalle and Jimmy Licavoli were also permitted to plead guilty to alleged extortion in the murder charge. Each served five years. Syracuse and Mirabella were never found.

The last defendant, Leo Moceri, remained at liberty until 1952 when he was arrested in California trying to put slugs into a telephone. Extradited to Toledo, he was also permitted to plead to the same alleged charge of blackmail or extortion and was sent to the Ohio Pen for five years.[13]

The voters of the city and county were grateful to Reams and his assistants for ridding the city of the Licavoli killers. Frazier Reams tried to become Attorney General in 1936 by capitalizing on the national publicity received. The rest of the state was not as grateful as Toledoans and his bid was lost as was his 1948 repeat attempt. In 1942 he became Collector of Internal Revenue for the Tenth Federal District involving 25 counties of northwestern Ohio. He lasted until January 6, 1944 when he accepted a position as State Welfare Director under Governor Frank Lausche.

In 1950 he ran for Congress as an Independent. He accused John P. Kelly (Democrat) and Herman R. Miller (Republican), county chairmen, of "irresponsibility to the voters." He said the Democrats have abdicated to appease labor racketeers." Two days after such remark, Kelly removed his name from the County Democratic Executive Committee. That did not stop Reams from declaring, "Congressman Tom Burke was controlled lock, stock and barrel by Richard Gosser."[14] Gosser, an international vice-president of the UAW-CIO was accused of attempting to strangle the city's economic life.[15] Referring to his election opponents, Burke, "as a racketeer and the other, Ramey as a common crook, he was elected twice to Congress

(1951-1955). He ended, with his law partners, being extremely wealth.

The electorate securely bound Democrats to the office of prosecutor for the next forty years. No Democratic candidate could lose. All assistants in the office were cinches to be elected. First, Tom O'Conner, then Rhinefort and Friberg were retained as prosecutor every time they chose to run. Their rewards, if any, are alternately revealed in subsequent chapters.

# 20 More Reform

Toledo was a sick city, financially and morally, during the term (1934-35) of Socialist Mayor Solon T. Klotz. His ineptitude brought clamor for change or reform.[1] Toledo, the critics claimed, needed a complete change from the old mayor council system to a city manager form of government as practiced in Cincinnati![2] Proportional representation (PR) was the name given to a system of election of nine city council men who would elect a mayor from their number. The duty of running the city would then be delegated to a professional city manager appointed by council. The campaign for a new form of city government was sluggish. Both newspapers supported reforms. 54.5% of the voters in the November 1934 election favored a charter amendment providing for a new plan for 1935.[3] Walter F. Brown criticized the proposal calling it "bewildering, fortuitous and un-American." Perhaps he was bewildered by the novelty himself. Brown eventually left the city in 1935. Nolan Boggs, a mediocre lawyer, as his temporary replacement, almost led the party to ruin. Because the Republicans were without strong leadership, they didn't make recommendations or endorsements that year. All candidates pledged nonpartisanship, honesty and efficiency.[4] Politicians claimed the new candidates were a bunch of "do-gooders" which is the term used for people they couldn't bribe or reach for favor.

## MORE REFORM

It took a week to count the ballots under the PR system. Nine high-minded citizens were elected to the first council under the new plan. John N. Edy came to the city as first city manager. A reform group known as the City Manager's League dominated city politics in the next two elections, 1937 and 1939. But then the fervor of reform subsided and like all reform, eventually went out of existence.

Mayor Klotz reinstated gambling and a segregated vice district. It was gambling and prostitution as usual, promoting "The old-fashioned horse sense of our fathers." So regardless of reform, there were a few ludicrous incidents the newspapers had to publicize.

Isadore Mitchell was an Aronoff associate. He operated the Buckeye Restaurant. It was located in front of Benny Aronoff's remodeled emporium. Entrance to the rear could only be through Mitchell's restaurant. Mitchell's lawyers got a temporary injunction against the police from passing through their client's place of business to go to the rooms in back.[5] After the order was granted, a motion was filed to hold police officers in contempt for visiting the gambling rooms in violation of the restraining order. The judge finally set aside the injunction on the grounds that Mitchell came into Court with "unclean hands." Judge Robert G. Gosline upheld the police actions, stating "They had a right to do what they did." [6] Aronoff's place became an object of great police interest. Since starting in craps, more police visits were made. Captain Timiney sought to harass Aronoff because of his Licavoli - Fretti connections. Iron crap tables were installed so that they could not be broken. The entries on horse races were changed. Instead of using portable boards posted against the walls, entries were printed on the walls so that they could not be destroyed.

To counter Timiney's arrests, Benny's connections reacted. The Social Club being run by Ed Warnke, after Hayes' murder, was raided. 45 customers were found guilty of gambling. A police officer dressed as a sailor shot crap in the place and became the chief winess.[7]

Aronoff became the city's biggest operator at his renovated new quarters. He wanted everybody who asked to get a bet in. He told his help to hold off calling a race until all bets were down. "Nobody is to be shut out." Consequently, Aronoff was often pastposted! Clerks found ways to flash known results by vocal and hand signals. Aronoff paid off regardless! Stories of past posting are legion as depicted in a later movie, "The Sting." Aronoff had a policy of discrimination. "No blacks were allowed to come into his gambling joint," Aronoff stated. If they wanted to wager, a clerk would go to the back room, return with a slip and collect for the bet. The reverse would be true in event of winning.

News of the size of Aronoff's operation reached underworld groups in other cities. One Saturday afternoon, six armed men broke into his upstairs rooms. He had no buzzer or look-out system for with Licavoli, Fretti and police, he felt safe. 250 patrons were forced to lie on the floor. All the money in the safe and table boxes was taken. Two customers complained that during the robbery Charley Shulkey, alias. Sulkin, Firetop's brother, had picked their pockets as they were laid out. It was customary for members of the vice squad to come up before the last race. This was to protect the bankroll from robbers and control the crowd in leaving. On that day, the robbers came a half hour before the cops.

Later Aronoff told the disappointed police, "Don't say anything about it. We'll make it up. Not a word is to be said because if they find out how easy it was, they may be back." When another gang tried a second robbery, Benny Aronoff's armed guards prevented the robbery but Benny lost part of a finger shot in the affray. The day after, the police were criticized by the newspapers for war on gambling.[8] Patrolman James Tafelski broke open the front door of Aronoff's Social Club with an ax.[9] It was also claimed he assaulted a porter in trying to get into the offices. Tafelski claimed he was working under "special secret orders." Chief Ray E. Allen and Merle Unkle, head of the vice squad, denied that orders of any kind were issued. Two days later, Patrolmen Tafelski, John Michalak and John M. McCarthy were transferred out of the vice squad.[10] They were Timiney men and Unkle claimed he differed with Timiney on matters of vice. Rifts, dissension, petty jealousy and bitter arguments developed in police ranks. Police Chief Ray Allen decided to start a police school in 1938. An entire school system was to be installed. Chief Allen wanted to improve the caliber and education of new officers. Salaries of $1,500 a year for patrolmen was increased to $150 a month or $1800 a year.

Twenty new patrolmen as a class were to receive training in an Academy dedicated to development of a highly trained professional officer.[11] A practice pistol range was erected at Bay View Park. A year later when the first class graduated, Service Director Edward DeAngelo, a former city councilman under PR plan, took the top half of the class, ousted the existing vice squad and installed such new Academy graduates under William Gray as head of vice. They were uncorrupted and remained so! DeAngelo ordered his new recruits "to rid the city of the gamblers and prostitutes." The story was told that when Gray went to the first whorehouse with his new orders, he knocked at the back door. "Who's there?" a voice cried. "Police, open up." "Go away. Allie Brown was here this morning." Gray laughed so hard he gave the place a week reprieve. Allie Brown was no longer a member of vice, but that didn't bother him; he still tried to get some of the action. For years, Allie advised younger cops, "Take all you can get, then look around for more." He was of the old school that believed "grift," the police word for "graft," was their just due. Shortly thereafter, Brown was pounding a residential beat. To attract publicity and attention, he tagged six hundred cars in his area for parking without lights, hoping publicity would get him back on vice. Even after retirement years later, Allie Brown double-dipped on pension and as a collector in Joe and Ben Fretti's J. and B. Realty Company.

There were all kinds of stories told about police transfers. Ex-vice member Harvey Kaiber was put on an inside desk because of making unauthorized pinball arrests.

Once Lieutenant John Power was assigned to a night desk because of attempted interference in vice affairs. A body had been found under conditions that indicated homicide. At 3 a.m., Powers called the home of former Coroner Dr. William Shapiro. "Hello," his wife Maude answered. "Is Doc there? This is the police. We got a stiff." "My husband hasn't been Coroner for years; go to bed;" she cried, as she slammed the phone in his ear.

William Gray and his crew chased the numbers men, craps and horse operators from the city. He allowed a few cigar stores to carry sports betting and handbooks but there was no evidence Gray was corrupted.

By the end of the year, all houses of prostitution were closed. One or two girls were allowed to sneak but they did so because Gray sanctioned it.

The sex action was transferred to Port Clinton, Ottawa County, Ohio where Dago Rose took over. Her place was one of the biggest in the midwest. Eventually, such operations moved closer to Toledo. At a point in Ottawa County closest to Lucas County, a big sporting house known as the Clock was established.

The Sheriff of Ottawa County was later indicted for his involvement in the illicit bordello. There is no evidence that the Toledo authorities got a cut of the action, which somehow seems anomalous, for Dago Rose had the largest and busiest House ever known in this section of the country, rivalling the best ever in Toledo's well-known line.

When World War II broke out, Gray enlisted in the Marines, but was restored as head of the vice squad on his return. He preferred working nights. In the after hours life of the city, bars, saloons, and supper clubs, he became known as the "cunt crazy cop." His custom was to enter an establishment; take off his coat, display two gun shoulder holsters on his 6'2", 235 pound frame, flex his back and shoulder muscles and try to impress the ladies. Years later, exotic dancer Rose La Rose, owner of a burlesque circuit, attached herself to him. She discovered that flashing genitals or breasts to the public paid off. Gray helped her eliminate Toledo competition at the Gayety Theater from Leroy Griffen by closing him for flashing while Rose remained open. Griffen, now a multi-millionaire Miami flesh promoter, is still in action. Rose La Rose also accumulated a substantial fortune prior to her demise.

For the city police, chasing the gamblers from the city into the county may have been killing the goose that laid their golden egg. For the sheriff, it was a financial boon. He could now dictate the number of operators and other conditions — any and all criminal activity in the county, outside of city limits, was solely in his jurisdiction.[12] Sheriff James M. O'Reilly, a former police officer, had campaigned in 1934 on a platform in which he stated he favored gambling and said so many times publicly and in print. In spite of his proclamations, O'Reilly was regarded as a good scout with many friends among the criminal element.

Serving as Chief Deputy under O'Reilly was Joseph Delehaunty, author of *Know your Profession, A Guide for Police Officers,* which had worldwide circulation.[13] Despite the altruistic members of his staff, Toledo remained a Shangri-la paradise for lamsters.

Early in May 1936, J. Edgar Hoover and seven agents, without a word to local police officials, flew into Toledo in a special plane from Cleveland, Ohio. Within an hour of arrival, they surrounded and stormed into a house near downtown to arrest Harry Campbell, one of the principal members of the Barker-Karpis gang, being sought for months by police all over the country for kidnappings in St. Paul. Just as he had candidly admitted approval of gambling, Sheriff O'Reilly also admitted drinking beer with Campbell for a period of six months before his apprehension. "I didn't know it was THAT Campbell," he said. This was scandalous! Criminals had used the city as a hideout for years. Except for the Cowboy Hill, alias Joe Muzzio, shoot-out on September 14, 1921 nobody ever got caught. Toledo police knew through tips Campbell was in town. J. Edgar Hoover was told exactly where to find him! Hoover listened to everything that was said but made no comments in return. When it came time for the arrest, Hoover grabbed all the headlines and left the local police without a word of credit on the case. Most police officers want publicity for their participation in arrests or solution of crime. Denial of such credits, was a national basis for dissension and distrust of Hoover. As a result of this lack of notoriety, some Toledo detectives absolutely refused to cooperate with Hoover. The result of J. Edgar's habitual headline hunting and upstaging of local police was that the F.B.I. never learned that the rest of the Karpis gang was hiding out on Middle Island, using various islands of Lake Erie as sanctuary.

Hoover blamed crooked politicians for his inability to capture Karpis. Karpis claimed," I made that son of a bitch"[14] This came out at a time when Hoover's personal courage was under fire in Washington. Many newspaper men claimed Hoover "would wait in he wings until the shooting was over and arrests were made" before he appeared to be photographed. Karpis claimed Hoover's reputation as a fearless lawman was not deseved.[15] Yet when the Karpis gang was finally captured, Hoover reaped national headlines.

At this time, while a senior in High School, I won a gold medal for journalism from the Newsboys Association. Joseph W. Robinson presented the award which also included a week vacation in Washington D.C. and Philadelphia. I met J. Edgar Hoover in both cities briefly posing for pictures with other youths. Hoover was cold, distant — and I had a distinct distrust of him. You can't fool kids. Karpis may have been right.

Upon my return to school, the publicity and pictures earned me the brief sobriquet of "G-man Illman". I hocked and lost the gold medal in a crap game trying to raise money for the Senior Prom. A gorgeous gal expected me to ask her to the Senior Prom. She put off others until three days before the event. When I failed to call, she accepted another date and never spoke to me again. I didn't know then that when you are a compulsive gambler, you do not love yourself, so how could I love anybody else?

It was always the same. Everytime I needed to win, I lost. Maybe I deserved to beat myself mentally, subconsciously enjoying the loneliness, self-pity and degradation. Anyway I lost the medal, never regained it and never seemed to care. This may have been an omen of things to come.

The Toledo *Blade* was up in arms over the Campbell arrest. This incident occurred a few days before the May Primary elections. O'Reilly was up for re-election. Daily front page editorials labelled "O'Reilly Must Go" read, in part, as follows:[16]

> Lucas County today has a sheriff who for five months has been meeting in friendly fashion one of the most notorious gangsters in

the United States. The name of that gangster is Harry Campbell, chief Lieutenant of Alvin Karpis, Public Enemy Number One. Lucas County ought not to have that sheriff in office tomorrow. He should resign today. Public decency and the reputation of Toledo demand it. It is the least O'Reilly can do to maintain self-respect and whatever respect he is entitled to from the people of Toledo. The reputation of our city demands this action at once.

"I've been drinking beer with Campbell plenty of times," said the sheriff yesterday, "but I never knew who he was. I hadn't seen a picture of him."

And in the meantime a picture of the criminal Campbell had been on the bulletin board in the county jail.

The sheriff says he has seen Campbell about once a week in every week or two since last winter.

In the annals of crime — in and out of fiction — is there a tale more amazing, a record more. disgraceful than this? It is said other officers of the law have known Campbell in this city. . . . 'I didn't know he was a criminal,' says the sheriff. 'I never saw a picture of him.'

And he never looked at the bulletin board in his own jail.

"O'Reilly must go."

The next day the *Blade* editorialized:[17]

J. Edgar Hoover, in Washington yesterday, declared to the *Blade* correspondent there that he could not possibly understand how a sheriff, who is supposed to know something about crook-catching, could associate with one of the Number One gangster of the United States for months and not know it." "The face of this Campbell," said Hoover, "was plastered on the walls of the county jails and police stations all over America." It was posted on the walls of the office over which Sheriff O'Reilly is suppose to rule.

No wonder Hoover in forceful, unmistakable terms condemns this man who is now on the ticket for a renomination for sheriff. No wonder people in all walks of life in Toledo were joining in the general and growing demand that O'Reilly resign at once.

It was too late for the *Blade* expose to defeat O'Reilly at the May primary. No write-in candidate could organize any full campaign on such short notice. O'Reilly became the Democratic nominee in the fall election. The election for the first time was for a term of four years. Nor could the Republican-oriented *Blade* stop the November election landslide. In 1936 FDR swept Democratic candidates, including O'Reilly, into office with him in his lopsided victory over Alf Landon.

Reform in the city stopped at the County Line. It merely took a little longer to get where the action used to be. For O'Reilly, the next years were to be prosperous, and it would get better — beyond all dreams when a syndicate was formed, but O'Reilly would not be sheriff to benefit.[18]

# 21 Industry and Labor

"Ohio has long been a state in the grip of big business and Republican satrapy," Steffens said. The story of C.C. Miniger growing rich from low-paid workers has already been told. Just as wages were limited by employers, self-important bankers, officious businessmen and civic leaders protected skilled labor as a commodity by keeping competitors from the city. Reasons why Toledo never grew to the size of Detroit varied. Most critics blamed selfish local interests or leaders, without vision or purpose.

Toledo might have been the center of aircraft and wireless radio manufacture if the ideas of inventions of two early pioneers were given financial backing.[1]

On June 30, 1905 Roy Knabenshue made a flight from an old Fairgrounds area to the roof of the downtown Spitzer Building in an airship named Toledo I. Hampered by high winds, his 58-foot-long dirigible, filled with hydrogen gas, made the inbound trip of two and one half miles in 37 minutes. With the wind at his back, he made the return flight in 13 minutes.

Every newspaper in the country carried a story on the historical flight.[2] In August 1905 Knabenshue took his airship to New York where he flew around the Flatiron Building, then landed in Central Park. Knabenshue was unable to commercially develop his lighter-than-air craft in Toledo. He eventually moved to Los Angeles where he remained active in aviation circles until his death.

The first broadcast of a sports event occurred in July 1907 under the ingenious skulduggery of Dr. Lee DeForest and Frank M. Butler, pioneers in development of a wireless telephone. The two scientists hoped to report and cover the annual Put-In—Bay regatta on Lake Erie.[3]

They placed a transmitter and radio receiver aboard a yacht, *Thelma,* with a similar outfit on shore. When their boat was a few miles out in the lake, two 100-inch sheets of copper were nailed to sides of the yacht, providing a perfect grounding for the current necessary in the communication process. The experiment was a success. On July 18, 1907 wireless telephonic history was made in reporting the yacht races as the first sporting event to be broadcast by radio.[4] The public thought the scheme was a fake. Efforts by Dr. DeForest and Butler to sell stock in a newly-formed company were regarded as fraudulent. Both were indicted on charges of fraud. The story of how the reporting was arranged was retold in court. After nine hours of deliberation, the jury found the men not guilty. The adverse publicity seriously impaired all chance of financing.

In 1903, Pope Toledo had the first internal combustion machine. Labor problems and strikes shut the plant down. With local financial help, John North Willys salvaged the plant and reorganized it into Willys Overland Company. After the famous Killets injunctions in the strike of 1919, the company became one of the area's biggest employers with 12,000 engaged in automotive production following World War I.

Henry Ford built his Model T in 1908. By 1914, the Ford factories were paying $5 a day salary with a profit sharing plan. His was double the average weekly wage in auto plants elsewhere. Rumors that Henry Ford wanted to put up a Toledo plant caused many Toledoans to believe that but for certain evil-intentioned businessmen, Toledo would have become the home of a huge Ford plant. Many were convinced that Ford was driven off by industrialists who feared his competition.

While such rumors have been denied by Ford Company officials and the Toledo Chamber of Commerce, it was a fact that Ford owned a railroad and land for a terminal in North Toledo, located for direct connection with the Lake Erie Harbor.[5] While the facts were that Ford was not discouraged to move, there is no evidence he was encouraged either.

Henry Ford's brother later built a 20,000-foot warehouse in Toledo under the name of William Ford & Co., Inc. It was one of the leading equipment distributors in Michigan and Ohio of tractors and equipment, commercial and dump auto bodies for all makes of trucks and accessories of automotive dealer and uses.

William Ford was quoted as saying, "He has long recognized the advantageous location of Toledo and believes that few cities in the United States occupy a position of greater strategic importance in the competition for business today."

With discovery of natural gas in northwest Ohio and availability of water, the growth of Toledo as the eventual glass center of the world has been previously told.

In 1910, Robert A. Stranahan and Frank Stranahan came from Boston to establish the Champion Spark Plug Co., the largest supplier of plugs in the world.

Favorable legislation and taxes to protect Ohio industrial interests were always taken. Enacted were the manner of laws that Mark Hanna, the businessman in politics, would have approved. In 1911, Ohio enacted a Workman's Compensation Act where employers gained advantage. The law allowed certain employers to become "self-insurers" under the Act.[7] All the Toledo glass companies, public utility corporations, Auto-Lite and big industrial employers became self-insured. Willys maintained a full staff of attorneys on its premises to handle claims. A number of abuses followed. Employers controlled the files. Claims were not timely or properly filed, delays were made in payments of benefits, files were lost or deliberately misplaced, rights were forfeited in death and disability benefits. Laymen were permitted to handle claims for pay while use of lawyers was not encouraged. Men on disability were ordered back to work by company doctors often before recovery as sweepers, guards or clerks so the company could avoid dual payments of compensation and disability pay. Wage earners received two-thirds of a weekly pay during disability. A maid, injured in a hotel accident, reportedly received $6 a week in 1930 to support herself and child. This was the typical case reported.[8] These abuses by employers were in the name of profit for disability payments, lost time or man hours were lost profits. Many lawyers claimed the enactments were profitable for the self-insured, for otherwise they would have allowed the state to handle all claims.

Before the end of World War II, most employers did not provide group health, accident or disability programs. No life insurance programs for employees were in existence at the time. Payments for death in the course of employment were meager. A survey after World War I showed 56% of the widows and 19% of the children were forced to go to work upon death or injury to a breadwinner father.

When the United States and Canada started talks in the early '30s for mutual construction of a St. Lawrence Seaway to allow oceanic vessels to use the Great Lakes, railroad interests and lobbyists obstructed action on enabling legislation for years by dilatory tactics. They knew cheaper shipping rates would cut revenues. Railroads early enacted roles precluding use of attorneys at disciplinary proceedings involving personnel so that injured employees' rights were often left unprotected. When trucking began to cut in on railroad transportation figures, legislatures were induced to enact weight and road taxes to keep freight rates competitive. Both railroad and trucking kept Toledo from becoming an early Great Lakes port, when foresight might have allowed for development in all three fields.

Upon repeal of Prohibition, employers needed all advantages and more to equalize or compensate for assaults later made by unions and labor racketeers. During the Depression, the economic picture for criminals was bleak: there was little or nothing available to steal. Each city was locked up. Local hoodlums would not brook opposition from outsiders. New revenues had to be located somewhere. An answer was found in organizing labor or labor racketeering. News of success of an operation in one city invariably passed on through Underworld sources immediately.

In Chicago, the premier extortionist, Willie Bioff, started a labor shakedown racket of Jewish butchers. Then he organized a motion picture projectionist union. Bioff threatened to put two operators in every theatre projection booth in the country unless tribute was paid through his union. Al Capone heard of Bioff's successes and insisted upon becoming a partner. Fear of Capone in the theatre paralyzed Hollywood producers, distributors and movie owners throughout the country.

For years before the Auto-Lite strike, Henry Ford in Detroit hired strong-arm squads under the direction of Harry Bennett, his enforcer, to prevent unionization or labor problems in his plants. In addition, big business always had the police on their side to protect their property rights and to crack a few skulls when trouble started. Where police were unavailable, employers paid Pinkerton police whenever labor problems arose.

The Auto-Lite strike saw laborers, Communists and Underworld characters on the same side fighting back at the company, guards and plant police.

Before this strike, Toledo industry had no organized muscle or strong arms. The local police were neutralized because of their illicit connections with the Underworld. The hoodlum element, however, had friends progressing in labor. The Communist leaders of the Auto-Lite strike were unable to find sufficient strength among the workers. Most employees with families already in need were fearful of eventual job loss or arrest, if caught using force. Under such circumstances, the Communist elements bargained with mobsters and muscle to provide a counter force to demonstrate strength and instill fear in management. A bonanza was found in the labor area when leaders of goon forces realized the strength of the union, the size of its treasury and the political potential, power and prestige. They stayed after the strikes to take control, using force where necessary. This was the beginning of the strange marriage of unions and the mobs which continues undissolved to this date.[9]

Mobsters thereafter assisted or financially backed union or business in exchange for "a piece of the action."

The Mob people learned very early that tributes could be exacted from both labor and employers. For employees, it was "No pay, no work."[10] Protesting victims were silenced by strong-arm tactics backed with sufficient political influence to quash any court proceedings. Organizing was now legal. Non-joiners would be coerced to join so that a whole group or factory could be controlled. Another common practice for "organizers" would be to take one month's or more of dues of all members or a percentage of annual dues as fees. Other "organizers" elected to remain on the union payroll as officials with strong-arm duties at substantial salaries.

The Toledo scene had its share of Mob assistance. Ties with Detroit's huge labor force were fortified by locals in both cities joining national organizations. Union officials linked to Mobs were the hierarchy of leadership. If a local union was successful in wresting control and ousting mobsters, the international stepped in, suspended the local and established another union in the same territory with the ousted officers returned to power.

Toledo and Detroit grew together labor-wise. Walter Reuther, reputed to have left-wing tendencies, became a frequent visitor to Toledo in the '30s.[11]

Reuther came to learn unionism from a true genius in labor relations, another carrot-haired Toledoan, Edward T. Cheyfitz, who was with the Communists in the Auto-Lite strike. Eddie rose rapidly in labor ranks. During his growth, an Industrial Peace Board was formed in Toledo. Its success in averting and settling strikes became well known throughout the United States.[12] While at the Doehler Jarvis plant in 1935, he was elected national secretary of the Die Casters Union. Cheyfitz helped organize the Toledo Labor Management Committee. He taught Michael V. DiSalle, future Toledo mayor and Ohio governor, and Reuther how labor and management could counsel.

An example to the state and county was set in April, 1945 when the Toledo Labor Management Citizen's Committee was formed to transform and retain wartime industrial harmony. It was called LMC by all media.[13] Composed of a conglomerate of 48 labor, clergy, industrial and public officials serving without pay, they formed three-man mediation panels to solve labor-management disputes, adopting an attitude that such problems were community matters requiring community leaders. Michael V. DiSalle was first chairman. The *Blade* labor reporter, Jerome Gross, became executive secretary and manager. Cheyfitz and Royce C. Martin of the Auto-Lite were among the original members of the panel. Cheyfitz helped draft the original charter.[14] When the die casters merged with the mine, mill and smelter workers, Cheyfitz became national chairman.

Eddie served as labor consultant for west coast shipping firms and helped organize labor in the movie industry. His talents were then transferred to the nation's largest union, the Teamsters, where he handled press relations for presidents Dave Beck and Jimmy Hoffa.

With the power of the Teamsters behind him, Cheyfitz was instrumental in breaking the Bioff-Capone hold on Hollywood moguls.

Warner Brothers, Twentieth-Century Fox and Loews were named as the movie victims in the March 1943 trials of the labor racketeers. Willie Bioff and his original partner, George Browne, turned informers on a plea deal. Convicted Capone henchmen were Frank (The Enforcer) Nitti, Louis Compagna, Philip D'Andrea, Charles Gioe, Paul (The Waiter) DeLucia, alias Ricca, Francis Maritote, John Rossells, and Louis Kaufman. Three years later, all were pardoned in a scandal that shook Washington.

After the 1943 trial, Bioff went to Phoenix. There, under the name of Nelson, he renewed political ties until his presence was reported to Chicago gangsters. Then on November 4, 1955, as he started his car in his remote rural home, Bioff was blown 300 feet away into the Arizona desert. His organizational abilities and threats to industry died with him.

The movie people were grateful to Eddie Cheyfitz. He was one of the few men able to greet and meet most Hollywood moguls on a reciprocal first-name basis. Pledging support of the National

Teamsters Union to the motion picture industry meant Hollywood would no longer be subjected to costly labor shutdowns previously experienced.

Aligning the teamsters with Hollywood was a shrewd move. In exchange for protection of theatrical interests, a good national press, better public image and exposure would be given to the Teamsters Union, badly in need of same.

The movie industry was delighted when Eddie became an assistant to Eric Johnston, president of the Motion Picture Association of America, in his Washington offices.

When a Congressional inquiry on un-American activity was begun in 1947, Eddie was accused of being a Communist. Roy E. Brewer, a Hollywood union official, had told a House subcommittee that Communists tried to capture movie unions as a prelude to taking over the industry.

Eddie's activities in helping movie unions organize created enemies. They opened up on him during the inquiry on the list of Communist leaders and writers in the movie world. In answer to the question, "Isn't he a Communist?"[15] Johnston defended Eddie by answering, "He was when he was young ... (age 18 in 1932) ... but broke his ties following the 1939 Hitler-Stalin Alliance."[16]

Character letters submitted to the committee in Cheyfitz's behalf came from the Most Rev. Karl J. Alter, Bishop of Toledo, John D. Biggers, president of the Libbey Owens Ford Glass Co., Charles Pack of Doehler Jarvis, William Hard of *Readers Digest* magazine and many others.[17] In gratitude to Johnston for saving his career, Eddie named his son Eric.

Eddie later bought the Teamsters Union into the law offices of Edward Bennett Williams and it was claimed Eddie later brought Joe E. Louis to be seen by the jury in Hoffa's first trial, which resulted in acquittal. Eddie was in charge of and virtual guardian of the growing, gigantic Teamster Pension Fund. After his death, huge assaults in unauthorized loans were made. Prior to his death, his controls and advice would have precluded such deals.

Richard T. Gosser, a diversified and flawed character of many faces, was a second Toledoan to emerge as a giant on the labor scene, local and national. In the '20s he had served a 23-month term in Michigan for armed robbery resulting from a conviction with his boyhood friend, Tony Paul alias Neufio Scott.[18] Gosser later started as an electician apprentice at the Willys Overland, the city's biggest employer. He began organizing auto workers in 1934. When the Wagner Act of 1935 gave labor "Magna Carta" rights, he enlisted a goon squad of strong-arm men to make employees join his union organization. These acts of muscle, with general knowledge of Gosser's friends in the Underworld in mind, kept workers in line. Tony at the time was a strongman associate of Joe Fretti, soon to be part of the new Aronoff venture into craps. Tony, like Gosser, was a good Catholic, supporting the church and sending his children to Nazareth Hall. Gosser knew the bishop well and had two priests, Brogan and Konts, as close associates. A Catholic action group further helped Gosser to power by favors to make him look good. In 1937, he became chairman of the Willys Unit of Local 12. Two years later, he became president of Local 12, then president of United Auto Workers Region 2 R, covering all of Northwestern Ohio.[19] He was appointed to the Labor Management Committee, where Monsignor M.J. Doyle also improved his public image. Dick, as he became known, worked hard, making friends with civic and industrial leaders. He developed a patronage system to reward loyal followers.[20]

Labor leaders John Quinliven and John Kelly, both staunch Democrats, indoctrinated Gosser in politics. In furtherance of political ends, a plush flower fund was set up. Then he organized a political arm of the union, delivering funds and votes for delegates aiding the causes of labor.

He turned the political relationship full circle. By 1950, it was claimed he literally owned Congressman Thomas H. Burke.

In 1939 Gosser became one of the earliest allies of Walter Reuther, an association that was to continue harmonious relations until 1960, when a split occurred. In 1946 Dick managed Reuther's campaign to become elected president of the United Auto Workers and headed a 371-member Toledo delegation that unseated R.J. Thomas by a close vote.[21] Gosser was elected International vice-president in return.

Gosser's greatest power came in the early 1940s, with the outbreak of World War II. Willys had a government contract for 100% of their jeep production. The war had a no-strike threat over factory employees. All the company wanted was to keep labor in line. Edwin C. McCleary, formerly associated with Harry Bennett of Ford Motor Co., came to Toledo Willys as superintendent of manufacturing. Later he was made plant manager. Gosser and McCleary became great friends. In business association, labor and management each became extremely wealthy. They bought Florida property jointly.

For keeping his local in hand and giving "sweetheart contracts," Gosser was able to take many advantages of his employer. He and Tony Paul owned a car wash where Willys contracted to wash every car off the production lines for two dollars each. Not every car was washed! Gosser had the run of the plant. At Gate 4 in a remote area near Swan Creek, each day number runners or football betting pools were distributed, and paid. Thievery of plant equipment occurred at regular intervals. Stolen goods would be recovered and sold back to the plant at a profit. In its desire to avoid later entanglements, management refused to complain. Willys was on a cost-plus basis with the government, so repurchase was being paid by the taxpayer. Gosser also sold scrap back to the plant for recycling. He formed a paint company with a Robert Rath and sold paint to his employer. It was claimed he was often paid for more than he delivered or for nondelivery.

He joined McCleary and Lou Poulos, a Greek importer-exporter, in getting records of Jeeps arranged for sale overseas at tremendous profit. By Underworld contacts with the Morelli brothers of New York, who controlled New York docks, the trio arranged large European shipments of Jeeps.

Gosser helped Virgil Gladieux become a giant in the food vending business. All the canteens in the Jeep plant were built by the unions for Gladieux, who maintained a monopoly on food supply in all the plant service areas, particularly during the World War II years.

Gosser organized a Sportsman Club for union members and took vending machine profits. He owned Colonial Hardware Company, which sold goods to Local 12 and Willys as its best customers. Owning real estate at Sand Lake, Michigan, he formed Will-O-Land summer health camp for children of union members. Then he leased it to Local 12.

An ostentatious display of wealth by Gosser and McCleary brought on problems that led to their eventual capitulation. Both were inveterate gamblers. McCleary, it was stated, owed a Cleveland syndicate thousands of dollars. Stories circulated that there was a contract on him because he didn't pay. McCleary went to Tony Paul and begged him to handle a settlement in his behalf. McCleary was known as "the Big Man" at Willys. This was more physical than factual. He stood six feet tall and weighed over 350 pounds. Special chairs had to be built to accommodate his large frame. McCleary entered Toledo society with a number of big affairs. Frequent lawn parties at his residence for 200 or more were staged. $25,000 or more was spent for his daughter's wedding at Inverness where Guy Lombardo's band played for the revelers. In 1962, when American Motors took over Willys, McClearly left town.

Gosser loved to go to race tracks in Toledo, Detroit and Florida with an entourage of guests which included his wife, two priests,

Frank Konst and James Brogan, his loyal aid Arnold Shenofsky, and three or four other stooges who would run his wagers for him. He often bet large sums on three or four horses in the same race so that he could boast of his handicapping prowess. His pockets were filled with $100 bills. When approached by his trainer, Gus Lonski, Gosser would publicly peel off thousands to buy a horse. He and his wife maintained several stake horses in their own stables. He was often known to bet $5,000 or more on a football or baseball game.

An outburst of publicity described as the "Civil War of Local 12" occurred in 1950, when 20 complaints against Gosser and his administrators were presented to the International Executive Board headed by Walter Reuther.[22] They contended, among other things, that Gosser was a dictator in union affairs and had mishandled or wasted union funds. The local war became a full-fledged issue after the huge Ford Motor Co. Local 600, largest in the union, called upon Reuther to conduct a full-scale investigation. Hearings in Toledo at the Secor Hotel, with Reuther in attendance, ended with the guarantee that rank-and-file members be given more say in union politics. This was tantamount to a whitewash.[23] *Blade* editorials and articles thereafter precipitated a running battle with Gosser. He defended himself by telling his foes "to go to hell." He sounded off against the *Blade* by saying, "For my money Paul Block can go to hell ... it's a scandal sheet." Gosser also resigned from the LMC accusing the *Blade* of lies in stating that his union tactics were "wrecking Toledo." The *Blade* had never maintained good personal relations with Gosser, but they wanted the goodwill of Willys so outward appearances were more congenial than the true situation.     John A. Bolman brought a suit against the Automotive Workers Building Corporation headed by Gosser charging gross irregularities in the financial affairs of Local 12. Four hours after suit was filed, Bolman was expelled from the union so that the claim was made he had no status to bring civil suit. The court made short shrift of such argument since he was in the union at the time of filing. When the court ordered an audit of the books, for Bolman's attorneys, an appeal was taken for delay but the order was upheld unanimously.

It was revealed that the *Blade* had advanced Bolman $5,000 for legal expense. A *Blade* editorial on the case stated, "There is finally the obligation of a newspaper to serve and safeguard the best interests of the community."[24] This was March 10, 1950 while syndicated gambling continued in the city and county.

As a consequence of the *Blade* intervention and pressure,[25] Bolman's case was settled whereby Will-O-Land Sportsman Club was deeded over to the Willys Overland Unit of Local 12; $82,000 debts allegedly owed by Automotive Workers Building Corporation to Local 12 was cancelled; Gosser resigned as president of AWB Corp. and sold his Colonial Hardware store to Local 12. Bolman received an award of $7,000 to cover his expenses and Gosser paid all the court costs.[26]

In an attempt to regain public favor in 1954, Gosser built the U.A.W.-C.I.O. Diagnostic Clinic for union workers, establishing a complete health and convalescent center for such employees and their families.[27] It didn't help.

Gosser's problems multiplied thereafter. In 1958 he was named in a Senate rackets committee investigation. Walter Reuther came to his defense saying, "He is a decent honorable citizen who wouldn't take a dishonorable dollar." Shortly thereafter, however, Reuther did not deny reports of sharp differences between him and Gosser over union operations.

His numerous financial transactions further invited attention of Internal Revenue. In turn, he attempted to obtain confidential information from IRS of what, if anything, they had on him. He instructed an employee, Ted Maison, to contact Patricia Niedomski, an IRS employee. She brought copies of papers to Gosser's office which had been marked with invisible ink for identification, discernible by ultraviolet rays. When apprehended with tell-tale markings indicating handling of the confidential IRS documents, Gosser was indicted with two of his associates, Don Pinciotti and Ted Maison. All were charged with conspiring to obtain confidential information from IRS.[28] Gosser, at trial, had many civic leaders appear in his behalf. The *Blade,* whom he accused of "knowing too much about his affairs," came out with an editorial supporting acquittal. The jurors felt otherwise.[29] Although Gosser was in failing health, the federal judge sentenced him to a three-year prison term beginning in November 1965.

Gosser resigned from the UAW after his conviction and remained in retirement until his death on December 1, 1969.

A third Toledo labor leader of prominence, locally and nationally, was Lawrence N. Steinberg, a Detroit transplant. Born in Russia, he came to the United States at age 16. When placed in the first grade with six-year-old students, he rapidly advanced in schooling but never obtained more than a fifth-grade education.[30] He became streetwise in the labor field at an early age, making friends in the same areas in Toledo and Detroit. Steinberg was director of the old CIO Retail, Wholesale and Department Store Workers Union. When that union was expelled from the CIO in the '40s on charges of Communism, Steinberg turned to organization within the Teamsters, also later expelled from the AFL-CIO.[31] Toledo Local 20 had the teamster drivers and the AFL-CIO had the factory workers. Any other laborers could be organized. The field was wide open. Steinberg successfully activated a second charter from the Teamster International, as Local 22, naming himself president. Steinberg consulted the firm of Fink and Canelli, lawyers who were representing most Toledo underworld interests after the deaths of McMahon and Marshall. His friend, Chalky Red, one of the big men in the local Syndicate, recommended such lawyers. Red became a staunch supporter of Steinberg's cause. Another Detroit transplant, Al Shnider, was appointed organizer and public relations man. Since they needed musclemen or goon squads to coerce labor into joining unions, Steinberg and Shnider turned to Red for help. With connections in Detroit through the Syndicate, Red brought in an ample supply of muscle. The average small employer had little or no means to combat Steinberg's organizing diplomacy.

Like the gangsters, fear and intimidation were his stock in trade. Any business having three or more employees was worth organizing. Steinberg or Shnider would go to the shops to talk to the help on unionism. When an owner refused to bargain with his union, a six to eight-man strong-arm squad arrived by Cadillac shortly thereafter. The muscular goons would usually break all plate glass windows of any establishment. Then, during business hours, for whatever duration, the paid goons would parade with placards announcing their protest and strike. Whenever customers tried to enter, they would be spit upon, cursed or threatened. "We got your license number, you fink. We'll get you too." Owners would likewise be verbally abused, taunted and attempts would be made to inviegle them into fist fights where the pugilistic goons could give the recalcitrant a going-over. Very few fought back.

Sometimes the Labor Management Citizens Committee would be called in to arbitrate the strike. Monsignor Doyle often stationed himself in the shops during the voting on the pretext of maintaining peace and decorum. Some owners complained that his tactics pressured the workers with voting for the unions. A few shops voted to join the Teamsters, but later rescinded the deal. Steinberg called such reversals "his greatest defeats." Despite criticism and setbacks, he persevered.

His local prospered as did the International. Dues were $5 per month out of which the International received $4. Originally starting with 500 members, the Teamsters International grew to two million as the biggest in the country. Steinberg forced Harry Card, president of rival Local 20, out[32] by exposing Card in *flagrante delicto* with another Teamster's wife, among other things.

Card received $10,000 in cash and a new car on resignation. Steinberg merged both locals into Local 20. He organized all loose and unattached labor in earnest, making his local the largest in Ohio — eventually 12,000 in number. In 1954 he built a new Teamsters Union Hall where he installed complete legal, insurance, credit union, pharmacy and other services for union members and families. Chalky Red had the run of his office, in and out, coming and going as he pleased.

Jimmy R. Hoffa of Detroit was also a frequent visitor to Steinberg in Toledo. Both had mutual friends in the Underworld of both cities. Both were experienced, early Teamster organizers. Police and Mafia strongmen employed by industry had cracked both skulls on more than one occasion. Steinberg and Hoffa had served time in jail for their early violence in labor.[33] It is claimed that Hoffa, in the early years, turned to the Purple and Licavoli gangs in Detroit for muscle to retaliate against employers. He owed them and they knew how to collect.

In 1955, Hoffa had 50,000 members in his Detroit union, only Chicago had more.[34] As president of their own locals, both Steinberg and Hoffa were qualified to run for office in the International and eventually take over national control. Continuous national ties with Underworld connections to unions were maintained.

By example, Chalky Red was called upon to get tickets for six Toledo friends during the first week of the opening of the musical "South Pacific" in 1949 at the Majestic Theatre in New York. Red called Steinberg for the phone number of Johnny Dioguardi (Johnny Dio). Scarcity of tickets did not deter Dio. Six front-section seats were ready for the Toledo group when they arrived to see the hit, then starring Ezio Pinza and Mary Martin.

In 1954, Dioguardi became a regional director of six unions and a friend of John O'Rourke, president of Local 282. O'Rourke was also a close friend of Hoffa. It was the same O'Rourke newspapers accused of "selling labor for a price."

Labor racketeering was sometimes used by employers to prevent some unionization. If an employer made a contract with a union, the law prohibited rival unions to breach contracts, so that the employer and union would be bound to the first deal.

Such arrangement froze labor conditions for the life of the contract even if pay was at substandard levels. Employers lucky enough to receive such deals paid labor leaders "consulting fees" for arranging the terms. Likewise, fees were paid to prevent unionization and keep organizers away. Sometimes employers were induced to grant concessions to union officials or their associates by allowing vending on the premises or allow football pools or policy members to run. Ads in union papers were coerced as good will gestures towards the unions. The evils of the practice were not unprofitable. After Dave Beck's conviction in 1957, connections in control of Teamster locals in all big cities were instructed to have their delegates vote for Hoffa as president. Hoffa took control with a firm hand on Teamster reins. Steinberg became his right arm, handling public relations and press affairs after the death of Cheyfitz in 1959. In the convention in Cincinnati in 1958, Steinberg appeared as personal representative of Hoffa.[35] Steinberg was with Hoffa in Nashville, Tennessee, during his federal trial there. He stood by Hoffa in all his tribulations.

In 1963, when the International offices in Washington, D.C. lowered their flag to half-mast in memory of the martyred President Kennedy, Steinberg called Hoffa to report what he had done. Hoffa, who was being prosecuted in Nashville by Attorney General Robert Kennedy, flew into a rage. He became very abusive to Steinberg and Harold Gibbons, another International officer. Both threatened to quit as a consequence of the abuse and insult to the President. Hoffa relented — but the breach created wounds that did not quickly heal. After Hoffa's conviction and imprisonment, Steinberg resigned on substantial pension. He left the Teamsters to return as a "labor consultant" to the Sheller-Globe Corp. and various Ohio politicians.

# 22 *A Detroit Suicide*

A bombshell suicide letter found August 6, 1939 gave Michigan newspapers and reformers new impetus in its war to stop gambling and avenge the death of Gerald Buckley. Before and during the 1930s Detroit, like Toledo, was a wide-open gambling city. The gambling and sporting populace had a greater variety of handbooks and crap joints than Toledo. Johnny Ryan's game was the biggest. Located at Elizabeth Street and Woodward Avenue in the downtown area, Ryan paid guards and manpower overtime wages to keep the bank below his headquarters open 24 hours a day to cash checks for his business or customers, if desired. Other prominent houses were Lefty Clark's, Wertheimer's, The Grand River Athletic Club, Merchant's Club, Metropole, Chesterfield, Chalet and Doc Grady's. At the latter, dealers themselves would indulge in play. Numerous Detroit policy numbers operators once paid 900 to one on winning numbers as there were three houses — Stock, Bond and Race — for players to wager. Later the odds dropped to 500 to one on on single numbers and 600 to one on doubles. Endemic of all large cities, the Detroit triumvirate was long established.

Politicians, sheriffs, prosecutors and mayors as well to numerous police officials became wealthy through the payoffs made for protection. Despite the Buckley murder and the brief period of reform that followed, gambling activity in Detroit continued without another major incident until August, 1939, when two poignantly written suicide note blew the cover on the entire operation.[1]

Janet McDonald, a 33-year-old divorcee, had been rejected by her married lover, William McBride, a handbook operator. She became desperate after he refused to continue their illicit relationship. While dejected and despondent, on August 5, 1939 she placed a blanket near the exhaust pipe of her car. She then laid down in her garage by the side of her eleven-year-old daughter, Pearl, to inhale the lethal fumes from a running motor. When discovered the next day, two letters addressed to the newspapers, governor, FBI, police commissioner and other authorities were found. She wrote that her erstwhile lover, William McBride, was a payoff and contact man between policy racketeers and the police and that McBride paid protection money through Police Lieutenant John P. McCarthy, head of the racket squad.

Mrs. McDonald was a clerk at the Great Lakes Mutual Company operated by her braggart boss, McBride. Two days after the letters were opened, Duncan C. McCrea, a worried Wayne County prosecutor, flew back to Detroit from his vacation to stop an investigation started by his assistant, William E. Dowling. Charging that "Hell hath no fury like a woman scorned" he tried to quash any further inquiry into police corruption or graft. The Detroit News saw the possibilities of reform and refused to keep the lid closed on the case. Two lives had been taken. Explanations were demanded particularly as to why the daughter was involved. State Attorney General Thomas Reed was a Republican. Prosecutor Duncan C. McCrea, Sheriff Thomas C. Wilcox and Mayor Richard W. Reading and his son were Democrats. These political fires kept burning as the News clamored for and investigation and cleanup.

In the ensuing five-year period from discovery of the McDonald notes to the end of court appeals, the *News* wrote or carried 738 different articles involving "The Detroit Policy Graft." This constant coverage prevented political "whitewash" and gave the public an expectancy of punishment. After some delay, all circuit court judges of Wayne County met in secret, electing one of their colleagues, Republican Judge Homer Ferguson, to act as a one-man grand jury in the case. While "one man grand jury system" was declared unconstitutional in some states, the law at that time permitted Ferguson great latitude to use sworn or unsworn testimony, punish for contempt, secrete witnesses, or grant immunities under a section of Michigan law entitled "Proceedings for Discovery of Crime." Judge Ferguson knew that sensational publicity and recognition from the case would enhance his political ambitions. He hired a special prosecutor, Chester P. O'Hara, at a pay scale of $100 per day.[2]

1,500 to 2,000 witnesses were called before Ferguson and O'Hara, who worked on the case 18 to 20 hours a day.[3]

Robert Dorrell, now a Lucas County Domestic Relations judge, was hired as a special investigator for the Ferguson grand jury after his graduation from the University of Toledo in 1939. After military service in the 40s, he became associated with Toledo city government. Law departments were the seat of local power in politics yet there is no evidence that Dorrell ever publicly manifested any efforts or desire to use his Ferguson knowledge or experience in Toledo underworld affairs. Pay off man McBride flew to Florida before he could be questioned. Three months later he died there of pneumonia. His wife wanted the police to investigate what she called "peculiar circumstances" of his death.[4]

During the investigation, the "one man grand jury" ordered Michigan Bell telephone service to cut off wire service on race results furnished by the Continental News Service Company which severely impeded race wagering.[5]

Immunity granted to various witnesses revealed that partners in a baseball pool in 1934 and 1935 paid Purple Gang protectors half of the thousands they received during those two years. After 1935, the police declared themselves partners of the promoters and pushed all Purple gangsters aside. Operators of gaming machines reported they paid $8 per month protection money for each machine and there were hundreds in the city and county.[6]

The eventual principal witness Raymond (Buddy) Boettcher, inadvertently mistook the investigation of gambling as a probe of a peculiar robbery that occurred in his precinct. Four young Purples allegedly robbed a Dr. Fred B. Robinson of $2,000, which mysteriously was lost from the police property room where it was to be kept as evidence. The Purples claimed the doctor had been shylocking money to various underworld sources and used the robbery for insurance purposes. When the Purples were acquitted, Police Inspector Boettcher, involved in both matters, accepted immunity and told Ferguson's team the facts that eventually led to indictments and convictions! Inspector Boettcher was known as "cash and carry Boettcher," The grand juror heard him say he delivered payoff money in neat white envelopes to the police station. As he passed the graft, he said, "Pay day, boys — money talks and everybody listens," or "While money is talking, nobody interrupts." Buddy became known as the "boy bandit" of the Detroit cops. Boettcher told how he delivered $333,000 in 33 months from handbooks.[7] He took orders on payoffs from Elmer (Buff) Ryan who controlled 225 handbooks through the Continental News Service.[8] "The mayor," he swore under oath "was paid off at a downtown hotel once a month." Payoff envelopes were referred to as laundry. Other payoffs from brothel keepers, numbers operators and slots were between $750,000 to $1,000,000 a year. The policy houses were estimated to have done $10,000,000 annual business.

The voluminous payoffs included police inspectors, $1250 to $4,000 per month, lieutenants and sargeants $200 to $250 a month, various patrolmen $50 per month.[9]

The prosecutor and sheriff received sums separately from the police. Prosecutor McCrea gave one-third to his chief assistants including Harry Colburn, chief investigator. Before the investigation was completed or charges could be filed, the desperate prosecutor tried to raid the grand jury files kept in secret headquarters. Leaks in the police department from the jealous, unpaid or honest factions allowed Ferguson to get help before the raiding party arrived. Seeing armed guards in the Ferguson offices, the raiders fled before being discovered. As a consequence of the Ferguson investigation, 135 persons were indicted.[10]

Among the persons named were 89 policemen, comprising such a large portion of the department that in some precincts there were not enough sergeants left unscathed to man the desks and call the rolls.[11]

Principals indicted included Duncan C. McCrea, Wayne County prosecutor; Harry Colburn, his chief investigator; Fred W. Frahm, recently deposed as Detroit Police superintendent; John Roxborough, co-manager of Joe Louis, world heavy-weight champion; Claude Roxborough, brother of John; Police Lieutenant John P. McCarthy, and Everett Watson, fight manager and reputed "King" of the numbers racket.[12]

Besides the 135 defendants, there were said to be 28 co-conspirators whose names were kept secret because they would be witnesses for the State. One hundred fifty-six more were indicted on August 8, 1940.[13] Eighty-one were civilians, including many handbook and gaming operators, and seventy-five members of the police department from ranks of patrolmen to inspector.[14] All gamblers closed down; those not indicted fled to avoid arrest or subpoena.

Lt. John P. McCarthy, named in the suicide letters as the collector, denied the charges. He was exonerated in a police and prosecutor's investigation held before Ferguson was named "One man grand juror." After such whitewash, McCarthy was called before Ferguson. There he refused to answer questions, was found in contempt, jailed for five days, then suspended. When the trials began, the proceedings were publicized daily. (Buff) Ryan named by the "boy bandit" as the pay-off man, was sure all the payoff money was distributed; yet 30% remained unaccounted for despite intensive scrutiny. It was surmised that certain political figures in the state or elsewhere went undiscovered and undisclosed in the proceedings.

Among the principals, Mayor Richard W. Reading and his son (who served as his secretary during 1938 and 1939) were found guilty of violation of public trust by accepting thousands of dollars to protect gambling rackets.[15] Prosecutor Duncan C. McCrea was convicted of taking more than $104,000 during the six years he was prosecutor.[16] Sheriff Thomas C. Wilcox was convicted of taking $37,000 during a shorter term of office.[17] These were Depression dollars; and were only the amounts allegedly proven because reports stated one-third of the ten million in annual policy receipts went for protection. No amount was mentioned of the take on craps. Imposing sentences of four to five years on the mayor, prosecutor and sheriff, sentencing Circuit Court Judge Earl C. Pugaley of Hart, Michigan who heard the cases by special assignment said, "It is my duty to discourage and suppress corruption of public office. The heart of the crimes are not gambling but public corruption through illegal graft payments to public officials."[18] In addition to the state charges, Mayor Reading also faced fraud and income tax evasion charges in the Federal courts.[19] The impact of the criminal proceedings also sent several other police officials, numbers operators, gamblers and brothel owners to jail. The cost to the taxpayers for the special prosecutors and grand jury was $392,351.[20]

The Michigan Republicans were grateful to Homer Ferguson. They sent him to the U.S. Senate in 1942 and re-elected him in 1948.

The gambling conspiracy case enabled Detroit reformers to close down gaming operations and chase every operator from the city. Lefty Clark went to Saratoga, New York, where he dealt craps during the month of August. Saratoga was given that entire month for the State racing season catering to the vacationing elite and sporting crowd of the world. It was reported Lucky Luciano also had a piece of the famous Smith Club action. Some of the highest rollers in the country assembled annually at Saratoga. A shooter could get faded there for any amount. If the bettors or players didn't cover, the house would, but asked a little percentage for doing so.

Jimmy Ryan, Detroit's biggest dealer, sent several employees and associates to Toledo. The closing of the Chalet Club, Charlevoix Club and others forced nationally-known gamblers as C.P. Samuels, Sleep-out Louis Levenson and his brother, Harry, to Covington, Kentucky, and subsequently to Las Vegas.

The Detroit betting public still demanded action. The wrath of reformers kept Detroit and environs too hot for any local operation.

The volume of action and the amount of tribute being paid was too much to go unnoticed or remain untapped. During the Ferguson investigation and trials, plans were being made to accommodate the Detroit players in a nearby location to the south, namely, Toledo, Ohio![21]

# 23 Formation of the Syndicate

Reform ruined big-time gambling in Detroit. All police and political connections were lost when the grafters were tried and sent to prison. Leaders in the reform movement would not tolerate a resurgence of vice. Toledo reform stopped at the city limits. The gamblers merely went out into the county where they paid the sheriff and his deputies instead of city police for protection. Since they already owned Sheriff O'Reilly and Hennessy, his successor, there was no problem in that quarter. In 1936, Democrat Tom O'Conner replaced Reams as prosecuting attorney. The Underworld supported him. Whether he took money from the gamblers is not known but he wanted to be liked and to continue public office. As a Casper Milquetoast, it was doubtful that he could thrive in a private practice. O'Conner, a small man physically and mentally, was weak, tractable and congenial. With no ax to grind he was easily manipulated by the politicians of the time.

Many people claimed "Tom O'Conner was a nice guy who was taken advantage of by his friends."[1] He was easy to reach for favors. One of his best supporters was another jailhouse lawyer, Eddie Foss, who stood to O'Conner as Firetop to Judge Cole. The Eagles Lodge maintained headquarters directly across from the courthouse. Foss ran that club as if he owned it. The lodge served food and liquor and had bingo and slots. When an entertainer named Jack Shea from

Buffalo lost his job, he was allowed to stay at the Eagles. Shea was elected trustee and entrusted to watch the proceeds from the operation. When he started to complain about Foss ripping off proceeds, he was taken to an initiation party, slipped a few Mickey Finns and when found in such drunken condition, evicted from his office with his membership revoked.

O'Conner was a daily visitor to the Eagles for free lunch or a few games of cards. Foss catered to his every wish and was always after judicial favors.[2] Stories are told when a few attorneys demanded the remainder of fees in cases, they would be told "I paid Eddie Foss; he did all the work on the case (with O'Conner) and I'm not paying anymore."

In September 1940, Pete Licavoli sent two friends from Detroit to influence Harry Craig, principal witness in his brother's murder trial, to change his testimony. A trap was set. Toledo police caught the two men in the witness' house. Arrests were made as they overheard the attempt to bribe the witness if he changed his testimony given at trial. Indictments of all three followed. Pete Licavoli retained veteran attorney Steve Fazekas to represent him, promising a $2,000 fee if he won the case. Steve graduated from old St. John's College of Law with O'Conner and knew he could get a break from him regardless of the reputation of his client. "Since the alleged conspiracy occurred in Detroit, Licavoli had not committed any offense in Toledo," Prosecutor O'Conner said. A nolle pros, dropping the case, was entered as to Pete with his consent. Armed with a certified copy, Fazekas called his client at a number in Detroit. Licavoli was fearful of Toledo police and was afraid his attorney might be followed and lead the police to him. Fazekas was instructed to go to a bar in that city. When he arrived at the bar, he was to ask for a certain person. Upon compliance, Fazekas was taken in a car by a circuitous route for two hours until Licavoli met him. Upon delivery of the dismissal order, he was thanked and paid in cash. For the other two apprehended in the bribe attempt, O'Conner had no objections to release.[3]

By 1940, Lucas County became saturated with gambling spots. Benny Aronoff had the Webster Inn — craps and horsebetting in the rear with steaks at bargain prices at the restaurant in front. Pat and Joe Morrissey opened the Old Dix, a half block away. A Syrian group — George Haddad, Al Jacobs, Charley Bassett and George Shamy — operated the Academy Club while Chalky Red and his buddy Louis "Paddock" Walker were in the Chesterfield Club. Tom Worland with Abe (The Muzzler) Shapiro dealt in the Vicory Club in Adams Township, which was later annexed to the city. So it went as political protection, payoffs and competition led to cutting each other's throats. Yet, they scrambled to attract action-hungry Detroiters.

The voluminous and extremely profitable Detroit gambling became chaotic, disorganized with slip-shod practices as the grand jury probe developed. Detroiters could not relocate in Toledo where conditions were saturated. Toledo gamblers, police and politicians would not permit it. Yet they remembered that Yonnie Licavoli had defied all the local Underworld, police and politicians and there were signs of danger of repetition. Killings and violence made politicians wary of publicity or public indignation. Talk of use of muscle, gangs or killings was taboo. No more blood was to be shed, for the public would rise in indignation and, through reform action, close them down. Detroit was proof of it!

Pete Licavoli, Pete (Enforcer) Carrado and Joe Massie were among the gambling big shots of Detroit. They were in with Tony Zarrelli and Anthony (Tony Jack) Giacalone. The Purple gang were allies. They all wanted to do business together in Toledo, arranging for their Detroit people to have outlets. They promised not to compete provided they could get "a piece of the action" in return. Meetings were arranged. The parties decided to merge. An organization was needed to carry out their program. Benny Aronoff went to John McMahon, his attorney on political affairs. The sheriff, prosecutor and newspaper allies were consulted. More conferences were held. The enormity of the proposition attracted willing listeners.

Joe Fretti called in John Canelli as his counsel, as the latter was prominent in the American Bowling Congress (ABC) and had nationwide connections.

The Underworld was aware of the success of the Barn, started in Bergan County, New Jersey, in 1937.

Until closed by the Kefauver investigation in 1952, the Barn was the largest money crap game in the country.[4] There, local patronage was discouraged because local talk, word of mouth or losses could lead to detection and involve problems with police or courts and publicity. There too, a system of transportation was devised for delivery of players to the Casino. Convenient locations off the highway were selected for parking of customer cars and then "fishwagons" carried groups of customers to the action. This arrangement would preclude traffic congestion around any casino, decrease problems with nearby residents or businesses and allow a low-key profile on the extent of operations.[5] The Barn plan would be copied by the new Syndicate.

Since this was to be an interstate operation, police, political and newspaper protection was needed to protect the operators. They felt Aronoff's brother Walter, as circulation manager of the Detroit *Times,* could suppress publicity in Detroit. It was no news to report that people of that city gambled in Toledo. The Detroit *News* could care less, but the *News* proved a paper could close down an entire city. Boss Tweed regarded it as essential to have most, if not all, city newspapers on his payroll. The Detroit *News* exposé proved the point to the schemers. The Toledo *Blade,* after the demise of the *News-Bee,* began calling itself "one of America's greatest newspapers."[6] It was, for all purposes, the only newspaper in town. The *Blade* owned and printed the *Times.* All the Syndicate wanted was for the editor and publisher to keep the lid on gambling. The organizers turned to Ray Kest, street sales manager and soon-to-be circulation manager of the *Blade.* As he grew in the newspaper world, Ray became a friend of Christopher Wall, fire chief, businessman and political boss.[7] Wall was his tutor in good press relations and encouraged Raphael in the new proposition.

The promise of getting on the payroll of the Syndicate intrigued Ray Kest. The absentee *Blade* publisher, Paul Block, Sr., loved him. His friends of the Underworld promised to supply booze, broads, football tickets, anything for favor. Ray let his friends on the city desk know where he stood. Fortunately for him, they didn't knock it. Years later, reporters stated, "We knew what Ray was doing all the time, but we didn't think he was hurting the city's image."[8]

In addition, Clifford T. Quinn, police reporter, was approached for a cut of the Syndicate payroll. A native of Plymouth, England, Quinn was raised in Toledo where his father Thomas was business agent for Local 7, Painters and Decorators Union. After graduation from high school, he became a reporter for the *News-Bee* in 1934 but joined the *Blade* in 1936 before his old sheet folded. Most police at the time regarded Quinn as "Paul Block's hatchet man." Generally, a chief never had a reporter around but Quinn was in and out every day getting the dirt. He was able to bypass the city desk and go directly into Block's office so that they could determine what to use or what to keep out in news stories. Quinn made a number of enemies among the police as he often refused to put names of officers in police stories. As courthouse and police reporter, Quinn was on a first-name basis with city hall, the law department, police officials, sheriff and prosecutor. Quinn would be the first to know what, if anything, was up! But Block wanted all scoops before being actually printed. The *Blade* could also help limit interference from Columbus.

In 1938, the *Blade* regarded Governor (later, Senator) John Bricker as Presidential timber. A reporter and political newspaperman for 20 years, John Joseph (Jack) Flanagan left the editorial staff of the *Times-Blade* to become publicity director for Bricker.[9] As a former attorney general of Ohio, Bricker uncovered actions of Governor Martin L. Davey that he would correct.[10] He blew the whistle on his predecessor.

In the years between 1936 and 1938, the public learned about their State in Davey's administration. It came out that the state's contract for trucking liquor had been let to a company that never owned a single truck. The dummy concern got the contract for 17 cents a case and sublet it to a bona fide trucking outfit at 11-1/2 cents. Eventually the contract was outlawed by the courts, and the state recovered $113,740 from the bogus company.[11]

During the legislative season of 1937-1938, a special committee of the preponderantly Democratic state Senate produced testimony substantiating the charges Bricker made against the Davey administration. In a formal report, the committee described the condition of the state government as "unbelievable." It had found "padded expense accounts, falsified reports, forged bills, pretended statistics, even punishment of those politically opposed, rake-offs and commissions and payoffs."

In the Department of Liquor Control, the committee found "the entire situation so shot through with forgery, corruption, graft, false reports, faked statistics and maladministration, as to be hopeless of cure."[12]

It was characteristic of Governor Davey to seek to excuse a specific charge on the ground that the act complained of was either "legal" or that "it always has been done and will continue to be done long after you and I are dead."[13]

When accusations were made, Davey answered charges with counter-charges, filing libel and slander suits against his accusers and quietly withdrawing them after public interest died down.

Most politicians and newspaper people claimed that beginning with Bricker's election as governor in 1938, the Republican Party in Ohio had the greatest chain of successes in half a century. No governor had interfered in internal affairs of a municipality and they doubted if political advisors would permit Bricker to differ. In addition to Flanagan, Toledo politicians had a great friend in Isadore Topper, elite Columbus lawyer, originally a native of Toledo.[14] In 1931, he was an assistant attorney general of Ohio and reappointed in 1933 by Bricker on election to that office. The attorney general had investigative powers to ferret out corruption or inquire into illegal activity.

Following the repeal of Prohibition, Topper helped draft Ohio's liquor control laws and served in the department of liquor control, when organized, under the attorney general. When he left that office he became legal counsel to the nation's largest liquor distillers. During Prohibition, many had become connected with Underworld financing. "Top," as he was frequently called, was an excellent lawyer — thorough, brilliant, yet concise in argument. He was openly praised for his briefs by the Ohio Supreme Court. Some called him "the power behind the Governor." He was also referred to as the "unofficial and unpaid attorney for the Republican organization." Top was a close personal friend of Harry G. Levy and other Toledo politicians and judges. With his brother Hyman, a prominent local Republican, they maintained a Toledo law firm. When local gamblers in taverns and bar businesses received citations from the Department of Liquor Control, they were invariably referred to a Topper office for answer. Top maintained contacts in the governor's and attorney general's offices. Daily he could be found dining at a special table reserved for him in the Neil House, often accompanied by Flanagan, Levy or friends in the governor's or attorney general's offices. Clients lavished gifts of liquor on him, keeping the bar in his basement of his Bexley, Ohio, home filled, as he entertained extravagantly. The locals felt there was no problem in the state capital that their lawyer friend "Top" could not handle.

Labor and industry respected each other and left well enough alone. They both knew the Mob had men like Steinberg and Gosser if pressure was needed. The mere threat of labor problems gave businessmen a headache; so industry was neutralized.

For politicians in Lucas County, there was little difference between the parties except in division of spoils. It was long established that opponents for office were never to "kick up traces" or raise this issue even in "a reform platform." Neither party would ever initiate such action or attack. Police, sheriff, prosecutor or other public official never pressed the gambling matters. Non-interference was part of the city's gambling tradition. Political connection from both parties extended from Toledo to Columbus thence on to Washington when the occasion demanded.

The arrangements were simplified. The Licavoli gang, with the Purple in Detroit, would arrange for players to come to Toledo. They would keep other gangs from the city and help local police control crime and criminals in Toledo. Moe Dalitz, a former Purple who moved to Cleveland in 1926, and Georgie Gordan promised no interference from that city. Covington, Kentucky, had enough action from southern Ohio to lay off competition. No one else was around. Pete Corrado would head the Italian faction with Maxie Stern for the Purples as labor-liaison connections. Maxie Stern was a Licavoli lieutenant in the '40s. Stern worked with Peter Lucido and Sam Scroy. When they had a dispute with Stern, both were murdered.[15] Accepting these promises of patronage and protection, a Detroit-Toledo gambling symbiosis was founded.

Some called it the Mob. Others claimed it was Mafia. The sophisticated called them "connected." In modern parlance, the associates are called "wise guys."

Their plans called for a new casino. There were war clouds in Europe. Girding for production of supplies, the country was in a period of prosperity. Bennie Aronoff advanced the cash with alacrity. He paid a $25,000 bonus to beat the government deadline on nonessential construction! When completed, all other county operations would stop except at the Victory Club, continuing primarily to handle Toledo clientele. Joe Fretti was to be local boss and payoff man for the new Syndicate. All others would work and have percentages of the take. The Licavoli gang predominated. They were in charge of protection. Pete had married into the Bommorito family of Detroit. Tony Paul's sister married into the Detroit families. They reportedly merged with the Purples, but the Licavolis called all shots. The new Syndicate took in Harry Soliski, aka Joe Wilson, of the Polish number house, on a percentage. Then all city, county, policy numbers and football pools were turned over to former Licavoli henchman, Whitey Besase. With Pete Bommorito, Whitey shared duties at the Victory Club with Toledoans Tom Worland, Abe (Muzzler) Shapiro, Nate Blumberg and Burdette (Skinny Lefty) Meemsoth. Whitey was to have first count. This device allowed the person counting to skim or take off unless detected doing so. It also set the amount collected to prevent other counting shortages.

At the new joint, Buster Lupica had first count. Chalky Red was boss of the night shift. Tony Paul, Joe Morrissey, Pat Morrissey, Pittsburg Lefty Kistner, Ed Warnke and Benny Cohen of Detroit were also top men.

The pieces or precentages of all the other merging partners were apportioned to be paid after the payoffs were made. For the first time, apparent agreement was reached in the gambling fraternity as they raced to build. These were minor problems that Joe Fretti had to iron out. He went to the Syrian group and told them, "My boys say you're out. Now I can't help you or save you if you don't get out. They'll kill you. So you better sell." They did.[16] Only Chalky Red's connections with Licavoli saved the new Jewish outfit from the same deal, but the sellers were given jobs in the new set-up. The authorities created a monopoly by the merger. Granting a Syndicate the privilege to operate a crap game openly is equivalent to opening a gold mine for them.

The site picked for the new club was on the first roadway in Ohio south of the Michigan Line. The Dixie Highway from Detroit ran right into it. A left turn as soon as one passed the Ohio boundary line and voila! There it was a short distance down the road. It was named the Club Devon. Some said it was named after a place of the same name in Detroit but others claimed that Ben Aronoff was very proud of his nephew, Chester Devenow. His sister's boy was brought to Toledo and introduced to Marilyn Fruchtman, daughter of one of the city's leading steel magnates. A merger and marriage ensued. With money and advice from both families, Chester was vested with legitimate business connections in the Sheller Globe Co. where he subsequently rose to president. In a moment of frolic, Aronoff, honoring his sister and nephew, named the establishment the Club Devon. The newspapers called it the "$135,000 Depression Memorial." Eight months before Pearl Harbor on April 21, 1941 the Toledo *Blade* feature writer, Tom Kenny, wrote his front page under a banner headline a half-inch high so that it couldn't be missed. "Old Glory Flies Aloft as Aronoff Opens Swank New Gambling Spot" was the headline. His feature read:

> Post time at the Club Devon was 1:00 P.M. today. In case you don't know it and are interested, the Club Devon is Benny Aronoff's successor to the Webster Inn, Dixie Highway gambling spot which Sheriff Charles Hennesay ordered closed some time ago.
> Situated on Benore Road, between Stickney Avenue and the Dixie Highway, adjacent to the old dog track, the $93,000 Club Devon is the most elaborate gaming establishment ever erected in or near Toledo.
> Its official opening was scheduled for this afternoon and this morning scores of workmen labored furiously to make ready for the resumption of gambling in the county.
> Equipment from the old Webster was moved into the new building and some of the tables were already placed under droplights preparatory to play.
> The Devon copies the style of the original Buckeye Social Club at 224 Superior Street, where Benny went the limit in streamlining.
> The Devon, which also will have a restaurant, this time serving full-course dinners, according to the restaurant operator, Isadore Mitchell, is dressed in light tan brick. Its restaurant section has windows of glass block and flat pane glass, trimmed in chrome. The

canopy still is under construction. A new American flag flies from a new pole in front of the canopy.

The interior of the restaurant, through which one must pass to enter the gambling room, is of a two-tone flat color job. The gambling room follows the same color scheme, the lower section painted a dark gray and the upper a lighter shade. The ceilings are pure white and from them are suspended indirect lighting fixtures and the long corded droplights which play upon the gaming tables.

Simultaneously today there were at work bricklayers, carpenters, sewer men, plumbers, electricians, restaurant fixture installers and amateur handymen.

The horserace chart also was moved from the old Webster and hours before the scheduled opening a marker was busy listing the races and the horses entered.

The Devon is equipped with numerous exits and firedoors. It has lookout posts, alarm chimes, numerous washrooms and a women's lounge equipped with overstuffed furniture. All rooms are air-conditioned.

The gambling room is 88 by 80, or 14 feet longer than the old Webster. The restaurant is about 40 by 80.

There is ample parking room and today workmen used rakes, shovels and hoes and even a heavy mechanical roller to prepare the grounds for the expected traffic.

Sheriff Hennessy, who ordered closing of the Webster and Dixie Inns, still is in Magnetic Springs, O., where he went recently for treatment of arthritis. He is not expected home for a week.[17]

Illegal activity cannot be legitimately advertised. This news item as an ad could not be purchased for a million dollars, yet it served as an announcement and invitation. The *Blade* connections performed a magnificent job. Reports were that at the end of the first day, the Syndicate was off the hook, Aronoff had his advances back and they were now operating in the black. From the very beginning it was a phenomenal success!

John Scarne, the world's foremost authority on gambling, wrote in his chapter on Casinos: "The largest number of illegal gaming tables in a single casino at one time in America were in operation during the early forties at the Devon Club, a sawdust joint in Toledo, Ohio. It catered largely to Detroit horse betters who were transported the intervening 50-odd miles in Greyhound buses at the club's expense. The Devon Club had 20 Bank Craps tables, 25 Black Jack tables and 8 casino side games — 53 gaming tables in all."[18]

Scarne also claimed that the New Jersey Barn had the greatest gross profit of any casino in the world. He claimed the largest night's take by the Barn operators was on September 1, 1946 when 11 gambling tables showed a gross profit of $1,250,251. Scarne's report was based on actual visits to the Barn but his estimate on Toledo was based on hearsay. The Syndicate tried to keep the entire operation low-key to avoid increasing demands of politicians or possible conflicts with other gangs or muscle. Scarne did not mention 50 or more slots or the Devon's boards covering horse racing at all the major race tracks. Betters lined up 15 minutes before post to bet to avoid getting shut out. People stood waiting at all spots. Stickmen kept yelling, "Make room for shooters — stand sideways — all you need is one arm and one eye" to play at the boiler-room type crap tables, which would accommodate up to 44 customers, side by side! The entire 10,000 square feet was wall to wall humanity.

The Devon had a captive audience. Players that came 60 miles or more to play did not "hit and run away." They came to play and play they did. The house limit was $50 on the line with double odds on points. Come bets were the same. The action became gigantic as the word spread in a few months. On weekends, trains brought players in from as far as Chicago to the west and Pittsburgh to the east. Bus terminals were packed. A cab would deliver a fare anywhere in the city for 50 cents. On delivery to the Devon, the doorman was authorized to pay the driver a dollar.

The Devon had no entertainment expense, no freebies, no stars and no shills, for on slow nights dealers from empty tables would act as shills. All the bosses worked. Estimates of gross profits of a million dollars weekly were regarded as low.

On weekends, the city was pregnant with betters. Within its limits, the Healy Brothers, George Haddad, Al Jacobs, George Shamey, "Monk" Antone, Irv Greenspoon, Meyer Greenberg and others had books for sport betting which had great impetus during and after World War II. Automobile production stopped late in 1942 to convert to the war effort. Gasoline was rationed. Factories in Detroit and Toledo were going three shifts, seven days a week. Recreational facilities were limited. A weekend in Toledo was the only action in the vicinity.

Pinball machines were in every restaurant, bar, drug store, cigar store, lobby or shop in the city. Football pools circulated in the factories and streets during season openly. Bingo games under Ben Weiss, authorized by Joe Fretti, attracted thousands every week.

Absenteeism from war plants was given as the reason James F. Byrne asked all the race tracks to close. Manpower and transportation were needed for the war effort. The volume of action in Toledo was never affected by the government order! Pay-as-you-go taxation was adopted in 1943, requiring withholding of taxes on employees. The Syndicate had to leave everybody on its own by reason of its illegal nature. Harry Manning of the IRS in Cleveland reported that each year after Joe Fretti gave him names of persons in gambling to be assessed, he raised the amount reported $5,000 each.[19] Since the tax brackets were 20-32% at the time, every altered assessment was paid. While objections to the "aerial figures" were made, the accountants recommended payment rather than an audit. Devon profits, a cornucopia of cash, could not be traced from the hands of the Underworld or politicians. It would wind up in somebody other than the owner's safety deposit box, in an investment under a front, or be washed out of state or through unnumbered Swiss accounts. In the Credit Suisse Bank scandal, the Italian government declared an amnesty for all citizens who brought their money back into the country. The response was magnificent.

Newspaper reports from all over the world reported a flight of capital from Swiss banks. If permitted in the United States, a like amnesty might produce a flood of cash dollars from "no show" to aid the economy and fight against inflation.

Hidden money became known as "no show dough." Nobody knows how much "no show" exists in this country. Economists have suggested that in hard times or shortages of cash that the government declare a moratorium on prosecution of tax evasion cases (the number of them are insignificant when considered in the light of benefit to the country) and allow this money to appear in circulation without inquiry or penalty.

Toledo's biggest business during the World War II was gambling and the newly-organized Syndicate, now called "The Mob," was its biggest moneymaker.

Scarne reported years later:[20]

> Gambling in the United States, despite all the Federal and State restrictions against it, is the leading industry in the country, both in the number of participants and the amount of money involved. Its handle surpasses the combined total money volume of the 100 largest industrial organizations in the country, including such giant corporations as U.S. Steel, General Motors, General Electric, Metropolitan Life, Ford Motor Company and any others you care to name. Today about 90 million adult Americans — of whom 43 million are men and 47 million are women — are gambling the astronomical sum of $500 billion annually.
>
> Almost 90% or $450 billion of this huge amount is wagered illegally; only $50 billion legally."[21]

Another student of gambling wrote, "50 million U.S. citizens gambled regularly in 1940."[22]

Toledo, though low in profile, was the real leader in the country.

# 24 The Payoffs

A system of payoffs was essential to the continuous operation of the Syndicate. Toledo politicians expected to be paid from every illicit operation. They insisted on dealing with a man who could be trusted to collect from every source and give them a square count. They all chose Joe Fretti. Joe became the number one man in the eyes of the public, police and politicians after the demise of Jimmy Hayes. For years, Joe, with his brother Ben, had been in gambling. Joe was extremely well-liked. A tall, bald man of a congenial, gregarious nature, he could be easily taken for a banker or business executive. Immaculately dressed in the finest tailored clothes, with expensive matching shoes, ties and vests, barbered, manicured and groomed, trim and thin, Joe was indeed an enviable figure. He always spoke softly, rarely in anger. The only words that provoked him was being called "Baldy." For years Joe was the most respected member of the local gambling fraternity. His word was good; the police confided in him and came to him when in financial straits. He rarely turned anyone down. He practiced charity in every police action, donating to their causes or social events, paying legal fees or expenses for them in any case, civil or criminal. His credo was "Buy 'em if you have to." He was able to get all types of favors in return. Many times, after making some "connected arrest," a cop would be asked by the captains to go out and see Mr. Fretti. "Do you have any objection to the bond being reduced?", the officer would be asked, after stating the nature of his mission. "No," was the usual answer. "Do you have any objections to the charges being reduced to a misdemeanor?" "No." "I take it you have no personal interest in the outcome of this case one way or another?" "Not really." "Thank you very much. Here is a little something to help you out." Then the cop would be handed a couple of hundred for his visit. It was obvious that each question was legally prepared and rehearsed. Each question was designed to increase the degree of involvement, criminality or culpability. Three "nays" usually resulted in a fixed case and a corrupted cop. It happened all the time.

Joe and his family were also well-regarded at the Board of Elections, the seat of political power in the city and county. His wife had become a heavy drinker. Friends claimed her lack of social life with Joe drove her to it. Whenever she wanted a bottle she would send word to the board of elections where Steve Shea, a Republican toadie, would promptly deliver it without any word to Joe. Joe was reputed to have been friendly with five girls, although none were ever seen publicly with him. Joe appeared ubiquitously in all the night life of the city, downtown restaurants or hang-outs, parties, sports parlors, funerals. Usually, his tag-along brother Ben accompanied him.

With an innate ability to provide solutions in internal dissension among underworld people, it was easy to understand why Joe was, by unanimous agreement, appointed to head the fantastic Syndicate as he became the payoff man handling the millions involved.

Joe originally had slot machines in the city and county. Pinball machines replaced slots. Joe knew that game. The city charged an annual license fee of $50 on each machine. It was easy to find out from the licensing agency how many units were on location. Merle Fike, of the Main Novelty Co., was appointed collector on the pinballs. Each operator had to pay the politicians $10 per month for each machine. The operators took off $3 per week in their split with the location, and paid regularly so that the city ordinances allowing pinballs would not be revised. Pinballs took up too much room and the take was too small for the space allotted. In all the games of the Mob gambling, contraband slots remained on the premises. Bingo was also big. Bennie Weiss had one of the biggest games in the county. He was to collect on bingo from all the dealers. All downtown gambling dens and sports betting houses were "advised" to contribute to Joe's pickup man a stipulated monthly figure for protection.

Anybody wanting to get into nefarious action here had to first see

Joe Fretti. He could give the word on whether any new operation went. When the word was "go," there was always a proviso for payments and protection. As a sideline for the dissidents who had no part of the Syndicate, Joe gave them an O.K. for fireworks sales in the county. What cost a stand a nickel to produce could be sold for a dollar. Occasional token raids by the sheriff took away $20,000 of goods a year but it only represented a mere $1,000 expense to the operators. A few locations operated year-round, but the majority operated from May through July 4. Most mushroomed, prospered and disappeared for another 10 months.

Little Frankie Gaustello of Detroit wanted to come to Toledo to bet or book a few games in sports. He was a likable, innocuous person without a criminal record of any kind. Pete Corrado gave him a note addressed to Joe Fretti stating, "This will introduce my friend, Frank. Anything you can do for him will be a favor to me." When Chalky Red wanted to collect on sports action from him, Frankie said he was only a small better and Pete had told him he wouldn't have to pay. That's the last Frankie ever heard of demands. His case demonstrated a manner of knowledge Toledo gamblers had on anybody or everybody in the city.

All manner of men tried to move Joe Fretti for privileges. Frankie Urban ran a small pinball route. He also owned a twin engine Cessna which he piloted. He took Joe Fretti and friends to Notre Dame football games, to Pittsburgh and Cincinnati baseball games and anywhere else Joe cared to go. Frankie wanted to get bigger and told Joe about it. Locations were saturated. If Frankie came up with something good, he knew Joe would help. In the cardrooms that he frequented, Frankie Urban met the Gould family and frequently played gin rummy with Jay Gould, an ex-pugilist. Jay had served time in the Ohio State Penitentiary for statutory rape. Upon release he tried professional boxing and got his brains beat out. He became a ne'er do well, a hanger on.[1] Jay and his brother Harry professed to being Jews, but their younger lawyer brother, George, renounced such faith. George felt Jews in the '20s would not be acceptable in big law firms. Upon graduation from Michigan, George joined a firm representing railroads including Pennsylvania and New York Central. The railroads, in turn, owned Greyhound Bus Lines. A newly-built Greyhound Bus Station had a large waiting room and plenty of space. Jay Gould and Frankie made a deal. If George, his lawyer brother, could get Greyhound to lease room in their station to them, Frankie would put in pinballs and make Jay a partner. In 1949 George Gould was elected president of the Toledo Bar Association., He played cards regularly with Joe Fretti and others. When Joe gave his O.K., it was easy for Gould to arrange a Greyhound lease to pinball operators, Urban and Gould, partners. Sworn testimony relating to this transaction was adduced in the Probate Court of Lucas County.[2] Jay had executed a will 20 years before, but it could not be found after his death so proceedings were held to prove the execution of such former will.

George testified, "Jay had a checkered career and a lot of peccadillos and unfortunate occurences...."

In 1949, he had just lost his job and was in desperate straits and found someone (Urban) who was knowledgeable in the amusement arcade business and who had proposed to Jay that, "If I could get them a lease of some vacant property at the Toledo Greyhound Bus Station that they would spend all the money, that is, this (Urban) friend of Jay's. To repair it, fix it up and remodel the place and could make a lot of money and I would have an interest in the business.

"This was a fifty-fifty deal between Jay and his partner, this man who was going to furnish the money, and I was to have 50 per cent of Jay's interest. In other words, a fourth of the interest.

"I had represented Greyhound Corporation since its inception in 1926 and I went to the President of Greyhound, Mr. Robert W. Budd, and made a full disclosure of this and they agreed to give him a lease so there was a lease given to the Amusement Arcade Company, which was on the surface legally, my brother, Jay."

Q. "Did you ever receive your share of profits from Jay?"

A. "No, I did not. That is the reason why he made out the will leaving his estate to me in 1952.

"I was supposed to get regularly half of $125.00 a week which was $62.50 a week and I did for about three months and this was starting in, say, the latter of '51, and then Jay became increasingly reluctant to pay my half of his half and made the proposal that he was ten years older than I and why didn't I just make out a will leaving everything to him so that he could be sure of something for his old age and then since I, in the normal course of events, would not die before he, he would then leave everything to me in lieu of which I was to waive my interest in the profits and also my half of what the proceeds were when the business was sold. That was done. That is how the will was drawn in March of 1952."

Jay's sister Minnie also testified that Jay "left everything to George because everything he was able to accumulate came to him as a result of his brother ... he owed everything to George."[3]

Jay Gould prospered as promised. He lived well, kept a woman and made frequent trips to Florida. When pinballs went out as games of chance to be played for amusement, he sold out in 1956 to Joe Yappolo, alias Joe Yapp, who was financed by his good friend Chalky Red. At the time of death, Jay left a $79,717 estate, all of which went to George. After collection, George retired and left the city being "hated by many," for reasons later related.

George Zilba was a likable, personable young athlete. While he was a partner in a 45-unit pinball route, he needed more to augment his income for a growing family. He asked Joe Fretti to allow him a pool room and poker game in a downtown building. Joe gave the O.K. The first night he was opened, Captain Gray of the vice squad raided Zilba and arrested everybody. Joe Fretti listened to Zilba's complaint. "Open up again," Joe said. Zilba opened again but locked the front door. A buzzer was installed for admission. After some delay in entry, Gray appeared. By the time Gray gained admission, the customers were seen lounging around. There was no action in sight. An angry Gray chased everybody out. He told Zilba to stay closed and not to defy his orders. Gray had sucker-punched other people when ordering them about. The vice-squad captain's philosophy of street life was to resort to force. "There's a class of people who don't understand anything else. Unless you whip them, they have no respect for you ... and they better listen."[4] Gray didn't try to manhandle Zilba. George was young, tough, could hit like the proverbial mule and had political clout. Gray had once broken the nose of Irving (Slick) Shapiro when he defied closing. A power struggle developed in Zilba's case! Fretti told Zilba to continue operation despite Gray. The show was on to see who really ran the town, Gray's vice squad or Joe Fretti and the politicians. Gray was honest but he still had to take orders. The next time he opened, Zilba operated continuously, without interference.

As for crime, the Syndicate actually told the local burglars and robbers what local jobs they could or could not perform, basically insisting that they take their larceny out of town but bring the dough back here for a cut, if they expected help or a fix in the future.[5]

The Mob knew who was operating by the modus operandi of the job. To their credit, it must be admitted that in the first formative years they kept the city clean from other criminal elements. When my brother Ben had a new topcoat stolen, a call to Chalky Red brought it back the next day. He atoned for his former act toward the family.

Pawnshops frequently were recipients of stolen goods in cases where fences were not used. Sometimes, if a person who gambled went a bit overboard, pawnbrokers would inform the Mob of such conduct. The police checked out pawned items daily. In one case, a burglary victim identified a typewriter as one taken from her home. She went to the police station to get assistance in its recovery. Before the police acted, a tip-off enabled the pawn broker to secrete the article. Where a victim in other cases identified stolen property and threatened to get a lawyer to replevy the same, the article would be gone before any papers arrived. Nobody had any rights in the property greater than that of the true owner! That's the law but the proof vanished! These favors paid off to the police and combination because the pawnbrokers, in return, would tip off information on buyers of guns or burglar equipment. To make the police look good, sometimes the Mob bought back the stolen article themselves at the price loaned and gave it to the cops.

A second Casino, Victory Club, was permitted to compete with the Devon Club syndicate in craps and horse betting. The purpose was to have a place for Toledoans while the Devon would cater to the Detroit crowds. "The Muzzler" managed the game and restaurant during the best hours.

To be called a "Muzzler" is to denigrate a person because the term has a foul, odious connotation meaning "no good" or "not to be trusted." Abe (Muzzler) Shapiro was a big, overpowering, officious kid from a family of means — *he* didn't have to hustle on the streets like many other gambling characters mentioned. They called him an overgrown dummy. At 16, he became chauffeur and factotum for Wittenberg, Jacobs and Berenson, the local bondsmen. One time, while drunk, he drove over a curb and killed a kid. There was too much publicity to allow a fix, so he had to go away. His contacts later permitted inveigling himself into the local mob. Friendships formed in the "can" under adverse conditions usually lasted a lifetime.

Perhaps the killing gave him a consciousness of guilt so that he felt a need for punishment and a desire to destroy himself. The Muzzler turned to gambling and became compulsive. Several of his associates complained, "Don't let him handle money. He's got the fever awfully bad."

While with the bondsmen, The Muzzler saw who put up the 10% on certain cases; knew who got tipped off in advance on raids or arrests and why. He learned which cops did favors for crooks or politicians (is there a difference?). Cases were marked off docket, affidavits for arrests or even search warrants were misplaced, delayed in filing, lost or destroyed. Money changed hands. Valuable Christmas presents were delivered. Bondsmen made a good living. The dummy was being wised up and getting a good buck for services in return.

There was always action around — sports, dice, cards. The Muzzler eventually became a high roller — he bet them all. He loved the role he played. Many gamblers, being typical loners, did not marry. Muzzler never did, but he bragged that he loved all broads with big tits. They held a fascination for him. He would do anything for one with massive mammalaries; he was obsessed. He stood 6'4" and spread 260 pounds over a large frame. With black hair, long bushy eyebrows and a perpetual elongated cigar in his "kisser," he appealed to many women. Others he bought. "Here," he would say, "if we are going out, buy something to wear." Then he would toss the broad a twenty or a fifty. One waitress wanted to get out of a date, saying, after spending the dough, "I have nothing to wear." It was pathetic to hear what a man of that size did to that little girl.

The Muzzler had to be in action. Whenever a fraternity or any organization had a smoker or stag at the Victory Restaurant adjoining, he was there booking the games, hogging all the bets. He was on stage — the star of the show. On baseball, football or sports, he laid the biggest bets. He could ruin a bookie. They knew it, yet he kept coming in — a real high roller!

In a skin game one night among the city rollers he won $100,000! The score was reputed to be the biggest ever in the city. He was advised to buy an apartment building or invest his loot. The owners of an apartment building wanted $107,500; instead of borrowing the rest, he reportedly blew all his winnings in two weeks. To complete his role as a big shot and showoff, The Muzzler had to have an audience. First it was Budrow's Delicatessen where he took his calls, made dates and played his scene. Later Brauer's Restaurant, where a larger crowd could watch his act, became his headquarters.

Despite his shortcomings, The Muzzler had police and political connections, so Joe Fretti used him. The Muzzler also knew that if he wanted to keep in action, protection had to be paid first. The manner of payoffs was the big thing. Constant care was required to this essential detail, else the entire operation could fold. The first count of the money was all-important. In Las Vegas, the siphoning off the top, or skimming, was done before the "profits" money was divided among the owners or partners. It presented an advantage to the parties counting, or having first counted, to steal what they could. If only one person counted, a danger existed. Here, the first count larceny, if any, would be in the nature and extent of payoffs that none could question as they involved, to a certain degree, matters of discretion and trust. Everybody trusted Joe Fretti on these problems.

The Detroit and Licavoli interests nominated their own Sebastian

(Buster) Lupica. He handled the first count for them with Joe Fretti. The ever-trusting Chalky Red was always present at the count for his segment of the combination.

In the Detroit scandals, after appeals were exhausted, there was a daily series of payoff stories of the "Boy Bandit" Boettcher.[6] He said "The payoff man, Elmer (Buff) Ryan took payoffs out of barrooms and alleys right into city hall and police headquarters. For Buff, it was a cold, methodical business proposition." The *News* printed more stories on the insatiable greed of high public officials, carefree immorality of police on the take, and the precision with which gambling bosses set about to keep their illegitimate industry alive. In Toledo, it would be the same.

Certain people had to be paid, regardless of winning or losing weeks. The "protection people" were not interested in hearing of losses. As long as they made no claims to the profits — the weekly cash envelope was to be delivered. The amounts set aside varied. Sometimes somebody on the list did a big favor and deserved a bonus or payoff; these were such situations Joe had to confront. Complaints would and did arise. When lawyers complained or made noises about gambling, Joe Fretti visited their offices. Then their shouting ended. Congressmen today use the same technique. Making noise about a company or an issue usually brought a lobbyist or spokesman with the wherewithal to end the controversy.

For unknown reasons, The Muzzler was given the assignment of settling claims with Toledoans. He used Ira Cole as the attorney. The Mob's prosperity allowed Dan McCollough to give up his police court practice to Morris Lubitsky, a well-liked criminal lawyer. Dan then became the society lawyer of the city. Big law firms did not relish divorce or criminal cases, and so referred such matters out to him. On settlements out of the city, McCollough and Harry G. Levy represented Mob interests.

Uninterrupted business required punctual, weekly payments. No lump sum payoffs for trouble were advanced. Past losses could be settled but nothing else. The logic and arguments were simple. The payee could collect in full and the joint could go under and be out in a week thereafter. The gamblers used "pay as you go" long before the Treasury Department adopted it as a policy in tax collections.

The town was under control. Unions, under Gosser and Steinberg, could hold industrialists at bay. Bankers were delighted with the large bank accounts and deposits. Only the church could be a source of concern. Dr. Parkhurst, in the New York of Lincoln Steffens' time, had routed the gamblers. In Toledo, the churches were tractable.

Contributions from the gamblers were not charity but purchase of peace. Yet such tithes made the contributors pillars of the church. Sheriff William Hirsch later wrote, "It was understood ... that professional gamblers would be tapped heavily for any and all charities. ... It was a comfortable arrangement all around, because many a civic improvement came from the gamblers, including new churches."[7] When Joe Fretti died, for example, four priests attended masses in an overflowing cathedral. Bennie Aronoff was later buried from his synagogue instead of the the usual funeral home. The Toledo Ministers Association stood against graft and corruption.[8] Walton E. Cole, D.D. of the First Unitarian Church, was the only clergyman the Syndicate feared. As minister from 1932 to 1941, his group grew to become the largest in the country. The church debt during his stay was reduced to nothing. As to whether the Underworld had anything to do with such achievement is conjecture. Cole's influence was so powerful that he undertook a series of radio rebuttal talks over station WSPD to counteract those of Father Charles E. Coughlin, head of the Shrine of the Little Flower in Royal Oak, Michigan. Cole's vigorous and outspoken denunciations in defense of social justice won him national prominence in 1939.[10] He was able to rid the air of Coughlin's influence. In 1941, Cole received a call to Boston's Second Church, established in 1649. In colonial times, Increase and Cotton Mather had preached there.[11]

There were even a few clergymen involved in "shakedowns." One would call every Monday if his envelope was not delivered on time. They referred to him as the "hypocrite" and rightfully so, but he was paid. Whenever he phoned, Joe would be told "the M.F. is on the line." Joe would take over: "Reverend, I am sending your money by cab right now." Joe was diplomatic, but the truth was he just couldn't face that kind of person. Whenever any business man was a big loser or made some complaint, a settlement had to be arranged with him or his attorney. A trustee in bankruptcy could sue for gambling losses. The Ohio law at the time permitted anybody to sue for gambling losses within six months of occurrence. A class suit could have been filed in those days — if one lived to collect! When a businessman went overboard financially, the Syndicate often arranged to loan money at 4% to 10% per month at Shylock rates. In this manner, Mob figures obtained interests in legitimate businesses when defaults occurred on the 48% to 120% interest per year!

If a dispute occurred, all settlements were to be reported so that the first count would deduct that figure. This is where the matter of trust entered the picture. A boss handling the complaint could tell the others "it cost twenty big ones" but actually only pay out five. Nobody else would check with his lawyers in Toledo or Detroit, so the matter ended on payment.

There was always chiseling and carping from within. Some politicians used spies during the week, to check on business done. Politicians wanted the biggest cut and insisted on being paid first.

When Joe and Pat Morrisey moved their operation out into the county at the Old Dix Inn, they employed Assistant Prosecutor Thomas J. Mattimoe's father as a clerk in their horse betting room. At Sheepshead Bay in New York, Mattimoe's dad had acquired the experience necessary to qualify. Tom Mattimoe occasionally would pick his dad up from work. Edwin J. Marshall of Marshall, Melhorn, Marlon and Martin and John McMahon had an affinity for the letter "M". It was natural to choose Mattimoe as an obscure attorney on the prosecutor's staff to do collections. He was assigned to evaluate the take through his father and other informants. Mattimoe was an ideal choice. He made so many new demands that Joe Fretti began to dread his calls, taking to swearing that Mattimoe was the toughest of all to settle financially. Prosecutor Tom O'Conner didn't have the stomach to cope with the political involvement. He feared a repetition of the Detroit scandal. Some said he was in deadly fear of exposure, particularly because of the amounts involved. When Joe Fretti came to brother Irv's office and put his name on the list of daily visitors, O'Conner screamed to remove Fretti's name and raised such clamor that his clerk-typist quit. Tom O'Conner resigned as prosecutor in 1942 to take a judgeship at $5,000 a year. His chief assistant, Joel Rhinefort, was selected by the judges of the county to replace him. O'Conner, they claimed, could not stand prosperity.

The prosecutor's position paid $5,000 a year. Rhinefort remained in office for 10 years, then he was replaced by Harry Friberg in 1952. They used an obscure black assistant prosecutor, Ben Fisher, to run bank deposits for them. Rhinefort had no children but reportedly sent a half million dollars during that period to nephews and nieces in Lawler, Oklahoma. Mattimoe also became wealthy, using his share to buy in real estate on foreclosure sales he handled through the prosecutor's office in his role as an assistant. The political shares for protection to the prosecutor increased proportionately after the deaths of McMahon in 1942 and E.J. Marshall in 1946. When Rhinefort was going to step down in 1952, there were political minds who favored Mattimoe over Friberg for the job. A settlement was reached that if Mattimoe withdrew, he would never be without a position on the prosecuter's staff as long as a Democrat held the office.

The first count men, Chalky Red and Buster, opened up a bank account as Lupica-Leonard, Inc. Creditors were paid in cash as were most business debts, but their accountant had to have some bank records. All dealer-employees received $20 a night in cash and had to pay their own income tax as shown on the 1099 statements annually distributed.

Pete Corrado would make weekly visits to pick up payoffs for the Detroit interests including Zarelli, Licavoli, Giaclone and Massie as principals of the Italian faction while Maxie Stern handled the Purple ends. On paydays, little white envelopes would be filled. Joe would order cabs to deliver to those he despised or those in whose company he could not or refused to be seen. Joe would be chauffeured around by a trusted driver. He would stop by each of his five lady friends to pay some financial favor. He would stop at the Safety Building and go into the *Blade* reporter's office, there to deliver an envelope. In that case, he didn't care whether the public knew or not. Steve Shea would pick up a package of envelopes for delivery to the boys at the Board of Elections. In the summer months, Joe would go to Sunnydale Golf Course, rent a golf cart and drive about the layout or to the pool or clubhouse dropping off his obligated pay. Irv Miller, owner of Sunnydale, was asked if he knew the people Joe gave money to on these visits. "Sure I do," Irv replied, "but I won't tell you."[12] In the winter months, Joe would meet his clientele at Bus Carbin's Recreation Center or at downtown hangouts such as Charley Bassett's or George Haddad's. When Timiney was sheriff, James McGrather, a bartender at the old Navarre Hotel, would be called over to the pay phone area and receive a weekly envelope from Joe. Later McGrather would brag, "See this envelope? It's got ten $100 bills for the sheriff and I'll get one."

Once a month Joe was driven to Columbus. There he met Firetop for the boys in the pen and others. Ex-*Blade* reporter John Jack Flanagan was asked, "Do you know who gets envelopes from Joe Fretti on his visits to Columbus?" "No," he replied, "but there were a lot of them."[13] The Miller and Flanagan statements, although negative in response, indicated knowledge that statewide payoffs took place. In addition to the regular police, prosecutors and politicians, the Mob retained a Christmas list for gratuities. Cases of expensive whiskey or Scotch would be delivered to most judges and courthouse personnel. Police and public officials would be invited to Whitey Besase's house or to Chalky Red's for special Yuletide envelopes. As long as money was being made, everybody was paid.

When people wrote or spoke of "second governments," in retrospect, they were referring to the Combination of that time. With labor on their side, with industry paralyzed by fear of strike reprisals, with political power and unlimited finances, the Syndicate controlled an entire city, and would continue to do so for a period of 15 years! Those who corrupted ruled the corrupted! The Mob eventually could call the shots on anything short of murder — and they usually did. Incredible, but true![14]

In 1967, the President's Commission on Law Enforcement and Administration of Justice issued its task force report on organized crime. The study focused on the politics of vice in a town the editors called Wincanton, USA.[15] Gambling and corruption were viewed as social forces and political issues. The problem was the same in any city of any size in this country. "Capone ruled Chicago because he controlled politicians. Politicians could always be bought."[16] To claim that the gamblers operated in Toledo without political protection is an insult to the intelligence of any student of American culture.

It takes no great stretch of the imagination to figure that if a public official is making $3,800 a year and sending his children to private schools costing $5,000 a year in tuition, such official is making money from another source. Or if one sees less-than-mediocre lawyers like Thomas Mattimoe and Joseph Jan Sr., who would have a hard time earning a living in competitive practice, accumulating wealth and fortune, then one can surmise that their funds are from sources outside the law.

I had all the elements necessary to write the chapter on payoffs. I was an "A" student of history, had the inquisitive mind of a journalist, had received the education of a lawyer and had had early and continuing exposure to the people and environment that supplied the necessary facts.

When I was transferred in the seventh grade from La Grange to Sherman School, it was reported that I had an IQ of 185. This qualified me for placement in the "A" class, among the best students. One day I was called out of the cloakroom, where I had been confined for "cutting up" in class, to take a surprise examination in history consisting of 103 questions. The highest grade would get to sit in the first seat in the first row on the right of the teacher, Daisy Knight. I got a perfect score in that extemporaneous test; the next highest score was 94. In grade school, high school, college and graduate school, I received A grades in all history or history-related courses. History was my forte!

My first venture into politics was my election as president of Claire Humphrey's freshman English class at Scott High School. My lifelong friend, David Seretsky, was elected vice-president. The only difference between the two offices was that the vice-president was required to clean the erasers and blackboard. Dave later became secretary of Local 12 at the Willys Overland, the activity of which has been previously reported. The only distinction I ever had at Scott was winning the foul-shooting contest of 34 out of 40. I received two season tickets to football games, but the team was so bad that I couldn't give the tickets away.

I never had time for high school activities, leaving early from last period home room to work. One great interest on the outside was in the Newsboys Association, where I was a member of the Boyville Council. I was involved in an election for Boyville mayor and while I thought I had won, Chief Cook announced Charley McCarthy as the winner. I learned then and there that the one who counts ballots in secret holds great power. All the members of the board of trustees, which included many business, industrial and political leaders, knew me from my speeches at their meetings.

Later I was elected president (Aleph Godol) of AZA, the junior order of B'nai Brith. We held raffles to raise money for basketball uniforms and road trips. I went into the offices of Benny Aronoff, Ben Harris, Joe Fretti and the card rooms and crap joints of the city to sell tickets. I knew all the bosses by name. One day I won a beautiful electric toaster in a sales contest. When I reported the news at an AZA meeting, it was suggested that the toaster be included as one of the prizes. Max Mallamad and Sol Sharfe told me not to worry. We raised the money to win the Ohio basketball championship at Cleveland and the Indiana championship at South Bend. When the raffle ticket winner was to be drawn, Sol stuck a ticket on the side of the box holding all the entries. The first two tickets won minor prizes. Then Sol reached in and plucked the ticket for the winning number on the toaster — Esther Illman The toaster never left the house. It was hard to be honest when prizes were at stake.

Now we wanted to go to Louisville for the Indiana, Ohio and Kentucky regional championship. Our order of B'nai Brith balked at our request for funds to make the trip. "All they want to do is play basketball," advisor Bernie Jaffe reported. "You have to enter the oratory contest if you expect them to help." "O.K.," I said, "We'll have an oratory contest at a B'nai Brith meeting." The winner would go with the team on the trip. Three orated. I won. The B'nai Brith supplemented our funds by $400. Seventy people, the largest contingent of members, coaches and friends in Toledo history, went by train to Louisville for the three-day tournament. I won again, and, with our team, the right to go to the national finals in Kansas City.

In the meantime I finished high school and had a job in a downtown garage, parking cars and running an elevator, working 60 hours for $15 a week. One day Mr. Robinson called for his car and I delivered it to him.

"Harry, why aren't you in school?" he asked.
"I graduated in June."
"What about college?"
"How can I go? I have to work."
"Nonsense, you come up to see me in my office. We'll arrange something."

I learned he had previously helped several others. My family decided it was an opportunity I should accept. Mr. Robinson gave me $100. $60 was for tuition, the rest for books. My family promised to help with the rest. I enrolled at Toledo University in February 1937 as a journalism-history major. Six weeks later, our AZA trip to Kansas City for the national finals in basketball and oratory came up. My mother asked me not to go, but I didn't listen, as usual. On a two-lane highway outside of a small town, Roberts, Illinois, south of Chicago, a 10-ton truck and trailer smacked into the car carrying our six-man team. It was St. Patrick's Day, March 17, 1937. I awoke on an operating table where a friendly doctor was applying a plaster of Paris cast from my chest down to my toes — "fracture of the neck of the femur," he called it. The operating table was also my bed as they had no other place. They didn't know about surgical pins then. Two days later my sister drove down in a two-bed ambulance to take me and Sol Sharfe, with a broken pelvis, home. Some farmers helped us into the ambulance. In gratitude my sister bought a crate of eggs — it was Passover — which she placed under our cots. About 15 miles from the hospital, the one-armed driver of Pierstorff Funeral Home (I didn't know it at the time) tipped over into a 20-foot ditch on the side of the road. He had been drinking. Sol flew out the back door; his cot hit me in the teeth, loosening 11 of them. The eggs splattered all over me and my cot on the impact. I was bleeding profusely. When the state police lifted us up to the roadway, I deleriously yelled, "Call Kansas City and tell them the champs are on the way!"

Another ambulance took us back to the hospital for repair of the shattered cracked cast. They gave me a large dose of morphine for pain and arranged our return to Toledo by train. My cast was now too big to go through the window of a compartment so I ended up in the baggage and mail car of a mail train. It took 10 hours to get to Toledo. When the dope wore off, I drove the mailman nuts.

Within a day after I was admitted to the hospital, bringing the most beautiful bouquet of red roses I ever saw, came Mr. and Mrs. J. W. Robinson. Wonderfully fine people! I was too emotionally involved to do anything. "We'll start all over any time you're ready," Mr. Robinson said. Then he shook my hand as though we had closed a deal. He made me feel wonderful.

I was a good patient. The nurses always had a laugh over what I said or did. I had phlebitis, pleurisy and other complications. My legs and veins swelled. My cast had to be removed. I was developing a shortening of one leg unless operated upon. So they put me back on the table — rebroke my hip with a hammer and chisel, then reset it. I wore a cast for months. Then when I was released, I used a brace and crutches and cane until healed.

My oldest sister Sadye again hired Harry Levison as family lawyer for my personal injury claim. The attorney hired Chicago counsel to file a suit in federal court against the trucking company who had the advantage of having an adjuster on the scene in half an hour after the happening. Levison settled the ambulance case for $1,500, his favorite figure. This was before our trial in Chicago. After a week of trial, we lost. The defense claimed all my injuries were due to the ambulance crash, not the truck. I was a minor, age 18. I had two years after becoming 21 to sue Pierstorff, an Ohio resident. Liability was clear. He had insurance and was collectible even for punitive damages for drinking. There was no valid reason for an earlier settlement. This was the second case Levison had loused up and the inevitable third would be the worst.

My journalism career consisted of editing the *Newsboy Herald,* for which I won the gold, and the *AZA Kibitzer,* which circulated in the Jewish community. Nat Charnas, publisher of the *Jewish News,* had me edit his paper where I had a feature column entitled, "Rebbi Says Good Shabbes." Nat owned a number of theatres and I got paid in show passes and entertainment. I became campus editor of the *Campus Collegian* — third name on the masthead — and had a shot at being editor but for the time lost due to the accident.

In my junior year I was elected to Alpha Phi Gamma, national honorary journalism fraternity. The journalism courses were taught by William E. Hall, an editor of the *Blade.* During the summer, I handled some publicity for the city recreation department, headed by Gordon Jeffery. My brother Ben helped with his political speeches, so Jeffery gave me summer employment. One year, while I was in charge of the tennis courts at Bay View Park, I fell asleep in the sun and was badly burned. I complained to the golf pro, Vern Royer, "If you don't send one of the caddies over to wake me up when the shade moves, I'm gonna tell Jeffery to fire you." It was our classic joke. I had free run of Jeffery's office and the *Blade* news room and city desk, submitting occasional copy.

One summer while I was handling publicity for the city playgrounds, Scott Park was going to open a new swimming pool. A beauty contest was to be held. As I gathered the publicity, Jeffery gave me a picture of the beauty contest winner two weeks before the event!

I was disillusioned. Toledo has so many pretty girls!

I didn't like it. Jeffery was going to be watched. I knew sooner or later something would be uncovered on him.

I was active on the Toledo campus: French Club, International Relations, Lambda Chi Fraternity, paper and yearbook. Since I was spending all my time at school, friends suggested I run for Student Council. My campaign manager did what no other candidate had done before or since. He had his uncle, Sam Fine, take my literature in his plane, fly west of the campus and drop my pamphlets into the east wind, carrying the flyers all over the area. I didn't get elected, but I did wind up in the dean's office on a charge of littering of literature. Knowing my physical condition, however, he let me off with a reprimand.

My AZA friends and college fraternity were kind. Once a month they came over to my house, hauled me by car to the still existing brothels, and chipped in the requisite dollar for me to get my ashes hauled. That was true fraternity. We had many enjoyable episodes. As the girls strolled around in their see-through diaphanous gowns, one would select a member of our group and lead him gently up the stairs to where the action took place. One guy started coming on the second stairway. The girl grabbed the dollar and led him through the living room to the john as we roared with delight. Another time I would hear my friend begging one of the girls as she washed him, "Don't touch it. Don't touch it. Awww ... you touched it." he spent his dollar in the basin. "Didn't we tell you to jack off before you went up?" "Yeah, I did twice, but it didn't help," was the usual rejoinder.

I was unhappy with the prospects of a journalistic career and told Mr. Robinson so. "Switch to law at Ohio State," he suggested. "Only three years of college credit is required ... so you make up the year lost."

My grades were about 3.3 on a scale of 4. If I had stayed at Toledo University for the final year, I might well have graduated *cum laude,* but I switched, so I never had a class year.

Mr. Robinson got me into the Buckeye Club for my first year in law. I lived in the stadium, walking all the way across the campus to get to class. There were only 106 freshmen. Half of you won't be back," the faculty warned. They were right — only 52 returned for the second year.

One of my best friends at Ohio State was fellow Toledoan Donald S. Teller. He was the driver of the car involved in the accident in which Isadore Topper's mother was killed. Donnie stayed with Top, in Bexley, a Columbus suburb. Many times he stayed over with me to study late into the night. After Pearl Harbor, Donnie got his draft notice. I was host for a surprise send-off dinner at the Topper home. All the Toledo graduate students in law, medicine and dentistry attended. Doctors Harold Poneman, Bernard Shuer, Dave Sheer and Sid Schall, and dentists Mel Cohn and George Shopneck were there. We gave Donnie a fur-lined jock strap, money clip, duffel bag, a gross of rubbers and other necessities. While George Shopneck and I told stories, it was really very sad. Six months later Master Sergeant Donald S. Teller appeared before me on campus. He stood 5 feet 6 inches, with wavy hair and dimpled cheeks; his formidable fighting weight of 140 pounds, without an ounce of fat, made me very proud of his presence against the enemy. "I made Officers Training," he said. "They are going to make me a bombardier in camp." He didn't have to go. I knew Top could have arranged through Harry G. Levy for him to stay in the States. "I'll write regularly, pal. Take care." Six months later he was in the European theatre. Then word came that in a 38th mission over eastern Germany or Austria his plane and entire crew was reported missing. Years later, the same group that had been present at his farewell smoker, including me, attended memorial services for Donnie in Toledo. I can't remember one word said because my mind was clogged with thoughts of what might have been.

I worked my way through school with the help of Mr. Robinson. His efforts to get me into Army Intelligence failed because I flunked three physicals. The 162 stitches on my right hip discouraged the medics. The best I could do was donate blood which I did regularly, giving a total of 18 pints during the war years.

My principal jobs were in the Supreme Court Law Library in my freshman year, Legislative Reference Bureau part of my junior year and as a page in the Ohio Senate in my senior year. Bureaucracy at work was always overstaffed and underworked, but I never analyzed the problem at the time. While working for the Supreme Court, I was reminded of my visit to the U.S. Supreme Court on the trip down to Washington, D.C. in 1936. Before being seated in the courtroom, I was able to obtain the autograph of the Chief Justice, Charles Evans Hughes. After the impressive entry of the Court, the justices proceeded to read aloud their decision declaring the Guffey Coal Act unconstitutional. People can't hear that fast. Judicial decisions are meant to be read, studied and perused — not heard. To me, it seemed that continued practice was a waste of the Court's time and the taxpayers' money. The Court got enough exposure and publicity without it. In this day of media coverage by radio, TV and newspaper, it is superfluous. The U.S. Supreme Court could do itself and the country a service by abolishing this long-standing precedent. The Ohio Supreme Court did not have a high regard for the U.S. Supreme Court, particularly after reversal. This was the impression I received in my work there. The judiciary, it seems, engages in a lot of carping. As Justice Oliver Wendell Holmes once wrote, "Lawyers spend a lifetime shoveling smoke."

My politics were Republican. I became president of the Young Republicans on campus, president of Tau Epsilon Rho legal fraternity, and senator from the Law College to the Student Senate. One of the later politicians I met while a student was Howard Metzenbaum of Cleveland. He displayed insatiable greed and love of money at college. Metzenbaum ran a bike rental business and charged his fellow law students, including fraternity brothers, a fee for his advice in answering examination questions.

Gambling was minimal at college — pitching pennies and betting on weekly football and basketball games. Edward (E.) Walker was stationed at Fort Hayes while I was at Ohio State. I often got to use his car in exchange for favors in driving him around. E. had been in the tire business, but he liked gambling better. I never knew how he could have made the physical. He was overweight, 250 pounds on a 6-foot frame with a pendulous girth. He wore very thick glasses and I felt that he couldn't see anything 10 feet away. I occasionally played Casino with Bob Milkman, a Columbus bookie. One day, E. wanted to make a big bet on an Ohio State game, but because he was in uniform, he was afraid he would be refused. I placed his wager and when I went in to collect, Bob asked, "Who's he?" I replied, "He's my heavy in case I have any problem collecting." Then I introduced E. The two gamblers became fast friends.

As president of the Jewish Legal Fraternity, I was the authorized agent for Abraham B. Gertner's Bar Review Course. In exchange for my services in recruiting students, I was given a free cram course for the Ohio Bar. Abe also had a legislative reference service where he followed the course of legislation in the Ohio House and Senate, and reported the status of various bills to interested parties or lobbyists. In my senior year as a page in the Ohio Senate, I learned a great deal about the legislative process. Most of the members of the Legislature were there to make money and most were men of small intelligence or intellect. The two senators from Lucas County, Virgil E. Cramer and Raymond E. Hildebrand, were nice guys but were "order takers" rather than leaders. The majority leader of the Senate was Stanley Mechem, a shoe salesman. Paul M. Herbert, Lieutenant Governor, and John W. Bricker, both lawyers in the executive branch, were of exceptional qualification, but the legislative branch, to my observation, consisted of a very poor lot who made much ado over some things to do.

One incident stands out in my memory. Frank S. Day of Cleveland, Cuyahoga County, used a well-known name to get elected. He was burly, heavy set and apparently uneducated. On the one occasion that he chose to introduce a bill, the Senate tittered with laughter. In fact they openly snickered. His speech was the shortest on record. His own 40 members ridiculed him. Day was one of the old school who believed that graft and privilege came with election. He later demonstrated such philosophy upon being elected county recorder. A deputy, granted immunity, turned him in to answer for 27 charges of swindling. Day got one to forty years. Politicians have a reason not to get educated people elected. People that are too smart are a danger.

The motto of Sir Francis Bacon was "Knowledge is power." Lincoln wrote, "You can't fool all the people all of the time, but you can fool enough of them to rule a large country."

"Democracy is the most difficult of all forms of government since it requires the widest spread of intelligence, and we forget to make ourselves intelligent when we make ourselves sovereign."[17]

Ignorance lends itself to manipulation by forces that mold public opinion.[18]

I received an LLB degree in June 1943. The only thing I was remembered for in law school (if indeed I was remembered at all) was my retort to Professor Frank R. Strong, the acting dean who taught Constitutional Law. One very foggy day I walked into class about 10 minutes late. "Sir, why are you late?" Professor Strong inquired. "To tell the truth, Professor," I replied, "I couldn't make up my mind whether to stay in the fog out there or come into the fog in here." He let out a roar of approval and I was forgiven.

I stayed in Columbus after graduation to study for the bar exams. The night before the three days of tests were to begin, I wanted to relieve the tension. I wandered into Roundies, a cigar store on High

Street with a crap game in the basement. I won $100. I thought winning was a bad omen, but I sailed through the exam with a grade in the upper third. After the third day many gathered to celebrate in the Deshler Wallick Hotel basement bar. I proceeded to pass out. The pressure and booze got to me.

On my admission to the privileged profession, Mr. Robinson suggested that I join the office of the attorney general of Ohio for experience. Topper recommended me. There was a shortage of lawyers; I could have gone anywhere. At a munificent salary of $1,800 per year, I became an assistant attorney general of Ohio. The title, plus the occasional use of a state car, filled me with a sense of pride. I was full of the proverbial vim and vigor, piss and vinegar, but became disillusioned within a year. The Attorney General was the lawyer and legal advisor for all State departments and agencies. His constituents constantly wrote in requesting opinions. Every morning a general meeting was held to evaluate the opinion being drafted by an assistant. I listened and learned. My real education began with our work as the collection agency for all state claims — taxes, insurance losses, hospital bills for state institutions and such. Whenever I would be on the verge of collecting a big amount, the file would be taken from me and forwarded to specal counsel in the city of the debtors. Special counsel would complete the collection and take one third as fees. They would be giving the taxpayers' or state's money away. This was the party method of rewarding its backers for raising campaign funds. They all did it. I didn't like it, but there was nothing I could say or do.

My boss, Thomas J. Herbert ("The General," as we called him), wanted to become governor. In Ohio, running for governor was equated with running for the Presidency. They year 1944 was a year for state elections. The General's slogan was:

Thomas J.<br/>
on the 9th of May.

I brought literature up to Toledo for him and campaigned among friends. At the scholastic level, the battle to get elected is fun, but in governmental politicis it is sheer warfare, for serious money is invested; losses are hard to take. I brought some fellow attorneys general up to Toledo for the campaign.

An alleged irregularity occurred in the primaries. My boss asked me to contribute one month's pay of my meager salary for a vote recount. Top said I had to comply. Already disillusioned by referral tactics and the preferential treatment given to certain lawyers in liquor board cases, I tendered my resignation. Neither titles nor positions of power impressed me. I vowed never to enter politics, for the party or bosses ruled in most instances. A man's mind was not his own. I felt I would never be able to comply with orders on a partisan basis alone. I planned to practice in Toledo.

The word "coif" originally referred to the white silk wigs worn on the heads of ancient English "Sergeants at Law." Later, the American Order of the Coif was established at all leading law schools as an honorary society for chosen students. Usually the top 10% of the senior class would be elected. Julius "Hodge" Jacobs made Coif at the University of Michigan College of Law, one of the best in the country. He was also a compulsive gambler. He had plenty of business for Bennie Berenson, a bondsman, was his uncle and referred numerous lucrative criminal cases. As soon as Hodge made a fee, he would rush out to the crap joints in the county to gamble, come back broke and repeat the process the next day. But marriage reformed him. He and his wife bought an Army-Navy store that did a thriving business in the war years and after. Julius tired of the law and had little zeal to practice.

Hodge's father Joe was a stalwart Republican, and Hodge's former partner was Clyde Deeds, later a Republican spokesman who became Toledo's best trial lawyer. Visitors to Jacobs' office talked of elections, disgruntled losers, politics and graft. I listened. When Jacobs wanted to go into the sale of fireworks, he talked to his friend Harry G. Levy, who got the O.K. for him. Hodge made a lot of money; he kept it in large envelopes in my safety deposit box. He was uxorious. He allowed his wife Marge to go to Florida for six months at a time. During her absence, he never resumed his compulsive habits and advised me repeatedly, "You can lose it a lot faster than you can make it."

I did part-time work for Fink and Canelli. I had known Fink since childhood at the newsboys. Even then in the distribution of Boyville money, he displayed greed and cupidity. The kids called him "Hungry Fink," and you can't fool kids. He used me. He had me sign documents which he filed and never paid me. When I complained he said, "Didn't I loan you $500 without interest?" Canelli was much kinder and a gentleman. I gave Fink a wide berth. It was in their offices that I learned of the role of Joe Fretti and the mention of Tom Mattimoe, previously mentioned in this chapter.

When I joined Jacobs' law office, he referred most of his legal work to me. I kept office hours form 9 to 3 and then took a job as an expediter on the second shift at the Spicer plant which manufactured gears and transmissions for army tanks and trucks. Mine was a white collar job. With an excellent memory for part numbers, I would chase (expedite) movement of critical material through the plant. My boss, Pat Casey, liked me. I began collecting money for his St. Agnes Federal Credit Union. I passed out cards to everybody, getting all kinds of legal matters — real estate closings, business deals, divorces, etc. I never missed a day and had more money than I had ever had before. I didn't have time to gamble. When the war ended, the tune changed.

I bet at every bookie joint in the city. I was a frequent crap shooter at the Devon and Victory Clubs. I knew most of the dealers and bosses by name. When I was losing at craps and had a winning baseball ticket, they called the book, paid the ticket and I simply continued to play.

One time I got lucky. After the last of the Sunday baseball games had ended, a large crowd remained at George Shamy's Academy. Charley Bassett, one of the partners, hustled a crap game. Since the craps in the county were primarily for Detroiters and Charley was a boss out there, he didn't think they would mind. The doors were closed to preclude interruptions. This was the first and last time a crap game was held in one of the downtown joints.

The reason was that the game didn't last over 20 minutes. Practically everybody went broke except me. I had the dice. I pressed and doubled every bet. I took all the odds anybody offered to lay. I made seven passes and was shooting over $2,000 when I came out with 10 as a point. Nobody wanted to lay the customary 2 to 1 odds. The money didn't mean anything to me. I said, "I'll lay everybody 2-1." I liked to gamble even if I took the worst of any bet. Many hidden twenties, fifties and hundred dollar bills were thrown on the table and covered 2 to 1. Like Big Julie in "Guys and Dolls," I made 10 the hard way. In disgust, Charley Bassett threw the dice over a wall in the back room and broke up my fantastic unfinished hand. I won $18,000 in cash, $4,000 in markers and title to a new black Cadillac convertible with a white glass spun top.

There was talk, envy and gossip and eventual adverse publicity. Enemies in the bar talked much about image. There was more to come. Thus I became a natural for writing a chapter on payoffs, combining my investigative reporter's instinct, good legal education and exposure to the milieu. I knew who and what to ask to produce the requisite information. Such are the facts of life.

## 25  A Toledo Suicide Compared

Early in 1944, George D. Wilcox, a 54-year-old Detroit businessman, became a desperate man. His gambling losses were driving him mad. For years he had been a compulsive gambler. As a reader of the Detroit *News,* he knew the Ferguson graft cases, and what it had done to gambling in that city.[1] From Detroit sources he was directed to crap games in Toledo. He began commuting in 1940. In two years, 1942 and 1943, he admitted dropping more than $30,000 at the Club Devon, losing as high as $2,500 in one afternoon. In 1941 he had obtained a loan of $2,100 from the gamblers here and signed a note or a release from all claims thereafter. His continued reversals and inability to cope with the constant problems of creditors, family and business drove this distraught victim to the verge of suicide. He contemplated such action unless he could recoup his losses by approaching the gamblers for more help.

On January 4, 1944, he called on Kenneth Tooill, managing editor of the Toledo *Blade.* At the time the court appeals were over in the Ferguson cases, the Detroit *News* printed daily stories of corruption as told by the "Boy Bandit," Buddy Boettcher.

The papers circulated on Toledo streets. Tooill reported "Mr. Wilcox was calm, reasonable and unreservedly intent on pressing one point home — that lives should not be wasted as his was." It was further stated that he gave no hint he intended to kill himself, yet no report was made on what Wilcox meant by "a wasted life."[2]

At 6:50 p.m. that same day, Wilcox sent a telegram to Ben Aronoff demanding an immediate meeting and restitution of funds. He threatened, "If you fail in this and do not make the refund Tuesday morning, I shall present evidence of your interstate operations in my case to the federal government. I demand the return of my money without further quibbling."[3]

He threatened suicide and enclosed a detailed affidavit of his dealings with the Club Devon and Webster Inn. More than 15 months before, he had tried similar tactics but backed down after rejection. In 1942, at the time of his former threat, he had gone to the office of Dan McCullough "to impress the attorney (for Aronoff) with the repercussions which might follow if I talked to the F.B.I. and the Grand Jury." He was given a brush-off then, according to his notes.

On September 17, 1942, he first stated an intention to do away with himself because of "mental anguish as a result of gambling losses." He prepared an affidavit which he sent to the F.B.I. detailing his gambling contacts in Toledo. He had a conference with an F.B.I. agent that year. He had also engaged a Toledo law firm who had taken up the matter in 1942 with the then-prosecutor of Lucas County, Ohio. The prosecutor advised "he would present the matter to the Grand Jury if Wilcox was prepared to testify." The investigations failed to proceed further as there were no records found of intervention by either state or federal authority thereafter. Whether this disclosed the strength of the Toledo organization is a matter of conjecture. Wilcox apparently was relying on the Detroit Ferguson results in making his demands. He did not know what Janet MacDonald knew about specific payments to certain police. Wilcox's voluminous correspondence laid no evidence to incriminate them. It was obvious he neither appreciated nor comprehended the local strength of political connections. In 1942, after reporting all he knew to an F.B.I. agent, he allegedly wrote to the President, U.S. Attorney General, Ohio Governor Bricker, the state attorney general, the mayor of Toledo, chief of police, the police prosecutor and like officials in the State of Michigan, who have no jurisdiction over crime in Ohio. Nothing ever developed from all such communications, strengthening the Syndicate's position in refusing his demands and overtures. Wilcox erroneously believed that the one-man jury of Michigan's system would produce a similar investigation from disclosures in Toledo.

In Ohio, the grand jury of 12 or more is called by the prosecuting attorney of each county to investigate alleged criminal activity. When such jurors are assembled, the prosecutor subpoenas such witnesses as he desires the jurors to hear. Such witnesses are not subject to cross-examination, for the proceedings are *ex parte,* one side only. The prosecutor generally advises such grand jury and his advice and recommendations are generally accepted. Consequently, the grand jurors can be manipulated. But a one-man juror like Judge Ferguson presented a far different picture. Had Wilcox been advised of these differences and of the strength of the Toledo organization, his life may not have been wasted. Yet who was there to tell him what many knew, but none would discuss? There was too much money being made to allow one disgruntled loser to spoil the entire operation. Homer Ferguson, the one-man juror of Detroit, was zealous, ambitious, desirous of a higher office, such as U.S. Senator or governor, and above all was not involved in the corruption and thus irreproachable. Wilcox also was not aware that Detroit reformers were active in 1939 while Toledo reformers were dormant. He also failed to recognize that the Toledo *Blade* was not the Detroit *News* in pursuit of gambling reform.

When the deadline Wilcox set in his telegram was ignored, he began at midnight to write the suicide note that would be delivered to the *Blade* at 3:00 p.m. the next day, with copies to the U.S. Attorney and to the Toledo chief of police. Wilcox wrote: "I am giving my life today for a cause worthy of your attention and relentless campaigning to rid this section of the country of the gambling racketeers who have preyed upon the weaknesses of such people as myself and who are destroying whole families without regard for the war effort."

The *Blade* was forced to print the story first, else recriminations would have developed elsewhere. Tooill reported "The records... in the voluminous correspondence mailed... are so explicit and make such direct accusations that public officials immediately set in motion efforts to utilize the information for crackdown on gambling."[4]

Wilcox, in poignant agony, before taking a powerful overdose of sleeping pills, concluded his death missive. "If they cannot legally convict the guilty parties on the evidence I submit, it is a sad commentary on American justice for never has any remorseful man persevered to a greater extent in his effort to make last-minute amends with no other hope of reward than that others may be saved from the torment brought upon my loved ones and the ignobility of my fate."

He died that those afflicted with the same disease of compulsion might be saved — Jesus would have approved, forgiven and loved him — anywhere but Toledo.

His attempt to become a martyr by calling upon the Toledo *Blade,* "one of America's Great Newspapers," to take up a crusade in his behalf could be regarded as ludicrous but for the solemnity that death brings to such events.

Unlike the Detroit *News,* where there was concern over a life being wasted, the *Blade* wrote one or two stories then put the lid on the case. The Syndicate public relations people with the *Blade* did a magnificent job under extremely adverse conditions. One reading the *Blade* story might have some sympathy for the gambling fraternity, in that portions of the articles indicated Wilcox was attempting to blackmail or shakedown the boys in return for his losses. Since they once paid him off, they felt he had nothing more due. Sheriff Hirsch, later commenting about the suicide, wrote: "He (Wilcox) had not gambled in Lucas County for over a year because he was refused admission to any of the joints. He lost about $30,000 at Detroit Race Tracks and the investigation confirmed this. He'd come to Toledo in desperation ... The poor fellow had been drinking, and he did take an overdose of sleeping pills."[5]

Had Wilcox survived his lethal dosage, then attempted to file charges, in all probability he would have been arrested for blackmail to counteract such move. In a gambling community, these situations are common. Where a loser complained to the police, the vice squad often told such complainant that he also could be booked for engaging in a game of chance. Usually that ended the matter. If a loser persisted, many times the gambler would be charged. Then police would charge the loser as threatened and both cases would be dropped on splitting of court costs. It happened in Toledo that way all the time.

From the few stories the *Blade* wrote after the death, public conscience, curiosity and interests were aroused. The public had to be satisfied that justice be done, which, in a gambling case, meant Toledo style! The Detroit *News* exposé series on the "Boy Bandit" ran coincidentally with the *Blade* stories on Toledo gambling.

The *Blade* headlined its January 16, 1944 issue "Bricker (Governor) Orders Gaming Shutdown After Suicide."[6] The governor's quote laid it right on the line when he said, "There is not a gambling place in the state that could not be closed if local officials want to act." Then hedging as the others did, he added, "Law enforcement is a matter for local officials as the state does not have any enforcement machinery." No one from that office had intervened for 50 years prior and Bricker wasn't about to be the first. Governor Bricker appointed Edward DeAngelo (Toledo Safety Director) and six police officers as special deputies to investigate gambling. The *Blade* reported these men went out to the Devon Club on January 27, 1944, opened a safe and took $24,000 as evidence to be used at trial,[7] but this evidence was never used.

The second-day story on the Wilcox suicide in the *Blade* had one line below the headline on the extreme left — "Michigan Patrons Urged to Stay in Own State" — while another line to the right read "Devon Reopens in 30 minutes after 2nd Raid." A Michigander reading such paper from left to right wouldn't know whether he was being warned or invited.[8] Detroiters knew where they could find the answers. The Devon remained open for months after the death with business as usual despite the publicity. A delay was necessary to enable the operation to be moved to a new location. The Webster Inn, Chesterfield, Pines and other locations were held in reserve in event of need. Finally Forest Park, a large hall used for roller skating, was renovated as new headquarters. "Fish wagons," a shuttle system to haul customers to the new scene of action, were installed. Customers on buses arriving from Detroit would be instructed to park or drive to designated areas from which fleets of vehicles would transport players to and from the new locations. Harry "Butch" Petler, who had testified against the Licavolis, was in charge of the "fish wagon" fleet. He was a good mechanic and driver so the Syndicate forgot all past problems and gave him a good job. One of the better 21 dealers was Sam Stein of the same trials who changed locations with his gaming employers.

After a few trial runs with "fish wagon" drivers, the Mob permitted the Devon to be padlocked, for it was business better than ever at new quarters.

Comments of other local officials were also published by the *Blade* on the Wilcox death. The U.S. District Attorney was quoted as saying that he "would carefully investigate the charges to determine whether or not Federal statutes have been violated." The "pay as you go" on withholding had recently been enacted. The income tax of the gamblers, whatever amounts, were being paid. There were no facts to charge any federal offenses. Also there was no desire to make a case where no complaint was filed. The skirts of the U.S. Attorney were clean.[9]

County Prosecutor Joel S. Rhinefort stated, "I would like to have anybody who has information get in touch with me so that they can appear before the Grand Jury." This was tantamount to asking for volunteers to commit suicide. Hedging further, he added, "If necessary, I will ask the judges for additional funds to make a complete investigation because funds allotted to this office are inadequate."[10]

Sheriff Charles E. Hennesey, a former police officer, was equal to the prosecutor. "We know, of course, that there is gambling in this county. We were out just the other night on other raids. We are handicapped by lack of men and equipment but we are constantly on the alert and intend to continue the campaign we have been waging. The public does not understand that we have 10 times more work to do than that involved in gambling control."[11]

For the public, to make sheriff and prosecutor look good, a token Devon raid was made but tipped off in advance. *Blade* reporters were permitted to inspect the premises and take pictures. As soon as the photographer packed his equipment, spectators and employees headed back to the covered tables.

Wilcox should have realized Toledo had more important issues and problems. Although the prosecutor allegedly ordered the sheriff to station men at gaming spots, the weekend wartime business was as good as ever — three shifts, 24 hours a day.

Resentment of suicide and death in gambling coupled with curiosity of the public would not permit the local authorities to drop the Wilcox case. Out-of-town reporters, visitors and several local civic leaders kept pressure on the problem. Somebody had to pay. The politicians were obliged to act to "make themselves appear to do their duty."

A theatrical production was to be enacted! The authorities had to protect themselves otherwise the protection for gambling would fail. If they exposed themselves it spelled the end of a very lucrative adventure. The fall guys had to be the gamblers! There couldn't be anybody else! If done through court procedures quickly, the public and press, if any, would be satisfied. Local gamblers were reminded of the Detroit debacle under Ferguson and how it got out of hand. Under such duress, the gamblers were at the mercy of the prosecutor. Arguments made by gamblers that "we're all equally guilty" were answered by the politicians stating, "so we all go to jail. You still have to go and do time for a felony. The fact that we don't go keeps everything alive." Although the inequities were obvious, the operators were promised a favorable deal. A court charade to make the politicians look good was to be staged.

Seven weeks after the suicide, on February 25, 1944, indictments charging 26 members of the gambling fraternity were returned by the Lucas County Grand Jury.[12] If ever a case existed for elimination of grand juries, this was one. The jurors were lay persons, they knew little or nothing of law, the machinery, mechanics, their rights and powers. A prosecutor could dominate such panel and usually did. Their function was a mere formality, for the prosecutor gave them what evidence he desired them to know, calling such witnesses as he wanted them to hear and prepared such charges as he thought fitting for them to sign. He literally led them by their collective noses under the guise of public service or duty. Further, the grand jury sessions were secret so that neither press, public, the defendants nor their counsel were entitled to know the nature or manner of proceedings, only the results. Indictments were made known when arrest warrants were issued for those named. When booked on the charges, $2,000 bond was set for the principals. Joe Fretti, Ben and Joe Aronoff, Joe and Pat Morrisey, Tony Paul and 20 others were named. In the Ferguson inquiry the prosecutor, sheriff, mayor, the mayor's son and numerous police officials were named in Detroit. In the Wilcox death in Toledo, no police or political figure heard a breath of scandal!

The Ohio law at the time contained certain bribery statutes as criminal offenses. One defined the crime, "if a person corruptly give or offer any officer of the state or judicial officer anything of value to influence him in respect to his official duty . . ." the penalty would be one to ten years and removal from office.[13] The Ohio law further permitted the State or prosecutor to give immunity to a party to a bribe in order to obtain testimony to convict the others.[14] Bribery was a felony, a crime punishable by a year or more in a penitentiary.[15] All other offenses, including gambling, punishable by lesser penalties, were called misdemeanors. This was before the Criminal Code of Ohio was revised and updated.

Several Ohio cases held gambling on horses or craps to be crimes under the Ohio definitions of wagering. Gambling laws were to be liberally construed.[16] Each day's violation constituted a new offense. The attorney general of Ohio had written a classic opinion (No. 444) years before in response to a query about dog-racing in Madison County. In this opinion, entitled "Methods available to local law enforcement officers in dealing with violation of Gambling Law," the attorney general advised: "The Sheriff has the duty of preserving public peace. It is his duty, when he had knowledge, to take proper action to secure punishment of all crimes committed in the County, within or without the city limits."[17]

"The Prosecuting Attorney is empowered to inquire into commission of crimes within the County and it is his duty to prosecute on behalf of the state . . . all violations of state laws."[18]

Listing the courts that could act and the various procedures available, the attorney general's opinion concluded: "Under statutes of Ohio, these officers are fully armed with the means to effectually enforce the laws against gambling."[19]

A series of interesting peculiarities occurred in the trial of the gamblers.[20] Ordinarily, when indictments are filed, the statute alleged to have been violated is cited on the charge. This was not done. A multi-court indictment charged all 26 with "Keeping a Room for Gambling" — a misdemeanor with a fine of $30 to $500 and 10 to 30 days or both — and "Exhibiting Gambling Devices", carrying a $50 to $500 fine and 10 to 90 days or both. Misdemeanors generally are filed in a court of lower jurisdiction, like the Municipal Court of Toledo, but that was not done either. The prosecutor did not want to lose control of the case in which he was duty bound by law to prosecute. He was being paid by both sides to do the job. He was indeed in an enviable position.

The frustrations in being duty bound to send the gamblers to jail while making the politicians look good entailed as many legal convolutions and machinations as the Watergate case.

Joel S. Rhinefort was a good actor and a shrewd prosecutor. He claimed to have won 98 of 100 murder cases including participation in the Licavoli trials. Many of his victories were questioned on appeal on grounds of misconduct of counsel where Rhinefort attempted to convert examinations into arguments. He continuously repeated damaging vital testimony, although this was legally impermissible. Repetition was tantamount to argument before the allotted time.

An Ohio statute specifically put a three-year limitation on misdemeanors, stating, "no person shall be indicted or criminally prosecuted for a misdemeanor unelss commenced within three years from the time the misdemeanor was committed."[21] Yet Rhinefort went back to 1938 in the gambler's case! In addition, he charged that gambling had occurred at the Webster Inn and Academy Clubs. Both of these were closed when the Devon Club opened, more than three years before.

The purpose of the multiple charges was to distract attention from the Devon Club. No mention was made of the Victory Club or its principals as it continued operation during this entire episode. In a subpoena issued to Sam Kaplan, an outstanding Toledo attorney, Rhinefort asked for Devon and other tax records since 1938. If he went back that far, did he know what was going on then? Yet trial counsel did not attack the indictment on technical grounds as statute of limitation being a bar to prosecution. Instead, the defense attorneys headed by Dan McCullough demanded separate trials, which motion was denied.

The defendants fought for time, arguing that the Wilcox suicide would have occurred regardless, but the politicians were equally adamant. Somebody had to go to jail to make the picture look right. The gamblers balked. They wanted a better deal for what they were paying. The gambling trial started on April 10, 1944.[22] Only 13 of the 26 charged went to trial. News of the trial crowded the war events on the beaches at Anzio, Italy, off the front pages. Counsel for the parties first fought over which side should have the table nearest the jury. Judge Lehr Fess, whose family had long-standing Republican ties locally and nationally, ruled in favor of the defense. An entire week was taken in selection of a jury. A new panel had to be summoned.

Rhinefort told the jurors in his opening statement that gambling profits at the Devon were $11,000 daily, but often as low as $4,139. He said the lion's share went to Ben and Joe Aronoff with Joe Fretti and Tony Paul getting 10% and Ben Fretti 5%. The trial dragged on slowly. When Special Investigator Edward DeAngelo took the stand two weeks later and PFC William Gray arrived from his Marine base at San Diego, ready to testify, a recess was called. The curtain was to drop on the farcical drama.[23] A compromise was reached. Out of public glare, Mob leaders remonstrated for only a few to go. "No, it was not enough to satisfy the public. Another stink could develop," they were advised. Conviction of all the defendants might have presented problems for the prosecution. But they knew the publicity had created a public conscience demanding punishment. Finally 13 of the 26 charged, changed their pleas to guilty.[24] Bennie Aronoff, whom Wilcox charged as most responsible for his death, got five months and a $3,500 fine, his brother Joe, 120 days, Joe Fretti 90 days and 10 others received 30 days each.[25] Among these were Dave Applebaum, who was alleged to have loaned the money to Wilcox. In effect, he was the Syndicate "bank man" arranging for deposits of out of town checks to be cashed for the gamblers. Out of loyalty to Aronoff, although neither gambler or owner, he consented to serve 30 days. Because he had slot machines in his restaurant at the Devon, Isadore Mitchell was involved and jokingly consented to go. While Mitchell was in jail, the Devon Club was placed in court receivership. All of his valuable silverware, dishes and kitchen utensils were stolen and had to be repurchased when he reopened his restaurant at Forest Park skating rink near Genoa a month later. Tony Paul and Al Schaub were among the other defendants receiving 30-day sentences and $1,400 fines. The court suspended sentences on remaining counts against Aronoff and Joe Fretti on the condition that they refrain from further operation.[26] Joe and Ben Aronoff already had new men fronting for their interest while Ben Fretti, who was not named, could easily protect his brother's interest. The fines totaling $20,125 were paid immediately by chief defense counsel, Dan McCullough, to Gordan Jeffery, clerk of courts. The prisoners were allowed time to arrange their affairs and report for confinement on May 1, 1944 at the city facilities at Whitehouse, Ohio. During the week between the sentence and incarceration, Prosecutor Rhinefort addressed an Exchange Club meeting in a downtown hotel.[27] The *Blade* reported that he spoke of gambling, stating, "Few people know the real character and evil of commercialized gambling ... the serious matter is what the gamblers and mobsters and others of their ilk do with their profits. ... They're not satisfied to let their huge returns flow into proper channels of business, but they use it to corrupt government and enforcement."[28]

When a person is convicted of a crime and sentenced in the Common Pleas Court of Lucas County, as the 13 were, the normal procedure would be to send such persons to the Lucas County Jail. There the county absorbs the costs. Only city prisoners are sent to Whitehouse. In a question posed to more than 20 veteran criminal lawyers of the city representing over 400 years of cumulative experience in criminal cases, they unanimously agreed it would be a most unusual procedure to send county prisoners to the city workhouse. None of those attorneys questioned had ever heard of another case like it!

The benefits of change were obvious. The county jail was overcrowded. It was old, filthy, with small cells and without outdoor recreational facilities. It housed felons awaiting trials or transfers to penitentiaries. The workhouse held only misdemeanants, mostly drunks. In the summer months, county jail conditions would be stifling. Furthermore the county jail was downtown between the court house and the police station. The public could see the comings and goings and guess about unusual activity in between.

The city workhouse at Whitehouse, Ohio, was out in the county, secluded. A high wire fence would keep intruders at a distance. There were few prisoners. One section of large rooms could accommodate the entire group in one area. They could bring in their own mattresses, bedding, fans, radios and have freedom of the grounds with unrestricted visitation and telephone privileges.

The unusual confinement for this unique plan was prearranged. The superintendent of the workhouse was William Hirsch. He was brought into politics by his boyhood friend, Harry G. Levy.[29] After serving for two years under Mayor Solon T. Klotz, a Republican ally, Gordan Jeffery, had him reappointed under the first city manager in 1936 at double his original salary.[30] Hirsch was indebted to Levy and Jeffery. For his role in arranging jail facilities, Jeffery was able to obtain his first funds for an investment portfolio.[31] The Mob could afford to be generous. In later gratitude, they contributed funds to all Jeffery campaigns to make him the biggest vote-getter in the county.[32]

As the group found Hirsch tractable they would later back him financially in a bid for sheriff.

Bets were made that the group would be allowed to go home at night or serve less than full time. Newspapermen came from all over the state to verify the confinements. Hirsch turned chicken. He was afraid that Fred Siebert, safety director, would raise Cain on absenteeism. If any prisoners were discovered on the outside, he felt there would be hell to pay.

In his book, Hirsch said, "The gamblers ate the Whitehouse meals and liked them. As for going home at night, they were much too tired after a day's work. There's a difference between shuffling cards or rolling dice and mopping a dormitory floor."[33]

This statement was not true. Most of the inmates had elevated themselves socially. From early coffee house menus and all-night eateries, most became addicted to filet mignon at high-priced restaurants. On first encounter, it was said, many drank the finger bowls until learning proper etiquette or protocol. They also matured in sartorial splendor in a style that included regular manicures. Few, if any, touched soap suds at home. When questioned on the sheriff's story, one stated, "Politicians should write comics instead of books." When asked if they ever mopped floors while confined, most grinned sheepishly and refused to answer.[34]

While those convicted in the Ferguson shake-up went to penitentiaries and were put to hard labor, the Toledo gamblers had a picnic at the workhouse.

They had one or two large rooms, good mattresses, bedding and fans. They had the freedom of the grounds. Many visitors came and went bringing rich foods, steaks, snacks, cigarettes, tobacco, fresh fruit and cards.

The summer weather was good. They were permitted outdoors. Al Schaub, one of the 30-day defendants, had the use of a farm tractor. He drove over to Whitehouse daily to buy 30 or more breakfasts which the prisoners ate or distributed to others. Friends brought in food at noon or night without surveillance.

On Sundays, Monsignor Jerome Schmidt said, "We had the largest collections ever in the history of the workhouse." Even the Jewish defendants went into Maumee or Whitehouse with the others on Sundays for Mass. The Jews stayed outside or in the vestibule. To pass time, they listened to sports on their radio or played cards. Some wagered on the games as lines were phoned or brought to them.

A barber was in jail on a drunk and disorderly charge serving 30 days. He shaved the gang regularly and gave weekly haircuts. Another inmate had a relative deliver a shoeshine kit and he also was in business. The Mob tips were generous. The leaders became extremely popular with the other prisoners because of their lavish spending. They were soft touches for gifts of food or money to help others make bond or release. "Mr. Fretti, please give me money to pay my fine," prisoners begged. They emptied the jail by giving court costs or fines to fellow inmates. When the barber's time expired, he went out to a public place, got stinking drunk and disorderly deliberately so that he could be recommitted to Whitehouse because he was making more in the workhouse than in a shop.

The Ferguson felons came out of penitentiaries broken in spirit and health. All of the Toledo 13 served full sentences, with time off for good behavior. They emerged in good spirits. Their business of craps and horses went uninterrupted. Seven or eight different locations were available if needed. A central parking system was devised to transport customers to and from such locations. A downtown parking area was also opened. Syndicate employees directed out-of-towners at bus and railroad depots to "fish wagons" on the scene. Taxicab companies were advised of changes. The new system of transportation and protection of cars of players worked.

After the Devon Club receivership, the Syndicate learned to put title to real estate of new locations into the name of a non-resident of Ohio. Hyman Chait of Detroit was a frequent owner of local real estate. This move was advised by the lawyers. Non-residents were entitled to notice before injunctions or padlocks could be applied. Precious time could be gained before legal service of process was completed. Service on out-of-state owners required publication by newspaper notice, another time-consuming action.

The Wilcox death taught the Mob a few beneficial lessons that enabled them to outlast all other similar establishments throughout the country.[35]

# 26 The Capone Connection

Wagering on the outcome of horse races has been big business in the United States for more than 100 years. In the early history of the sport of kings, three distance stake races for three-year-old thoroughbreds were inaugurated. They were the Belmont stakes at Belmont, New York, in 1867, the Preakness at Baltimore in 1873 and the Kentucky Derby at Louisville in 1875.

Racing a horse hitched to light sulkies at trotting or pacing gait began about 1850. Various fairs and racing circuits were established for sulkies in the formative years until the Hambletonian Stakes for three-year-olds was inaugurated in 1926. A circuit for harness racing nationwide then ensued. The origin of horse racing is lost in time, but it was evidently derived from warfare, chariot racing and the chase. Horse racing has flourished in every major country throughout the world. One of the earliest references to horse racing in England was given by the secretary to Thomas à Becket, Archbishop of Canterbury in the reign of Henry II (1154-1189), when he described how "the jockies, inspired with thoughts of applause, and in the hope of victory, clap their spurs to the willing horses, brandish their whips, and cheer them with their cries."

In America, horse racing reached maturity in the 1860s with the emergence of sire lines founded on importations from England.

Regulations by state commissioners protected the sport in early years.

The New York Jockey Club founded in 1894 issued the racing calendar, maintained the American Stud book and compiled handicaps. The Daily Racing Form became the house organ or the Bible for bettors in the bangtail industry. Its turf library on horses, breeding and racing was the most complete in the world. Among other classic items, it contains the Daily Racing Register beginning with the edition of 1709 and the British Racing Calendar beginning in 1743 and has every stud book ever printed. The Daily Racing Form was published in eight cities, including foreign editions in Toronto and Mexico City. At the time of this history in 1945, it had recorded results of 20,000 horse races a year. It had a circulation of 150,000 daily at the peak of the summer racing season. The racing form originally cost 25 cents and a purchaser received a small pencil with each purchase. Gradual increases were to 35 cents, 50 cents, 70 cents, a dollar and today's price of $1.75. The early development of this one sport which permitted wagering gave the horse racing industry tremendous advantage over all other sporting events. It was the biggest spectator sport in America, until surpassed by basketball in the 1950s. In 1946, 598 tracks were in operation for harness and thoroughbred meets. Some only held a few days of racing. In 1945,[1] the *Saturday Evening Post* reported that $1,306,514,314 poured through pari-mutuel betting machines, an increase of 16% over 1944 despite a federal ban that knocked out four lucrative months of the prior season.[2] Upon organization of a race track, many states began to tax their advantages by taking a percentage cut of gaming revenues. Large tracks flourished under state sanction. Legislatures refused to declare "pari-mutuel betting" constituted gambling, for that would be illegal. It was labeled a form of lottery to evade the constitutional provisions prohibiting gambling.

Before installation of pari-mutuel totalizer or tote machines at the race tracks in the 1940s, only one system of horse wagering was used.

Pari-mutuel betting was a system devised to compute the odds to be paid by the track to the bettors on each horse at the end of any race. From the total amount bet, the state's share was deducted and the balance divided according to the amount bet on each horse in the race. Such division determined the odds. Each track would have an employee count off the tickets at four or five windows. He would look at the number of the tickets remaining in the seller's box to determine the number sold. Such figures of sales would be quickly calculated and the odds changes would be noted every 90 seconds. Bettors purchasing through a seller's window would be paid odds calculated in such manner by the track. To accommodate large crowds, each track permitted bookmakers to operate at the track for a stipulated rent to be paid. Bookmakers would make their own lines on each race. Prior to the races, a morning line was established. If a bettor wagered on the morning line with a bookie, he would be paid such odds quoted regardless of the odds calculated by the track at the end of the race. In the days of Pittsburgh Phil and Bet A Million Gates, these stalwart gamblers would send 20 or more agents into the line of oral bet-taking bookies. When they all wagered at stipulated odds, the bookies would be stuck at such price. Betting coups could be manipulated because there was no way for bookies to change such odds. Often the bookies would rush to the windows and lay off as much money as they could. A horse that would pay 20 to 50 to one by a bookie often paid track odds of six to five or eight to five or less. This action taken by bookmakers to minimize losses on any given race was often necessary. Where the bookmakers themselves or runners went to the track windows to reduce the odds on a given horse, the action was called come-back money. Money bet off the track was coming back into the windows.

It was once reported that Gates won over two million dollars in the old days on a horse called Royal Flush while Phil became a multimillionaire through his race machinations. Eventually, bookies set a limit of 15 to one to win. Since there was no way to accurately compute place or show prices, an arbitrary limit was set and 15-6-3 became the general odds quotations. It meant six to one for place, three to one for show. Where a horse was held out at 6 to one odds, the morning line paid two to one for place and even money for show bets so "6-2 and even" became a familiar quotation.[3]

Horse betting parlors, called handbooks, accommodated bettors who could not go to the race track or those who lived in distant cities. Rooms were established in every city of the country. Many cities had several parlors, operating under political and police protection, for such wagering was illegal. To further service such action, wire service providing results immediately following each race was provided. The benefits of wire service were manifold. Bettors could bet on every major track in the country. Free race forms would be provided by the house for their use. With complete wire service results from each track, bettors could spend an entire afternoon and have action all day. Since each bet gave the bookie an edge, there was a tremendous advantage to hold bettors in the rooms throughout the racing day rather than allow a bettor to come in, make one bet, then await the results overnight and collect the next day.

Newspapermen played major roles in the early days of wire service. In the early 1930s, James M. Ragan was circulation manager of the Hearst newspaper, Chicago *Journal American*. Moses Annenberg was also a circulation manager. Annenberg bought into the Daily Racing Form for $750,000 and eventually became publisher. Ragen became his general manager and head of Nationwide News Service, which had monopolistic connections to supply race results to thousands of handbooks across the country on all major track race results. When Annenberg was convicted on tax evasion charges in 1939, Ragan took sole charge. The corporate name was changed from Nationwide to Continental Press, without duplication of service. To forestall Mafia interference and restrain underworld muscle, Ragan brought Arthur B. "Mickey" McBride of Cleveland into part ownership and management largely because of his connections to underworld syndicates. McBride had been head of the Chicago *News* circulation department in 1913. His experience in circulation — involving, as it did, use of gangland muscle and contacts — was similar to the conduct of the circulation wars in othe cities, including Toledo. Musky Wexler of Cleveland had a wire service direct from some tracks to handbook subscribers who paid $50 or more a day for such service. Others had similar services in other sections of the country. Ragan sought to monopolize such service through his McBride associations. Their income was phenomenal. McBride later became a millionaire, acquiring newspapers and control of the Cleveland Indian baseball club. When questioned later by the Kefauver committee in 1951, he denied underworld affiliations.[4] It was estimated that the amount of off-track betting was three to four times the amounts being bet in track windows. Each subscriber had to pay a daily minimum for wire data and often "spotters" from wire service would visit the operation, determine the volume of business, and demand a higher fee or proportionate share of the profits.

For years after Annenberg's incarceration, Chicago area bookies refused to pay Ragan for wire service. Instead they paid Hymie "Loud Mouth" Levin, lieutenant of Jack Guzik, nominal Syndicate head. The Capone Mob demanded 50% of all Continental income "or else." Ragan, in turn, demanded payment from Levin as Capone representative. When Levin refused to pay, Ragan cut off service to the area handbooks. Levin and Capone interests started reporting the same service through the formation of a corporation known as Trans-American Publishing and News Service, Inc.

Competition was costly to both sides: handbooks could choose to bargain and pay less. Each side was adamant. On April 29, 1946 two gunmen attempted to take Ragan's life. They pursued him from his home to a Chicago police station where he found refuge. Ragan told police he was marked for death by the remnants of the Capone Mob because of his refusal to cut them in on his service. Ragan was persuaded to hire two ex-policemen as bodyguards. On June 24, 1946 Ragan stopped his car for a red light in downtown Chicago. His two bodyguards were directly behind. A shabby delivery truck covered with a tarpaulin pulled alongside the right of Ragan's car. Quickly the cover was pulled aside and shots blazed from rifles or a machine gun. Bullets tore through Ragan's right shoulder.[5] The gunmen drove off as the guards followed with blazing guns. Twenty shots were exchanged but no one was injured as the gunmen escaped. Their truck was later found abandoned with two guns in it.

Ragan lingered in a Chicago hospital for weeks, finally dying from the bullet wounds on August 15, 1946. The police received a 98-page Ragan affidavit setting forth details of the Capone gambling operations in the Chicago area. He accused Syndicate members of large-scale income tax evasions. Ragan stated that his racing news organization paid $600,000 to politicians over the country for protection in Depression years between 1934 and 1936.[6] No prosecutions followed these disclosures. Ragan deliberately avoided naming current politicians for fear of retaliation in his business connections. His estate was estimated at $550,000 with no value being placed on his interests in the wire service "because of the danger of operating it," his lawyers explained.[7]

Ragan's heirs were not as adamant as their father. They capitulated to Capone demands, selling to McBride of Cleveland. The Trans-American competitor went out of business. Continental Service, with McBride and Chicago associates, became a monopolistic operation. For 10 years thereafter, the Cleveland wire services retained former *Blade* circulation manager Abe Joffa as a spotter to check on the amounts to be charged.[8] Informants stated $100 a day was paid for wire reports during the week days while Friday and Saturday payoffs were $500 to $1,000 or more. Georgie Gordan, formerly of Brooklyn Murder, Inc. and Moe Dalitz, a former Detroit Purple gangster who had moved to Cleveland, became the carriers and liaison of Capone shares from Toledo to Chicago. The Syndicate and operators of the Victory Club (which used such wire service) preferred to pay spotters' demands without quibbling rather than irk Cleveland and Chicago mobs into muscling in on what they knew was established as "a very good thing."

## 27 The Kefauver Investigation

The greatest show on television in its early formative years of the '50s was the Senate investigation into national crime, headed by Senator Estes Kefauver of Tennessee. His name became a household word.[1] TV exposure led to his being selected as vice presidential running mate with Adlai Stevenson in the campaign of 1956. Without pay of any kind to the principals, TV stations had a field day exposing Congressional hearings on interstate crime to the American viewer.[2] The big-shots of national crime were on candid camera. Many balked at public hearings, for they preferred a low-key lifestyle. Early witness Frank Costello of New York refused to be photographed on TV. His refusal was upheld. The TV cameras concentrated on his twitching fingers and hands, which moved continuously about his body and the table near his chair.[3] Later, betting commissioner James Carroll of St. Louis, who set the sports lines over the country at the time, also refused to testify before TV cameras.[4]

Kefauver took his show on the road, scheduling hearings in big cities all over the country.[5] In hearings in Detroit, he heard, "The people who run Toledo live in Detroit."

Twelve years later, Detroit Police Commissioner George Edwards told a similar McClellan Senate subcommittee, "Mafia is big business. Their principal product is fear. ... The Mafia front men are characterized by the smile, the glad hand, the tuxedo and ticket to the charity ball, but the basic Mafia tools are still money, murder and corruption."[6] In January, 1951, Kefauver issued subpoenas for Toledo principals to appear before his committee and counsel in Cleveland.[7] Subpoenas went out for the current sheriff, George B. Timiney, his predecessor, Charles L. Hennessey, Joe Fretti, Ben Fretti and Tony Paul. All were served and appeared except Tony Paul. The U.S. marshall notified Kefauver and his committee that they were unable to find the last witness. The missing gambler's wife told them her husband "just got in a car with a friend and went to Florida."

Ohio governor Frank J. Lausche voluntarily appeared to tell the committee Detroit gamblers recently tried to get into large-scale operations in Lucas County. He said, "There was a Webster Inn and Benore Club there. I closed the Benore Club a couple of years ago."[8] The statement could be misconstrued. While the Benore Club could have been closed, the shuttle "fish wagons" brought players elsewhere or that the closing of one or two locations did not mean cessation of action.[9] Lausche's other attempts to close down Toledo gambling a year later were also frustrated.[10] The governor's statements relative to Lucas County were made while he was relating his experience and difficulty in getting all sheriffs to cooperate and stop gambling.

The first witness called was Sheriff Timiney. Kefauver had made a personal visit to Toledo months before, and observed several gambling places in full swing in addition to slot machines being played "by children in restaurants outside the city limits." Now he confronted the witness who was sheriff at that time.

The Senator repeatedly asked Timiney to explain continuance of wide-open gambling in view of his election campaign on a reform ticket. The sheriff insisted he had campaigned to drive gamblers out of the county and had done so. Timiney was kept on the stand until midnight.[11] His testimony, in part, was as follows:

Q. Have you ever heard of any gambling in Lucas County?
A. What do you mean?
Q. Have you ever heard of the Pines?
A. There is no gambling there. A fellow lives there. (The Senator failed to follow-up to ask who "the fellow" was for the answer would have been, Whitey Besase.)
Q. Do you know Joe Fretti?
A. I have known Joe Fretti since I was eight or nine. Yes, he has been in my home.
Q. Do you know anything about the Webster?

A. No.
Q. Ever raid it?
A. No.

Lucas County records showed that on March 19, 1941 Timiney had arrested the financial secretary of the Carpenters Union for embezzlement of $4,073, which he told Timiney he had lost at the Webster.

After listing a number of locations, Timiney was asked, "Are these places listed as disseminating racing news?"

A. Yes, I guess so!

Q. Have you ever been offered any bribes to keep these places running?

A. No sir.

Q. Didn't I ask you last Saturday whether you, and your tenure, had been offered bribes, and didn't you say you had?

A. I've been offered bribes for years, but they don't mean a thing. I've never received any.

Q. Can you name anybody who ever tried to bribe you?

A. No, I can't think of anybody now.

Timiney had given the committee a list of his campaign contributors and a copy of his tax returns.

Q. Who is James McGrather, who contributed $1,000?

A. He is a retired tavern keeper.

This is the braggart mentioned earlier in the payoffs who handled the sheriff's weekly envelopes at the old Navarre Hotel.[12]

Q. Are you a gambling man, Sheriff?

A. I play the horses once in a while. I won about $6,000.

Q. Didn't you get that money from the gamblers for allowing them to operate?

A. No.

Q. Weren't the Frettis and Aronoffs glad when you became sheriff?

A. They are always glad to get along with the sheriff.

Q. The places are wide open. Why didn't you close them down?

A. We go out there and chase everybody out.

Q. Did you ever arrest anybody?

A. You have to have evidence. We can't get evidence.

Q. Where did you win this money on horses?

A. At Hazel Park in Detroit and Fort Miami.[13]

The Toledo Junior Bar, in its annual Gridiron show lampooning the political life of the city, had a story on Timiney in its newspaper, the *Bar Rag*. "The Sheriff won at the races because he was able to bet with the bookie after the races were over."[14] This is called past posting. Sheriff deputies would go into the clubs, look at the race results of the day and then write out a three or four horse parlay. It would then be turned in for cash payment. In that way the sheriff could truthfully say he won money on the horse wagering.

Kefauver took Timiney as the first witness because he claimed to be sick. He had been hospitalized four times during his term of office and appeared to be ill during examination. For these reasons, further pressure was not applied. Two days before he was to leave office the largest jail break in Lucas County history occurred.[15] Nine inmates escaped by sawing their way out. The jail had concealed microphones to record noises but his "deputies weren't using it to the fullest extent," Timiney claimed.[16] He called it "wanton carelessness." The men squeezed through two sets of sawed-off bars after filing for 12 hours. Five of the escapees were recaptured within two days. Timiney died within a week thereafter on January 8, 1953.

Charles L. (Spike) Hennessey was the second Toledo witness. Hennessey became a captain on the Toledo police on October 17, 1932. He served on the vice squad and knew the Mob. He was induced to run against Democrat James O'Reilly in 1940 and won two four-year terms (1940-1948). Kefauver wanted to question him about his large farm near Grand Rapids, Ohio, stocked with choice cattle and other property acquired after his election.

Hennessey said he closed down the Webster, Benore, Chesterfield and Victory Clubs, but they would start up again in a few days. He said he and his deputies had given all the time they had to anti-gambling work and had broken up "more than 400 pieces of gambling items." Hennessey swore his net worth included a 116-acre farm, which he purchased for $14,000 or $15,000 and added about $6,000 for improvements.

Wood County farms were valued at $400 to $1,000 an acre, but the sheriff was not questioned on the price per acre. The house on the farm itself was worth the amount stated. Nor were questions asked about the value of the herd of cattle or the dairy farm Hennessey purchased two years after his election.

Hennessey stated his annual salary was $4,888. He admitted building a $12,000 home in Toledo and owning a late-model Dodge.[17] When Hennessey died on November 15, 1961 it was rumored that more than $200,000 in cash was found under the rugs in his farmhouse.

Joe Fretti appeared without counsel. He explained he didn't need any attorney "to tell the truth." He was perfectly candid with Kefauver. He said he had been in the gambling business since the repeal of Prohibition and that he had control of or an interest in eight gambling casinos. Included were the Benore, Devon, Webster, Pines, Chesterfield, Victory, Westwood and Evergreen, all in Lucas County. He did not mention any current place of operation nor was he asked whether he had offered to bribe any public official. Even without counsel, the Kefauver committee suspected the witness could then invoke the Fifth Amendment and refuse to answer any question that might incriminate him. Fretti said that he had been a former taxi driver and virtually all his present estimated net worth of $300,000 or more came from illegal ventures. The one time he tried legitimate business was in the '20s, when he attempted to establish a recreation area like Cedar Point on Lake Erie called Willow Beach. The deal nearly bankrupted him. He labeled his one try at legitimate business a "fatal mistake." He lost about a million dollars.[18]

The committee was so surprised at Joe's truthful revelations that they excused his brother Ben from testifying but continued to ask about the errant Tony Paul. Kefauver was disturbed by his obviously willful absence and said he intended to do something about it, as he subsequently did.[19]

The last Toledo witness was Gerald Eldridge, chairman of a gambling action committee that started a grand jury investigation of Toledo gambling in June 1949. Although Prosecutor Rhinefort heard from a dozen witnesses, no indictments were returned. The public affairs committee of the Toledo Council of Churches took over the work started by Eldridge but their efforts, if any, were also fruitless in purging the county of gambling.

At the same hearing, Arthur B. (Mickey) McBride, owner of the Continental Press and of the Cleveland Browns football team, was called to testify about wire service. Joseph L. Nellis, the committee chief investigator, offered evidence of a chart showing 170 cities in four states where wire service was piped, including Toledo. Such records were easily ascertainable from the Western Union or Bell Telephone systems.

Every county prosecutor had access to such files, if he wanted them. A state attorney general also had the right to inquire through the Public Utilities Commission.

The Toledo testimony was only a fragment of the national investigation in which claims were made that crime and gambling in the United States was controlled by Mafia families.

Labor people were called to testify on Mafia influences. Later Harry Bennett, the ex-Ford strongman, admitted hiring felons for the Ford Company but denied using them for labor troubles.[20]

Two significant pieces of Congressional legislation resulted from the Kefauver inquiry. In 1951, Congress enacted a law making transportation of gambling information across state lines a federal offense. This made the wire service of giving race results from various tracks to bookies illegal. In Detroit, the Homer Ferguson grand jury had closed down the wire service 12 years before. While the law was enforced in other parts of the country, Toledo gamblers continued to benefit until 1956, when the Syndicate finally closed out operations.[21]

A second law, enacted in September 1951, required all persons engaging in gaming to pay $50 for a tax stamp. Such persons were to also pay the government 10% on all bets taken. Dice, roulette and casino games were exempt because of the difficulty in keeping track of such wagering. The I.R.S. kept a record 10, a public record of persons purchasing tax stamps, and later made a record of taxes paid. Such records contained the address of the operator where the operation in gambling occurred so that any prosecutor could easily obtain the names and addresses of all gamblers in the city and county, if desired.

Throughout the country, bookies began closing shop rather than registering under the new federal tax law. They feared compliance would be a public announcement of gambling activity, while noncompliance would be even worse in facing consequences of possible tax evasion prosecutions. As a direct result of the new law, the sources of "lines" in sports — baseball, basketball and football — supplied to the nation's bookmakers from Minneapolis and St. Louis were cut off. An influx of gamblers to Las Vegas occurred. There, the legality of wagering was not impaired under the new law! Kefauver was indirectly responsible for the impetus given to sports books growth in Las Vegas.

At the time of enactment of the tax law, Congress estimated a yield of 10% of the four or five billion annually wagered would be collected., They anticipated receipts of four hundred to five hundred million dollars annually.[22] Like Prohibition, morality in human behavior cannot be legislated. The first quarterly returns required to be filed in January 1952 showed national collections of $265,000. The state of Kansas bookies paid $23.40 while Ohio led the nation in contributions of $79,385.[23] 18,913 tax stamps were purchased within the first year. Two-thirds of such purchasers failed to renew the following year. Less than nine million dollars, instead of the estimated four hundred million, was collected in the top tax year. The estimated volume of illegal betting may have been correct but the estimated revenue was disastrously understated. Like Prohibition, there was not sufficient manpower to check or enforce the act. Toledo had 16 stamps buyers in the area. The Syndicate had "fronts" or employees purchase stamps and they paid a small tax rather than risk a fight or federal charges. No arrests were made in the area in five years after the laws were enacted. Ohio city and county officers had access to the exact location of gambling and gamblers through stamp purchases, yet took no action, civil or criminal, in the ensuing years.

In 1967, the United States Supreme Court declared the tax stamp law unconstitutional as an encroachment on the right against self-incrimination.[24] Again like Prohibition, the Tax Stamp Congressional Enactment, for the time and money spent, proved worthless, unenforceable and ill-advised.

# 28 Denaturalization Plea Bargaining

The Kefauver committee wanted to make an example of Tony Paul's conduct in failing to respond to attempted service of a subpoena on their scheduled hearings. Some felt his flight was a deliberate evasion of process by a material witness. The Senatorial committee was indignant. Orders were sent to the Toledo Immigration Office of the Government to investigate this reluctant witness. The case was assigned to Kelsey Bartlett, an 11-year veteran investigator who was also attending the law school nights at the University of Toledo.[1]

Kelsey Bartlett found prior naturalization papers which made Tony Paul a naturalized citizen of the United States. When called in by Kelsey, Tony was warned that if he had obtained his citizenship illegally, he could be deprived of it and perhaps be deported as part of the discretion of the court. The investigation revealed that Neufio Scott (alias Tony Paul) was born under the name of Onofio Scotti in Naples, Italy in 1904. He claimed to have been brought to the United States shortly thereafter by his parents. He obtained the equivalent of a second or third grade education. Most of his education took place on the streets, where he acquired a reputation for toughness while a newsboy hustling at the Union Station. In the early 1920s, he was convicted with Richard Gosser in Monroe County, Michigan, of highway robbery (armed robbery) and sentenced as a felon to the

Michigan State penitentiary.[2] Even then he had some influence, receiving parole nine months before Gosser.

Tony registered to vote in Lucas County in 1940, claiming to be a citizen born in Pennsylvania. In 1950 he again registered to vote in Lucas County, giving his birthplace as Italy and claiming naturalization through his father in 1920. 1950 was his first registration, he said.

In criminal case No. 8609, filed in the U.S. District Court in Toledo on October 15, 1942, one Antonio Pulifeico, also known as Tony Paul, was convicted on a plea of guilty to the offense of failing to register under the Selective Service Act.[3] The court ordered him committed to imprisonment for one hour and to pay no costs. He thereafter was placed in custody of the U.S. Marshall to register as an alien for selective service. Tony filed an affidavit at the time claiming he was 46 years old.[4] Some prior statement indicated he was 38 years old.

Good conduct for a period of five years prior to filing for naturalization is all that is required by law. Two prior felonies was grounds for deportation. The felony conviction in Michigan was not fatal. The draft registration failure was a misdemeanor. On March 9, 1948 attorneys John J. Barone and George C. Bryce filed papers for naturalization, stating in an affidavit that "they had known Tony since March 1, 1947 and since that time he was of good moral character, attached to the principles of the Constitution of the United States and well disposed to the good order and happiness of the United States and in their opinion he was in every way qualified to be admitted to citizenship."[5] The Immigration Act specifically excludes persons whose income is derived principally from illegal gambling. At the time of filing, one of the attorneys, John J. Barone, was U.S. Commissioner appointed by Judge Frank Kloeb to act on behalf of his court primarily in setting bonds in federal criminal cases. On the basis of the affidavit, citizenship was granted on June 16, 1949[6]

John J. Barone was a transplant from Jamestown, New York. After graduating from Ohio State College of Law in 1936, he came to Toledo and was appointed by Judge Kloeb as U.S. Commissioner in 1943. He was replaced by action by the same judge 20 years later in 1963. A year before, his name was brought out during the trial of U.A.W. vice president Richard Gosser and two others who were later convicted of conspiring to defraud the United States by obtaining confidential documents from the Internal Revenue Service. Barone's name was brought into the Gosser trial when the government placed into evidence confidential tax investigation reports as among those copied and sold in the conspiracy.[7]

*UNHOLY TOLEDO*

At the time of Gosser's arrest and apprehension at his local U.A.W. offices, in November 1962 his life-long friend Tony Paul was in the place.[8] Tony Paul was never linked to the conspiracy. Pat Greclak, the same Patricia Niedomski of I.R.S. intelligence, the government employee who delivered the marked documents to Gosser, was formerly in the Immigration Department with Kelsey Bartlett and knew of Tony's prior involvement.[9] A second felony conviction could have meant deportation.

Kelsey Bartlett said he inquired of Warren Reidel, local head of the Immigration Department, "Warren, nothing gets by you. How did Tony Paul get naturalization?" Warren replied, "I recommended his petition be turned down, but the decision in his case came from the top. The Commissioner of Immigration in Washington, D.C. wanted him to be naturalized, so I was overruled."[10]

When talking to Kelsey in the investigation, Tony admitted his felony record. Tony never wanted to apply. He contended he went to the third grade and was never in a good position to read or write. He trusted those who presented papers to him. "I was getting along fine without citizenship papers. I was talked into applying by politicians and my friend, Dick Gosser." His wife, Rose, of a Detroit family, wanted to visit Italy. They couldn't go without passports, so he filed at her behest.

Tony made admissions against interest by going into Canada several times. Re-entry was based on citizenship. He candidly admitted lying about gambling, connections and income. When sentenced to the workhouse in 1945, he stated he ended his gambling activity. He testified he had quit.

To the question, "Have you any interest in gambling in Lucas County, Ohio?" he answered, "No."

"Have you told us everything about your activities and income?"

"Yes."

Yet there was evidence before the court that he was in gambling from 1945 to 1956.

Joe Fretti testified that Tony was a partner in his gambling business. He produced books from his accounting firm which carried on a gambling business known as the North Street Club. This was one of the fronts used to conceal distribution. Tony Paul, at investigation, admitted gambling actively until 1950. His income from 1945 to 1950 on the club books was:

    1946 — $ 9,295.00
    1947 — $27,560.00
    1948 — $27,300.00

1949 — $44,850.00
1950 — $35,100.00

On January 1, 1951 he had a credit balance of $15,973.00.[11]

In addition, there was an interest in an Alan Furniture Co., where Tony had advanced and invested $50,000 in cash.

Kelsey stated Tony further admitted he was connected to the "Syndicate" as he termed it. Kelsey turned in his papers recommending denaturalization after the Eisenhower election of November, 1952, as he recalls the date. He told Tony and his attorney John Barone at a conference that the lies about income, illegal association and voting were grounds for deportation.

Kelsey claimed he kept his desk locked. Nevertheless, his files were disturbed during his investigation. Two months after making his recommendation, Kelsey Bartlett was committed by his wife and at some other unknown urging, to the Toledo State Hospital for the mentally ill. There, against his will, he was given electric shock treatments which he claimed impaired his memory and destroyed his sex drive. Later, on obtaining his release and admission to the Bar, Kelsey maintained a series of suits against Dr. Doty, superintendent at the State Hospital, and others for his illegal confinement and care. He never alleged or sought to prove sinister influences were behind his confinement, done to destroy his testimony or to affect his credibility as a witness in event of a court hearing. The stay in the hospital would have such affect, for his testimony could be impeached. In April of 1953, Bartlett's file was sent to the U.S. Attorney General.

Finally, after futile attempts to forestall filing, the Republican Assistant U.S. Attorney, Clarence Condon, filed a complaint on January 26, 1954 to cancel the citizenship of Tony Paul on grounds of unlawful conduct in obtaining his papers.[12] If the truth had been told in the first intance, he would never have been admitted to the privileges of citizenship. In line with his evasive tactics of the past, his counsel filed a motion to quash service on him as he had been served in Florida instead of Ohio.[13] The court overruled his motion, for service anywhere in the United States would have been proper in such proceedings. Thereafter in a brief Tony contended that the Truman administration had indicated no civil action was to be taken, but the present Attorney General insisted on the denaturalization. Tony fought the charges. On May 2, 1955, in preparation for trial, the government subpoenaed Joe Fretti and two accountants for all tax returns and records of the North Street Club, the clerk of courts of Lucas County to bring over files of four civil suits arising out of gambling in which Tony Paul was named, Harry G. Levy of the Board of

Elections and the records of the White Manufacturing Co. of Midville, Michigan on all evidence of income of Tony Paul in 1951.[14]

Kelsey Bartlett, who had taken all the self-incriminating statements, was available, but was not subpoenaed as the court records show!

Plea bargaining is a form of dealing in court-accepted pleas in criminal cases. Naturalization proceedings or denaturalization are not subject to plea bargaining, for the citizen is either guilty or not guilty. Kelsey claimed "Tony had received a great deal of bad advice in handling these papers which had probably cost him a lot of money."

In lieu of trial, where the outcome was obvious, Tony Paul consented to surrender his certificate of naturalization for cancellation. The consent order was entered on the court docket on May 5, 1955. Four days later a copy was mailed to the Commissioner of Immigration in Washington, D.C. to preclude issuance of any passport.[15] Tony could leave if he liked but he couldn't re-enter legally without a passport. No further orders were made as Tony was permitted to remain in the United States. Such penalty was discretionary by the court.

When questioned on this result, Kelsey said, "It's the only case of its kind in the country." Asked if it was unusual, he replied, "I never heard of another like it before or since."

When he started the Tony Paul case five years earlier, Kefauver declared, "The big operators even reach members of Congress in efforts to stop deportation proceedings against undesirable aliens who are working for the Syndicate."[16] The Senator knew what he was talking about!

# 29 Licavoli Tribulations

Just as Frazier Reams tried every trick in the book to put Licavoli behind bars, conversely Yonnie went the same route to try to get out!

He had a great number of people go to bat for him. They touched all the bases but it took a long, long time to finally bring him home.

Tribulation is defined as "distress or suffering resulting from oppression, persecution." After the trials, Yonnie had his share.

A *Blade* reporter with the party taking Licavoli to the Ohio State Penitentiary in Columbus after his conviction in 1934 stated that he received the distinct impression Licavoli did not intend to spend the rest of his days in a prison cell.[1] "It is believed licavoli will depend on the leniency of some future governor for an opportunity to reshape destiny."[2] Licavoli planned two courses of action, one to get preferred treatment and the other to get out of jail.[3] With his partner Joe Fretti now in craps, Yonnie had connections for a continued supply of funds. The relationship between warder and prisoner is the most abrasive in the human experience but Yonnie knew that a well-placed dollar could smooth the situation.

When admitted as #68,912, Yonnie immediately put plan one in operation. In his first two months, prison records showed 383 recorded screen visits for 3,600 inmates. Licavoli received 17 of them, far more than any other prisoner. Visitors with criminal records spoke to him at length in the semi-privacy of the visitors' box. Reports of privilege and favors reached Frazier Reams. He became incensed.[4]

Early in 1935, Reams went to Columbus unannounced and witnessed Licavoli lounging in the prison hospital as a patient.[5] The ruckus raised by Reams lead to an investigation. Warden Preston E. Thomas called Reams the "platinum blond carpetbagger from Toledo," accusing him of being "a helpless victim of an exaggerated ego."[6] Following the report of an investigation, Warden Thomas resigned.[7]

Later his successor, Warden J.C. Woodward, also departed for having granted Yonnie repeated privileges which included smuggling in fried chicken dinners for his private table.[8] With his connections and bribes, Yonnie got a job as porter in the prison chapel. The few prisoners attending services left no debris in such places. Except for occasional dusting of furniture, his job required little attention. In 1939 fellow prisoners reported he regularly ate steak for dinner. Yonnie later became an attendant in the psychiatric ward as an honor prisoner but lost his job for passing $20 to a prisoner inside the walls.

In September 1940 Yonnie's brother Pete and two Detroiters tried to get Harry Craig, a principal witness, to change his story. Pete was discharged and the two others fined and released, as previously reported.[9]

After years of privilege, Yonnie undertook a public relations scheme. In February 1950, he conceived the idea of enlisting the support of Drew Pearson, syndicated newspaper columnist and radio commentator. His plan was to donate $5,000 from the Licavoli family to the J. Edgar Hoover Foundation, a project in which Pearson was involved.[10]

On March 7, 1950 Pearson sent a telegram to the *Blade,* which carried his columns stating "the donation will not help."

Reports circulated throughout the underworld and political circles that $100,000 or more was available to "spring Yonnie."[11]

A man who only identified himself as "being from Cleveland" approached Judge McCabe in 1955. He offered the judge $100,000 if he would write a letter to the governor urging pardon or parole. When questioned by a reporter from *Life* magazine, the judge said, "Do you think I would do that? Only a damn fool would agree in conviction and then ask for the man to be set free." The offer disturbed the judge. Sensing that, the man "from Cleveland" departed in a hurry, according to McCabe.[12]

Judge McCabe said, "Licavoli doesn't belong out of prison."

Governor Frank Lausche was elected to the United States Senate in November, 1956. He was a maverick Democrat, basically honest. He could get early preference in Senate Committee appointments if he resigned his office as governor and went to Washington 11 days earlier. Before doing so, it was reported he obtained an agreement in writing from Lt. Governor John Brown that he would neither pardon nor commute Licavoli's sentence. In the absence of such agreement, Lausche refused to resign. In the 11 days that Brown served as governor he acknowledged that "overtures were made to me to consider Licavoli's case and they were flatly refused."

Another governor approached was Toledoan Michael V. DiSalle who twice refused clemency for Licavoli during his term of office. In the fall of 1962, after suffering defeat for reelection by James Rhodes, it was felt that as a lame duck, DiSalle's attitude would soften. Late in 1962 Mike DeAngelo, a Columbus connection to the Mafia circles, appeared at the executive mansion with another man. The offer was $100,000, with the implication that it could be bargained upward, if the outgoing governor would take action favorable to Licavoli before the governor-elect took office.

DiSalle, who had been forewarned by federal agents that a bribe attempt might be forthcoming from Detroit sources acting through DeAngelo, rejected the offer. Though this was the only direct bribe attempt during DiSalle's four years in office, he acknowledged that "there were lots of calls. I was contacted by lawyers from all over the United States — some acquaintances, some not — all feeling me out on the possibilities for a fix in the Licavoli case."[13]

While outsiders made appearances on his behalf, Yonnie was giving orders to his gang during the 1950s from his cell in the Hocking Honor Camp in the southern Ohio hills. Anthony (Whitey) Besase and his brother Pete visited with unimpeded regularity. Yonnie was an organizer, a brain, and his associates used him. These meetings were top flight conferences on Ohio racket operations.

Jimmy Hoffa was also a visitor seeking Licavoli aid in Teamster affairs, for Ohio and Michigan were their strongholds.[14]

In a front-page story dated November 6, 1958, the Columbus *Dispatch* reported that Licavoli was "being given special treatment to assure his personal comfort and pleasure" at the honor camp.

Among the privileges that the *Dispatch* said were granted to Licavoli were:

unlimited visitors on days other than regulation visiting days;

meals served apart from other prisoners with special food provided by his family;

uncensored mail, both incoming and outgoing;

receiving boxes by mail and personal delivery without inspection by a guard for possible contraband;

use of the camp telephone;

permission to take visitors to a small cabin for private talks and permission to wear non-regulation clothing.

Other privileges reported included trips to Logan, Nelsonville and Athens.

In response, Maury C. Koblentz, Director of the Ohio Division of Corrections, commented, "No special privileges have been granted to any prisoner and they will not be tolerated."[15]

Mr. Koblentz said that "as far as this division knows, special treatment for individual prisoners is still not being done."

He said that when published reports came out, Warden Alvis sent his camp supervisor, Capt. Frank Morcel, to investigate conditions at Hocking Honor Camp. Captain Morcel then labeled the reports untrue.

In an investigation that followed in 1958, Warden Alvis protested that Licavoli was not being credited with the fine things he had done to spruce up the Hocking Honor Camp. The Warden said, "Licavoli purchased a television set, donated a pool table, a cash register and adding machine. He had given asphalt tiles for the dining room floor, venetian blinds and draperies for the windows and a sandbox for children visiting fathers or grandfathers." Evidence adduced was that the superintendent accepted gifts from Licavoli's friends and showed up as a guest at the Detroit wedding of Yonnie's daughter. Following the hearing, the superintendent, Lt. Thomas Crowe, resigned and Yonnie was ordered to return to Columbus.

While Licavoli's conduct was constantly scrutinized, Firetop's privileges went unnoticed by the media. Firetop had his boyhood Republican friends, Harry G. Levy and Isadore Topper, pulling strings for him. Levy was in Columbus during many years of Firetop's incarceration as a member of the state executive committee of the Republican Party. Within a few years after admission to the pen, Firetop was able to get an easy job as postal clerk and messenger duties with privilege of driving a state car as a trusty on the streets of Columbus. For 24 years, beginning in 1941, he had outside privileges which included permission to wear civilian clothes, avoiding the stigma of prison in such detail.[15] Firetop claimed that except for nightly lock-up, he had almost every other privilege.

On May 15, 1965, Governor Rhodes, acting on the recommendation of the seven-man adult parole authority, commuted Firetop's first degree murder charge to second degree, making him immediately eligible for parole since Firetop had served three times the 10 years required under the lesser charge. The official reason for the commutation entered in the governor's book was that Sulkin "was convicted of murder as a conspirator, but did not himself kill anyone."[16] A commutation was necessary before parole could be given on a first degree murder conviction.

When his death penalty was reduced in March of 1936, Governor Davey explained that "the chief conspirator and head of this crime gang (Licavoli) was given a life sentence; the actual triggerman was given a death sentence by the jury which later was commuted to life by my predecessor. . . . Since that time, two other members of the same gang have come to trial and have been given life sentences.[11]

"This leaves Sulkin as the only one to face the death sentence. While there is no doubt about his guilt, or his active participation in this conspiracy, and in other lawless activities, yet it does seem a bit unfair that he alone should have to pay the supreme penalty."

Upon reaching his 75th birthday, Firetop was granted parole on July 9, 1965. The Mob had taken care of his financial needs in jail but now the rackets were down and he was on his own.

Firetop had fallen and broken his hip a year before his release. He recovered sufficiently to walk with the aid of a cane. He came to Toledo under parole, crippled by arthritis and arthritic physical changes. He was slightly bewildered, decrepit, hating and being hated, filled with envy on seeing the wealth and status of the Toledo members of the gang like Red and Whitey who had prospered after their five-year tenure in prison. Firetop could not cope with the new generation. There were no rackets for him to get into, nor would his parole permit it, if he could. He no longer held political prestige for few, if any, wanted any part of him. Politicians wanted a low profile without publicity. Using Firetop wouldn't do. He had no future, no opportunity to repay favors or money lent, if any. No one seemed willing to do anything for him. "Schmuck" they called him behind his back for getting the guns that Licavoli needed like he needed more red hair. But nobody said that to his face. If Firetop dared to strike or to plead with anybody, they could refuse with impunity for he was not the feared Firetop of old. He was on lifetime parole and if he got out of line he could return. He didn't dare do or say things about the years before. Confronted with such frustrations from all sides, his spirits weakened, his mind declined and failed. He began to battle himself from within. Eventually he had to be placed in a strait jacket to restrain his tantrums. Racked by pain of arthritis, this now sadly disillusioned madman had to be finally confined in the Toledo State Hospital for the mentally ill. His wasted life ended there seven years after his release.

The release of Firetop spurred Yonnie's friends into action. In 1965 Ohio enacted a "post conviction remedy statute" that permitted belated appeals in criminal convictions to be taken in the original court rendering the judgment. Yonnie saw the opening. He knew of the millions paid by his associates to the prosecutors and politicians. His gang "owned" them. If he could only get a new trial, Yonnie felt there were plenty of grounds for the state to drop further proceedings. Moses Krislov, a Cleveland lawyer who represented Teamsters, filed proceedings for a new trial under the new statute. He claimed prejudicial pretrial publicity had deprived Yonnie of a fair trial and, secondly, that a charge of conspiracy to commit murder was a nullity under the law of Ohio. The common pleas judge who replaced trial judge McCabe, George Kiroff, studied the record of 1,200 pages and the newspaper clippings supplied by Krislov.[17] On June 2, 1966, Yonnie's motion for a new trial was denied.[18] He appealed to a higher court from that ruling. On November 30, 1966, the court of appeals of Lucas County unanimously affirmed Kiroff's decision.[19] Undeterred, Licavoli counsel went a step higher to the Supreme Court of Ohio but, on April 27, 1967, that court refused to review the lower court actions.[20] Still undeterred, he went the final step, a petition for certiorari to the U.S. Supreme Court. They likewise refused review.

Yonnie did not give up easily. His counsel decided to start a fresh attack on the constitutional questions in the federal courts. Since Yonnie was confined in Columbus, Krislov filed a writ of habeas corpus on March 1, 1968 in that city.[21] He engaged F. Lee Bailey of Boston to join the Licavoli counsel team. A writ of habeas corpus is a procedure used to bring the court's attention to a claim that the warden (having the body of the prisoner) is holding him unlawfully, wrongfully or unconstitutionally.

Bailey had received nationwide publicity in freeing Dr. Sam Shepard from the penitentiary on similar grounds. Shepard had been convicted of second degree murder of his wife by a Cleveland jury. His murder trial received sensational reports daily from the media. Although his appeals through the Ohio appellate courts was denied, Bailey was successful in the U.S. Federal Court procedures. Shepard obtained his release on habeas corpus through the federal courts, went to Cleveland for a new trial, and won an acquittal. So the right of review of criminal convictions in federal courts after state appeals have been exhausted still remained. The result is a double chain of appeals, first in the state system and thereafter in the federal. Having used all the state procedures, Yonnie was now in the federal chain.

While his writ was pending, Governor James A. Rhodes exploded a bombshell of vibrations on January 28, 1968 when he commuted the sentence of Licavoli to second degree, making him eligible for immediate parole![22] To the deluge of cries of payoff and bribe, the governor's assistant, John McElroy, produced a letter, instead of affidavit, from Mrs. Licavoli, stating, "Neither I nor anyone with my consent or knowledge has paid or promised anything of value ... in the commutation of sentence."[23] The parole board set up a hearing a week later. The media screamed. A furor of public criticism ensued. While the case was being considered, *Life* magazine came out with its story on "Leniency for a Hoodlum." The magazine retraced the Licavoli history with specific charges of IRS tax problems and "slush fund" manipulations by the governor. The parole board delayed Yonnie's hearing for further studies. Rhodes over-reacted to the charges made. He ordered the highway patrol to investigate the case.

The patrol found no hard core evidence of bribery in a six-month investigation. To the surprise of nobody, they found nothing to criticize in the governor's decision.[24] Rhodes proclaimed he was going to sue *Life* through attorney Louis Nizer, claiming their story "was designed to eliminate him from the race for the U.S. Senate. ... It was a politically motivated article. ... I am going to follow the suit and punish the perpetrators of it."[25]

Since *Life* magazine did business in Ohio, they could have been sued in that state. Rhodes did not use Isadore Topper's office in his complaint even though they were the Republican trial lawyers of the state. (He later retained them for his defense in the Kent State trials, where the legislature authorized a substantial six-figure fee for their legal services.) A suit for 6.3 million dollars in damages was filed by Nizer[26] in behalf of Rhodes against Time, Inc. in New York.[27] The suit charged that *Life* implied "the Governor took a bribe and acted in concert with the Mafia."[28]

A spokesman for *Life* said, "The article says no such thing."[29] Nizer commented, "The suit is an attempt to establish the principle that there is such a thing as a public official not having to run this kind of gamut."[30]

The magazine's statement was that "The information was thoroughly researched and documented by the editors before it was published. The article would not have been published unless the editors were prepared to defend it in court."

The article made no accusation that anyone accepted a bribe in the

Licavoli commutation, but it mentioned that up to $250,000 had been available to anyone who could get the gangster out of prison.[31]

Years later, Nizer commented on the Licavoli-Rhodes controversy in his book, *Reflections Without Mirrors*.[32] He wrote: "(Rhodes) had been mayor of Columbus four times and was selected in 1962 to run against the popular Democratic Governor Mike DiSalle. Ordinarily this would be an invitation to disaster."[33] Nizer was mistaken about these Republicans. Republican C. William O'Neil beat DiSalle in 1956,[34] but DiSalle reversed it in 1958.

Ohio traditionally was a Republican stronghold. Beginning with its first governor in 1803 as a Republican, 20 of the 30 governors preceding Rhodes were Republican.[35]

Nizer claimed, "The innuendo (of the *Life* story) was unmistakable.... The clear implication was that Rhodes had yielded to temptation."[36]

The author and magazine both claimed they made no such statement.

Again Nizer argued, "Licavoli had been convicted of conspiracy to kill two people. His confederates were sentenced to be electrocuted.[37] The facts here in this research reveal that Licavoli was found guilty of complicity and conspiracy in four murders, with four times that number attributed to him and his gang. Only English and Firetop were sentenced to death but had their sentences commuted to life 30 years before. Nor did Nizer reveal that Rhodes, as governor, had personally commuted the sentence of Firetop in 1965, allowing him to be eligible for immediate parole.[38] When *Life* magazine wanted to take Rhodes' deposition, he backed away. Discovery would have opened a Pandora's box of troubles.

Rhodes withdrew his suit with a press release stating, "*Life* Magazine has now acknowledged that it did not state or intend to state that I acted illegally or dishonorably in commuting Licavoli's sentence. Its attorney has written my attorney, Louis Nizer, that 'you are correct that *Life* did not state in its article that Governor Rhodes commuted the sentence because of any illegal involvement.'" That's what *Life* claimed all along. Rhodes made no issue on the *Life* stories about his tax problems or use of slush funds.

Ohio history indicates it was inimical to all Republican political policy to grant favor of such magnitude without something in return. Nobody bothered to check whether the parole board members or members of either party got any or all of the money available or spent to get Licavoli released. There is no question in the mind of this author that money was paid. As to the recipient, that's another question and story.

Ironically, Rhodes lost the race for the Senate. In the heat of disclosures and adverse publicity, the parole board delayed two more years on approval of Licavoli's parole. This meant he would have to stay in prison another five years; no new appeal could be taken before then.[39] Michigan and federal authorities also hindered a release. Licavoli told the board that he planned to move to Michigan to live with his wife and daughter but Michigan authorities refused to supervise him. Vincent W. Piersante, a chief investigator for the Michigan Attorney General's Office working with the U.S. Justice Department's crime strike force in Detroit, frustrated any ideas of Ohio officials to parole Licavoli to Michigan. Piersante discovered that Michigan parole authorities had made only a cursory investigation before agreeing to accept Yonnie as a resident. They paid no heed, for instance, to the fact that son-in-law Jackie Lucido, listed as living in the same Grosse Pointe house in which Yonnie would live, was himself active in Mob business. Piersante took his case to Michigan Attorney General Frank Kelley.

"This is no ordinary prisoner," said Piersante. (The New York *Times* articles named Yonnie the leader of the Detroit-Toledo Licavoli and Purple gangs. He headed a syndicate. Despite jail, he ruled two cities.) "The Mob in this area today needs a shot in the arm. We've been hitting them at the management level and they're feeling it." (As a result of a strike force investigation, Pete Licavoli's right-hand man, Matthew (Mike the Enforcer) Rubino, was sentenced in March to 10 years in prison for income tax evasion.)

"We are beginning to get witnesses," said Piersante, "even some from the Mob's own community. If Yonnie comes out, it will be a feather in the cap of every Don in Detroit — especially Pete, who is already too strong. And Yonnie? Yonnie Licavoli has nowhere to go but to the Mob. He wouldn't want to go anywhere else."[40]

Detroiters were also reminded that it was Yonnie Licavoli at a meeting at the Hotel Pick-Fort Selby in 1927 who told Al Capone personally "to stay the hell out of Detroit" and made it stick. Yonnie's organizational abilities were a legend in underworld circles.

Stymied after the payoff stories, Yonnie resumed his fight for freedom through the federal court case. The Licavoli team hammered the federal judge on three constitutional arguments.[41] His attorneys Bailey and Krislov claimed witnesses for the state in the original cases were coerced by the prosecutor; there was a carnival atmosphere at the trial a la Shepard and, third, the prosecutor's comments in final argument on Licavoli's refusal to take the stand by stating "he hides behind his lawyers" were all sufficient to grant a new trial.

His counsel claimed witnesses Ed Beck, John Brown and Sam Stein were coerced into testifying. Ed Beck originally testified at the murder trial that he worked at an illegal still but he could not remember who got him the job, who paid him or the names of any persons he was working for. Reams told the trial court he was surprised by this testimony so he asked the court to order Beck to remain in the courtroom. Beck was then arrested for perjury and jailed. When recalled to the stand two days later, he contradicted his original story as he remembered the names of his employer and co-workers.

John Brown, the black Licavoli gardener, said his white wife was told unless he returned to testify she and her child would go to jail. Brown was also arrested on perjury charges after his original testimony but also returned to the witness stand to recant.

Stein's three versions had already been reviewed.

Mindful of the fact that he had not taken the stand at the murder trial, the federal judge allowed Licavoli to testify on the habeas corpus hearing. Licavoli was given his day in court and was permitted to make a hearsay statement that his trial lawyers told him, "if he won an appeal, he might get a new trial and the electric chair." So he dropped any appeal. When asked if he ever attempted to win his freedom by payments to the executive branch of the government, Licavoli answered, "I never attempted to bribe anyone at any time."[42] No cross-examination of the petitioner was made by Attorney General Paul W. Brown.

U.S. District Judge Joseph P. Kinneary asked defense counsel, "Who were the witnesses afraid of, the prosecutor or the defendant?" "That's a good question," was the answer, and they let it go at that.[43] In a 17-page opinion the judge said there was no evidence that the witnesses' testimony was false or that the prosecutors knowingly presented perjured testimony. The law was that the prosecution may not knowingly employ false testimony to convict.[44] Nor can the prosecution conceal exculpatory evidence from the defense.[45]

The federal judge distinguished Shepard's first trial from that of Licavoli. The newspaper accounts of events at the latter's trial did not approach the sensationalism or magnitude of publicity of the Shepard case. The Licavoli jurors were not treated as celebrities. No photographs were taken. No motion for change of venue was made. Most importantly the case was tried in the courtroom, not in the newspapers.[46]

They also argued that the original prosecutor told the jury "he (Licavoli) hides behind his lawyers... behind alibis. He doesn't take the stand to testify, as he would if he were a man... he hides behind them."

While a decision of the United States Supreme Court held that a prosecutor cannot comment on the failure of a defendant to take the stand, the federal judge held such decision was not to be retroactively applied.[47] Judge Kinneary commented briefly on the ruthless prosecution tactics by stating, "Obviously the Prosecuting Attorney relied upon techniques which are not consonant with the rights the Constitution accords... yet these facts do not give rise to the level of right to constitute denial of due process."

On July 10, 1970 the judge's written opinion was filed dismissing Licavoli's writ for being without merit. Such decision was again affirmed by the Sixth Circuit Court of Appeals. His later appeal was again denied by the U.S. Supreme Court. Licavoli had run the gamut of federal courts without a word of encouragement anywhere! To his credit and that of his lawyers, such constant appeals on Constitutional questions affecting a defendant's rights were a bulwark of safety in preventing zealots from turning the country into a police state. Many of the landmark decisions of the U.S. Supreme Court involved "not such nice people."

Yonnie persevered. Although the outlook was bleak he continued to make headlines. In May 1971 he received two first place awards in an international stamp collectors exhibit. A New York stamp dealer flew to Columbus to personally present the "Hissman Space Award" to Licavoli at the Ohio pen. Still later he won recognition for 50 songs he composed under the pseudonym of Tommy Thomas.

Finally in August 1971, George Denton, chief of the adult parole authority, said that although Licavoli's case was continued for five years after the former rejections, it was normal to conduct a review after an inmate had served at least half of the time of his continuance. Despite the statute stating a five-year interval, the parole board again considered his case.[48] Yonnie was then 67 years old. He could become physically dependent at any time. He had been hospitalized with a bad heart, cataracts and was generally in poor health.

In a letter to the governor, Yonnie poignantly pled as a supplicant. "I have a daughter who was born three months before I came to prison. Now she is married, with two lovely girls and a little boy of her own, and none of them have ever seen me except behind bars. My first born daughter was killed, along with my father, while they were on their way to visit me one day." Yonnie withdrew his promise to live in Michigan, stating an intention to open a stamp business in the Columbus suburb of Gahanna. Based on this new evidence the parole board announced Licavoli was eligible for parole. The statutes of Ohio required "the prisoner have a good prison record (Licavoli's activities were the basis of three wardens being fired) and further that such action recommended by the Parole Board to the Governor "would further the interests of justice and be consistent with the welfare and security of society." The controversial gang leader was ordered released! The board made a rare stipulation in his case by requiring him to remain on parole for the rest of his life. This meant he could not leave Ohio without permission.

On January 6, 1972, 37 years, one month and 27 days after entering the Ohio Pen, Licavoli emerged at the head of a line of parolees.[49] Eighteen newsmen tried for an interview. Licavoli stepped quickly through the crowd to enter a 1971 vehicle that waited with motor running. The car bore Michigan license plates listed to Euro Homes, Inc. of Southfield, Michigan, a Detroit suburb. The company was one of the enterprises owned by Anthony (Tony) Giacalone, of the Detroit family.[50] Yonnie's release enabled the remaining three of his faithful gang, English, Rai and Carsello, to receive benefits of parole within a year.

Less than two years after gaining freedom, Yonnie died in Gahanna on September 17, 1973. His struggles were over. His parole expired. The family could take him wherever they desired. Three days later, his body was taken to the Bagnasco Mortuary in St. Clair Shores, a Detroit suburb. The New York *Times* obituary carried his picture in their death story as he was a national figure. At the funeral home in Detroit under watchful eyes of F.B.I agents checking attendance and cars, Yonnie was buried in services befitting a Don. A 60-car procession of luxury vehicles followed the hearse.

Most bore Ohio license plates.[51]

# 30 Gambling Characters

"Gambling is a form of self-flagellation and masochism. Many gamblers come from broken homes. ... Most had little affection when young. The compulsive gambler is buying love or a substitute form of love."

"Obsessive gamblers are self-destructive ... they have a subconscious wish to lose."[1] It is hard to convince the public that many who gamble deliberately or subconsciously want to lose.

Gamblers Anonymous came into national existence after the syndicated gambling was on its way out in Toledo. In 1957 the new organization would be to gamblers what Alcoholics Anonymous was to drunks. Some lives might have been saved, had victims been called "Jerk" or "Jack-off" by their peers. "Look in the mirror and see one who plays with himself," may have been used to deter those allergic to the first bet as a drunk to the first drink.

There was no way of measuring the nature, extent or effect of gambling on the many lives, businesses, professions, marriages, educations or life styles that crapped out on the gaming tables of the city. Since man is a creature of his environment, a perusal of some of the illustrative stories of gambling characters and the forms of action is appropriate in a book of this nature.

Not all of the gambling of the city took place in casinos and sport parlors. Inverness Country Club attracted its share of attention beginning with its inception of the famous invitational tournaments in the late '30s. Every professional golfer in the country wanted to participate because of a Club guarantee of a good fee, win or lose. Betting on the winners or Nassau was insignificant in contrast to the betting in the Club room crap games. Member Andy Reynolds won worldwide attention in World War II for breaking an Officers Club crap game in Paris. In the late '40s it was reported that he repeated a six-figure win at Inverness. The Club then boasted the world's leading golf amateur, Frankie Stranahan, of the Champion Spark Plug family. In addition to golf action, golfers were regally entertained by the fairer sex of Toledo who enjoyed the reputation of being both cooperative and hospitable in that regard.

Men in the Armed Forces during World War II stationed in Toledo or traveling through claimed it "was the greatest liberty town in the country."

At one tournament during the '40s, a young professional from New York questioned the congeniality of the local fair sex. Older golfers on the tour bet him they could prove the point. With two local lovelies and two imported beauties from Dago Rose's as hostesses, they locked the New Yorker in a room at a local motel for a weekend orgy. They refused to let him out to practice. Monday morning, he complained he couldn't grip his putter. Informants reported he abandoned the Invitational to take two weeks off to recuperate. "Whoever bet on Toledo sex," he said, "wins my bet." The sexcapades of the golfers were notorious even then.

Membership of Inverness consisted of the most prominent business and industrial people of the city. Most were very kind to the help on the grounds. Bobby Kay, who eventually developed into one of the city's finest amateurs, started his golfing career as a caddy at Inverness. Some said Bobby was once struck in the head by a club or ball driven by a Stranahan. Regardless, that family was very good to Bobby. They gave him an excellent job at Champion. Stranahan paid his expenses and fees as sponsor in statewide tournaments. When Frankie married, Bobby tutored his lovely wife, Ann, in putting — his play on the greens matched that of any professional. Bobby, like many others in the city, was hooked on betting at an early age and became a compulsive gambler. He made up golf matches with spots where he could not win. He bet heavily on sports of all kinds. He became self-destructive. When he did have a winner, he saved the money to bet it all back. The few times he did win, Bobby would gloat, "The cream is coming to the top." He never kept a dollar, depriving himself of necessities to have funds to bet. His Friday paycheck would be squandered by Monday. Frankie Stranahan always could be counted on to lend him money. Frankie also gave Bobby and his kids Christmas and birthday gifts. Even with Frankie's help, it was never enough. Bobby always owed at least three different loan offices at the same time. His marriage ended in divorce. His kids became alienated because his gambling activity never allowed him to spend money or time on them. Such problems were endemic of all compulsive gamblers. Joe Fretti and Tony Paul liked Bobby. They golfed and played cards with him. When Bobby lost, he would often be unable to pay off. He came up short. Joe and Tony would merely laugh when he couldn't pay. They understood. His money meant nothing to them. They knew Bobby would play with them again. Whenever Bobby won a tournament in the city or the senior golf titles of the state, the first people to view his trophies were the habitants of the sports gambling rooms. They became his only friends and social companions. Such was his life in later years, work all day and hang around the card and sports hangouts at night. In all the years of losing, neither Joe, Tony or any other gambling or industrial figures ever took Bobby aside to stop his plunges by counsel. It seemed nobody understood or was interested in any gambler's problems.

The saddest day in a gambler's life is when he goes to bed at night without knowing where the money for the next day's bet will come from. Bobby had many sleepless nights.

He contemplated suicide. Two attempts were aborted by friends. His sister became alarmed. "You can't live at my house," she told her brother, "unless you go to Gambler's Anonymous." A chapter that had begun in Detroit sent missionaries to Toledo. Bobby attended a few weekly meetings. He converted the group to his own ends. On the day of a scheduled meeting he would go to a few bookies and say, "Let me have two dollars for dues." No dues were ever collected or charged. Bobby would then take whatever he had collected in donations and make a bet on something going, someplace. When asked about his progress, Bobby would in solemn sincerity reply, "Gamblers Anonymous is helping me. They cut me down from betting four teams to two. Don't ever bet over two teams, they told me."

When he won, friends would ask about his progress at Gambler's Anonymous. "I'm only supposed to go when I'm losing, never while winning," Bobby replied. Bobby never really recognized any personal problem; compulsive gambling is a progressive disease. A drunk in A.A. must first admit he has a drinking problem. Then he can relate to it and be cured. Bobby could neither admit nor relate. Without such action, he was beyond help. In a city of vice, nothing helped. While saddened by the news of cancer in the Stranahan clan, whom he loved, new tragedy struck Bobby. In two separate auto accidents a day apart, one of his boys was killed and another severely injured. Bobby decided he wouldn't take any more. In a friend's trailer, he performed the ultimate act of a self-destructive personality. He laid down on a couch, crossed his arms with a revolver in one hand and put a bullet through his heart.

Compulsion had no racial barriers. Intelligence or lack of it was no detriment. It is a disease of people who cannot control an obsession to bet. As later told, 10 Toledo lawyers — including me and the "Redhead from Cleveland" Benjamin F. Sacharow — were suspended or disbarred for the Toledo gambling involvement. Joseph Val Knack came to Toledo from the Kansas City *Star,* and got into trouble with bookies over his inability to pay. His rivals at the *Journal Post* said he was like the baseball team the Kansas City Blues — spelled B-lose.

In Toledo, he became news and sports editor of the *Blade*. His compulsion continued. Like all habitual horse handicappers, he died broke.

Dr. Pat McCarthy performed abortions for as little as $10 if given a sob story. Money meant nothing to him. He carried large packages of losing tickets bet on the horses in his medicine bag. "Look," he said, "what I lost." He wanted people to feel sorry for him or to pity him. The good doctor lost his marriage, his home and would have lost his career if his brother John, a prominent lawyer, had not intervened. He made a deal to give up practice and join the staff at the state mental hospital. One who needed psychiatric help was dishing it out, a classic case of the blind leading the blind.

After the holocausts of World War I and II, male interest gave great impetus to all sports. Betting on the outcome of athletic events or handicapping of games was the macho thing to do. The fabulous forties were even more sensational than the roaring twenties — it was an era of wartime and post-war prosperity. Many of the gambling parlours of the city had Western Union tickers to bring in sport results. With the increase in night games, entire rooms would be crowded with betters, pockets filled with money, to bet among themselves or the book or anything on the boards. Lines on all major baseball games and two minor leagues, American Association and International League, were made. Without double headers, there would be 32 different games a night. Sundays would often bring twice that number. Football and basketball weekends were even bigger. Betting on the outcome of each game was not enough for the new betters. They required even more action, for most gamblers were of a shallow nature and easily bored. "Bet A Million" Gates, the story was told, on return by train from Saratoga Races, would often bet on which raindrop hitting a pane would beat another to the bottom. Inmates of penitentiaries bet on the speed of cockroaches and rats. Anything that moved could evoke some wager. Each game, even of little-known, obscure colleges, had a line. Every inning a new bet could be made. For example, if the Yankees were two to one to win and fell behind by two runs, the bookie would make a new line of even money. Each inning brought new prices and changes where a better could go either way. Half-time of football and basketball also brought new spots so that hedging or increase of individual bets were constantly made, particularly where games were tied at any stage.

   The most popular bookie catering to the handicappers of the city was George Haddad. This short, heavy-set, dark-complected man with a bulbous nose made a line on anything as long as it appeared fair to both sides. In his large downtown restaurant, he set off an outer portion for dining while the inner half held a blackboard for sports, a nearby ticker, a long counter for his clerks and a back office for privacy or paying off. Evenings and weekends would find the inner sanctum one of wall to wall humanity. Bettors crowded the ticker or lined the counter to bet every time a new line was called out as the score was posted. Short wave radios on major games were going full blast in three different areas of the room. Many bettors carried pocket radios to get instant results. Others would go out to their nearby cars to listen and return. Most of the bettors of the city at the time could easily recognize the voices of New York sportscaster Red Barber, Dan Dunphy or Connie Desmond of Toledo. Bob Prince of Pittsburgh, Harry Carey of KMOX St. Louis, Bob Elson and Jack Brickhouse of Chicago or Ty Tyson and Harry Heilman of Detroit came in loud and clear as they reported their own games and other major league action as it came over tickers in their booths.

   Dissemination of information on sports reached every better in the country. Two-dollar betters talked about small colleges like Gustavus Adolphus of St. Peters, Minnesota. Their great center Olsonoski was a national figure. They all knew when unknown basketball guards, centers or quarterbacks were injured or out of a lineup. Few knew the value of such information; but conversations would begin with "No Blanchard, No Davis, Budreau is hurt, etc." Radio play-by-play reached new heights in coverage. Listeners not only knew the lineups but could also easily identify Patsy O'Toole, the Jewish rooter for the

Detroit Tigers and his female counterpart in Brooklyn. Everybody became a wise guy and they congregated to prove the point.

There was good natured camraderie among the betters. Jesting and wise-cracking was common as was name-calling — a male chauvinistic personality trait. Odd names as "Pear-shaped," "U-Boat," "Front Row Jack" or "Nose-picker" were used. Haddad went with all gags. His customers were his business. He enjoyed a joke even if on himself. He always paid off promptly and with a smile.

One time a syndicate was formed to fix a number of 915 in stock, of the three houses. Strangers began betting early in the day. Clerks were becoming alarmed. Haddad was warned to lay off some of the action, but he refused to do so. When the number hit, some places in the city refused to pay; others folded. Haddad paid out $5 to a penny, a total of $75,000, without complaint. A bookie's reputation, he knew, depended on his ability and willingness to pay. The next day, one of the top members of the stock exchange issued a corrected statement indicating that an incorrect number of 915 had been wrongfully issued. Yet, even though the fixed number was a fraud, Haddad made no effort to collect from those who had won on it.

Number or policy betters had a morbid intuition on odd numbers arriving out of death. When a woman leaped 20 stories from a downtown building numbered 315, those digits also resulted in a large payoff but no fraud was suspected or found.

One of the consistent long-shot betters of that era was Emil Marks, credit manager of a local jewelry store. He always bet $5 and $10 parlays. One Saturday night, Emil bet 10 baseball teams, all long-shots. When nine of the 10 won, the bookies went searching for Emil to make a settlement of $6,000 for his parlay, figured at more than $18,000 if the last team remaining won. Emil was at the ball park at Swayne Field but the bookies couldn't find him. After Emil's Chicago Cub team took an early four-run lead, the bookies quit the search, figuring that they would have to pay. But luckily for them, the Phillies overcame to win 9-6, shattering every sports player's dream! After the experience with Emil, bookies set a 30 to 1 limit, regardless of the number of events bet.

One of Haddad's regulars was Benny Aronoff. He had one salient trait that was common to all professional gamblers: a desire for an edge in his favor. He had it in his numbers, horses and craps and wanted it when he bet. He was an avid better on sports, betting thousands on baseball and football. His favorite team was the Yankees. "They were cinches," he always declared.

In football, Bennie originated a unique system while betting with George Haddad. If a team was a 14-point favorite, Bennie wanted to lay 2 to 1 instead of the usual 11 to 10 if he could take the favorite minus seven. Haddad said, "I'll do even better, I'll give you six points either way on any two games, for even money. Both must win." As a result, the two-team teaser, as the bet became known, was born. later it was expanded to three or four teams at bigger odds as new variations of old betting styles were created in football and later basketball.

After his jail sentence in the Wilcox case, Bennie had plenty of time to bet. He promised the court he would quit gambling. he had to stay away from the syndicate while others fronted for his interests. To show the city he meant what he promised. Benny converted his downtown Buckeye Club location into a swank jewelry store named Lindel's. A short time after opening, the store manager became innocently involved in an unsolved murder. The public stayed away. They ridiculed Aronoff's business enterprise into oblivion. Benny moved to a new location in the Secor Hotel. The public still refused patronage. Bennie decided to go to Las Vegas after the syndicate closed out. In 1957, it was reported he invested five million dollars in the El Rancho Vegas. But Bennie did not have the political or police protection out west that he had had in Toledo. The gamblers in Vegas proved to be more shrewd and untrustworthy than Bennie had contemplated. A year later, he sold out his interest at a substantial loss rather than be involved in protracted litigation. He returned to Toledo but found that the teasers he had loved to bet and short prices were no longer "cinches." His family and advisors started to budget his finances. When Bennie lost $18,000 in a few sessions playing gin rummy, he told the winner, "I have a limited income because of IRS problems. I have to pay you a thousand a week." It took three months for the city's biggest operator to pay off this gin rummy loss.

Jakey Patlin was probably the city's most lovable gambling characters. In the '30s, he worked for and played pinochle regularly with Bennie Aronoff. Jakey always was in action and played all games. In an effort to attract players, one establishment honored Jakey by naming the place after him using his name spelled backwards, Niltap. The notoriety and love displayed for Jakey was only surpassed by that given to his well-known dog, Rusty. This canine of dubious breeding loved beer. He had his own special mug in his master's bar. Rusty had the run of downtown Adams Street for years. Every bar owner kept a mug for Rusty. When he came in, his mug would be promptly filled as if for a regular customer. Once a month, Jakey or his wife would make the rounds paying Rusty's markers. Nobody could claim the beer diet hurt, for Rusty lived to the extraordinary age of 18.

Catty-cornered to Jakey's Bar, Al Vollmer, a former city councilman, maintained a pool room for billiards with poker and card games in the rear. Many of the poker players came from the Ohio Clover Leaf Dairy nearby. One of the milkmen was once stuck in a poker game. He refused to quit to go to work until he was even. Pleas of friends were ignored. In desperation, a colleague went over to the dairy barns, unhitched the milkman's horse and brought it over to Vollmer's. As he looked up from a losing hand into the forlorn white face of his faithful equine helper, the milkman rose, saying, "It looks like I gotta go to work boys, cash me in." The game proceeded as though no interruption ever occurred.

Another avid and colorful character among the city betters was Meyer (Dream Prince) Friedman. In his youth he was one of the the best softball pitchers in the city. This was the time of fast pitch when Toledo had outstanding players including the Crimson Coach Tobaccos, world softball champions. Meyer could kick a football or hit a softball the proverbial mile. He was also the sorest loser and the biggest beefer in the game. If anything went wrong, he fumed, argued, cussed, attacked in all directions. He just couldn't stand to lose. He enjoyed the role. To him, it was a way of life.

A heart condition sidelined the Dream Prince from sports as an adult so he transferred his interests to handicapping. During the day, Meyer dealt 21 for the Syndicate. Women players loved to drop tokens and chips into the shirt pocket of this tall, muscular, and handsome dealer. He acquired his moniker from his manner of dancing in the Trianon crowd. The girls loved his style. He would smother his dance partner in his arms, hold her close and tightly, body to body, cheek to cheek, eyes closed, his mouth close to one ear. The Dream Prince would make his pitch as he danced, in his own corner, slower and slower regardless of the rhythm of the band.

As Dream Prince became compulsive, a second personality emerged in gambling. Every bookie was a mortal enemy. Meyer hated to lose, yet he rarely won. He was always in debt, borrowing yet rarely paying back any markers. The Dream Prince dominated the ticker. He stood by it all the time. When a favorable score came in, he kissed it, otherwise he hit it, spit on it or carried on a continuous stream of vituperation until the games were over.

One day Haddad made the Yankes 2 to 1 over the lowly St. Louis

Browns. A 20-game winner was going to start for the Yanks. Handicapper Meyer thought the price was way out of line. "Let's go co-sign for each other," he asked a friend. "Don't change that line, we'll be right back" he told Haddad. Together they borrowed $400 and laid it down to win $200. When the Yankees had a 5-0 lead in the early innings both were elated. "Let's take a walk," they agreed. After a few blocks, they entered another handbook The score board showed the score now 6 to 4. "Get out of here. This joint is jinxed," Meyer cried. They stopped for a sandwich.

After the snack, Meyer went into a handbook a few doors away. He peeked at the ticker. The score came in tied 6-6 at the end of seven innings. He spit all over the ticker and left. He was still cussing when they encountered a couple of girls a few blocks away. Twenty minutes passed. They couldn't wait for a score any longer. The ticker now became his mortal enemy. He would avenge himself on it if he lost his bet. Meyer and his friend went into a stranger's book store. There on a high shelf was a ticker with its tapes cascading into a waste basket below. Meyer scanned the tape. "The Browns are ahead 8 to 6 top of the ninth," he reported angrily to his friend. "How long have they been out?" he asked the store clerk. The kid didn't know. "If it's more than six minutes we got a chance" Meyer said. Anything beyond that for a half inning indicates action, but in the last of the ninth, time meant nothing for the results were being totalled in runs, hits and errors. They waited. The final score came in 8-6, St. Louis. Meyer took a ladder, climbed up the shelf to the tortious ticker, spit on it, broke it, and with a vituperative barrage of bitter words to the perplexed employee, left the store. Only his partner later apologized.

In hustling bets on sports, little Frankie Gaustello of Detroit was in his prime. He would take each half inning and bet a team to score or not at certain odds. Frankie is credited with having added, in the '40s, a new dimension to betting: the over and under. Since betters were not happy with wagering on the outcome alone, a number was made in each given game. In baseball, it was over or under a certain number of runs to be scored. The game had to be a full nine innings. In basketball and football the total number of points to be scored was set. If the total scores of both teams added together went over a stipulated figure set by the bookie, the over won, under lost. Most players liked the numbers betting better than the spot betting, for a bet could be won or lost on the number before the game result was determined. Today, over and under in pro football often exceeds the betting lines.

Big shooters came from all over the country to engage in skin, a game of luck, rather than skill. Nightly winnings of $40,000 or more were frequently reported. The biggest single winner reported was the Muzzler's $100,000 which he promptly lost back.[2]

The wide-open city also attracted many of the best handicappers in the country. Robert Saul Black, a youngster in his early twenties, came from Brooklyn, New York to make his living off the local bookies. At first they called him Brooklyn Blackie, then Boston Blackie, then shortened it to plain Blackie. Bob, as he preferred to be called, had an innate ability to handicap sports. He constantly read newspapers from every major city in the country. On baseball, he made extensive notes and kept books on pitching records, number of walks versus strikeouts as a key to pitching control. While in high school, he was consistently able to put over six or seven team parlays on a quarter bet. Handicapping baseball and basketball games was his forte. The significance of injuries to key players could be evaluated by him in determining the odds, point spread or price of any given game. Bookmakers in Minneapolis, Miami and Montreal in later years called upon him for his line on games to determine whether or not their own lines had any games which were out of line. The bookmaker relied on a two-way betting of any given event. If the betting was lopsided, all one way, it was gambling and a book could be ruined. The idea of a line was to balance the action as evenly as possible so that the bookmaker could then collect his percentage without any gamble. In Brooklyn, Blackie knew Bobby Goldsmith, Salvatore (Torto) Sallazzo and Eli Klukofsky, alias Eli Kaye. These three were instrumental in arranging the early "fixes" or point shavings in the basketball scandals of the early '50s.[3]

Such scandals broke in 1951 when Junius Kellogg, a New York player, went to the police. They set up Kellogg as a go-between with fixer Sallazzo. Kellogg claimed the scandals went back to 1949.[4] After Kellogg's testimony, three Long Island University players admitted taking bribes of $16,500 from Sallazzo to shave points in games he bet. Other schools' players — Manhattan, City College of New York, Bradley and Kentucky players, among others — also became involved. Whenever a team played badly, it became customary for fans to chorus: "the dump is on." In 1951 Sidney A. Brodson, an attorney in Milwaukee, appeared as a witness on television before the Kefauver committee. He claimed he bet a million dollars a year on sports. He said "I quit New York because of abnormal results of three years' standing."[5] He placed bets all over the country by telephone, averaging $2,000 per bet. Brodson's helper, Ted Gagliano, reportedly read 100 newspapers a day and reported important information for 15% of his action.[6] It was inevitable that basketball scandals would also involve the University of Toledo. For years before actual acceptance of bribes by members, T.U. players were aware of spots on games and wagered through intermediaries locally. One classic tale involved a game against Michigan in 1950, where T.U. was an eight-point underdog. Certain members of that team felt that the spot was too high. Some felt they could win even. Rather than ruin the spread by local betting, they pooled $2,000 and sent a friend by plane to Minneapolis to make their lay down. With 10 seconds to go, Michigan was leading by nine points. T.U. called time out. They called for the Jerry Bush famous roll play, where all players but one break away from the basket. The out-of-bounds pass would go to the one player breaking for the basket. It would be one on one. The play worked perfectly. The pass came right down the middle to a guard, Eddie Leroy, who wasn't told about the bet. The man guarding him was three feet behind. Eddie laid the ball up for a bunny shot and blew it! The trailing Michigan guard retrieved the rebound and dribbled unguarded to a corner. In the final seconds, Leroy, unaware of the cost of his error, was seen lying on his stomach at the foul line kicking his feet wildly in the air in frustration as the final gun sounded.

News of T.U. involvement in the basketball scandals saddened Toledoans in July 1951.[7] Co-captains William J. Walker and Carlo John Muzi and captain-elect Robert McDonald, a law student, told District Attorney Frank Hogan their story in New York. Eli Kaye had wired $1,700 to Walkers' wife for T.U. to shave the points in the Niagara game of December 14, 1950. Toledo was a seven-point favorite at home. They were paid not to win by more than seven points. With eight minutes to play, T.U. led 60-45. Time out was called. The trio were worried. They felt something awful would happen if they didn't perform after receipt of the money. Coach Jerry Bush called his play-making guard, Muzi, "the greatest little defensive player in the country."[8] Muzi had allowed Zeke Sinacola, Niagara sharpshooter, the outside shot, but gave his opponent plenty of room so that he couldn't drive around him. These were Bush's instructions. Now heat was on. Muzi now guarded his man more closely; Zeke easily drove around him to the bucket in the last minutes. Walker fouled frequently, passed badly, turning over the ball several times. McDonald did not rebound as he had earlier in the game. T.U. looked inept. Except for some game-saving play they would have lost. The final score was 73-70.[9] New York gamblers were jubilant over their new success.

While the gamblers thought they had T.U. in their pocket, the proud playeres twice refused to dump games with Big Ten teams. When Kaye became belligerent, he was cut off. A T.U. freshman, Joseph Mazza of Brooklyn, set them up with Jack (Zip) West for further payoffs.[10] In two other games, the players told Hogan, there were dumps. As a seven-point favorite at home against a bigger team from Bowling Green, Kentucky, they lost 66-59. When favored by 13 points over Cincinnati, they also dumped, 79-59. The guilty trio tried to avoid implicating sophomore forward Jack Feeman. Many Toledoans called Feeman the greatest player ever to play at the University. Tall, agile and rangy, Feeman could dribble and shoot with either hand. He was an excellent set shot and foul shooter. Feeman had scored 31 points in the Niagara game. Some claimed he could "out-Cousy Cousy" as a playmaker. Because of the threat of his shooting, Feeman was called into the conspiracy by the trio. He suffered their same ostracism, although involved in only one game. Hogan said, "bribery of an amateur in Ohio was not a crime." Laws were enacted to make such conduct a felony.[11] Local bookmakers often took bets from the college crowd. After the third fix, student betters were asked to stay out. No local grand jury convened but safety director Edward DeAngelo ordered bookies to take all T.U. games off the board. Feeman went into service and played on several championship teams. He was of professional caliber but the rule makers excluded him and many other All Americans from professional sports because of their point shaving involvement.

When enacting a bribery bill covering sports in New York, Thomas E. Dewey said, "The young men involved in this scandal have suffered greatly by their exposure and have irreparably damaged their future lives."[12] McDonald never returned for his senior year or pursued law, for his conduct might have precluded admission to the bar. For Feeman, it was social ostracism and complete financial disaster.

Blackie knew the games Sallozzo, Kaye and Goldsmith would bet. He was a regular winner at the local offices. Blackie was the most devious of gamblers. Whenever anybody, including some close friends, would ask which side he favored, he would often deliberately lie to them hoping the price, odds or points on the side he liked would change in his favor. Handicapper Edward (E.) Walker got wise to Blackie's action and profited from it. Whenever Blackie wanted to bet, E. limited his action to $500 per game. Then E. would bet thousands out of town himself on the same games. Blackie and E. bet with confidence. Now the out-of-town bookies taking E.'s basketball wagers became alarmed at his percentages of success. They discovered how he was getting his information. Blackie was in the middle. His own bookie friends told him, "Bet the games we tell you to bet with E. We'll cover your losses." E. was victimized for a week. He might have never discovered the scheme but for a bit of vanity on the part of Blackie. After telling E. of four games he had to bet in which E. followed him, he turned around and made a four-team $50 parley on the opposite sides. The parley won. Blackie could not risk collecting such bet so he sent Bennie Pollock, a local hanger-on, into E.'s place to collect. Walker happened to be there when the ticket was presented for payment. He became suspiciously critical for Bennie was not a $50 better. Under threats of violence, Bennie admitted the source of the parley. E. was furious. E. warned Bennie not to report their discussion.[13] He laid for Blackie and pounced upon him when he came through the door. Without listening to a word of explanation, E., a large, heavy-set man weighing 250 pounds, then lit into the lighter and younger man, dragged him to the back room, ripping off his tie and shirt, tearing his clothing and beat him severely. Blackie was told to leave town. He did so but returned after the scandals ended the fixed games.

In the interim, E. Walker became one of the outstanding handicappers in the country. He saw the potential of having an edge on other bookies. From Blackie, he learned the importance of evaluation of injuries to key players. To solidify his position, he called upon Bobby (Hunchback) Berent of Cleveland. The Hunchback had a reputation among many bookmakers as being the best handicapper in the country. He avidly read many newspapers to discover helpful information. Many of the country's bookmakers would call on Bobby to give them his line. In exchange, they would give him a free $300 bet on any game he named. They usually followed his selection. E. Walker changed all that. He went to Cleveland to induce the Hunchback to become his partner. E. had knowledge of certain teams in the Southwest conference. He had leads from trainers in certain pro football locker rooms. He knew what players themselves bet and had reliable inside reports from the team doctors of the New York Giants. He gleaned information of importance including injuries to starting players. With the Hunchback, E. could book their own lines and bet other lines before they were adjusted. E. and his team had phenomenal success. They won 21 out of the first 22 bets. Every weekend during football and basketball seasons of 1953 and 1954, his men ran to pay phones to bet "outs" (out of town) on selected games. They soon ran out of bookmakers, who were being killed by the fantastic win streak.

E. became known as "the big man" in the sports world. When the tax stamp law threatened exposure or problems, E. and the Hunchback looked westward to Nevada.

There they established themselves as a team to be reckoned with in sports betting. Years later, the two were joined by Blackie. The trio continued to be among the best informed sport handicappers in the United States.

With the expansion teams in baseball and football, it was said, "Jimmy (The Greek) Snyder got all the publicity in the newspapers and TV but in the early years, E. and his crews probably got all the money."

From the Minneapolis-St. Paul area, Dave Bohn brought his younger brother with him to start a handbook in Toledo. Dave was a shrewd handicapper of baseball. "An amateur could handicap one game of a team he knew, but to make a line in four different leagues, day in and day out during season required some special talent," Dave said.

The tall, lanky newcomer was extremely nervous. He had two habits, one was to lock his hands behind his head with his elbows protruding upward like two TV antennas while parading about the room, always with an eye on the blackboard. The wise guys couldn't think of a name for this habit but for his second characteristic of picking his nose in public, they dubbed him "nose-picker." During the daytime, when things were slow, Dave liked to drive around listening to the radio broadcast of Chicago Cub games. Sometimes reception was poor. Outside of the city one day, Dave drove up a knoll in a farmer's yard. Reception was perfect, but the farmer objected. Bohn's team was winning so he tossed the farmer a double sawbuck for the trouble. When the game turned around, it was reported Dave was seen chasing the farmer for a refund.

One day Dave walked a block over to Haddad's to peruse the line. A friend cornered him and said, "One of the games he's got listed as a night game is over. I know the score." Dave went into the back office and past-posted Haddad for $200. While he remained on the premises, he forgot to tell his brother of the error in the games. A customer who had overheard the bet ran down to Dave's and past-posted his brother for $500.

Another well-known handicapper came to Toledo in the middle '40s. Richard (Boston) Cogswell, originally a native of Boston, worked for books in Detroit where he made the line on National Hockey League games, charging 13 different Detroit bookies $5 a week. After the McDonald suicide he moved to Toledo. His innate acumen on hockey started when Boston became the first American entry into the National Hockey League. Most American bookmakers did not understand the fundamentals of the game so they refused to make wagering lines. Hockey on Sunday night was the only game open. After football or basketball was over, betters still clamored for action. Cogswell obliged by making a line for years. Apparently the locals were satisfied, for they continued use of his services without interruption. This made the cycle complete. There was not a sporting event of any kind in the country, college or professional, that one could not wager on in Toledo. There was always a line on boxing events, particularly when on TV.

Years later, Blackie brought Teddy Brenner of Madison Square Garden to Toledo. They were to look at some fighters in an exhibition at the Hockey Arena. Both chuckled when they talked about winning on Mohammed Ali as a 6-to-1 underdog against Sonny (29 months in the can) Liston. Brenner claimed he "never lost a bet on a fight in the Garden in his life."[14] Blackie remained silent when later questioned on that score.

The biggest compulsive loser, financially, in Toledo that I knew personally was tobacconist Sherman Sharwell, a Cleveland transplant. During World War II, Sharwell sold off-brand cigarettes as Homeruns and Wings retail for $2 a carton. Sherman was always in action. He played gin rummy, bridge and pinochle for high stakes. He would bet every game on the board. During World War II, he bought the Jamra Tobacco Company and shipped extra quotas of cigarettes to Cleveland for sale at a higher price. He sold his tobacco company and signed an agreement not to compete for five years in the Toledo area. Suit restraining his competition through a new Cash Wholesale Tobacco Company forced his sale to the forerunners of the Star Vending Company, a national corporation. Sherman next bought a laundry. In 1948 he became a partner with George Haddad at the biggest book in town. Sharwell did not bring any luck to the partnership. Fate never meant Sherman to be a bookie; he preferred to be a sucker or a better. Some say the compulsion to punish himself by losing took over. He never tried to learn the intricacies of bookmaking. In Haddad's absence, he ran the store, but he was always caught out of line. In the winter of 1948, Haddad went to Florida for a long-needed vacation. Sharwell had the usual roomful of basketball betters every night of the week. The opening line wasn't enough for him. During the half of any game on his board, he would make a new spot for the second half of play. If a team at home was a 13-point favorite and tied at half as an example, Sharwell made them minus seven. Betters jumped on the bargain of a favorite at half the opening line. Sharwell was honest with his partner but useless as a bookmaker. Haddad had to rush back home to stem the losses. Sharwell sold out within eight months. Thereafter, in order to remain in the tobacco business, which he knew, Sharwell moved Sharwell moved to Columbus and established the Sharwell Tobacco Company. Cigarettes are fair traded in Ohio. A retailer made 6%. A wholesaler made a 6% gross profit and at least 10% of that was net profit. Cigars and candy were not taxed by the state so the wholesale figures did not relate to such items. Local politicians and bookies told Sharwell that Isadore Topper was the lawyer to use in event of any legal entanglements. From the start, Topper became his attorney. Sharwell's betting received national attention. His name came before the Kefauver Committee but that never deterred his betting. Stories about Sharwell's activity were legends. He was generous to a fault. When he took a group of friends to the College All Star football game at Soldier's Field, Chicago, he ordered the cab driving them to the game to wait at the gate until the game was over as he handed the driver a $50 bill. To a compulsive gambler, money meant little or nothing. Sharwell's name came up again in the federal investigation of gambling in Terre Haute, Indiana in 1959.[15] The government alleged that Leo Shaffer, Jules Horwick and Charles L. (Buck) Sumner of Chicago with others handled $3,263,150 in World Series and football bets in the fall of 1957.[16] Sharwell would bet a $10,000 round robin and $5,000 parley with the boys. If one of the teams involved in his bets played on the West Coast, Sharwell would call a colleague on the phone and listen to the game as it was played over the telephone. His extravagances were story-like.

    Like all compulsive losers, Sharwell encountered trouble with creditors. He preferred to pay his bookmakers ahead of legitimate creditors. Gambling debts were debts of honor and, consequently, received preference. Besides Sharwell wanted to stay in action. He knew that he was like a bookmaker in such respect, his reputation depended on being punctual in paying off. In 1960, his place of business was totally destroyed by fire. His books and records were destroyed, he claimed. Reynolds Tobacco sued him for $192,623 the following year.[17] the State of Ohio claimed Sharwell's Company was delinquent in payment of cigarette excise taxes.[18] They were continuously in his offices for there was a substantial amount of money in arrears over the years. The State filed a criminal proceeding charging a felony in false reports and in failing to file.[19] Topper's office displayed their brilliant legal minds in defending. On Sharwell and his company's behalf, a civil suit was filed[20] asking for an injunction and damages against tax commissioner Stanley J. Bowers and the attorney general of Ohio.

A public employee ordinarily cannot be enjoined from performing his official duties. That rule of law did not deter his counsel.

His complaint alleged: "Plaintiffs further say that defendant Stanley J. Bowers in attempting to coerce plaintiff the Sharwell Tobacco into submitting to said purported tax assessment without contest or resistence has repeatedly caused rumors and stories to be circulated both by word of mouth and in the newspapers of Columbus and central Ohio, alleging, by innuendo and otherwise that plaintiffs are guilty of criminal acts, and by so doing has utterly and completely destroyed the credit and business reputation of plaintiff.

"Plaintiffs say that as a direct and proximate result of said circulation of stories and rumors, deliberately and maliciously conducted by defendant Stanley J. Bowers, lines of bank credit have been withdrawn from plaintiffs; accounts receivable have been made difficult or impossible to collect; lines of trade credit have been cut off from plaintiffs; and plaintiffs have been held up in the community to ridicule, scorn and opprobrium, all to their damage in the sum of One Million Dollars (1,000,000.00).''

The State asked for a continuance of the criminal charges on the grounds that 200 subpoenas would have to be served and six chief executives of the major tobacco companies would be required to appear for the prosecution. By his own admission, Sharwell had sold at least 99 million units each year. The criminal case was tried eventually, with Topper's office as counsel. Sharwell was found guilty of a misdemeanor on five counts and found not guilty of felony charges. He was fined $50 on each of five counts and ordered to pay the court costs of the prosecution.[21]

Sharwell then left Ohio to become a bond salesman in New York. Since the criminal case was concluded, he could not be extradited for debt. When questioned by his Toledo cronies about his tax problems, Sharwell said, "I didn't have to pay the State of Ohio the two and a half million I owed, but it cost me about a quarter of a million to beat the case."[22]

While the State of Ohio may have lost millions, friends and relatives claimed that Sherman, in his 25 years of gambling, lost at least $15 million as one of Ohio's most compulsive losers.

No story on political corruption and gambling would be complete without an anecdote about Harry F. Sinclair. Operating on the motto "oily to bed and oily to rise," he acquired oil leases in Oklahoma, Texas, Kansas, Missouri and Illinois with 2,800 miles of pipelines costing $30 million. In 1919, Sinclair's corporation merged into Sinclair Consolidated Oil Co.

With 5,000 tank cars, ships, steamers, tugs and barges he held interests in ports all over the world. His company had more than 1,000 service stations for gasoline and natural gas. His personal estate was valued in excess of $300 million.

Sinclair was a devotee of the turf. In 1920 he was appointed a member of the New York racing commission. He owned the Roncocas Stable. His horse "Zev" defeated the English Derby winner "Papyrus" in the International Race at Belmont on October 20, 1923. He was a principal owner of a team in the Federal Baseball League — and he was without question the biggest gambler of his time.

Harry F. Sinclair contributed heavily to the Ohio Gang in the 1920 election of President Harding. The Teapot Dome transaction was the most sensational of all the Harding scandals. Control of national oil reserves was transferred from a weak Navy Department to the Department of the Interior under Albert B. Fall, the first cabinet member ever to go to jail.

For bribes in excess of $200,000 or more, 9,500 acres of oil reserves in Teapot Dome, Wyoming were leased by Fall to Harry Sinclair. An exclusive right to extract gas and oil for a period of 20 years was granted. Sinclair anticipated a profit of $35 million.

The Justice Department sued to rescind. In civil actions, Sinclair had to repay millions for the oil taken from the reserves. When brought before a Senate Committee investigation, Sinclair contended the government had no right to question him because he was being sued for cancellation of his oil leases, and cases were pending in court. He was cited for contempt of Congress, fined and sentenced to three months in the District of Columbia jail. In the federal courts, he received an additional citation of six months for criminal contempt. After he entered the District of Columbia jail to serve his two contempt charges consecutively, an enterprising bookmaker arranged to be committed for a like term. With regular bribes to the guards, the daily racing form and baseball line were brought in for Sinclair's selection. When released at the end of seven and a half months for good behavior, it was reported that Sinclair paid off his wagering losses, which ranged from a reported $750,000 to $2 million. Years after, *maitre des* (or pit bosses) in casinos around the world were fired on the spot if they failed to immediately recognize Harry F. Sinclair or offer him red carpet treatment.

Today, it is common knowledge that 80 to 90% of all Americans gamble in some form! New giants replace the old as the action continues worldwide. By gambling we lose both our time and treasure, two main things most precious to the life of man. *Sic transit gloria mundi.* Thus passes the glory of the world.

# 31 Some Interesting Cases

Continuous generous payoffs to political and law enforcement officials led to even greater corruption than that of Prohibition days. The Syndicate let it be known that it had huge election funds available to candidates seeking public office. Their ties to local labor and union leaders gave them further vote-producing power. They wanted people in office that they could control or from whom they could demand favor or privilege. Within a few years after formation, such ends were accomplished as Syndicate members virtually controlled the city. They possessed the power to make or destroy any person or business if they called the shots. Their influential ties extended into the judiciary of the city as well, as this chapter illustrates.

In the 15 years of Syndicate operation from 1941 to 1956, numerous individuals owning bars, taverns, restaurants and businesses sustained losses from alleged arson and deliberate setting of fires in their establishments. Yet in all that time, no person involved in gambling was ever indicted or convicted on arson charges of any kind.

In a few cases, Syndicate members arranged for experts to assist destitute businesses who needed to get out desperately. These same experts were often used by labor leaders who wanted destructive demolition of employers' property to induce strike settlements or better bargaining positions. Dynamite and nitroglycerine were favorite tools of the arsonists. Charges could be detonated in a series of relays by use of timing devices. Criminals could perform their assigned duties miles away from the scene of destruction. Such gimmicks established an alibi in event of investigation. There was little or no way for experts examining nitro ruins to determine whether a relay system had been used or not. Evidence was hard to come by. Nitro spread fast and left an acid fume that could be detected but by the time of police arrival there was nothing left to smell.

Homeowners were advised to place matches near an electric iron set on low. An amateur arsonist could be miles away by the time the iron heated sufficiently to ignite the matches. The mistake of an iron accidently being left on, like a stove, could be readily understood by insurance and arson investigators. Homespun advice was given freely to gamblers in debt who could not afford to pay expert fees.

Equally vulnerable to punishment under law were the habitual drinkers of the city. Aside from the regular bars and taverns, two prominent watering holes for the regular imbibers were the Urban Club, a private drinking club organized after the repeal of Prohibition, and a bar at the downtown Secor Hotel. John Sullivan, a hefty 300-pound prankster, held forth at the Secor to a group with the same camraderie of Haddad's. Occasional visitors to the group included Judge Harvey Straub and his political friend and patron, Harry G. Levy, among the regulars.

Dan McCollough often told clients, "Bring in $500 for me and $500 for the prosecutor." But when he couldn't fix a case, he often encountered disasterous results. One of the most publicized drunk driving cases involved Lawrence C. (Larry) Lennon, a 54-year-old federal court reporter. On Saturday April 16, 1950 he plowed his Cadillac into a group of pedestrians at the Secor Hotel Bus Stop.[1] One was killed and six were seriously injured. The driver took off but was stopped a block away. At trial on manslaughter charges, his attorney, Dan McCollough, contended Lennon was unfamiliar with the new automatic transmission. The prosecutor proved him to have been under the influence. At the time of accident, Lennon admitted having five or six drinks. After a one-week trial he was found guilty of second degree manslaughter and sentenced on June 27, 1950 to the Ohio pen.[2] The slight, frail defendant had high blood pressure at the time of his admission. He could not cope with the tension and stress of prison life. Less than two months after entry, Lennon suffered a heart attack and died nine days later.

Trouble-prone Nazarene R. Cochrane owned his own bar known as Rene's Cafe. He followed a customer to another bar. Then as the man was seated on a stool, Cochrane "sucker-punched" him from behind in the jaw or in the back of the neck with his fist. The victim fell, hit his head against a chair and died. A murder warrant was issued. With Dan McCollough as counsel, the state got in evidence of the defendant's vicious temper and bad character to obtain a verdict of guilty of murder in the second degree.[3] It meant a life sentence. Cochrane switched lawyers. He obtained the services of Paul Herbert, an outstanding Columbus trial lawyer, former Lt. Governor and father of a later Ohio Supreme Court Justice. Herbert obtained a reversal and new trial.[4] Subsequent plea bargaining led to a plea of manslaughter and a lesser jail sentence for the accused.

One of the daily regulars at the Urban Club was former Toledo Mud Hen pitcher Carl E. (Danny) Boone. After leaving baseball, Danny inherited about a half million dollars from his sister, Hazel Archer, which enabled him to finance daily drinking sprees. He was constantly drunk. Boone was also consistently getting rolled for everything he had. His second wife reported he came home more than once in shorts alone. Like most drinkers, Danny loved to drive a car. Taking driving privileges away from Danny would be equated to amputating his pitching arm. One night Danny knocked over a city parking sign on the corner of a high school building. The sign cost $30. Danny was arrested for driving under the influence. This was one of several scrapes he had with the law, all minor offenses. Reliable reports stated that Danny paid Norman Cohen, a less than mediocre lawyer, $15,000 in General Motors stock he had inherited to retain his driving privileges.

Like Danny Boone, another Mud Hen Baseball player (unnamed at his request) love to booze. One day at the Fort Meigs Hotel, a hooker from Cincinnati slipped him a Mickey Finn in his hotel room. He was out for hours. All of his clothes, jewelry, and cash totaling $1,800 was taken. Hours later, he told police that "She took everything but my shorts because I was still in them." The girl was apprehended. A $15,000 bail was set. The case was scheduled before Municipal Judge Edgar W. Norris. Judge Norris was an avid baseball fan. Autographed pictures of Connie Mack, Babe Ruth and others were prominently displayed about his office. He refused to lower bond. The judge was determined to have this girl bound over to the grand jury on felony charges, but the girl had Syndicate backing and counsel. The accused asked for a preliminary hearing to determine probable cause. That meant the baseball player as complainant would have to testify. At the first scheduled hearing, he failed to appear. The girl's counsel moved for dismissal. Judge Norris continued the case to subpoena the ball player. Before the order could be enforced, the Toledo Baseball Club announced his sale to a team in the International League. Teams in that league played in cities along the Atlantic seaboard. No team came through or near Ohio. Subpoena power was ineffective outside of the state. An infuriated Judge Norris could not refuse to order dismissal.

True to their promise to keep the city free from crime, the Syndicate kept major crime under control. Local hoodlums were adequately warned not to create problems. Out-of-state hoods were advised not to seek the old-time sanctuary in Toledo. If they came to the city, they were pointed out to the police. Presence of nationally known criminals might involve F.B.I. or federal inquiry. Nothing was to be done that would jeopardize the operation.

Yet when they did act, the Mob protected them. At the height of the Syndicate power following World War II, political critics contended that the prosecutor's office fixed more cases than local jewelers fixed watches. The Libbey-Owens-Ford Employees Federal Credit Union was victimized by armed robbers. Three armed men roughed up manager Al Godfrey and three women employees. They escaped with $36,000 in cash that was on hand to cash payroll checks. Godfrey and his help claimed they could positively identify the culprits. Godfrey went to Akron, Ohio to personally identify a man he claimed was the gangleader who was on trial there for other felony charges. Despite LOF witnesses' sworn testimony, Chief Assistant Prosecutor Joe Jan claimed it was a case of mistaken identity and refused to indict. Godfrey was furious. He threatened to go elsewhere but there was no avenue open to him. Federal Credit Unions later came under federal jurisdiction but the local prosecutor disposed of the case. It was later reported that the trio had taken most of the $36,000 to Chalky Red, who spent the money "to beat the case." Some judges of the Common Pleas court referred to Jan's handling of grand jury proceedings as a joke, stating, "If there are 19 cases being investigated, Jan would probably indict about three."

Joe Urbaytis, principal in the million-dollar post office robbery, became a model prisoner at Alcatraz where he served 19 of his 25-year sentence ordered in 1924. He was eligible for parole in 1943. Upon release, he returned to Toledo during World War II. Unable to find work, he engaged in the illegal sale of food and gas ration coupons and goods. Joe was envious of the Syndicate operators. He demanded a piece of the action but the organization was too long established to admit new interests, particularly a convicted felon. Threats by Joe were unanswered and ignored. Joe became a pest. The Syndicate did everything possible to prevent bloodshed. Joe decided to compete with the Syndicate. Without police or political protection or an O.K. from Joe Fretti, he opened an after-hours unlicensed boot joint known as the Bon-Aire Super Club on Woodville Road in East Toledo. There he established a well-stocked bar replete with stock from Michigan, Illinois and untaxed Ohio liquor. A dice table and several slot machines were available to customers desiring action. Joe was joined by an equally tough Polack as assistant and partner, Edwin (Big Edge) Wojnarowski, alias Wagner. This duo was a formidable pair for any muscular opposition. Both were big, tough and handy with fists or guns as the occasion demanded. The police, politicians and Syndicate were in a quandary about this new operation. If they made an arrest, Joe would claim he was being discriminated against because others were operating illegally. This would raise a stink and the situation might get out of hand or lead to some type of gangland rivalry that the politicians knew could arouse reformers or change. Something had to be done. On November 5, 1946 at about 5:00 A.M. Joe Urbaytis opened the double-door rear entrance of his club to admit a male customer. As he did so, three shots rang out. Joe fell to the floor with bullet wounds in the chest and right shoulder.[5] Patrons who crowded the front room of the converted 2½ storey frame home, fled to escape questioning. Felix (Jimmy) Grudzinski, the bartender, and Big Edge rushed to the rear door. They told police they found Joe sprawled at the foot of the stairs leading to the upper story. He was unarmed and wearing the same topcoat and hat he usually wore about his place. Big Edge told police he asked the dying Urbaytis if he knew who shot him. Urbaytis nodded that he did, but with his last gasp shook his head to emphasize refusal when Big Edge asked in Polish for names.[6] Perhaps Joe felt he was too tough to die. He had been shot years before and recovered rapidly. After his escape from the Lucas County Jail in 1921 he was free for three years. Questioning of a suspect in an armed robbery led Columbus detectives in May 1924 to a rooming house where Joe and his brother Frank were staying. Frank attempted to escape as detective Harry Carson, Columbus, chased him. Joe rushed into the house to fight the officer. As he reached the top of the stairs, Carson struck him in the jaw. Joe went crashing downward over a stair railing and fell backwards one flight, landing in the street on his shoulder. When Carson leaped downstairs, Joe pulled a revolver and fired wildly, missing the detective. Carson drew his pistol and hit Joe in the back but it did not stop his fury as he closed in on the detective. In the ensuing melee, Carson's gun was kicked from his hand. A moment later, Joe's revolver also went flying. The detective managed to pick up his gun and crashed it down on Joe's head. Joe kept coming back at him. Urbaytis was struck three more times on the head before falling to the floor. Joe relived that scene again as he refused to name his assailant.

No witnesses to the shooting were found. Friends and family said that Joe was in good spirits and they did not know of any threats on his life. The victim had $784.12 in cash in his pockets so police ruled out robbery as a motive. Powder burns on his left hand indicated that Joe had struggled with his killer. A .38 caliber bullet was removed from a wall and another was taken from his body. Homicide Detective Captain Ralph Murphy said both bullets were traced to a gun allegedly stolen in June from Detective Captain George Timiney, who had reported it missing from his car.

Two weeks after the slaying, a secret indictment was filed charging Frank Burns with the first degree murder of Joe Urbaytis. On September 30, 1947, federal authorities apprehended Burns in a Chicago hotel.[7] He was transferred temporarily to the federal prison at Milan, Michigan to be held on a federal warrant charging unlawful flight to avoid prosecution.[8] Conviction on this charge carried a maximum penalty of five years' imprisonment and $5,000 fine. On October 9, 1947 federal charges were dropped as Burns was turned over to Toledo authorities.[9] In a surprise move during a six-minute hearing held an hour after the court house official closing time, Burns, through the Syndicate attorney John Canelli, was allowed to plead guilty to a lesser charge of manslaughter.[10] It was the only time I know that Canelli made a court appearance. Prosecutor Joel Rhinefort consented as he told the court, "Justice would best be served by accepting the lesser plea." The prosecutor then made an oral motion to strike the words "purposely and with deliberate premeditated malice" from the indictment. John Canelli told Judge John W. Hackett his client was willing to plead guilty to the now adjusted manslaughter count, which would make Burns eligible for parole in 10 months. The judge had the power to inquire or go behind the plea of guilty as neither the prosecutor's recommendation nor request was binding. Instead, Judge Hackett granted the prosecutor's motion, sentenced Burns to one to 21 years in the Ohio penitentiary, and stepped down from the bench. "That was the fastest murder trial I ever saw," he said laughing.[11]

Burns was taken to the Bureau of Identification in the Police Department. Veteran detectives crowded around the ex-con and congratulated him on escaping with a comparatively light sentence. Returning to the county jail, Sheriff Lieutenant Alfred Bartkowiak remarked to Burns, "You've got a lot of friends around here." "I've always had a lot of friends here," Burns replied. "They like me." "They must," Bartkowiak answered as he referred to the fact that only aged pictures of Burns, who had an extensive criminal record, could be found in police records when he was sought as Urbaytis' killer.[12]

Bartkowiak charged Prosecutor Joel Rhinefort had ignored evidence he had accumulated during his 11-month investigation of the murder. He claimed, a day after the plea bargaining, that he had uncovered a witness who claimed he saw the stolen Timiney gun being handed to Urbaytis on the night it was allegedly stolen. He also revealed that he had an eyewitness to the shooting, claiming James R. McCawley, Bon-Aire bartender, had admitted to him that he was an eyewitness. Police found a note in McCawley's home reading, "If anything happens to me, call the police and tell them Frankie Burns killed Joe U." The officer said he felt there was enough evidence to convict Burns on the first degree murder charge. He claimed he left a message in the prosecutor's office before any plea was accepted seeking a conference on the Burns case, but the prosecutor never returned the call. The prosecutor denied there was any deal on the Burns case yet the *Blade* later reported that a manslaughter plea was arranged the night of October 1, 1947 in a conference that Burns, Canelli and Rhinefort held just after his commitment in Milan, Michigan. To 64-year-old Burns, it made little difference as he would have to serve time under either the state or federal charges. Underworld and Syndicate intermediaries for Burns carried a stipulation in arranging the plea that he was not to be questioned about the gun. Left unanswered by the six-minute trial were questions as to how the slayer came into possession of a police revolver. Also left unanswered was the motive for such murder.

Why? Nobody asked! Was Burns paid and if so, by whom, were also questions that could have been asked. Some judges might have asked how Burns supported himself in his 11-month flight. Burns served five years in the Ohio Pen. The Bon-Aire Club closed. No other action was taken. Reports were that Joe Fretti paid off Big Edge.

The Urbaytis murder caused grave consternation among the politicians and Syndicate. Fear of publicity and public indignation resulted in an admonition that killing would no longer be tolerated. If there was to be a murder, let it appear to happen elsewhere to take heat off locally. The lawyers said, "Of course, if there is no body found, then there is no corpus delecti and no murder can be charged or proved."

Leonard Gross, also known as Leonard Mandel, was a nephew of Charles (Schnick) Gross, a member of Richard Gosser's goon squad.

Leonard had a criminal record but his uncle was able to get him a job working for the Syndicate through Gosser's friendship with Tony Paul. Leonard proved to be talkative and a trouble maker. A local pawnshop tipped off the Syndicate that Leonard had purchased a gun. This was a taboo among crap game employees. Under physical grilling, Leonard confessed to a plot to knock off the crap game. The plan was to overcome the armed guard in the booth above the second double-guarded entrance doorway. This guard controlled entrances to and from casino doors by push button switches. If an accomplice could control that room, the gang could line up the customers and make a substantial cash heist without interruption.

"Sometimes employees are not patted down by the guards," Leonard told his captors. "I was to pass inspection; if I got my gun inside, I would hand it over to accomplices. They would do the rest."

Nobody said anything to Schnick Gross. Leonard was now beyond salvation. Who could say what motives he might have had in buying a gun. His death could not occur in Lucas County. Politicians ruled out local murder. In a field 20 miles outside of Cleveland, six months later, a farmer discovered the badly decomposed half-nude body of Leonard Gross. He had been dead for months before discovery.

Harold "Chink" Goldberg was alleged to have been another troublemaker. After serving overseas in World War II, he became involved in numbers and pinball rackets in the county. He told Syndicate people that he wanted more. His demands were ignored. One day he accosted Bennie Aronoff on the streets, held him and threatened him with personal bodily harm. That didn't help. Chink took to drink. Some said he was starting on dope too. In frustrated rage, Chink threw a brick through a plate glass window of Aronoff's jewelry store. Chink was getting out of line and was told to back down, but he refused to do so. On a warm June night in 1950, Chink was standing on a corner outside of a night club waiting for a friend to pick him up for dinner. At about 10:45 P.M. a car double-parked in front of him. Four men were in it. One man motioned Chink over to their car. He got in and was never seen again. Soon after, a detective said, "Chink's gone. Don't bother looking for him." Another facetiously remarked, "For all I know Chink eloped with another Chinaman." After seven years of absence, under the Ohio law, Goldberg was declared legally dead on October 3, 1957.[13]

Harvey G. Straub came from a poor family. His father, William E. Straub, had been a barber in the city since 1897. Haircuts were 15 cents then and were raised to a quarter 20 years later. His father expanded his business to haircuts and billiards in the partnership of

Straub and Haggerty in the downtown area. Still it was tough to make a living. Son Harvey was a good athlete, particularly excelling in baseball. He won an athletic scholarship at the University of Michigan where he was captain of the baseball team that went to Japan in the 1920s. Later he attended their law school, graduating in the depression years. Harvey became one of the boys drinking and hanging around Schuchmann's Tavern where gambling and card playing was permitted. He also hung around the Eagles where he developed alliances with many Republican political leaders. Isadore Topper and Harry G. Levy became close friends. Harvey could not afford to support his father on his earnings as a lawyer. Friends encouraged Harvey to seek political office. They promised to help his father financially. In 1939 he was elected to the bench of the Municipal Court. As a judge, Harvey was able to secure sinecure political jobs or appointments for his father who retired in 1940 but lived to over 90 years of age. The father became a hanger-on, seen around the smaller gambling spots, Eagles, Schuchmann's, Stag Grill, Elks, Republican Club and others of the city. He reported what he saw and heard in such places to his son, the judge.

In his retirement of 20 years or more, William E. Straub lived a seedy existence. He had very few friends. He never owned an automobile. He appeared shabbily dressed in one of two suits of clothes that he owned over such years. He was seen eating alone for the most part in the cheaper downtown restaurants as a regular habitue of such places. Except for the vicarious recognition given because of his son's position, William E. Straub was a loner. Members of the Syndicate whom he had barbered over the years and political friends of his son befriended him with financial pittances over his declining years. Many times I saw the assignment clerk in the Court of Common Pleas hand over a check to Billy on payday. Once I facetiously asked, "What kind of work are you doing now, Billy?" He reported my joshing and downtown antics to his son.

After a few terms in the Municipal court, Harvey ran for judge of the Court of Common please and was elected in 1944. He joined his political friend Gordon Jeffery who was clerk of courts. When Chester Urbaytis was accused of embezzling $6,000 of his ward's money, he waived a jury and consented to be tried by a man he knew personally, Judge Straub. He thought Harvey would treat him justly. There was enough evidence to justify acquittal, but instead Harvey found him guilty of embezzlement and sentenced him to the Ohio Penitentiary. An appeal was taken by Urbaytis to the Supreme Court of Ohio. That court said, "There was no direct evidence that he

(Urbaytis) had appropriated or converted his ward's funds to his own use...."[14] The accused produced two witnesses who swore positively and unequivocally that he had delivered the funds to his ward, and one of these witnesses was the ward to whom such funds belonged. Harvey Straub in a written opinion disregarded the entire testimony of these two witnesses on the basis it was a fabrication, pure and simple, to save a relative from conviction."[15] The Supreme Court further stated, "The fact remains that such evidence stands uncontradicted and unimpeached and constituted the only explanation in the case of what became of the $6,000." The trial court (Harvey) had no right to substitute his judgment of the facts to the actual facts in the record. The conviction was reversed. Urbaytis was discharged.[16] Harvey's arrogant know-it-all attitude was reflected in the comment: "I've built an immunity to reversals." He had also built up a record of cases where his decisions required appeal or reversal.

Joe Wolvek, a transferee to Toledo from Brooklyn, wanted to marry Julius Jacobs' sister Thelma. Joe was married at the time. He claimed his wife refused to come to Toledo where he had employment. The Wolveks had no children, no property and had been separated for over two years. There were no real issues or problems in the case. The wife said that she would not contest the divorce nor demand alimony. Since the wife resided in New York, service of notice of divorce proceedings would have to be by publication in the legal news. Julius Jacobs prepared the legal documents and requested me to appear as an attorney of record because of the family involvement.[17]

During the 1940s Lucas County had only one Domestic Relations judge, Paul W. Alexander, a Harvard graduate. A huge backlog of divorce cases arose during the war years. The Domestic Relations court assigned uncontested matters to the common pleas judges. The Wolvek case was assigned to Judge Harvey Straub. On the date of the trial, I appeared with the plaintiff, Joe Wolvek, and one collaborating witness, as required by law. Judge Straub refused to grant the divorce or sign the prepared decree which was a formality in 99% of the cases. "I want to know how they got along in New York," the judge said. Even when told that the case was that of Julius Jacobs, Straub was adamant. Wolvek and I were furious. I said to the judge, "You mean to tell me that Julius Jacobs and I don't know enough to prepare a simple uncontested divorce? There's enough evidence here to warrant it." But the judge insisted on more testimony. A request was made to continue the case for another day. Wolvek phoned his father in New York who agreed to fly in that night to testify. The money used for his fare would have been used to pay my fee. Now it was gone. The father testified the next morning. The decree was signed, but I was not paid and because of the expense, didn't ask.

No reason was ever given for Straub's conduct.

Bar associations have always been held in high regard by the public and press because of their traditional concern for truth, honesty and fairness. Any iconoclastic effort to shatter this image of respectability is more difficult than the task of Sisyphus. To attack such status or try to convince the media or public of error is equated to impeaching motherhood, knocking apple pie or disputing the Pope's dogmas while seated ex Cathedra where the same is infallible and irrefutable. In disciplinary proceedings of Bar associations, press and public alike are totally unaware of the nature of the procedures, the complexity of the rules and the secrecy in hearings; consequently when any decision or "end result" is announced, the press and public accept it as a considered judgment, not subject to scrutiny or criticism.

George Gould, the lawyer described in the chapter on payoffs who put his client Greyhound in the pinball business, was the president-elect of the Toledo Bar Association in 1948.

As a trial lawyer, Gould was vain, vindictive and ruthless. He fought to win every case at any cost. He loved attention. He swaggered when he walked. Riding a bicycle downtown from his home to his office, womanizing or making friends with many gays in the city, were tactics that he used to become the subject of conversation. "I don't care what they say or write as long as my name is spelled correctly," he said. A newspaperman once told me, "Gould is a powderkeg of dynamite ready to blow up in the face of anybody who resists him." Another person later told me, "One of the worst days of my life occurred when I was introduced to George Gould. I told him repeatedly that I would like to take back the introduction."

When Harlan Britz married into the Gould family, many people told his father, "Your son has married into the worst family in the city." Gould frequented the gambling places of the downtown area. He was seen betting on most sports events and liked to play bridge or gin rummy. One day in Niltap's card room he asked me to play gin rummy with him at 10 cents a point. I consented. His ne'er-do-well brother Jay wanted to bet a nickel a point against me. I consented. I liked being challenged.

Gould was tricky and had to be watched, I was told. Forewarned, I scrutinized his every movement in playing. The game started auspiciously with an argument when Gould picked up his hand which I dealt. He saw he held a bad hand of 11 cards. Instead of discarding the 11th card, he drew a 12th card, declaring a misdeal. An argument ensued. While keeping score, Gould would add 19 to 22 and put down 31. I corrected him. He would throw his cards into the deck, saying "Twenty points" when he really had 30. I had him retrieve his hand to properly account for the cards and the points. He was infuriated at being accused of cheating before the large audience of kibitzers that grew and watched the game. He fumed, fretted and played poorly. I blitzed him all across the board, Hollywood style, which mean about 1,800 points or $180. To Jay it meant $90. "That's all for today," I said as I rose from the card table. George wanted to play another game, but I was adamant because of his many arguments. "Pay up. We'll play again some other time," I said. George angrily wrote out a check. Jay had $30 or $40, but refused to part with it. He became abusive and insulting and made derogatory remarks. I countered with a remark: That "Don't call me names. You should be back in the penitentiary." Jay had served time for rape. The reference to his brother's crime and incarceration for rape and a public accusation of cheating, which was warranted, was more than George Gould could bear.

He openly boasted of his plans for revenge. He knew from his experience in the Bar that "a disbarred lawyer is a lonely man." He knew what the Toledo gambling had done to other attorneys who had gambled locally. He knew that the gamblers and the politicians would cut down and destroy anybody who posed a threat or invited Bar scrutiny into their affairs. The political fixers could not tolerate a Bar inquiry, for they knew a Bar group would not be as gullible as the public. The Syndicate removed the victim rather than remove the cancer. Gould knew all this, but I didn't.

When Gould became president of the Bar the following year, he appointed all the members of the Grievance Committee, and he personally went around gathering evidence to strike down and destroy my career and me in my chosen profession. Since the big law firms controlled the Bar, Gould knew the strength of his position.[18]

Unfortunately for me at this time, I went overboard financially due to my compulsive gambling. I commingled the funds of my clients with my own. My bank account showed it. This was a dangerous practice because it could lead to losses and problems with clients in event of death. The canon of ethics warned against such practice. Complaints were filed. The Grievance Committee of the local Bar undertook an investigation. A *Blade* lawyer on the Grievance Committee broke his oath of secrecy and leaked information to his paper. In turn, the Syndicate, or Mob, was put on notice. Chalky Red called me.

"Come on out to the joint," Red said. "Joe Fretti and I want to help you." I trusted him and wanted help. The Syndicate was looking out to protect itself and its business. They did not relish Bar associations looking into their affairs or making inquiry about gambling or gambling losses. It could be embarrassing, could lead to criminal action and/or closing.

"Find out how much you need and we'll give it to your lawyer," Joe Fretti said. "Just don't involve us or mention gambling. Promise." I promised. They didn't even trust me enough to give me the funds. I could have borrowed the $3,500 to cover up, but I thought they were going to help.

I hired George Effler, a prominent trial lawyer, to represent me before the Bar. His doctor brother had similar problems over drug charges, so I felt he could identify with my case. I paid a requested retainer and turned over several personal injury cases on a split fee arrangement. Effler suggested that I refrain from appearance in court.

For some unknown reason Joe Fretti turned over the financial aspects of our agreement to Abe (Muzzler) Shapiro, who by now was the city's most compulsive gambler. Usually Harry G. Levy looked in on settlements, over the shoulder of the attorneys. I was told to refrain from gambling, so I did not learn that the Muzzler went into every bookie and gambling joint in town under the aegis of Joe Fretti and told them to contribute to the settlement. He claimed that I had lost thousands, yet the $3,500 was a matter of record.

The Muzzler raised over $60,000 yet loaned 10%, or $6,000, to me. Attorney Morris Lubitsky, who replaced Dan McCullough in police court gambling cases, later told me, "I don't know what settlement he made, but the Muzzler made a big profit on you." Syndicate attorney Ira Cole prepared both a release and loan agreement which I signed, and $3,500 was delivered to George Effler. Maybe the Mob owed Cole a fee or favor, but the Muzzler pocketed over $50,000 with impunity. Levy, I was told, was furious over the matter.

Restitution of the $3,500 was made immediately. Nothing was said about the extra sum in the attorney's possession.

George Smith, a member of the Grievance Committee and of a big law firm, took over completion of all cases of my clients, appearing before the Grievance Committee before any decision was made. This is highly unusual. He also kept the entire fee. I was powerless to protest. Character witness Homer Hanham, who appeared in my behalf before the Grievance Committee, later said, "I never saw a colder bunch. I knew I didn't help."

The courts of Ohio had often said: "Restitution has its rewards" particularly where younger lawyers are involved. The Grievance Committee went on record that complaints against me merited nothing more than dismissal from the bar association, but the committee was never discharged.

Finally in February 1952, more than three years after complaints and two years after restitution, the committee wrote a letter to the Common Pleas court judges asking that a committee be appointed to prosecute charges.[19] Every other disbarment case in Lucas County was kept secret. Dan McCollough's file disappeared. The clerk of courts, Gordon Jeffery, had a special vault to keep such cases under seal. The reason for such action was based upon a decision of the New York Court of Appeal where Judge Cardozo wrote, while on the bench in New York:[20]

> Where the court is given power of Inquisition, we put into its hands a weapon whereby the fair name of a lawyer, however innocent of wrong, is at the mercy of the tongue of ignorance or malice. Reputation in such a calling is like a plant of tender growth and its bloom, once lost, is not easily restored. The mere summons to appear at such a hearing may become a blur and a reproach. Dangers are indeed here, but not without a remedy. The remedy is to make the inquisition a secret one in its preliminary stages.
>
> There is a practice of distant origin by which disciplinary proceedings, unless issuing in a judgment adverse to the attorney, are recorded as anonymous.

Publicity creates a public expectancy of punishment. Absent publicity, the courts or juries are more likely to be lenient rather than punitive.

Lawyers despise publicity of an adverse nature. One lawyer to the public is all lawyers. The Alger Hiss cause celebre was then in the headlines. Fellow lawyers on the Carnegie Enforcement claimed Hiss's conduct "ruined their reputations."[21] Ethics was an issue in the Presidential campaign of 1952. Lawyers, like Congressmen, despise adverse publicity or scrutiny. Columnist Jack Anderson is the man most feared by Congress.[22] The clerk of court knew or should have known all this but he didn't care!

Regardless of law, Clerk Jeffery let the media repeatedly publicize the bar letter. I had done journalistic work for Jeffery. I helped write his speeches and made cash contributions to his political campaigns. A blistering letter to Jeffery followed. It went unanswered. Jeffery reported its contents to his friends, Harry G. Levy and Harvey Straub.

From the financial assistance received in the gambler's trial from which he started a stock portfolio in 1944, Jeffery then became The Political Golden Boy. Mob backing and contributions made him the biggest vote-getter for the Republican Party in the county. By 1952, he had become vain, pompous and drunk with power. Jeffery was named to head the Eisenhower for President campaign in Lucas County. His annual salary as clerk was $5,545 a year. The county prosecutor made $45 less.[23] Beginning in 1952, U.S. government bonds were being purchased in Jeffery's name. Before he left office in 1956, $55,000 in bonds, 10 times his annual salary, had been purchased for him.[24] He kept the bonds without redemption. At the time of death, he left an estate of $220,903, exclusive of an $80,000 home in his wife's name.[25] In Toledo, crime paid and so did politics! Jeffery got his share.

When the court did appoint a committee to prosecute, it included my nemesis, George Gould. I couldn't believe they didn't know of his vengeance. Jeffery allowed more publicity to ensue. The first court committee appointed refused to act. Whether the members were reluctant to be privy to Gould's revenge is unknown. A *Blade* story stated a Grievance Committee member said: "They might be witnesses so they couldn't act in dual capacities." Gould told the court he had investigated the matters and might testify! This was not true. A second committee with renewed publicity was appointed. Finally, more than three years after the grievance proceedings started, a hearing was scheduled.

Friends went to Ray Kest for help. They knew he could get favor from the Mob. Ray had previously saved Joseph (Yussel) Friedman from their anger. When the Mob discovered a series of unusual winning tickets on horse racing, they became suspicious and hired Pinkerton detectives to investigate. Unknown to the help, detectives spied on the clerks. They discovered Yussel, in charge of horse race payoffs, past-posting them by slipping in a winner once in a while and having a cohort collect. Raphael saved his friend but after conferences on my case, said, "The attorneys call the shots in these cases. Everybody is afraid of them. It's up to Dan McCollough as far as I know."[26]

Raphael couldn't complain too strenuously for his own pocketbook would be affected. The Mob had treated him fairly. When he died in 1964, Kest left a gross estate of $212,000 without evaluation of Florida or other out-of-state property.[27] Considering the salary paid to a circulation manager of the only newspaper in town, where there was no competition as before, Kest didn't fare too badly.

A few weeks before final hearing on my professional life, Effler refused to divide a $2,200 fee as agreed. He deliberately provoked an argument with me because he had now undertaken representation of two members of the Syndicate, Joe Yappolo and Louis (Paccock) Walker. There was a conflict of interest. When confronted with this in a violent argument, Effler wanted to drop out of my case. I refused to speak to him. After the publicity my sister called in her favorite attorney, Harry Levison, who was going to save me. I didn't want him. I told her the two previous family cases had turned me completely against him. "The family has an interest," she said. "Who else can you get? Effler is a crook, you know that." I remained silent but I had a premonition about lawyers who take cases without preparation. Effler resented Levison's intrusion.

Levison never consulted with me. He persuaded Effler to come to court, but was told Effler did not intend to speak out although he was more familiar with the facts than Levison.

Effler had promised not to mention gambling but didn't tell Levison of his pledge, showing more favor to the gamblers than to me.

The judges were Tom O'Conner, the former prosecutor, John M. McCabe, Licavoli jurist, and Harvey G. Straub. Ordinarily a judge who has any leanings of partiality to either side should disqualify himself but such ethical considerations of fairness were ignored by Straub.

By that time, the milk of human kindness had soured the jurists into bitterness.

In an earlier case, these Lucas County jurists, sitting as a panel in place of a jury, also sentenced a 17-year-old to death in a rape-murder trial.[28]

A defense team of five attorneys, headed by McCollough, was unable to save the boy from electrocution. The jurists based their decision on the fact that during the entire trial, the youthful defendant failed to show any signs of remorse. In a recent television murder trial, "A Death in Canaan," another jurist used the same argument in ordering sentence. Howls of protest followed. Many psychiatrists claim that such youths are so overcome by the enormity of the nature of the crime and circumstances that they are rendered incapable of emotion.

The principal charge against me was commingling of funds of clients. No losses to any clients occurred. Levison told the court I was involved in gambling and produced a letter written that morning to me to sign promising to quit gambling. I cringed. He was not supposed to go into that! I signed without reading. It looked hopeless.

No witnesses were called nor sworn testimony given. The case was based on written statements of counsel. I did not testify nor could I be compelled to do so![29] No record was made so that an appeal could be taken. No law or briefs for guidance by the court were filed by either side. The three-judge panel ordered a suspension from practice for five years effective from the day of trial. The months of prior pretrial publicity, tantamount to disbarment, were not considered to reduce such judgment. Levison had strike three called while at bat for our family.

A loss of such right of appeal was prejudicial. About the same time as this decision, three jurists on the Court of Appeals of Lucas County, which could have heard my appeal, if taken, heard a Leiberman appeal of a bar decision by assignment from the Ohio Supreme Court. Attorney Leiberman had been previously suspended and indicted. He had several charges against him. The Court of Appeals resisted Bar recommendations of disbarment and imposed a one-year suspension![30]

The Mob had all the power and influence to save me, if they desired. No one came forward to advise me to go elsewhere to save my damaged reputation or professional career. I was sickened by this betrayal. I could not say a word about it at that time.

There were reasons why Chalky Red and Joe Fretti broke their word. They could claim I crossed them by mention of gambling.

Later investigation revealed that Straub was in Columbus the week of the disciplinary hearing and had conferred with Harry G. Levy and Isadore Topper. Both knew of my predicament and one favorable word from either could have turned Straub. They did nothing. The Columbus conference included the pending case with Effler and counsel where Straub could also be helpful.[31]

My brother Ben is one of the most intelligent men I have ever known. As a senior at Woodward Tech High School, he had his picture in the 1928 yearbook 14 times, more than any other student in the entire school. He was the starting guard on the city championship basketball team which later went to the state regional finals in Bowling Green, where his man in the playoff game was Ivy B. Williamson, later athletic director at the Universities of Wisconsin and Oklahoma. Ben was sports editor of the Woodward *Tattler,* president of the Pueper Club and the senior class; everything that he did resulted in favorable publicity. He was witty, had a keen sense of justice and was unquestionably honest and truth-telling.

A choice of friends led him to go into education, in which he received his degree at the University of Toledo during the Depression years. Since there was no advancement in education, Ben decided he would accept employment in the then forthcoming Social Security Administration. The training process took him to Baltimore, Maryland. There he entered the University of Maryland night law school. He received excellent grades. After one year, he returned to Toledo for field work. With the advent of the second world war and ominous threats of draft, he was advised to join the Red Cross as an athletic director. After spending 17 months with the Lightning Division at Camp Butner, North Carolina, which was about to embark for the European theatre of war, Ben received his draft notice. He returned to Toledo, was drafted and assigned to the Navy. While in training at the Naval Hospital in Bethesda, Maryland, a nodule was noted on his neck. The surgeon recommended surgery. After a second opinion, it was performed.

Following discharge from service in the Pacific, he entered the College of law at the University of Toledo. Dean Charles Fornoff taught Civil Proceedure, a very tough course. He was droll, dull and could put any student to sleep. Ben became inattentive, lethargic, his grades fell. He withdrew from school rather than flunk out. It was at this time that I was undergoing the publicized disciplinary proceedings mentioned before. Ben sought medical attention for his problem. It was discovered that he had a latent reaction to the nodule surgery performed while in service. It could have killed him if left undetected. He knew now that the grades that he had obtained in Maryland would, in all probability, have been the same at the Univesity of Toledo but for this injury. He could have gone to the dean and asked for an opportunity to repeat the classes, or be reinstated. He had the best excuse in the world — service disability. But he was embarrassed vicariously because of my predicament. He felt that he might be overruled or rejected and did nothing. He had all the qualifications for the making of a fine lawyer: acute intelligence, integrity and knowledge of human frailty.

Thus did George Gould's venom contribute to the demise of two professional careers — one entirely blameless.

I went to San Francisco to help my sister Jean whose husband George was an unemployed drunk. He had neglected her and their three kids. George Gould, George Effler, George Smith, Harvey George Straub, Harry G. (Could the "G." have stood for George? No one ever told me.) Levy and brother-in-law George. The name became an anethema to me. I took a job with Bancroft-Whitney, law book publishers. I was assigned to write the syllabus of California decisions. While working in their library, I discovered that California surpassed every other state with an integrated Bar where all disciplinary actions were heard by the California Supreme Court. That court would have imposed a one-month suspension on me, given the same facts. A survey and extensive search of all the cases in the country revealed no attorney received more than a six-month suspension for commingling and related matters. Five years was tantamount to disbarment.

Thorough research of California law also revealed procedural errors that violated principles of due process or fundamental fairness. I felt that the local judges erred badly, so I sent my findings to Toledo.

In the interim, Effler had recovered a $27,000 verdict for one of my clients. Originally he had agreed that the one-third contingent fee of $9,000 was to be 50/50. Effler filed a suit against me asking for a declaratory judgment as to the ethics of splitting with a non-lawyer.[32] This case was assigned to Harvey Straub who should have withdrawn but failed to do so. At a pretrial conference, both former attorneys were present with my sister. Judge Straub told them: "I (Straub) had held out for the five-year suspension against the other two judges who favored a six-month suspension." He based his ruling on a "spite fence case" decided some years before the hearing.[33] This was clear to counsel that Straub had decided on evidence outside the record. Veteran trial lawyer Morris Britz attended the "spite fence case." Afterwards he said, "I never saw a judge (Straub) castigate or berate an attorney (Illman) worse in any case as he did." Yet I received a favorable verdict which was sustained on appeal and the greatest compliment of all when the parties I sued switched from the lawyer used at trial to me as family counselor. What was Straub talking about?

The braggadocio and remarks of bias and hate were repeated by Straub in several public places thereafter. Armed with affidavits from my sister and Levison, which disclosed this apparent error on its face, I sought counsel to vacate the former order and reinstate me to practice, citing numerous errors with legal citations in support of my position. No lawyers were willing to tackle the Bar with these assertions. I filed a motion to be reinstated myself. It was one man against the system.

The committee was imperious, adopting the rule "The King can do no wrong." Many lawyers felt they were above the law, or a law unto themselves! I claimed voluminous errors in conduct of their prosecution. California judges might agree but Toledoans would not tolerate the integrity and authority of Bar being impugned! Likewise, it never paid to buck the Hill powers or insult Congress! "Crossfire with one judge and the whole pack will help him get even."[34]

Ordinarily, a self-respecting judge would withdraw from any case where partiality was shown. I filed an affidavit of prejudice against Straub. We flew to Columbus on the same plane as he insisted on a hearing before the Chief Justice. The next day he stated in court, "I'm not prejudiced against him. He's prejudiced against me." After an extended self-protecting argument, Straub finally withdrew from the original three-judge panel. Upon his final withdrawal, I orally requested a new judge to replace Straub, "Otherwise the panel might be illegally constituted." This was too much! The two remaining sustained a motion to dismiss my motion as "a stray paper" having no right to record in such proceedings.[35] The California precedents were useless!

Friends in the legal fraternity in other cities in Ohio could not understand why a five-year suspension was ordered in a case where restitution had been made. Absent the gambling influence, in other Ohio cities one to six months would have been the worst penalty. No explanation was made of Straub's bragging about his unnecessarily severe action. Some lawyers who knew him claimed that either the Mob or the Bar or both were so firmly entrenched that they could not be subject to criticism and Straub wanted people to know he was part of it!

While Mayor of Cleveland, Frank Lausche brought Eliot Ness from Chicago to clean up the city, they closed up every joint in town. The city was clean and the police uncorruptible, all untouchables. In 1949, Governor Frank Lausche organized an undercover group in his office to investigate commercialized gambling "joints". Anthony A. Rutkowski was placed in charge. Under a carefully mapped plan, Mr. Rutkowski explained: "I sent undercover agents to make investigations preparatory to a projected raid. When the agent discovers gambling, reinforcements are requested and a raid ensues." Such procedure was successful in 1949 and 1950 raids on the Colony Club in Lawrence County and the Pettibone Club in Geauga County. Mr. Rutkowski stated his actions were authorized "as chairman of the Governor's Anti-gambling Committee."

On October 25, 1951 Rutkowski sent two of the governor's men, Donald Van Horn and John R. Hall, on a mission to ferret out evidence of gambling in Toledo. Before his state service, Van Horn had spent three years overseas in World War II where he won a Distinguished Service Medal, a Presidential citation and the French

Croix de Guerre. He was the third man to land in Normandy on D-Day, was wounded twice and captured by the Germans. At the time of his Toledo visit he was still under treatment for shrapnel wounds at the base of the spine. Mr. Hall was a veteran of naval service in the battles of Guam, Iwo Jima, Saipan and Okinawa.

Leaks from Columbus preceded their arrival in Toledo. The local Mob was prepared for Hall and Van Horn. When the two agents went to the New Dix Gambling Casino on a Saturday night, law enforcement authorities and Underworld characters knew they were there to obtain evidence of gambling. There was ample evidence to authorize a raid as the Casino was crowded with weekend business as usual. At about 1:20 A.M., when the two agents went to get their coats, six Syndicate employees, including Joe Yoppolo and Louis (Paddock) Walker, surrounded them. The agents were handed their coats without being asked for their check or its number. The agents were told they could not leave the building "until there was a little checking done." Later Yoppolo escorted the agents out of the building and ordered them into his car.

From there the agents were escorted by Walker and Yoppolo to the Library Lounge downtown. There a few phone calls were made. The agents were then driven to Ka-See's Theatre Night Club, the city's outstanding entertainment spot. There the four men allegedly watched a stage show. While there, the Club photographer took their pictures seated together. This was under advice of counsel for the Toledo duo were too naive to think of it themselves. The photo showed the two agents at a table flanked on both sides by their two "hosts." At three o'clock the two undercover men were then dropped off at a downtown news stand. The detention prevented the agents from going to the judges at that hour for an order to justify a raid. The disgusted agents returned to Columbus and notified their superiors.

A few days later, the governor's men said, "This kidnap incident brings our anti-gambling effort to light and upset immediate plans for a raid." A furious Governor Lausche immediately instructed Prosecutor Rhinefort to locate and prosecute the men involved.

Paddock and Joe were picked up. Both agents identified them in a police lineup. They were charged with being suspicious persons, a misdemeanor carrying a sentence of 30 days and a $50 fine. "This is a temporary measure," Prosecutor Rhinefort explained, "until the evidence is heard by the grand jury."[36] The grand jury was then in convenient recess for two weeks.

Mr. Rutkowski then refused to make any comments because he

had agreed to a conference with Safety Director DeAngelo and Mr. Rhinefort to keep the matter in confidence. The confidence request was made, he said, to prevent prejudicial bias. It was evident then that local officials realized pretrial publicity was damaging and created public expectancy of punishment. In Columbus, the attorney general, C. Willion O'Neill, could be made to look bad for the governor's men had bypassed his office as chief law officer of the state. The governor also could be placed in a bad light and even worse the Syndicate could be ruined!

In the preliminary conference with Safety Director DeAngelo and Prosecutor Rhinefort, the two defendants gave the same version of having encountered the two agents downtown and "believing to being acquainted" took them to Ka-See's as a "guest of Mr. Walker." At this conference, the picture taken at the night club was shown to the prosecutor. Mr. Rutkowski and the two agents were summoned from their hotel.[37] Mr. Rutkowski declared, "I suppose you are going to show us a picture?" Five days later, the picture appeared in the *Blade*.[38] The picture made the defense look good as it disclosed Van Horn seated west on the left side of a small table, Hall on the east end or right seat with Walker behind the first and Yoppolo behind the secret agent. None of the four appeared to be in distress!

Eventually the grand jury did return a felony indictment.[39] The Mob hired George Effler to defend while he was still representing me! When I asked for an accounting on the Muzzler's money "loaned" for my benefit, Effler replied, "It's the gambler's money and I am keeping it for their fees." I got nowhere.[40]

After charges were filed, the Walker case was assigned by Clerk of Courts Jeffery to Judge Straub. Effler filed a motion for a bill of particulars. The outcome was never in doubt. Paddock was a lifelong friend of Harry G. Levy, Straub's political patron. In his will, Levy on death left jewelry and personal property to Paddock and $5,000 to Straub.[41] Joe Yapp had showered drinks on Straub when a partner in Jakey's Friendly Bar. Neither defendant would ever be in jeopardy but it had to be staged to look good in the public eye. Assistant Joe Jan answered Effler's request for particulars on January 3, 1953. At that time the case was already 14 months old. The defense could claim denial of a right to a speedy trial but that would not set right with the public who would smell a fix.

The law under which the abduction charge was filed read: "No person, without privilege, shall knowingly ... by force or threat ... restrain another of his liberty under circumstances which create a risk of physical harm to the victim, or place him in fear."

The Bill of Particulars stated: "On several occasions, the agents wanted to leave but each time were ordered to remain for further checking. On several occasions the agents wanted to use their own cars, or even a cab, but in each instance they were told that the defendants would drive them in the cars of the defendants when the defendants were ready."[42]

Agents Van Horn and Hall were educated, well-trained men, trusted to do a job ordered by the governor. They were prevented from completion of their duties by detention, if they were to be believed. Six men surrounded them at the New Dix. Only two escorted them about the city. The agents knew that the Toledo Syndicate had Purple Gang and Licavoli connections. They knew of the unsolved murders. Both remained calm rather than risk physical acts of escape that would place either in jeopardy or cause violence. They had been disarmed! Their escorts may have been armed! They didn't know. They couldn't confer or agree on a plan of action. They couldn't use a phone. If they could, whom would they call? The police and sheriff were not on their side. The prosecutor would stall for time! They could become frustrated and not know what to do, hence do nothing.

Neither Gracie and Hy Segal, photographers at Ka-See's who took the pictures, were ever called as witnesses. They said "Both agents appeared nervous. Both originally refused to take the picture. Both refused to buy a picture." Both personally knew Paddock who bought the pictures and "gave a tip." The *Blade* picture did not show the table at which the four were seated was next to or against the stage. A small railing blocked movement to the stage. There were other tables on both sides. Neither agent could go to the rear for each flank was guarded by Walker or Yoppollo. The agents were small or medium-sized. Walker was over 6 feet tall and weighed over 240 pounds while the equally behemoth Joe outweighed him by 40 pounds. A jury might have believed the agents were "in fear" or restrained, but Judge Straub didn't have to.

By February 1953, Lausche was reelected governor. O'Neill was back as attorney general. Harry Friberg had replaced Rhinefort as prosecutor. Republican William Hirsch was the new sheriff. It was like old times.

On February 21, 1953, Judge Straub ruled that the information contained in the bill of particulars and other testimony presented to the grand jury was insufficient to warrant an indictment.[43]

Both defendants were discharged.[44] If dissatisfied with the order of dismissal, the prosecutor, on behalf of the state, could appeal. It was not a hearing on the merits nor were the defendants in jeopardy. No appeal was ever taken.

The Attorney General, the Governor and his untouchables lost their court case! The mob had won through the efforts of the attorney they had stolen from me. When I heard about this dismissal, I went to Effler's office, which he was sharing with John Barone, and said, "Now that you have been paid by both sides, why not do the decent thing and help me get reinstated." I felt a self-respecting Court, upon learning that the decision in my case was Mafia-tainted, would expunge such record from its files. Effler, however, was furious. He whisked me out of the office, belittling my claims that his conduct was a denial of effective assistance of counsel.

The dismissal was a big feather in the Syndicate cap. The whole state learned about it. The mob political power was ascending. Business people and criminals alike sought out Mob leaders for help in civil and criminal matters. The Syndicate kept operating for four more years, changing locations when required.[45] They outlasted every other joint in the country as this dismissal enabled them to continue until 1956. With money, labor connections, and union strength, the Mob became the city's real power. In the old days the Underworld worked for the police and politicians.[46] In Toledo the low point of the triangle representing the gangsters was reversed and turned half circle. Now the police and politicians worked for the Mob!

An assessment of mobster wealth, power and influence was recently reported: "The mob's hold on the economy stifles competition and siphons off capital, resulting in loss of . . . jobs, an increase in consumer prices of 0.3 per cent, a reduction in total output of $18 billion and a decrease in per capita disposable income of $77 a year.

"Americans will pay $6.5 billion to the Internal Revenue Service because organized crime figures cheat and do not pay their fair share of the tax burden.

"Rarely has the press examined the mob as a business, one that has its own management style and culture."[47]

When the Mob and Syndicate later phased out, Walker went to Las Vegas, where he became a boss at the Riviera Hotel. Judge Straub and his wife were allowed to visit and enjoy his grateful hospitality away from the scrutiny of curious tattle-tale Toledoans.

# 32 The End of Syndicated Gambling

1956 began and ended in stories of crime. Problems of all kinds marked the finale of syndicated gambling in Lucas County. Prior to a January murder that aroused the community, a series of newspaper articles the year before did not auger well for the Underworld, which relied on political favor and prominent attorneys for protection. Bob Considine, reporter of note, copyrighted a series of articles unmasking Las Vegas, revealing criminal alliances of politicians and lawyers with underworld characters.[1] Public opinion regarding such attachments changed. In Las Vegas, leading law firms held gambling franchises and did make deals with the Underworld. Thus comments on the ramifications of Considine's serialized stories made many politicians uneasy.

In 1952, William Hirsch began his first four-year term as sheriff. He was up for reelection in the fall. In his own book, Hirsch told of his response to a question by the clergy. When a minister asked, "Bill, did you know the gambling is still going on in the county?" "Sure," Hirsch answered. "I can name the spots for you."[2] This colloquy occurred within 90 days of his taking office.[3]

Like his predecessors, the sheriff complained that his "staff was too small to keep a steady check on gambling."[4]

Harry Friberg was allowed to run in 1952 in place of Rhinefort as prosecutor. The job paid $5,500 a year. The prosecutor and his staff were also permitted to maintain the private practice of law so long as there was no conflict of interest. Such side practice allowed members of the staff to cover up income from illicit sources. Then they could claim that all income was from legitimate sources.

In a deal with Rhinefort, Thomas J. Mattimoe was named chief assistant prosecutor on December 9, 1952. He took office on January 5, 1953. His salary of $3,600 a year was increased to $5,280.[5]

Ironically, Azar in Lebanese means hazard. In 18th-century England, the game presently known as craps was called "Hazard." Philip Azar led a dangerous existence. He was arrogant, mean and sadistic. He often chained his nymphomaniacal girl friend, Margie, to her bed while he left their apartment on his own errands. When she escaped, he took up with a Mary Lou and placed her under a madam. On Saturday, January 7, 1956, Azar was shot to death in a bordello located directly in front of the inn used by the Syndicate.

Three women were alone in the place when a group of five youthful gangsters entered. They had robbed the same house previously and felt safe, because the house madam could hardly report a crime on such premises. Azar entered to pick up Mary Lou. During the crime an argument and scuffle ensued between the bullish Azar and the youthful gang leader. A shot was fired. Azar fell fatally wounded as the youths fled.

If the deaths had been reported promptly, it would have ruined Syndicate weekend business. Saturday was their best day of the week, so reporting was delayed.[6]

Sheriff Hirsch stated that he knew nothing illegal about the house. He had considered it a tourist home. He expressed surprise to hear it had operated as a vice resort for more than 25 years.

The *Blade* was furious over the delay on the report, the murder and the weak explanation. A week after the murder, when three of the five youths were identified in a police lineup, the *Blade* ran a front-page editorial, "The Community was Alarmed."[7]

A front-page headline was, "Toledo-Detroit Gambling Ties Bolstered as Former Licavoli Helper Moves In."[8] Chalky Red's partner of bootlegging days, Frank (Rough Manuel) Empactato, age 52, alias Emanuel Badalamenti, had been given an O.K. under Red's new rules of order. At this time Chalky had replaced an ailing Joe Fretti as front man of the Syndicate.

Rough Manuel had been ousted from the city by police in Prohibition days. There was testimony in the Licavoli murder trials that he was one of the three men leaving the Bancroft Grill to intercept the Lubitsky trio in the double murder that followed.

Underworld sources, the *Blade* stated, alleged that Rough Manuel "moved in" on Tom Cochran and other operators of a horsebook known as "The House."[9] The "muscling in" was reminiscent of Licavoli tactics. Since there was no room for Manuel in the Syndicate, only outside operators could be victimized. When an objection was made, Rough Manuel was set up in a new venture as a partner with Joe (Yap) Yoppolo and Irving (Slick) Shapiro in operation of a downtown restaurant called Guiseppe's. Captain William Gray of the police morals squad began harassing the restaurant after receiving reports that a back room bar was serving stronger drinks than their wine and beer license permitted. A dice table and other gambling paraphernalia that bore evidence of heavy use, were also ordered removed.[10]

When another ex-convict friend needed work, Red approved of Ray Gentile of Cleveland to run a poker game at the Stag Grill. Gentile, a fellow prisoner during Red's stay at Mansfield, was a nephew of Nicola Gentile, part of the Cleveland faction associated with Joe "The Boss" Masseria. Captain Gray contended the operation was an attempt for craps "to get back into the city."[11]

This was taboo. Such action, the *Blade* stated, had been barred from downtown spots for nearly two decades. The *Blade* now laid out the entire story as though it was a report to the attorney general or governor. After 15 years, the sleeping watchdog of the public began to bark!

Chalky Red's action was creating dissension in the ranks. The boys at the House horsebook were all friends of Ray Kest. Tommy Cochran, Tony Rosen and Nick Abrams had helped Ray quash the strike at the Block wholly-owned Pittsburgh *Post Gazette* in 1941. Now Raphael was returning a favor when he blocked Rough Manuel's action.

Grove Patterson, *Blade* editor for more than 30 years, had gone to California that winter and returned in poor health.

New blood, dissension and jealousy on the editing end of the paper made Ray's position and that of police reporter Cliff Quinn difficult to sustain.

The *Blade* was able to continue its disclosures.[12] On January 20, 1956, they claimed the local gambling markets "lured caravans much like the U. of M-O.S.U. games." The House and Dixie Inn, operating outside the city limits, count their Michigan clientele by the thousand on Saturday.[13] For the first time, the front-page stories named city and county gambling emporiums and listed the names and addresses of all persons holding federal gambling stamps at each place[14]. This evidence had been available to the sheriff and prosecutor for four years. This was the first meaningful exposure.

The fear of Licavoli tactics evoked *Blade* comments: "The number games or policy houses are under the supervision of Anthony "Whitey" Besase, another former Licavoli mobster." Besase's picture was in the story.

The sheriff, in the spotlight and under pressure, reported gambling in the county "closed." Later it was reported that all the paraphernalia was moved to the cement-block building where the alleged kidnap incident of state agents had occurred in 1951 almost five years before. *Blade* disclosures on Mob action, particularly the fishwagon technique of transportation, gave clear evidence that such tactics enabled continuous operation until these new attacks.

Now the Mob had to sneak. There were interruptions. New locations opened, closed and moved. Sheriff's deputies reported when they drove into a suspected game site, they would be informed, "we're closed" but regular customers received instructions where to go. The Mob had to use devious tactics to avoid publicity. Weekend business thrived as usual! Within a few months, *Blade* attacks abated but Mob problems increased from other sources.

Captain Ralph Murphy was an excellent police officer. After serving on the vice squad, he resigned in 1928 and returned a year later to become what the Bar and prosecutor's office called "the perfect witness." Many good police officers refused homicide detail. They complained of being awakened at any hour, day or night, to inspect putrified, decomposed bodies. The job was distasteful, involved long hours and constant study. Yet Murphy's squad solved 18 homicides investigated that year and every one of 16 committed the following year.[15] Gradually, others left the squad and Murphy had to work alone. He liked his job!

The care with which he prepared evidence and his ability to translate his findings in simple language understandable to a jury won him local acclaim. *Blade* police reporter Clifford Quinn had a run-in with Murphy. When Murphy was unable to solve a slaying of a hospital nurse early in 1956, Quinn wanted Murphy to get more men on the job. Murphy resented the intrusion. he told Quinn, "I'll let you know when you can have a story." An angry Quinn retorted, "I'll get your job!" Then Quinn wrote a series of stories on unsolved murders in the city. This brought pressure on the chief of police and safety director. They called Murphy in and demanded he get more help. Murphy knew where the pressure came from. He refused to yield. Instead, he resigned.[16] Captain Owen Green punched Quinn in the mouth for his ouster of Murphy. Quinn now had enemies in the ranks of the police and sheriff's offices.[17] His ties to the Mob were also weakened. Police and sheriff's deputies were less likely to give advance tips of raids as they had in the past. With Murphys retirement, a collective hatred of Quinn asserted itself. Many police rallied to complain about Quinn's past refusal to give credit or publicity for meritorious work. His usefulness, with *Blade* editor Patterson absent and ailing, was limited.

Word finally embarrassed state officials in Columbus. Republican Attorney General C. William O'Neill began to send agents to Toledo to harass Democratic Prosecutor Harry Friberg. Democrat Governor Lausche countered with agents to goad Republican Sheriff Hirsch to action. In 1954, a city law director and later city manager, John McCarthy, had named George Gray safety director to replace Edward A. DeAngelo. Democrat McCarthy then joined the predominantly Republican law office of Walter Brown. In 1956, McCarthy also picked Anthony Bosch to replace Ray Allen as chief of police.[18] The move to dominate both political scene and parties locally was bound to backfire. Former Toledo mayor Michael V. DiSalle was seeking the May 1956 Democratic nomination for governor while the same office was being sought by Attorney General C. William O'Neill. Governor Lausche was running for the U.S. Senate. All three got past primary May tests. When newspapermen asked DiSalle, "Will corruption be an issue in the gubernatorial campaign?". He replied, "I suppose, but I don't know who will argue the affirmative."

At the local level, Straub resigned as Judge to run against Lud Ashley for the Congressional seat from the Toledo district. The Syndicate was told to support Straub and DiSalle. After the primaries, O'Neill sought to smash the Syndicate to cut off support to DiSalle.

Chalky Red was unsophisticated, disliked, untrustworthy. The political scene was disorganized, hectic; there was no clear way out. The Mob was to suffer its first political defeat.

The budding TV industry was competing with the *Blade* for the election advertising dollar. At the time, local network policy was not established. Most political issues were controlled by the home offices but it would be only a matter of time before TV exposure would also become a factor.

After the May primaries, downstate political heat was intensified. Pressure was on both the sheriff and prosecutor. Both were being supported by the Mob for reelection.

On June 6, 1956 the Mob received another setback: the Ohio Supreme Court, in a 6-0 decision, held "pinball machines which rewarded players with free games were gambling devices." The decision was based on state law rather than local ordinances, so it affected all pinballs in Ohio. Slots had already been declared contraband.

Clarence Condon, U.S. District Attorney in Toledo and Gilbert Hooks, Director of the I.R.S., said they would seek convictions because the court ruling "was something we were waiting for a long time." Pinball operators could now be arrested for failure to purchase a $250 federal wagering stamp for each unit. It was estimated that 5,000 pinball units were on locations in 25 northwestern Ohio counties. A crackdown on those not having stamps or those giving false information for tax purposes began. The city law director and Prosecutor Friberg met on July 1, 1956 in court chambers with Dan McCollough, attorney for 38 pinball operators, to set a deadline before banning the machines.

On July 26, 1956, "Mr. Toledo" Grove Patterson, editor of the *Blade*, was taken to the hospital with a serious heart ailment. A few weeks later he died. The *Blade* policy of continuous support of Republican Presidential candidates was to be finally altered. A way of life in Toledo of accepting gambling and prostitution was also near an end. The *Blade* influence, if any, in favor of continuance was lost. The Syndicate knew it was in for further trouble.

Late in July, Chalky Red was supervising action at a new location called "The Pines." Customers' cars spilled over onto a highly traveled road, impeding traffic. Businesses complained to the sheriff. The sheriff called out to report these complaints. In the background, the sheriff could hear his message being repeated to Chalky Red. "Fuck 'em," the uncouth Red shouted into the phone. The sheriff's office was enraged! He wouldn't listen or cooperate! That was the end. An unannounced raid ensued. Patrons were dispersed with warning of arrest on return. Pictures were taken. Equipment was destroyed. Red was emphatically told "That's enough. We won't take any more." Threats of padlocks and forfeiture of all real estate were made. Red capitulated. He had to consider his role in protection of the handbooks of the city and the numbers games. He would become the liaison man for the next 14 years for city crime and gaming parlours. He was mollified in knowing he would collect and he would pay off. He was still the city strongman.

In the race for governor, DiSalle lost by 400,000 votes.[19] Both Hirsch and Friberg were reelected and were supported for their respective offices for an additional four-year term each. Harvey Straub was defeated soundly. After taking a position in the law firm of E.J. Marshall for a short time, the Republicans gave him a position with the U.S. Pardon and Parole Board. In 1958 he ran for Common Pleas court judge against Friberg. The Mob backed Straub because they wanted Friberg to continue in the prosecutor's position where they would be protected if anything arose. Friberg was helpless to change a system he helped to create. Four years later he was again defeated in a race for Probate judge.

In 1958, DiSalle reversed the defeat by O'Neill by 400,000 votes. By then gambling had been closed for two years and there was no chance of reopening. Just as 1956 began with a story on crime so it ended.

A city service director is rated higher than the chief of police. Former safety director Edward A. DeAngelo was charged on December 1, 1956 in federal court with luring or baiting migratory birds in an area proscribed by the U.S. Secretary of the Interior.[20] On the last day of the year, he signed a consent order to be tried on misdemeanor charges before John J. Barone, U.S. Commissioner. He pled guilty and paid a $50 fine and costs.[21]

DeAngelo and vice squad captain William Gray were basically honest and forthright men. Both rendered a useful service to the community. DeAngelo was subject to calumny in the quips of the regulars at the Secor Bar for he heard "quack-quack" all Christmas season. "Gray," they always said, "was kept in pussy by his friend Rose LaRose as long as he kept her in business."

As the Syndicate folded, none of the gamblers publicly heard words of abuse. Perhaps the public was afraid. In the status-conscious culture that had developed in the city, gang leaders were more respected than government officials.

The constant threat of violence from the Detroit muscle subsided with the close of operations by the Syndicate. Local police and politicians were grateful for such an end. All made money and had attained position and stature in the community. They were secretly relieved in knowing nobody in Toledo was ever publicly exposed or penalized. Now they began to relax and spend their hoarded loot on themselves and families.

# 33 Conclusion

Boss Tweed's famous challenge was: "Now that you know, what do you intend to do about it?"

After 20 years, there was no backlash or feedback of any consequence. During the malaria and cholera epidemic of the 1850s, Toledo was called the "Graveyard of the United States."

The name Toledo became a source of more gags. "If the country ever needed an enema, there's where they should stick the hose." On the inter-city relationship, gagsters said, "If Detroit has a headache, Toledo takes an aspirin." Vulgarians put it, "If Detroit farts, Toledo shits."

Most of the larger American cities changed after World War II. In Toledo, plastic newcomers shoved themselves into positions of prominence as natives still took backseats in their lifestyle. The Beat generation of the 1950s and 1960s never really developed in the city, the lifestyle remained the same!

Toledoans continued singing praise of their hometown. City songs contributed to its national fame. Since 1906 the lyrics of "We're Strong for Toledo" were known by most inhabitants.[1] The words:

> "We're strong for Toledo, T-O-L-E-D-O.
> "The girls are the fairest
> "The boys are the squarest
> "Of any old town that I know."

1906 was the year of the famous San Francisco earthquake. Herb Caen of the San Francisco *Chronicle* claimed that North Beach residents sang the same tune after the earthquake using the word, F-R-I-S-C-O. Plagiarism anybody?

Other songs of the city also contributed to national fame. The Jones Junior High March[2] written to John Phillip Sousa's "Stars and Stripes Forever" and "Scott High Forever" were sung by servicemen in every combat area during World War II.

The University of Toledo also lead a rousing marching song with stirring lyrics.[3]

> "The Indians roamed the Maumee River Land
> "'Till along came Anthony Wayne.
> "Old England was the rule of the Lakes
> "'Til Perry gained his fame.
> "They were fighters and victorious
> "And drove back every foe,
> "Gave their legends and traditions
> "To the School we honor so..."

Years later, union leader Lawrence Steinberg reminded state politicians they owed him something. Consequently he was appointed to the board of trustees of the university for one term.

The College of Law at the University invited Dan McCollough to lecture and teach criminal law.

When Dan McCollough died at age 77 on August 20, 1976, his obituary suggested contributions be made to the University of Toledo.[4] Yet Dan did not devise any money to them himself. He had represented many society matrons in divorce cases within two years of his death where millions of dollars were involved. Rumors circulated that he obtained fees in excess of six figures in some cases. Several millionaires were established from earnings of the Syndicate. Many thought Dan was among them. He wore special hand-tailored clothes of English woolens and had a plush office. When letters of administration were issued, his estate was approximately $150,000.[5] It consisted of treasury bills in the amount of $75,000, bank accounts of $26,695, personal property of $11,000 and his home valued at $36,000. In a will dated June 2, 1976 he named his son beneficiary of World War I insurance of $10,000. He referred to his brother Thomas, commonly called Owen, of Houston, Texas as a successful businessman to whom he left nothing. To his former wife Virginia O'Connell, who also had cancer at the time of his death, he left nothing. He left his long-time secretary Bernice Shaffer $2,500 while a newer girl in his office received $7,500. After gifts of lesser amounts to other lawyers sharing his office, he left the balance of his estate to an associate, Richard T. Secor, attorney. This Secor name was not one of the early Toledo families but that of a Michigan transplant of Polish origin who had anglicized the former name to Secor for social and business reasons.

Poles in politics in Toledo were exemplary candidates for civil and judicial offices. Change of name for most would be superfluous.

"Where had the money, if any, gone?" critics asked. Dan lived high. Others claimed that Dan had to be watched during his last year, after cancer was discovered He burned with the desire to edit his novel on the women in his social conquests and the number of husbands he had made cuckold. If Dan wanted to be remembered as a ladies man to his society friends and a cocksman to the boys at the Y, his will never showed it.

While in the hospital fighting cancer, Dan kicked and beat a nurse, Helen Ackerman, severely. She claimed permanent injury and filed suit against McCollough.[6] There were no other witnesses to the incident. Some claimed Dan siphoned off assets to prevent her recovery. While the case was pending, the attorney for the injured party did not take Dan's deposition to preserve his testimony. When Dan died, the Dead Man's statute of Ohio[7] prevented the plaintiff from testifying since the other party was deceased. Plaintiff Ackerman lost.

An embittered son reported his dad was "a tough one to live with." His ex-wife stated, "Dan was a private person, a loner and difficult to live with." His son reported, "He sent $10 on Christmas and birthdays and some briefs he filed." A perusal of all legal documents revealed most were mediocre, none ever outstanding nor compelling. Virginia and Dan, Jr. were disappointed by McCollough's will but chose not to contest it.

Another story circulated that one of Dan's lady friends, immediately following his death, destroyed all letters and 14 pictures of Dan in her home. Then she quickly disposed of her property and went west. Dan had bought her love, not won it.

Others claimed Dan still paid huge forwarding fees to the lawyers who helped him back to the bar.[8] Many claimed that for 45 years, from 1931 to 1976, he was still paying off.

To many, his last will was Dan's best joke. Associate Secor shared his same warped sense of humor of performing pranks on fellow lawyers. At a Christmas meeting of the Ohio State Bar Association, Secor facetiously announced, "I want to introduce Harry Illman's best friend, the chairman of the Grievance Committee." Comments were, "There are Polish jokes and Polish jokers." Quintilian (103-35 A.D.), great Roman advocate of the first century, said "A joke at the expense of the unfortunate is inhuman."

A *Blade* obituary called Dan "a living legend." Dan had powerful patrons and a favorable press. On lawyers, the power to print was the power to destroy. In an era of status-conscious society, Dan had assets none could buy. His track record as revealed in this history, however, makes him much more myth than legend. When Dan Jr. died a few years later, the obit merely read, "son of a former attorney."

Fifty years before, at great personal cost in health, John W. Davis, "Lawyer's Lawyer," spent weeks in defense of criminal and disbarment matters of two Jewish lawyers, without fee. He claimed it was his duty as "a brother of the bar."[9] Since Watergate, the camraderie of the bar has been shattered. The joy of practicing law has been lost, many claim, as dog-eat-dog financial competition ensued. Today the few giants remaining are secluded on their self-made Mount Olympus pontificating, rather than advising, counting their money or scheming of new ways to make more. Only pygmies remain below.

Boss Tweed was buried in lambskin, the symbol of innocence.[10]

Good connections in labor and politics can lead to becoming a millionaire. The American dream came true for many members of the Syndicate.

Chalky Red died on September 26, 1975. The F.B.I. was present at his funeral to check license plates and look over the mourners for Mafia records. With his brothers, Louis (Paddock) Walker came from Las Vegas to be a pall bearer. Most of the crowd in attendance could hardly believe their ears when two Rabbis eulogized the deceased by saying "he was a good man." The *Blade* obituary that day traced his Licavoli ties and was less complimentary.[11] Red died a resident of Lambertville, Michigan. He owned a luxurious home over the state line. He left, among his Ohio assets, the house where he was born at 725 George Street where county records disclosed title in Harry Nemorowski aka Harry Leonard at $4,500.[12] He had $66,500 in other real estate, $200,000 in cash in the First National Bank and 357 shares of stock valued at $286,000. This was the book value. Actual sale value of the closed corporation stock was three to four times such amount. His Michigan and other property was administered in such states.

Co-worker Tony Paul put a great deal of his property in the name of his wife, Rose, who was a good housewife and mother. When she died on July 27, 1976, she left a gross estate in Ohio of $883,915.[13] Her 357 shares in the same company as Red was evaluated at $289,978. Her real estate in San Bernardino, California, Palm Beach, Florida, and Michigan areas required ancillary administration. The other outstanding shares in the corporation were owned by Louis (Paddock) Walker. All three partners came out of the Syndicate as wealthy men.

Whitey Besase kept his money in the family before death. When he passed away a year after Red, all the Detroit families attended services. Again, F.B.I. checks were invoked. In the floral showering, the largest bouquet was of white orchids from pal Tony Paul. Unlike the Rabbis, the priests held masses for Whitey, but no eulogy. Mourners later reported gratitude for this lack of hypocrisy by donating twice the amount to the church than that which might ordinarily have been donated otherwise. After the New York murder of Carmin (Lilo) Galante, the church began to refuse burial services for Mobsters because of "the public scandal that would ensue."

Another millionaire, Pete Licavoli, hosted a wedding for his daughter at the Sheraton Cadillac Hotel in Detroit. A thousand guests attended as Pete brought in a $1,500 wedding cake and four orchestras to play.[14] At last reports, Pete was convicted in Arizona in December, 1976 for receiving a stolen Ohio painting.[15] It was a 16th-century portrait called "Lucretia" by Italian artist Dominici Pulige.

After the end of syndicated gambling, the *Blade* and Prosecutor Friberg tangled when charges of "fixes" were involved. The *Blade* reporter goofed on making one erroneous claim. Friberg met with *Blade* reporters in January 1958. An employee of a contractor stated he was present when his employer offered a county official $4,000 to alter a sewer contract. A *Blade* reporter was supposed to have made a copy of the conversation but when called by the grand jury, the employee denied having told a *Blade* reporter such story.

The reporter alleged to have a secret recording later revealed the recording device failed to function.

Friberg's office then conducted a grand jury investigation. In their report filed April 2, 1958, "the evidence was not of sufficient credibility to return indictments." The grand jury concluded with its unanimous opinion, "We want the public to know that as far as Mr. Friberg is concerned, he has conducted the investigation in a fair and impartial manner. . . . We are impressed by the way he handled the jury investigation." They failed to mention Friberg's office handled the jurors and prepared these findings.

A former assistant U.S. attorney for Virginia, Rodney Sager, warned a House judiciary subcommittee behind closed doors, "The simple fact is today our system clothes the prosecutor with virtually unbridled powers. It's interesting to note from the historic comments that the so-called "function of the grand jury" is to act as a protector of the individual's rights. It began as a bulwark of safety against the crowd. Need for such protection today has vanished. In modern-day practice that term of protector of rights is completely meaningless. To the contrary, the person protected by the modern-day grand jury is the prosecutor."

The *Blade* refused to print Friberg's self-laudatory remarks.

Instead the battle between *Blade* and Friberg continued. The *Blade* refused to endorse Friberg for reelection in 1960, claiming he was not up to "proper standards."[16] Instead they endorsed a Republican, Paul Leahy, for the office for the first time in 30 years. But it didn't help Leahy. Later the *Blade* intimated impropriety in the acceptance of a reduced plea in the criminal charges of Bernard R. (Terry) Kazmierski, an ex-convict.[17] Friberg countered by filing charges of criminal libel against the *Blade*. If he had filed a civil suit for libel, the *Blade* attorneys could have taken his deposition, but Friberg was too smart for that. Both had evidence in their files that could be damaging to the other's reputation. Three months after filing the libel, Friberg *nolled* the case as "it would be in the best public interst." In an editorial after dismissal, entitled "The Blade and Mr. Friberg," the *Blade* stated "This newspaper never questioned Mr. Friberg's personal honesty and integrity or that of his staff." It probably was part of the settlement!

While the name of the principal city is eponymous to most newspapers, the name "Toledo" was dropped from the front-page banners of the *Blade* on January 3, 1960.[19] No reason was given for the change. The public didn't like it. Many Toledoans said the *Blade* felt its name wasn't good enough for the paper. Management is reported to have claimed that since the paper circulated throughout northwestern Ohio and southeastern Michigan, the name was not fair to all subscribers. The Detroit newspapers treated Toledo's image as a crime center or gambling mecca to get national TV and newspaper advertisers away from the Toledo area. The *Blade* action, some said, was to counteract such poor image.

While the name Toledo was rejected by the *Blade,* two other organizations who did not deserve the name, adopted its use, the Toledo Country Club and the Toledo Club.

The former was an elite waspish country club that rejected Jews and blacks. For more than 50 years it maintained a strict WASP ethic in status and membership.

Examples of snobbishness of Toledo Club members were legion. Dr. George A. Goroush was the city's leading internist. A fellow physician, Louis A. Levison, was introduced to him in the club bar as a candidate for membership. Goroush, in a rage, threw a bottle at Levison as he stormed out of the room. Paul Block, Sr. was among many other jews rejected for membership.

The Trianon Ballroom was a mecca for the youth of Toledo for over 30 years. All name bands of the jazz era of the '30s and '40s played there for school or college proms. Hundreds of friendships were formed in its atmosphere of romance and camraderie. For years after, "a Trianon style" dancer could be detected on any other dance floor of the city. In 1952, the Toledo Club (none of whom probably ever were Trianon regulars) tore down the dance hall for use of the land as a parking lot. Thus ended another era in the city.

The height of supercilious snobbery occurred when the Toledo Club experienced a fire in its kitchen. The downtown department beat the fire chief to the scene. The doorman told them that he was under strict orders not to let "anybody in." Finally, when the chief arrived in full white uniform and asserted his authority for safety reasons, the doorman relented and admitted them.

While Toledo citizens may have been provoked by the *Blade,* its fickle politicians were not.

The editor and publisher had a political policy of interviewing candidates for city and county offices. They befriended many by endorsement for winning the endorsement of the only newspaper in town went a long way toward election. The *Blade* made many friends in city council.

Cablevision was rapidly becoming America's newest growth industry. Cablevision involved the use of public utilities as telephone and electrical lines. Special enabling legislation to use such public facilities and to be permitted to operate within cities required the vote of city councils. In 1965 the *Blade* formed the Buckeye Cablevision Company, which was wholly owned by the Block family. Toledo's city council then approved go-ahead legislation for Buckeye Cablevision. A court battle ensued, but the *Blade* won.

The militant attorney of the Auto-Lite strike, Ed Lamb, was now a millionaire industrialist and radio station owner. He claimed he had a contract with Ohio Bell for cablevision and was first in Toledo. Lamb claimed further that Buckeye Cablevision with Cox Broadcasting

Company violated the Sherman Act by conspiring to monopolize and restrain trade in supplying TV service. He also said the Buckeye contract with Ohio Bell conflicted with his deal and caused them to break his contract. Lamb filed suit for 68.6 million dollars damages against the *Blade* and others.[20] A federal jury in Cleveland, after a five-week trial, held Lamb had no contract and there was no conspiracy. Successive appeals by Lamb were rejected in the federal system.

In another damage action against Buckeye Cablevision, the company comptroller testified under oath that Buckeye was used as a tax shelter to offset millions of profits in other Block family enterprises.[21]

The Block family fortune then was estimated to be between $50 to $75 million, so they wanted all the tax deductions available. Today it is three times that amount.[22] Buckeye had 40,000 subscribers at the time of the litigation of 1975 and had grown to 59,000 by September, 1979.[23] Other Toledo suburban communities, through their respective city councils, granted similar enabling legislation to assure continued service and insure further tax shelters thereafter. After settling the $150,000 judgment, Buckeye raised monthly charges.

As the corporation in politics, Buckeye received favor through city council again in the fall of 1979. Its original franchise was to expire in 1985. Buckeye's attorney wrote to city council requesting an extension based on a $5 million plan in capital expenditures in an expansion program. The extension was sought because Buckeye would not be able to recover capital costs of planned expansion by 1985. A month before election of a new city council, legislation extending the Buckeye franchise to the year 2000 was enacted.

After such legislation, the technical and maintenance workers represented by Teamsters local 20 voted to strike Buckeye. The ties and links of former years in the era of Ray Kest, Chalky Red or Larry Steinberg were lost. Otherwise such action never would have been taken!

Randy Sparks, organizer of the New Christy Minstrels, wrote a song entitled "Saturday Night in Toledo."[24] Minstrel singer John Denver capitalized on it. Three stanzas were:

> "Saturday Night in Toledo, Ohio
> Is like being nowhere at all.
> All through the day how the hours rush by
> Sit in the park and watch the grass die.
>
> "Ah, but after the sunset, the dusk and the twilight,
> Shadows of night start to fall.

## CONCLUSION

> They roll back the sidewalks precisely at ten,
> And people who live there are not seen again.
>
> "You ask how I know of Toledo, Ohio,
> Well, I spent a week there one day.
> They've got entertainment to dazzle your eyes,
> So visit the bakery and watch the buns rise."

Downtown Toledo proceeded to be what the lyrics claimed. Downtown died!

Chalky Red was still calling the shots in gambling for 15 years after the close of the Syndicate crap game until his death a few years later.

Red wanted to go into legitimate business. With political connections he started a King Road landfill deal. His plan was to eliminate competition and then raise prices on garbage pickup and disposal. A *Blade* reporter got details of the plan and ran one paragraph of the entire story. It was sufficient to stop the enterprise.

Detroit connections in the Mob sought Red's aid in convincing Foodtown, a local grocery chain, to handle their products, particularly pickles. An unwilling grocery chain president balked even after his home was bombed. The F.B.I. was called into the case. Lawrence Steinberg aided Red in making a statement to the Feds and they withdrew their muscle.

The F.B.I. was now gathering gaming evidence in all the city gambling action. A new federal conspiracy statute had teeth. As part of the F.B.I. threat, Red told all operators of handbooks, "I can't help you anymore. The new federal law is too tough. Close down or else." He quit collection of payoffs. F.B.I. agents brought local gamblers into federal court under the new laws. Most pled guilty and were fined. No jail sentences were imposed. All closed shop. Hundreds of night people and bettors had nowhere to go.

A new city manager, James Daken, wanted to keep the city clean. He appointed Corrin J. McGrath of Boston new chief of police. Civil service records disclosed that this was the first chief ever to be appointed from outside the city. The new appointee had been division director of the General Services Administration and a former police chief. He owed no favors to any officer in the ranks below him. Norbert DeClereq, a 1954 graduate of the Toledo Police Academy, was retained as captain of the morals and narcotics squads. In addition, the city manager and new chief appointed Detective John Mason to be head of Internal Security to investigate charges of bribery or corruption of city employees. This work later enabled Mason to become chief. DeClereq was a complete square, according to the local gambling fraternity. He and the new chief could not be approached. The threat of Internal Security investigation under Mason deterred all thought of graft and corruption. The new tactics insulated the police from such charges. The police department was as clean as their proverbial whistles and now the press and public knew it. For those citizens who sought or previously had action, the city was not the same. John Denver's ballad rang true to them.

After the demise of Chalky Red in 1975, Prosecutor Harry Friberg was free to resign. The city was free of vice. There was nothing more to protect. James E. McCormick, an experienced assistant prosecutor and ex-police officer, wanted to succeed him. William Boyle, head of the Democratic party and also an ex-police officer, favored McCormick. Boyle ran the local party with the same iron fist that was displayed in the O'Dwyer leaders from 1904 to 1932. Boyle's domination created problems at the board of elections and with the secretary of state's office, which acted as overseers of election boards. To his credit — perhaps fearful of adverse ramifications of a prosecutor-political alliance now that the city was clean — Friberg threatened to fire McCormick if he took out papers for election. When McCormick failed to file, the prosecutor recommended that Tony Pizza, another long associate, fill his unexpired term. This would give him an edge as an incumbent at the polls.

In the 1976 election, Tony Pizza won a four-year term over the Republican nominee. Friberg was given a recognition dinner. Then he retired to Florida. Later Tom Mattimoe also retired. The state public employees system permits 2% of an annual salary to be contributed toward retirement pensions. Thirty-three years of salary earned is used in computing average. Both Friberg and Mattimoe enjoy public employee pension checks from the state of Ohio of 66% of their highest salary, along with all the other moneys each accumulated during their many years in the prosecuting attorney's office.

The city still remains free of vice. Civic leaders want to keep it that way to overcome the poor image of the past. The Citizens for Decent Literature maintained headquarters in Toledo with Robert Anderson, of the Anderson grains and retail family, as its head.

Glass Company officials snatched John Andrews from his executive position with the Ohio State Republican Party in Columbus after approval of governmental regulations permitting loans for glass home insulation as part of the energy conservation program. Andrews later returned to Toledo to be guest speaker at a retirement banquet in honor of Judge Straub. Harry G. Levy served as honorary chairman.

In his will, Levy gave Andrews $25,000, five times the amount devised to Straub. Some say it was for favor in help getting the son of his first law partner appointed to the federal bench.[26]

Toledo was no exception to the downtown blight of many American cities in the late 1960s and '70s. Civic improvements took place in many cities. With the help of local industry Detroit undertook its famous $350 million Renaissance Center. In Toledo, Owens Illinois, Inc., called O.I. by the industry, wanted to make Toledo the glass capital of the world, and established headquarters in buildings which would revitalize downtown.[25] O.I. employs 80,000 people to operate 221 manufacturing facilities in 23 countries. In 1978 it had record sales of $3.1 billion and $85.2 million in earnings. It planned to spend over $100 million to improve the downtown city. Ohio law permitted cities to grant tax abatements. O.I. made a crucial feature of its Letter of Intent on downtown improvement, that a full tax abatement be granted on the project site. Abatement meant no taxes would be paid for a specific time. A 10.8-acre downtown site was sold to an O.I. subsidiary for $2,127,000. Congress had awarded the city $12 million for public improvements. This money had to be spent for public improvements which would not include parking. The money so spent would increase the value of downtown properties. The city council gave O.I. the abatement. The Toledo Trust Company united to get into the act but the city donors had gone far enough. No other American city reported such action. Mark Hanna would have loved it. Two years later special levies had to be approved by the voters to prevent the closing of public libraries, curtailment of police and fire activities and closure of some schools. Yet the abatement remained untouched. Some claimed the glass companies owned and ran the city.

In today's economy, the need for privilege and favor has been changed from the individual to the corporation. The United States Supreme Court gave corporations the same right of speech as individuals. This included the right of political expression. The number of corporations with political action committees has soared. Many corporations owe their very existence to governments. They need privilege and favor. When not obtained by lawful means, they must resort to lobby, influence, bribery, foreign and domestic. We have seen the transition of political power from the party boss (Tweed) to the businessman (Hanna) to the lawyer (Brown) and now to the corporation (O.I.). Many claim that the government is now run either by

## UNHOLY TOLEDO

political pollsters or by artificial persons, namely corporations.[26] It is my impression all the powers proliferate at all levels of government as parasites on the public tit.

Politicians have made suckers of their electorate. They have treated the voters as Falstaffs, fools, I dare say schmucks. It is often stated, "The American people are the only animals that can be screwed twice.... Their ignorance can never be exaggerated.... They have mortgaged the future of their children with trillions of dollars in deficits and debt.... There is no end in sight."

More than seventy years have passed since Brand Whitlock urged the voters to "Elect a man you can trust." Political parties have refrained from use of this aphorism for years. Democracy and capitalism are self-defeating. Whether the two-party system can continue with wanton corruption remains to be seen. The politician who wants to be honest won't last. His own party won't back him. William Saxby of Ohio, former Senator, U.S. Attorney General and Ambassador to India, said, "Persons disgruntled with the system must settle for what solace they found in the most hoary of political excuses. Both parties do exactly the same thing."[27]

Everybody has a song to sing, a story to tell. I have sung a song or two that some may not like; others may become angry. I have told a story that some may not care to hear. I have brought shame and sorrow on my beloved family and city.

Jack Anderson wrote, "Institutions will not reform themselves, and a nation dependent upon them for equity, will disintegrate unless the wrongdoing is exposed, arousing a public furor which forces compromised politicians to clean house. Every success of an investigative reporter means ruin for some human being. The trade-off is necessary to maintain a free society."[28]

I am now an investigative reporter and a member of the prestigious Press Club of San Francisco. The ERA (Editors & Reporters Association) and Media Alliance protect investigative reporters. I am told that they will equally get mad in event of violence. A furor greater than that of the Bolles case in Phoenix will ensue. A costly lesson was taught there. Neither the *Blade* nor the Arizona *Republic,* that state's largest newspaper, carried the 100,000 words written by the 23 investigative reporters who converged on the city to write about the crime.

I've been a gambler all my life. I'll have to take a chance on adverse reaction, if any.

Now, they want to chase me out of my own home town. The mood of the city is somber. The sounds of laughter seem stilled. Residents and the powers that be cannot forgive or harbor a sinner as in the old days. To me, Toledo has become a city without a heart. I pray for change.

I think I'll get in front of the crowd, carry a baton, like Firetop, and make them think it's a parade! Some will go along.

Then we'll all sing the last stanza of the city's most famous song,

>"In any old weather,
>We'll all stick together
>In T-O-L-E-D-O."

# Notes

### Chapter 1

1. Burton Memorial Collection, Detroit Public Library, Purple Gang File No. 7404-364.
2. Purple Gang, Burton Memorial Collection No. 29766, Detroit *News,* February 9, 1928.
3. Detroit *News,* September 26, 1971, Burton Library and Archives.
4. Detroit *News* Library Files and Archives.
5. Dennis Lynch, *Criminals and Politicians,* Chapter XII (New York: The MacMillan Co., 1932), p. 125.
6. Interview with Abe Joffa, a Toledo *Blade* circulation manager.
7. Lynch, op. cit., p. 136.
8. Detroit *News,* September 17, 1931.
9. Interview with Irving Mieland, a Detroit court reporter.
10. Detroit *Free Press,* October, November, 1931.
11. Lynch, op.cit., p. 137.
12. Dennis Walsh, "Leniency for a Hoodlum, Slush Fund Income," *Life Magazine,* May 2, 1969, pp. 21-26.

### Chapter 2

1. Dennis Walsh, *Life Magazine,* May 2, 1969, p. 21.
2. Burton Memorial Collection, Licavoli files, Detroit Public Library Archives, file E & M, 7404-364, Toledo *Blade,* May 5, 1957.
3. Detroit *News,* July 23, 1930. Burton Memorial Collection, Detroit Public Library Collection and Archives.
4. Detroit *News,* October 6, 7, 1931.

5. Detroit *News,* June 16, 1932.
6. Detroit Library, files and archives.
7. Detroit Library, files and archives.
8. Otto L. Bettman, *The Good Old Days — They Were Terrible* (New York: Random House, 1974), pp. 97, 184; Andy Logan, *Against the Evidence* (New York: McCall Publishing Co., 1970), p. 341.
9. Stephen Longstreet, *Win or Lose.* (Bobbs Merrill Co., Indianapolis, 1977) p. 143.
10. Thomas E. Dewey, *Twenty Against the Underworld,* (Doubleday & Co. Inc., Garden City, N.Y., 1974) p.388; *State of Ohio v. Sulkin* 22 N.E.2d 42, 30 O.O. 548.

## Chapter 3

1. Thomas R. Case, "The Battle of Fallen Timbers," *Northwestern Ohio Quarterly,* Volume XXXV, No. 2, Spring 1963, pp. 54-68. Clark Waggoner, *History of the City of Toledo and Lucas County,* (Munsell & Co., New York, 1887), pp. 40-47. Nevin O. Winter, *History of Northwest Ohio* (Lewis Publishing Co., Chicago and New York, 1917), p. 68. John M. Killits, *Toledo and Lucas County* (S. J. Clarke Publishing Co., Chicago, 1923). pp. 101-103. Charles E. Slocum, *History of the Maumee River Basin* (published by author, Defiance, Ohio, 1905), p. 207. Simeon D. Fess, *Ohio — History of a Great State* (Lewis Publishing Co., Chicago, 1937), Vol. I, p. 109.
2. Killits, op. cit., Vol. I, p. 116; *Ohio Archaeological Historical Quarterly,* 1909, Vol. 18, p. 127; Waggoner, op. cit., Vol. I, p. 61; Fess, op. cit., pp. 202-216.
3. Toledo *Blade,* January 14, 1953; Toledo *Times,* January 21, 1953 and February 24, 1953.
4. Toledo *Blade,* August 7, 1953.
5. Winter, op. cit., pp. 227-239. Harvey Scribner, *Memoirs of Lucas County and the City of Toledo* (Madison, Wisconsin: Western Historical Association, 1910), pp. 45-67. Killits, op. cit., Vol. I, pp. 133-152.
6. *Escanaba Daily Press,* Escanaba, Michigan, April 26, 1967.
7. George V. Fuller, *Michigan: A Centennial History of the State and Its People* (Chicago: Lewis Publishing Co., 1939), Vol. I, p. 223; Sister Mary Karl George, *The Rise and Fall of Toledo, Michigan* (Lansing: Michigan Historical Commission, 1971), p. 4. Clarence M. Burton, *How Michigan Came Into the Union,* bound manuscript, Burton Historical Collection, Detroit Public Library, pp. 25-26.
8. Fuller, op. cit., p. 236.
9. L.M. Boyd, San Francisco *Chronicle,* Sept. 27, 1980.

## Chapter 4

1. Scribner, op. cit., Vol. I p. 87.
2. Vol. 19, *World Book Encyclopedia,* Field Enterprises Educational Corporation, London, 1967, pp. 106-113. Randolph C. Downes, *History of Lake Shore Ohio* (New York: Lewis Historical Publishing Co., p. 193.
3. Alexis de Tocqueville, *Democracy in America* (New York: The Henry

Reeve text as revised by Francis Bower, Alfred A. Knopf Co., 1945), Vol. I, p. 275.

4. *Ibid.*, p. 278.
5. *Ibid.*, p. 270.
6. *American Bar Association Journal,* November 1977, p. 1578.
7. J. W. Hurst, *The Growth of American Law: The Law Makers* (Boston: Little, Brown, 1950), p. 319.
8. *New Mexico v. Credit Bureau of Albuquerque,* 42 U.S.L.W. 2176. John T. Flynn, *Men of Wealth, Mark Hanna* (New York: Simon & Schuster, 1941), pp. 389, 419.
9. Nathan Miller, *The Founding Finaglers* (New York: D. McKay Co., 1976), pp. 199, 200. Hank Messick, *The Silent Syndicate* (New York: McMillan Co., 1967), pp.7-10; Allen O. Myers, *Bosses and Boodle in Ohio Politics* (Cincinnati: Lyceum Publishing Co., 1895). Boodle is a term for graft.
10. Toledo *News Bee,* October-November 1922 editorials on the mayoralty campaign of Bernard Brough, "A mayor must be considered tractable by a machine headed by Walter Brown for Brown was a man whose business is to make money out of politics;" Harvey S. Ford, "Walter Folger Brown," *Northwest Ohio Quarterly,* Summer, 1954, pp. 200-209.
11. Miller, op. cit., 295, 302, 303, 307, 310, 312; Joseph Nathan Kane, *Facts About the Presidents* (New York: Ace Books, 1976), pp. 216-220. H. J. Eckenrode, *Rutherford B. Hayes, Dodd* (Dodd, Mead & Co., New York, 1930, pp. 305-309.
12. Miller, op. cit., pp. 240-242, 246, 247, 259, 256, 277, 260, 342, 343; Kane, op. cit., pp. 216-223. T. Harry Williams,*Hayes' Diary of a President* (New York: David McKay Co. Inc., 1964), p. xviii.
13. Stephen Longstreet, *Win or Lose* (Indianapolis: Bobbs-Merrill Co., 1977), p. 63.
14. Samuel P. Huntington, *American Politics: The Promise of Disharmony* (Cambridge: Harvard Press, 1981). "Americans have always tended to view government as inherently illegitimate."

## Chapter 5

1. New York *Times,* October 3, 1974.
2. *Ibid.*
3. *Ibid.*
4. John J. Connors, *Badges of Toledo and Lucas County, Ohio* (published by author, Toledo, 1973), p. 21.
5. New York *Times,* October 3, 1974.
6. Connors, op. cit., p. 29.
7. *Ibid.*, p. 9, 61.
8. *Ibid.*, p. 31, 32.
9. Department of Local History and Genealogy, Toledo-Lucas County Public Library, police records and archives.
10. Herbert Best, "Why the Police Fail," *Harper's Magazine,* January, 1933, pp. 204-210.

11. Department of Local History, etc., op. cit., police archives.
12. Best, op. cit., p. 210.
13. Bettman, op. cit., p. 97. M. R. Werner, *It Happened in New York* (New York: Coward, McCann Co., 1957), pp. 36-110.
14. *Ibid.,* p. 97.
15. *People v. Hines,* 284 N.Y. 93, 29 N.E. 2d. 483, where the New York Supreme Court recognized the role of a fixer.
16. Ohio became a Code state over 100 years before. The Codes underwent periodic revisions from General Code to Revised Code as enacted today.
17. Fred J. Cook, *The Muckrakers* (New York: Doubleday & Co., Inc., 1972), p. 13.
18. *Ibid.,* p. 10.
19. *Ibid.,* p. 10.
20. *Ibid.,* p. 32.

## Chapter 6

1. Samuel Milton Jones Papers, Toledo-Lucas County Public Library Archives, Department of Local History and Genealogy, microfilm edition, roll 1.
2. Lincoln Steffens, *Autobiography* (New York: Harcourt Brace and World, Inc., 1931), p. 365-392.
3. *Ibid.,* p. 374.
4. *Ibid.,* p. 422.
5. *Ibid.,* p. 430.
6. *Ibid.,* p. 399.
7. *Ibid.,* p. 407.
8. Fred J. Cook, *Mob, Inc.* (New York: Franklin Watts, 1977), p. 20.
9. Samuel Milton Jones, III. "Brand Whitlock and the Independent Party," *Northwest Ohio Quarterly,* Winter 1958-1959, Vol. XXXI, No. 1 p. 98. Lincoln Steffens, *Letters* (New York: Harcourt Brace and Co., 1936), p. 149. Steffens *Autobiography,* op. cit., p. 470. Brand Whitlock, *Forty Years Of It* (New York: D. Appleton Co., 1914), p. 164.
10. Police archives, Toledo-Lucas County Public Library, Department of Local History and Genealogy; Ralph L. Peters, Golden Rule Jones, p. 3. The mayors of Toledo, Toledo-Lucas County Public Library Archives.
11. Interviews with Archie Rubin and numerous other personal sources.
12. *Ibid.*
13. John S. Crosbie, *The Incredible Mrs. Chadwick* (New York, Toronto, Montreal: McGraw-Hill Ryerson, 1975), pp. 116-139. Alvin Karpis, *The Alvin Karpis Story* (New York: Coward, McGown Geoghegan Inc., 1971), pp. 113, 252.
14. Andy Logan, "Against the Evidence," *The Becker-Rosenthal Affair* (New York: McCall, 1970), p. 73.
15. Toledo *Blade,* September 14, 1920.
16. Peters, op. cit., p.3.
17. *American Magazine,* July 1911, pp. 306-308.
18. Justin Kaplan, *Lincoln Steffens: A Biography* (New York: Simon & Schuster, 1974), p. 133.

19. Ralph E. Phelps, *Profiles of Toledo Mayors* (Toledo-Lucas County Public Library Reference Book, Department of Local History and Genealogy).
20. Kaplan, op. cit., p. 133.
21. *Ibid.*, p. 134.
22. *Ibid.*, p. 134, Phelps, p. 3.
23. Toledo *Blade,* November 18, 1951.
24. Toledo mayor archives, supra.
25. Toledo *Blade,* July 13, 1904.
26. Phelps, p. 3, 4, 5.
27. Brand Whitlock, *Forty Years of It,* (D. Appleton & Co., New York, 1919), pp. 269-270.
28. Fred J. Cook, *The Muckrakers* (Doubleday and Co., Garden City, New York, 1922), p. 11.

**Chapter 7**

1. **Phelps, op. cit.,** *Toledo Mayors,* No. 30, Toledo-Lucas County Public Library Archives; Samuel Milton Jones III, The Early Years, *Northwest Ohio Quarterly,* Vol. XXXI, Winter 1958-1959, pp. 7-20.
2. *Ibid.,* Toledo Mayors, Scrapbook; Jean L. Stinchcombe, *City Politics in Toledo, (Belmont, California: Wadsworth Publishing Co., Inc., 1968) pp. 33-37.*
3. *Jones III, Northwest Ohio Quarterly, op. cit., p. 9.*
4. *Ibid.,* p. 11.
5. Whitlock, *Forty Years Of It,* op. cit., p. 88.
6. *Ibid.,* p. 89.
7. Jones III, *The Early Years,* op. cit., p. 16.
8. Toledo *Bee,* December 11, 1902. The Blade opposed him when he was mayor but always acclaimed his abilities as a trial lawyer. Jones III., op. cit., p. 28.
9. Samuel Milton Jones III, "Brand Whitlock and the Independent Party,", *Northwest Ohio Quarterly,* Vol. XXXI, Winter 1958-1959, p. 98; Toledo *News Bee,* January 28, 1922.
10. Toledo Bee, *January 1, 1900.*
11. Kaplan, *Lincoln Steffens Biography,* op. cit., p. 110.
12. Paul Lloyd Stryker, *Art of Advocacy,* (New York: Simon and Schuster, 1954), p. 109; H. Montgomery Hyde, *Oscar Wilde, a Biography, (New York: Farrar, Straus and Giroux, 1975), pp. 191-295.*
13. *Brand Whitlock scrapbook and papers containing many undated and unidentified clippings from newspapers of the 1890's; Toledo-Lucas County Public Library Archives, Department of Local History and Genealogy.*
14. *Jones III, op. cit., p. 97.*
15. *Ibid.,* p. 97.
16. *Ibid.,* p. 97.
17. Whitlock, *Forty Years Of It,* op. cit., pp. 163, 164.
18. Samuel Milton Jones III, "Brand Whitlock: Novelist, Muckraker, and Progressive," *Northwest Ohio Quarterly,* Vol. XXXI, Winter 1958-1959, p. 161.
19. Whitlock, *Forty Years of It,* op. cit., p. 164. Justin Kaplan, *Lincoln Steffins biography,* op. cit., p. 130.

20. Jones, op. cit., p. 96.
21. Steffins, *Autobiography,* op. cit., pp. 472, 492.
22. Toledo *News Bee,* November 3, 1905.
23. Whitlock papers and scrapbook clippings, op. cit.
24. *Ibid.*
25. Ibid., Stinchcombe, op. cit., pp. 26-37.
26. Kaplan, op. cit., p. 135.
27. Ibid, p. 135.
28. Jones, op. cit., p. 106; Brand Whitlock, "Enforcement of Law in Cities," an article published by him, Toledo, 1911, p. 93.
29. Jones, op. cit., p. 106; Whitlock, *Forty Years Of It,* p. 290.
30. Whitlock, "Enforcement", op. cit., pp. 23, 26-27, 43-46, 50.
31. Kaplan, op. cit., p. 97.
32. Brand Whitlock, "Elimination of Graft," *World Today,* June 1918, pp. 594-598.
33. Nathan Miller, *The Founding Finaglers,* op. cit., p. 303.
34. Stinchcombe, op. cit., pp. 36-37; Kaplan, op. cit., p. 173.
35. Kaplan, op. cit., pp. 172, 173.
36. *Ibid.,* p. 173.
37. Toledo *Blade,* June 29, 1968.
38. Toledo *News Bee,* January 26, 1922.

**Chapter 8**

1. Humbert S. Nelli, *The Business of Crime,* (New York: Oxford University Press, 1976), p. 111.
2. *Ibid.,* p. 111.
3. *Ibid.,* p. 111.
4. *Ibid.,* p. 112, John Cooney, *The Annenbergs* (Simon and Schuster, New York, 1982), p. 32.
5. U.S. Congress, Senate, hearings before the Special Committee to investigate organized crime in Interstate Commerce. 82nd Cong., 1st Sess. pt. 6, pp. 43-47, later cited as the Kefauver Committee, Cooney, supra, p. 34.
6. See the chapter on the Capone connection, infra. John Cooney, op. cit., pp. 59, 63.
7. Newspaper archives, Toledo-Lucas County Public Library, Department of Local History and Genealogy.
8. Cornelia Otis Skinner, *Life With Lindsay and Crouse,* (Boston: Houghton Mifflin Co., 1976), pp. 94-95.
9. Grove Patterson, *I Like People,* (New York: Random House, 1948), pp. 119, 121.
10. *Ibid.,* pp. 102-107.
11. *Ibid.,* p. 85.
12. Chapter on formation of the syndicate, infra. Cooney, supra, p. 54.
13. Patterson, op. cit., p. 117.
14. *Ibid.,* p. 126.
15. *Ibid.,* p. 133.
16. New York *Times,* March 10, 11 and 19, 1941.

17. Patterson, op. cit., p. 147.
18. New York *Times*, June 23, 25, 1941.
19. John E. Gunckel, Boyville, (Toledo, published by author, 1900).
20. Newspaper archives, Toledo-Lucas County Public Library, Department of Local History and Genealogy.
21. See Chapter on Formation of Syndicate, infra.
22. *Ibid.*

## Chapter 9

1. Ralph E. Phelps, *Blade* Staff Writer, "Toledo's Most Exciting Day," Toledo *Blade*, March 31, 1957.
2. Seymour Rothman, "A Fight to Remember," The Toledo *Blade Sunday Magazine*, June 29, 1969, p. 4; Robert B. Considine and Bill Slocum, *Dempsey*, (Simon and Schuster, New York, 1960), pp. 101-105.
3. Rothman, op. cit., p. 4.
4. *Ibid.*, p. 4.
5. Barbara Piattelli, "Dempsey, The Destruction of a Giant," *American Heritage*, Volume XXVIII, No. 3, April, 1977, p. 77; Considine, op. cit., p. 204.
6. Rothman, op. cit., p. 6.
7. Dempsey-Willard fight newspaper archives, Toledo-Lucas County Public Library, Department of Local History and Genealogy; Rothman, Toledo *Blade*, June 29, 1969, p. 6.
8. Rothman, op. cit., p. 5.
9. New York *Times*, June 29, 1919.
10. *Ibid.*
11. New York *Times*, June 27, 1919.
12. New York *Times*, June 28, 1919.
13. *American Heritage*, op. cit., p. 77.
14. Rothman, Toledo *Blade*, op. cit., p. 6.
15. *Ibid.*
16. *Ibid.*
17. Toledo *Blade*, May 30, 1919; Dempsey-Willard library archives, supra.
18. *Ibid.*
19. Toledo *Blade*, March 31, 1957.
20. Rothman, op. cit., p. 8.
21. *Ibid.*
22. *Ibid.*
23. *Ibid.*
24. *American Heritage Magazine*, "Doc Kearns' Last Dirty Trick," April, 1977, p. 80.
25. Considine, op. cit., p. 189.
26. Dempsey-Willard Fight newspaper archives, Toledo-Lucas County Public Library, Department of Local History and Genealogy; Sydney Australia, *Daily Mirror*, August 1, 1966.
27. Rothman, op. cit., Toledo *Blade*, June 29, 1969.
28. *Ibid.*

## Chapter 10

1. Newspaper archives, Toledo-Lucas County Public Library, Department of Local History and Genealogy; Toledo *Blade*, February 17, 1921; Toledo *Blade*, February 15, 1953; Toledo *News-Bee*, February 17, 1921.
2. *Ibid.*, Toledo *Blade*, February 15, 1953.
3. *Ibid.*
4. *Ibid.*
5. *Ibid.*
6. *Ibid.*
7. Toledo *Blade,* September 6, 1921; Toledo *News-Bee,* September 6, 1921.
8. *Ibid.*
9. United States v. Zimmerman and Szemtko, Cause No. 3063, U.S. District Court, Northern District of Ohio, Western Division. Trial held on March 15, 1922.
10. Toledo *Blade,* June 18, 1923, June 23, 1923.
11. Docket of the U.S. District Court, op. cit., U.S. v. Zimmerman.
12. Interview with Attorney Stephen Fazekas, 1977.
13. See Chapter on Interesting Cases, infra.

## Chapter 11

1. Harvey S. Ford, "Walter Folger Brown", *Northwest Ohio Quarterly,* Vol. XXVI, No. 3, Summer 1954, pp. 200-208; Newspaper archives, Toledo-Lucas County Public Library, Department of Local History and Genealogy.
2. *Ibid.*, p. 203.; Charles L. Mee, Jr., *The Ohio Gang,* (M. Evans Co., N.Y., 1981), p. 118.
3. John M. Killits, *Toledo and Lucas County, Ohio,* (Chicago and Toledo, S.J. Clarke Publishing Co., 1923), Three Volumes.
4. Toledo *News-Bee,* October, November, 1922.
5. *Ibid.*
6. Ralph Phelps, Mayors Scrapbook, Toledo-Lucas County Public Library and Archives; Toledo *Blade,* June 16, 1959.
7. Toledo *Blade,* September 18, 1918; newspaper archives, Toledo-Lucas County Public Library, Department of Local History and Genealogy.
8. Statements of Joe Jacobs, Julius Jacobs, Ralph Ziegan, Clyde Deeds, and many others.
9. Related by Louis Epstein, President of LaSalle and Koch Co., a party to the litigation.
10. Edward Lamb, *No Lamb for Slaughter,* (Harcourt, Brace and World, Inc., New York, 1963), p. 28.
11. Toledo *Blade,* January 23, 1946.
12. Killits, op. cit., pp. 88, 654. Biographical scrapbooks and newspaper archives, Toledo-Lucas County Public Library, Department of Local History and Genealogy.
13. See Chapters on Formation of the Syndicate and Payoffs, infra.
14. In the Common Pleas Court of Lucas County, Ohio, In The Matter of Dan McCullough, Cause No. 124008.
15. See Chapter on Interesting Cases, infra.

16. Related by Jack Clancy, a lifetime McCullough neighbor and friend.
17. Toledo *Blade,* August 20, 1976.
18. *Ibid.*
19. *Ibid.*
20. Related by Attorney Ben L. Levine, one-time associate of Dan McCullough in the practice of law.
21. Office of the Clerk of The Supreme Court of Ohio, Proceedings in the Court of Common Pleas of Lucas County in the Matter of Dan McCullough, Cause No. 124008.
22. Toledo *Blade,* August 20, 1976.
23. Related by Court Bailiff, Edward Newmark and Attorney Ben L. Levine.

**Chapter 12**

1. *Oxford English Dictionary.*
2. Rufus King, *Gambling and Organized Crime,* (Washington, D.C., Public Affairs Press, 1969) p. 23.
3. *Ibid.,* p. 24.
4. M.R. Werner, *It Happened In New York,* (New York: Coward McCann, Inc., 1957), p. 116.
5. See Licavoli Murder Trial, infra.
6. See Chapter on Formation of Syndicate, infra.
7. Ed Reid/Ovid Demaris, *The Green Felt Jungle,* (New York: Trident Press, 1963) p. 111.
8. *Ibid.*
9. Frederick Lewis Allen, *Only Yesterday,* (New York: Harper and Row, 1931) p. 98.
10. *Ibid.,* p. 74.
11. *Ibid.,* p. 79.
12. *Ibid.,* p. 95.
13. *Ibid.,* p. 96.
14. *Ibid.*
15. Reported to author by David Littin, Driggs Dairy driver.

**Chapter 13**

1. Toledo *Blade,* May 24, 1919; Toledo *Blade,* January 17, 1960.
2. *Ibid.*
3. *Ibid.*
4. *Ibid.*
5. *Ibid.*
6. *Ibid.*
7. Frederick Lewis Allen, op. cit., p. 82.
8. *Ibid.*
9. *Ibid.*
10. *Ibid.*
11. Toledo *Blade,* September 30, 1918.
12. *Ibid.,* and Newspaper archives on Prohibition, Toledo-Lucas County

Public Library, Department of Local History and Genealogy.
13. Cleveland *Plain Dealer,* February 12, 1921.
14. *Ibid.*
15. *Ibid.*

**Chapter 14**

1. Stephen Longstreet, *Win of Lose,* (Bobbs Merrill Co., Indianapolis, 1977), p. 143; *Ibid.* Thomas E. Dewey, *Twenty Against The Underworld,* Doubleday Co. Inc., Garden City, N.Y. 1974) p. 388, State of Ohio v. Sulkin, 33 N.E. 2nd 42, 30 O.O. 548; Fred J. Cook, *Mob Inc.* (Watts, N.Y. 1977) p. 19. Thomas E. Dewey, op. cit., p. 335.
2. Toledo *City Directory, 1917-1930,* listed Sarah and Jacob Nemerowski at 725 George St.
3. Toledo *Blade,* May 5, 1931; Toledo-Lucas County Public Library, Department of Local History and Genealogy, Licavoli files.
4. Toledo *Blade,* July 17, 1931.
5. Library files and archives, licavoli files.
6. Toledo *Blade,* October 6, 1931; Toledo *Blade,* May 12, 1957.
7. In the murder of Police Chief David Hennessey in New Orleans in 1891 the same cry, "the Dagos did it," aroused the city. Cook, *Mob, Inc.,* op. cit. p. 35. With the exception of this murder, the Mafia did not molest American police officials. Dennis Lynch, *Criminals and Politicians,* (McMillan Co. N.Y. 1937), p. 11.
8. Related by Sam Schuster to author.
9. Josephine Fassett, *History of Oregon and Jeruselum,* (Hurley Co. Inc., Camden, Arkansas, 1961) p. 220.
10. Toledo *Blade,* October 24, 1932, Toledo *Blade,* May 12, 1957.
11. Intimidation of witnesses was very common. George E.O. Johnson of Illinois, who later prosecuted Al Capone for tax evasion, told the U.S. Senate that in one case (D.C. No. 14677) six defendants and eight witnesses for the government were murdered. Proceedings before the U.S. Senate, March 29, 1932; Lynch, op. cit., p. 119, 120.
12. Toledo-Lucas County Public Library, op. cit. Licavoli files, In the Court of Common Pleas of Lucas County, Ohio. State v. Licavoli, et. al. No. 21529.
13. *Ibid.*

**Chapter 15**

1. Testimony in the Common Pleas Court of Lucas County, Ohio, State v. Licavoli, et. al No. 21529; Ralph Coll, "Trapping Toledo's Murder Masters," *Startling Detective Magazine,* April, 1934, pp. 17, 18, 63; May 1934, pp. 45, 48.
2. *Ibid.*
3. Marcia King, "The Gangland Killing of Jack Kennedy," *Bend of the River Magazine,* Perrysburg, Ohio, September, 1973, pp. 6, 7.
4. Testimony at trial, op. cit. witness Sadie Gromintz.

5. Toledo *Blade* and Toledo *News-Bee*, November 30, 1932; December 1, 1932.
6. Toledo *Blade*, January 2, 1933.
7. See the Chapter on the Wop English Trial, infra.
8. *Ibid.*
9. Toledo-Lucas County Public Library, Department of Local History and Genealogy, Licavoli files.
10. Testimony at trial, op. cit.
11. Toledo *Blade*, July 8, 1933; Toledo *News-Bee*, July 8, 1937.
12. *Ibid.*

**Chapter 16**

1. Toledo *Blade*, July 11 to July 23, 1933.
2. *Ibid.*
3. Related by subsequent owner of the Licavoli residence, Sidney Mostov.
4. Toledo *Blade*, November 2 to November 9, 1932.
5. Don Wolfe, *Frazier Reams*, (published privately, Toledo, 1977), p. 57.
6. Kenn Hamel and Hubert Dial, "Toledo Terror," *True Detective Magazine*, July, 1936, pp. 52-55, 118-120; June, 1936, pp. 82-84; "The Damned Fool Who Saved Toledo," *Male Magazine*, August, 1958, pp. 16-19; *Daring Detective Magazine*, April 1934; Ralph Coll, "Trapping Toledo's Murder Masters," *Startling Detective Magazine*, April 1934, pp. 17, 18, 63; May 1934, pp. 44, 45, 48.
7. Toledo *Blade*, August 8, 1933.
8. Toledo *Blade*, August 10, 1933.
9. See Chapter on Firetop Trial, infra.
10. In the Court of Common Pleas of Lucas County, State v. English, et. al. No. 21312; Toledo *Blade*, November 8, 1933 to November 18, 1933.
11. Akron v. Ney, 2 O.Abs. 36; and numerous Ohio case citations.
12. Hayes v. Smith 62 O.S. 161, 56 N.E. 879.
13. Toledo *Blade*, November 18, 1933, Toledo *News-Bee*, November 18, 1933.
14. *Ibid.*
15. Toledo *Blade*, December 13, 1933.
16. Toledo *Blade*, December 9, 1933. The government is required to turn over records relating to credibility. U.S. v. McCrane, 527 F. 2d 911.
17. Toledo *Blade*, December 13, 1933.
18. Toledo *Blade*, December 11, 1933.
19. Toledo *Blade*, December 13, 1933.
20. Telephone interviews with Dan McCullough, Jr., February, 1978.
21. Toledo *Blade*, February 7, 1933; Toledo *News-Bee*, February 7, 1934; In the Court of Common Pleas of Lucas County, Ohio, State v. Bruno, No. 76473.

**Chapter 17**

1. Based on personal interview and material in scrap book entitled *Auto-Lite Strike* of Brandon Schnorf Sr., now deceased.

2. Toledo-Lucas County Public Library, Department of Local History and Genealogy, Auto-Lite clippings; Toledo *Blade,* Toledo *News-Bee,* Toledo *Times Union,* May 1, 1934 to June 5, 1934.
3. *Ibid.*
4. A.J. Muste, "The Battle of Toledo," *The Nation Magazine,* June 6, 1934, Vol. 138, No. 3596 p. 639.
5. *Ibid.*
6. Toledo *Blade,* May 18, 1934.
7. *Ibid.*
8. *The New Republic,* "What is Behind Toledo," June 6, 1934, p. 86.
9. *Ibid.*
10. Ibid; "Street Fighting Marks Toledo Strike," *Literary Digest,* June 2, 1934, p. 6.
11. *Ibid.*
12. A.J. Muste, op. cit. p. 639.
13. *The New Republic,* op. cit. p. 86.
14. *Ibid.*
15. *Ibid.*
16. *Ibid.,* p. 87.
17. Newspaper archives, May 15 to June 5, 1934.
18. Statements of Brandon Schnorf Sr. and scrapbook, op. cit.
19. Lamb, op. cit. pp. 40-42.
20. Louis F. Budenz, *This Is My Story,* (McGraw Hill Book Co., New York, 1947) p. 96.
21. *The Nation,* op. cit. 639; *Literary Digest,* op. cit. p. 6.
22. Heywood Broun, "It Seems To Me," Toledo *News-Bee,* May 28, 1934.
23. *The Nation,* op. cit. p. 639.
24. *The New Republic,* op. cit. p. 18; Toledo *Blade,* Toledo *News-Bee,* Toledo *Times,* May 21, 22, 23, 1934.
25. *Ibid.*
26. *Ibid.*
27. Lamb, op. cit. p. 42.
28. *New Republic,* op. cit. p. 87.
29. *Literary Digest,* op. cit. p. 6; Library archives, op. cit.
30. Toledo *Blade,* and Toledo *News-Bee,* May 31, 1934.
31. *The New Republic,* op. cit. p. 87.
32. Toledo *News-Bee,* May 31, 1934.
33. Toledo *News-Bee,* May 26, 1934. The final edition carried a front page picture of the crowd and naked scab (see photo).
34. Heywood Broun, Toledo *News-Bee,* May 28, 1934.
35. Brandon Schnorf, Sr., interview and scrapbook.
36. *Ibid.*
37. *Ibid.*

**Chapter 18**

1. Olmstead v. U.S., 277 U.S. 438, 470 (1928).
2. Katz v. U.S. 389 U.S. 347 (1967).

3. Toledo *Blade,* March 13, 1955.
4. Ohio Code Section 3467 enacted in 1892.
5. Don Wolfe, op. cit. p. 75.
6. Toledo *Blade,* March 8, 1934 story with pictures of all defendants; Toledo *News-Bee,* March 8, 1934 story with pictures of all named defendants. In The Common Pleas Court of Lucas County, Ohio, State v. Licavoli, et. al. No. 21529.
7. Toledo *Blade,* October 7, 8, 1934.
8. Burton collection, op. cit. Detroit Public Library. Licavoli collection and archives.
9. In The Probate Court of Lucas County, Ohio. In the matter of the Estate of Gerald James Hayes No. 28366.
10. Toledo *Blade,* October 8, 1934, October 22 to November 8, 1934; Toledo *News-Bee,* October 8, 1934 to November 8, 1934.
11. Toledo *Blade,* October 22, 1934 story and front page picture of Licavoli home.
12. *Ibid.*
13. State v. Licavoli et. al., op. cit., record.
14. *Ibid.*
15. *Ibid.*
16. Chapter on Licavoli Takeover, supra.
17. *Ibid.*
18. State v. Licavoli, op. cit. Testimony of record.
19. *Ibid.*
20. *Ibid.*
21. *Ibid.*
22. *Ibid.*
23. *Ibid.,* Toledo *Blade,* November 5, 1934.
24. State v. Licavoli, op. cit. Argument of record.
25. Chapter on Licavoli Tribulations, infra.

**Chapter 19**

1. Toledo *News-Bee,* August 10, 1933
2. Toledo *News-Bee,* February 26, 1935; State v. Licavoli et. al, op. cit. Record of proceedings.
3. Edward Lamb, op. cit. p. 29.
4. Toledo *Blade,* March 16, 1935.
5. John McDonald of the Detroit police was called Little Clarke and Leonard Smith was Big Clarke but the record indicates Stein may have been beaten by both.
6. Toledo *Blade,* March 19, 1935.
7. Dewey, op. cit. pp. 388, 474, 475. People v. Hines, 284 N.Y. 93.
8. State v. Sulkin, 33 N.E. 2nd 42; 33 O.O. 548.
9. State v. Licavoli, op. cit. docket and journal entries.
10. Toledo *Blade,* August 13, 1936.
11. See Chapters on Formation of the Syndicate and End of Syndicated Gambling, infra.

*UNHOLY TOLEDO*

12. See Chapter on Licavoli Tribulations, infra.
13. Toledo *Blade,* March 26, 1953.
14. Toledo *Blade,* September 10, 1950.
15. See subsequent chapters on Industry and Labor, infra.

**Chapter 20**

1. Stinchcombe, "The Reform Movement in Toledo," p. 39.
2. *Ibid.,* p. 40.
3. Toledo *Blade,* November 6, 1934; Toledo *News-Bee,* November 6, 1934.
4. Stinchcombe, op. cit., p. 40.
5. Toledo *Blade,* September 25, 1935.
6. *Ibid.*
7. Toledo *Blade,* June 29, 1935.
8. Toledo *Blade,* January 13, 1937.
9. Toledo *Blade,* January 14, 1937.
10. Toledo *Blade,* January 16, 1937.
11. Toledo *Blade,* August 10, 1937; Toledo *Times,* April 28, 1940.
12. See the Chapter on the Formation of the Syndicate, infra.
13. Toledo *Times,* October 14, 1935; Toledo *Blade,* October 28, 1947.
14. Alvin Karpis, *The Alvin Karpis Story,* Coward, McCann & Geoghegan, Inc. N.Y. 1971. pp. 113, 252.
15. *Ibid.,* p. 257.
16. Toledo *Blade,* May 10, 1936.
17. Toledo *Blade,* May 11, 1936.
18. See the Chapter on the Formation of the Syndicate and Payoffs, infra.

**Chapter 21**

1. Toledo-Lucas County Public Library Business and Industry archives, Department of Local History and Geneology.
2. Toledo *Blade,* June 30, 1905.
3. Toledo *Blade,* June 26, 1947, on 40th Anniversary of re-enactment of first sports broadcast by Bill Stern, NBC reporter.
4. *Ibid.*
5. Toledo-Lucas County Public Library, Department of Local History and Geneology, Industry sections; Toledo *Blade,* March 2, 1952.
6. Industry archives, op. cit., Toledo Business June, 1929.
7. Ohio General Code Section 1465-61, now Title 41, Chapter 4123, Ohio Revised Code, first enacted in 1911.
8. *Ibid.,* annotations reported and annotated under the statute.
9. Toledo *Blade,* November 17, 1937; *The Nation,* "Labor Racketeering," August 10, 1935, pp. 137, 177-180.
10. *Literary Digest,* "How Gangsters Work,", August 5, 1933, p. 30.
11. Toledo-Lucas County Public Library, Department of Local History and Geneology, Labor Unions.
12. *Ibid.*
13. *Ibid.;* Scrapbook of clippings on LMC.
14. *Ibid.;* Lamb, op. cit. p. 156.

15. Toledo *Blade*, October 28, 1947.
16. *Ibid.*
17. *Ibid.*
18. Circuit Court Calendar, Monroe County, Michigan, June 6, 1921, p. 463, The People v. Tony Paul, Richard Gosser, et. al. No. 6602. Toledo *Blade*, December 1, 1963.
19. Stinchcombe, op. cit. p. 152; Labor archives, LMC clippings and arcives; Toledo *Blade*, May 3, 1964.
20. Labor and GMC archives, op. cit.
21. Toledo-Lucas County Public Library, Department of Local History and Geneology, Labor Unions; Toledo *Blade*, May 11, 1970.
22. Toledo *Blade*, May 18, 1950; archives, op. cit.
23. Toledo *Monitor*, March 31, 1960, April 7, 1960, April 14, 1960.
24. Toledo *Blade*, March 10, 1950.
25. In the Court of Common Pleas of Lucas County, Ohio, John A. Bolman v. The United Automotive Workers Bldg. Corp. Richard Gosser et. al. No. 172025 filed November 7, 1949.
26. *Ibid.*
27. Labor Archives, op. cit.
28. Text of Trial. Toledo *Blade*, January 30, 1963.
29. Toledo *Blade*, February 9, 1963.
30. Toledo-Lucas County Public Library, Department of Local History and Geneology, labor scrapbook and archives.
31. Review of labor in Toledo, Toledo *Blade*, May 3, 1964.
32. Stinchcombe, op. cit. p. 153; archives, op. cit., Toledo *Blade*, September 18, 1969; Toledo *Blade*, September 21, 1969.
33. Archives, op. cit.
34. Sam Romer, *The International Brotherhood of Teamsters*, (New York, John Wiley, 1962) p. 67.
35. *Ibid.*, archives, op. cit.

**Chapter 22**

1. Detroit *News*, February 22, 1940, February 25, 1940; Detroit *News* Record Librarian files on "Police Graft and Grand Jury Inquiry," New York *Times*, February 22, 1940.
2. *Ibid.*
3. *Ibid.*
4. *Ibid.*
5. Detroit *News*, March 7, 1940, March 9, 1940.
6. *Ibid.*
7. *Ibid.* New York *Times*, March 6, 1940.
8. Detroit *News* Archives, op. cit.
9. *Ibid.*
10. New York *Times*, April 25, 1940.
11. Detroit *News* Archives, op. cit.
12. *Ibid.*
13. New York *Times*, August 8, 1940; Detroit *News* Archives.

14. *Ibid.*
15. Detroit *News* Archives.
16. *Ibid.*
17. *Ibid.*
18. Detroit *News* Archives; Detroit Public Library, Burton Collection, Mayor Reading files; T & M, B R227; Detroit *News* articles on inside story of Mayor Reading, Jan. 2 to Jan. 18, 1944, inclusive.
19. *Ibid.*
20. *Ibid.*
21. See Chapter on Formation of The Syndicate, supra.

**Chapter 23**

1. Related by Attorney Ben L. Levine in interview.
2. *Ibid.*
3. Related by Stephen Fazekas, attorney in interview.
4. John Scarne, *Scarne's New Complete Guide To Gambling* (Simon & Schuster, N.Y., 1974) p. 228.
5. *Ibid.*; Hank Messick, *The Silen Syndicate,* (Macmillan Co., N.Y. 1967) p. 7, 8.
6. See Chapter on Newspaper Game, supra.
7. Ray Scheets to author, told by police officers Owen Green, Felix (Phil) Purcell.
8. Reported by Joseph Knack and Ray Jankowski, *Blade* reporters, in interview.
9. Statement of J.J. (Jack) Flannigan to author.
10. Marl B. Paily, *Bricker of Ohio* (G.P. Putnam's Sons, N.Y. 1944) p. 83.
11. *Ibid.*, p. 83.
12. *Ibid.*, p. 83.
13. *Ibid.*, p. 79.
14. Toledo-Lucas County Public Library, Department of Local History and Geneology, newspaper clippings and archives.
15. Detroit *News,* October 11, 1963.
16. Statement of George Shamey to author.
17. Toledo *Blade,* April 21, 1941.
18. Scarne, op. cit., p. 229.
19. Statements of Harry Klapfish, accountant, made to author.
20. Scarne, op. cit. p. 1.
21. *Ibid.*, p. 1.
22. Igor Kusyszyn, *Studies In The Psychology of Gambling,* (Simon & Schuster, New York, 1972) p. 1.

**Chapter 24**

1. See Chapter on Interesting Cases, Infra.
2. In the Probate Court of Lucas County, Ohio. In the Matter of the Estate of J. Jay Gould. No. 119520, transcrit of record of secret hearing to prove lost will of decedent.
3. *Ibid.*

4. Toledo *Blade*, obituary of William J. Gray, July 3, 1974.
5. Steffens' *Shame of the Cities, op. cit.* Chapter on on "The Shame of Minneapolis," as one of the cities muckraked showed similar criminal activities.
6. Detroit *Free Press*, January 2, 1944; January 4, 1944.
7. William Hirsch, as told to Victor Ullman, *Treat Them Human* (Crown Publishers, Inc. N.Y. 1964), p. 68.
8. Toledo *Blade*, March 25, 1938.
9. Toledo Lucas County Public Library, Department of Local History & Genealogy, Church and Radio Archives.
10. *Ibid.*
11. *Ibid.*
12. Statement of Irv Miller to author.
13. Statement of Jack Flanagan to author.
14. See Chapter on Interesting Cases, Infra.
15. Task Force Report on Organized Crime, U.S. Government Printing Office, Washington D.C., 1967, pp. 61-78.
16. John Cooney, *The Annenbergs* (Simon & Schuster, N.Y. 1982), p. 69.
17. Will and Ariel Durant, *Lessons of History* (Simon & Schuster, N.Y. 1968), pp. 77-78.
18. *Ibid.*

## Chapter 25

1. Detroit *News*, January, 2, 3, 4, 1944.
2. Toledo *Blade*, January 5, 1944 to January 27, 1944.
3. *Ibid.*
4. *Ibid.*
5. Ullman, *op. cit.*, p. 168.
6. Toledo *Blade*, January 16, 1944.
7. Toledo *Blade*, January 27, 1944.
8. Toledo *Blade*, January 5, 1944 to January 27, 1944.
9. *Ibid.*
10. *Ibid.*
11. *Ibid.*
12. In The Court of Common Please of Lucas County, Ohio. *State of Ohio* v. *Ben Aronoff et. al.* No. 26181; Toledo *Blade*, February 25, 1944.
13. General Code Section 12823, now Sec. 2917.01 O.R.C.
14. General Code Section 12824-1, now Sec. 2917.04 O.R.C.
15. *Ibid.*
16. *Snyder* v. *Alliance* 41 O.A. 48.
17. The Attorney General opinions served to advise all state and county officials. Any state official could ask for an opinion from the lawyer for the state and its officials.
18. *Ibid.*
19. *Ibid.*
20. *State* v. *Aronoff et. al., op. cit.* Transcript of proceedings docket and journal entries.
21. *Ibid.*, General Code Section 12381, now Sec. 2901.13.
22. Toledo *Blade*, April 10, 1944.

UNHOLY TOLEDO

23. *Ibid.*, Toledo *Blade,* April 24, 1944.
24. *Ibid.*
25. *Ibid.*
26. *Ibid.*
27. Toledo *Blade,* April 29, 1944.
28. *Ibid.*
29. Hirsch, *op. cit.,* p. 68.
30. *Ibid.,* p. 100, 101.
31. See Chapter on Interesting Cases. Infra.
32. *Ibid.*
33. Hirsch, *op. cit.,* p. 168.
34. Interview with Isadore Mitchell.
35. Chapter on End of Syndicated Gambling, Infra.

**Chapter 26**

1. *Saturday Evening Post,* August 17, 1946, p. 17.
2. Edict of James F. Byrne, as mobilization director, asking all race tracks to close on January 3, 1945 to save manpower and transportation needed for the war effort; New York *Times,* December 23, 1944.
3. Interview with Ray Douglas, Track Steward, at various tracks in the United States for 40 years.
4. See Chapter on Kefauver, Infra.
5. New York *Times,* June 25, 1946.
6. New York *Times,* August 15, 1946.
7. New York *Times,* September 13, 1946.
8. Interview with Abe Joffa while enroute to DRC on many occasions. Joffa originally owned a horse book of his own which he sold to Aronoff and Harris.

**Chapter 27**

1. *Newsweek,* March 12, 1951; *Saturday Evening Post,* April 7, 14, 21, 28, 1951; *U.S. News,* April 20, 1951, April 4, 1952.
2. *Ibid.*
3. Fred J. Cook, *Mob Inc.* (Franklin Watts, N.Y. 1971), p. 92, New York *Times,* February 15, 16, 17, 1951; March 7, 13, 14, 17, 19, 22, 30, 1951; April 3, 4, 6, 10, 1951.
4. *Ibid.*
5. *Ibid.*
6. Detroit *News,* November 21, 1950; Detroit *Free Press,* October 11, 1963.
7. Toledo *Blade,* January 17-19, 1951.
8. Toledo *Blade,* January 17, 1951.
9. *Ibid.;* See Chapter on Interesting Cases, Infra.
10. Chapter on Interesting Cases, Infra.
11. Toledo *Blade,* January 19, 1951.
12. See Chapter on Payoffs, supra.
13. Toledo *Blade,* January 19, 1951.

14. *Bar Rag,* edited by author for Junior Bar Association, Toledo, May, 1951.
15. Toledo *Blade,* January 2, 1953.
16. *Ibid.*
17. Toledo *Blade,* January 19, 1951.
18. *Ibid.*
19. See next Chapter on Denaturalization Plea Bargaining, Infra.
20. New York *Times,* February 9, 1951.
21. See Chapter on End of Syndicated gambling, Infra.
22. New York *Times,* January 5, 1952.
23. *Ibid.*
24. *Marchetti* v. *U.,S.,* 390 U.S. 39; *Grasso* v. *U.S.* 62; Marchetti held: "requirements for registration and payment of the occupational tax would have the direct and unmistakable consequence of incriminating petitioner," p. 48.

## Chapter 28

1. Personal interview with Kelsey Bartlett.
2. See Chapter on Industry and Labor, supra.
3. In the U.S. District Court, Northern District of Ohio, Western Division, *U.S.* v. *Pulifeico,* No. 8609, docket and journal entries.
4. *Ibid.*
5. U.S. District Court, Northern District of Ohio, Western Division, Matter of Naturalization of Neufio Scott, No. 13437; associated with Civil Action 7129 on docket of same court.
6. *Ibid.*
7. Toledo Lucas County Public Library, Department of Local History and Genealogy, Gosser and labor clipping and archives.
8. *Ibid.*
9. Bartlett interview.
10. *Ibid.* 11. Transcript of portion of record Civil Cause No. 7129, supra.
12. *Ibid.*
13. *Ibid.*
14. *Ibid.*
15. *Ibid.*
16. Detroit *News,* November 21, 1950.

## Chapter 29

1. Toledo *Blade,* February 26, 1950.
2. *Ibid.*
3. *Ibid.*
4. *Ibid.*
5. *Ibid.*
6. Wolfe, infra. op. cit. p. 100.
7. Toledo *Blade,* February 26, 1950.
8. *Ibid.*

9. *Ibid.*
10. Denny Walsh, "Leniency For a Hoodlum, Slush Fund Income," *Life Magazine,* May 2, 1969, p. 21-32.
11. *Ibid.*
12. *Ibid.*
13. *Ibid.*
14. *Ibid.*
15. Toledo *Blade,* July 9, 1965.
16. Toledo *Blade,* May 15, 1965.
17. Toledo *Blade,* May 27, 1965.
18. Toledo *Blade,* June 2, 1966; *State v. Licavoli,* Court of Common Pleas #21529, transcript.
19. Toledo *Blade,* November 30, 1966.
20. Toledo *Blade,* April 27, 1967.
21. In the U.S. District Court, Southern District of Ohio; In the Matter of Thomas Licavoli, No. C-2-68-79.
22. Toledo *Blade,* January 28, 1968.
23. *Ibid.,* Toledo *Blade,* January 29, 1968.
24. Toledo *Blade,* October 28, 29, 31, 1969.
25. Toledo *Blade,* April 2, 1970.
26. New York *Times,* April 2, 1970, May 26, 1970.
27. New York *Times,* May 26, 1970.
28. *Ibid.*
29. *Ibid.*
30. *Ibid.*
31. *Ibid.*
32. Louis Nizer, *Reflections Without Mirrors* (Doubleday and Co., Inc., Garden City, New York, 1977) pp. 161-168.
33. *Ibid.,* p. 161.
34. Chapter on End of Syndicate, Infra.
35. The Ohio Historical Society, *Governors of Ohio* (Stoneman Press, Columbus, 1954).
36. Nizer, *op. cit.,* p. 162.
37. *Ibid.,* p. 163.
38. Toledo *Blade,* May 15, 1965, June 6, 1965.
39. There is no legal duty on the state to grant a parole. *Wells* v. *Haskins,* 24 O.S. 2d. 36, 263 N.E. 2d. 311, cert denied, 402 U.S. 910. Under Ohio revised code Section 2965.14 where a prisoner under life sentences for a murder does not have favorable action taken by the parole board, he may make application for another hearing in five years.
40. Walsh, *op. cit.,* p. 31.
41. Re Licavoli, Case No. 68-79, *op. cit.,* transcript of record.
42. *Ibid.*
43. *Ibid.*
44. *Pyle* v. *Kansas,* 317 U.S. 213 (1942) *Mooney* v. *Holohan,* 294 U.S. 103; *Chambers* v. *Florida,* 309 U.S. 227; *Napue* v. *Illinois,* 360 U.S. 264.
45. *Brady* v. *Maryland,* 393 U.S. 196.

46. In re Licavoli, No. 68-79, transcript of record.
47. *Griffen* v. *California,* 380 U.S. 609 (1965).
48. Toledo *Blade,* December 7, 1971.
49. Toledo *Blade,* December 6, 1972.
50. *Ibid.,* Detroit Public Library, Burton collection, Licavoli Archives.
51. Detroit *News,* September 21, 1973.

**Chapter 30**

1. Longstreet, *op. cit.,* p. 240; Igorkusyszyn, *Studies in the Psychology of Gambling* (Simon & Schuster, N.Y. 1972), p. 15; E. Bergler, *The Psychology of Gambling* (Hill and Wang, N.Y. 1957).
2. Chapters on the Sundicate and Payoffs, supra.
3. New York *Times,* March 25, 1951; Jackie Goldsmith pled guilty on May 8, 1956, New York *Times,* May 8, 1956; Toledo *Blade,* July 25, 27, 28, 31, 1951.
4. New York *Times,* January 18, 1951.
5. New York *Times,* March 22, 23, 1951.
6. *Ibid.*
7. Toledo *Blade,* July 25, 27, 28, 31, 1951.
8. Toledo *Blade,* July 25, 1951.
9. *Ibid.*
10. Toledo *Times,* July 28, 1951.
11. Sec. 3773.15 of the Ohio Revised Code was enacted, effective October 1, 1953.
12. New York *Times,* March 22, 1951.
13. Related to author by Ben Pollock.
14. The author was present in person; see also *Sports Illustrated Magazine,* May 7, 1962; July 21, 1969, pp. 49, 50; Teddy Brenner, *Only the Ring Was Square* (Harper & Row, N.Y. 1983).
15. New York *Times,* June 23, 1959, July 12, 28, 31, 1959.
16. *Ibid.*
17. In The Court of Common Pleas of Franklin County, Ohio. *Reynolds Tobacco Co.* v. *Sharwell* No. 201771 filed April 20, 1961.
18. Sections 5743.02 to 5743.99, Ohio Revised Code.
19. In The Court of Common Pleas of Franklin County, Ohio, *State of Ohio* v. *Sherman S. Sharwell,* No. 41326.
20. In The Court of Common Pleas of Franklin County, Ohio. *Sharwell Tobacco Company and Sherman Sharwell* v. *Stanley J. Bowers, Tax Commissioner of Ohio and Mark McElroy, Attorney General of Ohio,* No. 210964. Filed May 11, 1961, later voluntarily dismissed at Sharwell's costs on April 25, 1963.
21. *State* v. *Sharwell, op. cit.,* transcript of record of docket and journal entries.
22. Declaration against financial interest made by Sherman S. Sharwell to author and others.

## Chapter 31

1. Toledo *Blade,* April 16, 1950; In the Court of Common Pleas of Lucas County, Ohio; *State* v. *Lennon* No. 29933.
2. *State* v. *Lennon, op. cit.,* transcript of record.
3. In the Court of Common Pleas of Lucas County, Ohio. *State* v. *Cochrane,* No. 27953. Transcript of record.
4. *State* v. *Cochrane,* 151 O.S. 128.
5. Toledo *Blade,* November 5, 1946.
6. *Ibid.*
7. Toledo *Blade,* October 1, 1947.
8. *Ibid.*
9. Toledo *Blade,* October 10, 1947.
10. *Ibid.*
11. *Ibid.*
12. *Ibid.*
13. Toledo *Blade,* July 6, 1950; Toledo *Blade,* October 16, 1974.
14. In the Court of Common Pleas of Lucas County, Ohio *State* v. *Chester Urbaytis,* No. 29743.
15. *State* v. *Urbaytis,* 156 O.S. 271.
16. *Ibid.*
17. In the Court of Common Pleas of Lucas County, Ohio. *Joseph Wolvek* v. *Dorothy Wolvek,* No. 27631.
18. Ralph Nader and Mark Green, *Verdicts On Lawyers* (Thomas Crowell Co., N.Y., 1976), p. 309; Chapter by Garkus and Seligman: "Sanctions and Disbarment: They Sit in Judgment", pp. 47, 48, 53 and citations p. 309. "Disciplinary Agencies will not proceed against prominent lawyers or law firms." "They don't get the Fat Cats ..., or the Fat Cats refuse to get themselves etc."
19. In the Court of Common Pleas of Lucas County, Ohio; In the Matter of the Complaint Against Harry R. Illman No. 175689.
20. *People ex rel Karlin* v. *Culkin* (1928) 248 U.S. 162, Matter of H, an Attorney, 87 N.Y. 521. Matter of An Attorney, 83 N.Y. 164.
21. William Henry Harbaugh, *Lawyers' Lawyer, Life of John W. Davis* (Oxford University Press, N.Y. 1973), pp. 445-453.
22. William M. Miller as told to Francis Spatz Leighton, *Fish Bait* (Prentice Hall, Englewood Cliffs, N.J., 1977), p. 156.
23. Toledo Lucas County Public Library, Department of Local History and Genealogy, Records of Wages of County and State Employees.
24. In the Probate Court of Lucas County, Ohio. In the estate of Gordon T. Jeffery, No. 138300.
25. *Ibid.*
26. Statements of Max Mallamad and others to author and others.
27. In the Probate Court of Lucas County, Ohio, estate of Raphael Kest No. 92590.
28. *State* v. *Schreiber,* 12 O.S.2D. 183.
29. *Spevak* v. *Klein,* 385 U.S. 511.
30. In re Leiberman, 165 U.S. 35.

31. In the Court of Common Pleas of Lucas County, Ohio, *State of Ohio* v. *Lewis Walker et. al.* No. 30965, Infra.
32. In the Court of Common Pleas of Lucas County, Ohio. *George Effler* v. *Harry Illman* No. 178074.
33. In the Common Pleas Court of Lucas County, Ohio *Kern* v. *Hitchcock et. al.* No. 173555; In the Court of Appeals of Lucas County, *Kern* v. *Hitchcock et. al.* No. 4653.
34. Joseph C. Goulden, *The Benchwarmers* (Weybright & Talley, N.Y. 1974), p. 18.
35. In re Illman, *op. cit.,* transcript of record.
36. Toledo *Blade,* October 26, 1951.
37. *Ibid.*
38. Toledo *Blade,* October 31, 1951.
39. *State* v. *Walker et. al., op. cit.,* No. 30965. Item 12 of Bill of Particulars.
40. In the Court of Common Pleas of Lucas County, Ohio *Illman* v. *Effler,* No. 182416.
41. In the Probate Court of Lucas County, In the Estate of Harry G. Levy No. 157890.
42. *State* v. *Walker, op. cit.* No. 30965. Item 12 of Bill of particulars.
43. Toledo *Blade,* February 21, 1953.
44. *State* v. *Walker, op. cit.,* No. 30965. Transcript of docket and journal entries.
45. See the Chapter on End of Syndicate, Infra.
46. Andy Logan, *Against the Evidence* (McCall Publishing Company, N.Y. 1970), p. 341.
47. San Francisco *Chronicle,* October 28, 1986.

**Chapter 32**
1. Bob Considine, "Las Vegas Unmasked", fifth article in series copyright property of International News Service, San Francisco *Examiner,* January 27, 1955.
2. Hirsch, opp. cit., p. 183.
3. *Ibid.*
4. Toledo *Blade,* January 20, 1956.
5. Toledo *Blade,* December 9, 1952.
6. Toledo *Blade,* January 9, 1956.
7. Toledo *Blade,* January 14 to 20, 1956.
8. Toledo *Blade,* January 19, 1956.
9. *Ibid.*
10. *Ibid.*
11. *Ibid.*
12. Toledo *Blade,* January 20, 1956.
13. *Ibid.*
14. *Ibid.*
15. Toledo Lucas County Public Library, Deparment of Local History and Genealogy, Police Archives.
16. Toledo *Blade,* May 16, 1956; Toledo *City Journal,* April 7, 1956, p. 424.

17. Related by Felix (Phil) Purcell, police officer friend of Clifford Quinn.
18. Toledo *City Journal,* April 2, 1956, p. 648; June 30, 1956, p. 778.
19. Toledo *Blade,* November 7, 1956.
20. In the United States District Court, Western Division, Northern District of Ohio, Commissioner's Case No. 8701.
21. *Ibid.*

**Chapter 33**
1. Joe Murphy wrote "We're Strong for Toledo" in 1906, library archives, *op. cit.*
2. Marjory Stottler, class of 1931, wrote the lyrics to the famous Jones Junior High song. Toledo Lucas County Library, Department of Local History and Genealogy, archives of songs of Toledo.
3. Library archives, Songs of Toledo, *op. cit.*
4. The *Blade,* August 20, 1976.
5. In the Probate Court of Lucas County, Ohio. In the Estate of Dan H. McCollough No. 133757.
6. In the Court of Common Pleas of Lucas County, Ohio. *Helen Ackerman* v. *Dan H. McCollough* No. 75-1683. Court of Appeals No. 6-78-26.
7. Section 2317.03, Ohio Revised Code provides "a party cannot testify when the adverse party is deceased."
8. The disbarment was ordered on March 9, 1931 but reportedly rescinded on Dec. 29, 1931. (In re McCollough, *op. cit.*) The papers are no longer in possession of the Clerk of Courts.
9. William E. Harbaugh, *Life of John W. Davis, Lawyer's Lawyer,* (Oxford University Press, New York, 1973), pp. 298-318.
10. Nathan Miller, *Founding Finaglers* (David McKay Co. N.Y. 1971), p. 261.
11. The *Blade,* September 27, 1975.
12. In the Probate Court of Lucas County, Ohio. In the matter of the Estate of Harry Leonard No. 130876.
13. In the Probate Court of Lucas County, Ohio. In the Estate of Rose Scott, deceased No. 133868.
14. Burton collection, *op. cit.,* Licavoli files.
15. Detroit *News,* December 12, 1976.
16. The *Blade,* November 3, 1960.
17. The *Blade,* June 1, 1961, June 6, 1961, December 11, 1961 and February 21, 1962.
18. In the Court of Common Pleas of Lucas County, Ohio *State* v. *The Blade* No. 40814 filed March 27, 1962; nolle pros entered July 26, 1962.
19. Toledo *Monitor,* January 14, 1960.
20. In the U.S. District Court, Eastern Division, Northern District of Ohio, *CATV-Edward Lamb Enterprises, Inc. et. al.* v. *Toledo Blade Co. et. al.* No. 66238.
21. In the Common Pleas Court of Lucas County, Ohio *Charles Raymond etc.* v. *Buckeye Cablevision, Inc.* No. 75-1330, transcript of record.
22. *Fortune Magazine,* "In Search of the Elusive Big Rich," January 12, 1979, p. 93.

23. The *Blade,* September 3, 1979.
24. The *Blade,* July 5, 1978.
25. The *Blade,* October 15, 1978, November 21, 1978, December 31, 1978.
26. Larry J. Sabato, *Rise of Political Consultants* (Basic Books, N.Y. 1981); New York *Times,* December 17, 1981 p. 2.
27. Goulden, *op. cit.,* p. 35.
28. Jack Anderson and James Boyd, *Confessions of a Muck Raker* (Ballantine Books, N.Y. 1979), p. 362.